HAPPY SAD LAND

MARK McCRUM

Happy
Sad Land

A Journey Through Southern Africa

SINCLAIR-STEVENSON

First published in Great Britain in 1994
by Sinclair-Stevenson
an imprint of Reed Consumer Books Ltd
Michelin House, 81 Fulham Road, London SW3 6RB
and Auckland, Melbourne, Singapore and Toronto

This paperback edition published by Sinclair-Stevenson in 1995

A CIP catalogue record for this book
is available at the British Library
ISBN 1 85619 515 5

Typeset by CentraCet Limited, Cambridge

Printed and bound in Great Britain
by Mackays of Chatham PLC

for Katherine,
without whose encouragement I wouldn't have gone;
for the people of Southern Africa, black and white,
without whose hospitality and kindness
I wouldn't have kept going;
and for the Reading Room of the British Library,
without which calm oasis I would never have got this
written . . .

CONTENTS

He was grave and silent, and then he said sombrely, I have one great fear in my heart, that one day when they are turned to loving, they will find we are turned to hating.

Alan Paton, *Cry, The Beloved Country*

The past is a foreign country: they do things differently there.

L. P. Hartley, *The Go-Between*

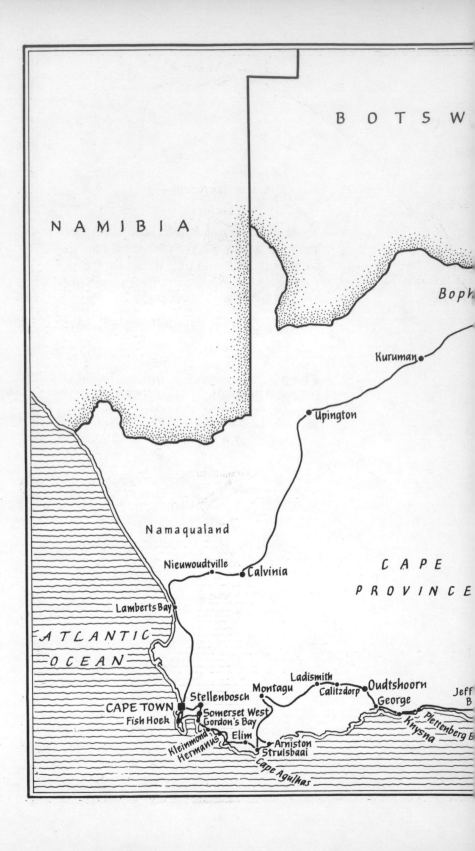

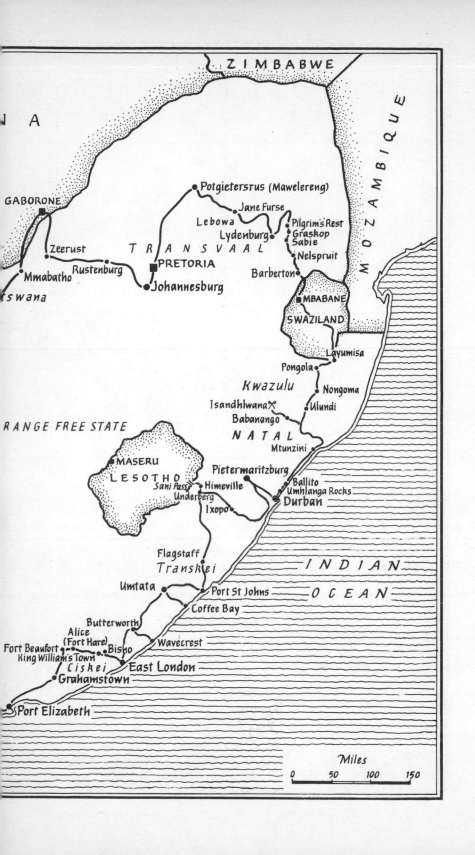

Acknowledgements

This trip was done on a shoestring and would not have been possible without the gambling instincts of Christopher Sinclair-Stevenson, or the generous support of British Airways, who provided me with a free Club Class ticket and the material for page one. Pauline Young of G & O Public Relations organised this for me with great efficiency, and thanks are due also to Southern Africa Travel of York (0904 692469) who specialise in tailor-made itineraries to Southern Africa.

Sherri Bailey of Dolphin Cars of Cape Town amazed me by giving me a free hire car for three months – my beautiful Dolphin. By the end we were closer than man and car have ever been.

On the road, I met with enormous hospitality and kindness from endless strangers and 'contacts', not to mention the old friends I found in Botswana. Some feature in the book; many do not – I am deeply grateful to them all. Likewise to the people in England who put me in touch – in particular, Sue Tomson, Nicola Lush, Mark and Tessa Katzenellenbogen, Matthew Campling, Michael and Sarah McCrum.

Back in England, when conditions were not exactly inspiring, my mother sustained me with a weekly phone call, James Richmond and Catherine Loewe became more than good friends, my brother Stephen was his usual generous and supportive self. A number of kind people looked over my first draft and offered encouragement and suggestions: my parents, my brother Robert, Katrin Macgibbon, Emily Stubbs, Lilia Bylos, Sarah Milwidsky. My agent Mark Lucas always phoned back within the week, and at Sinclair-Stevenson, Emily Kerr skilfully and tactfully excised the excess.

Author's Note

Some of the conversations that appear in this book were tape-recorded: many were not, and in those instances where I memorised what people said to me, I endeavoured to get something down within a few hours, so as not to misrepresent them.

I have changed the names of many of the private figures who appear in the book, though clearly public figures, and people who gave 'on the record' interviews remain the same.

Throughout my journey, I made it very clear that I was writing a book, and when my tape recorder was used, it was, with one harmless exception (Nomsa and Cynthia: Chapter 18), always with the permission of the speaker. If any of what follows should cause offence to those who were so kind and hospitable to me, I can only apologise. This is what I heard and saw.

1

THE GAP

So here I sit, in this armchair in the sky, watching a video screen where a woman in London is interviewing a man in Manchester about events that have taken place this very afternoon in the Middle East; and if I turn to my left and peer out and down through the darkness, there is Paris, looking like an illuminated spider's web in the night, the Eiffel Tower a tiny toy.

I'm drinking Ballantyne's Finest Scotch Whisky and Schweppes Soda, with a complimentary pouch of peanuts, and a complimentary plastic swizzle stick, and I'm deciding whether to eat the Collops of Prime Beef Fillet with a Pickled Walnut Gravy Garnished with Potato and Brown Lentil Pie (created by Alan Hill, Executive Chef of Gleneagles), or the Monkfish and Prawn Presented in an Oriental Style with Ginger and Soy and Served with Stirfried Vegetables . . .

By the time we are over Ethiopia I am drunk. I've been through the lot: the aperitifs, the champagne, the white Cape Riesling, the Australian claret, the port, the brandy, and the liqueur; not to mention three cans of still water all the way from Malvern.

Still I feel a tremble in my toes at the thought of all that space beneath me, above the huge continent where people are dying of starvation at this very moment; but no, I am thirty-three and I can handle flying; and more, I can handle

being alone, entirely alone, for the next three months, away
from my girlfriend Sarah who I've just kissed goodbye at the
airport. She has long dark hair that reaches to her waist; and
as I backed away and she stood there with her hands shoved
into the front pocket of her jeans, her eyes shone with tears.

The morning comes, and we haven't crashed into the
jungles of Chad; indeed we've landed at Johannesburg ahead
of time. There's an hour's wait, and some new passengers.
South African newspapers appear, and the three chubby
South African businessmen who've been making friends in
the centre section are discussing the news. *The Citizen* has a
front page picture of Nelson Mandela's new 500,000 rand
house in Houghton (one of Jo'burg's smartest suburbs) which
they're passing around. I can't *quite* hear their conversation,
but it's clear they don't approve. I hear the sentence 'Ah sed
to 'im, you dan't want to 'ave a siparate bell for the maid,'
and then the word 'kaffir' . . .

It's an expression I've not heard for fifteen years. It means,
literally, 'unbeliever'; and though it isn't quite as offensive
as 'nigger', it's not a polite way to talk about people who are
black. Even the most Right wing South Africans will tell you
that they'd 'niver call a keffir a keffir to 'is faice'.

I looked out of the window at a white with a mobile phone
making a gesture to a black in a boiler suit that would have
caused a strike in England, and suddenly I felt bitterly alone.
What the hell was I doing? Coming back to this part of the
world where there was such violence and cruelty and
prejudice; leaving everything safe and comfortable and English behind?

I'd last been in Southern Africa in 1977, when I was
eighteen. There was a period between leaving school and
going to university which was known as 'the gap'. We were
strongly advised to 'do something positive with the gap'. It

wasn't a time to lie around in London getting stoned and working in wine bars; it was a time to get out to far flung places and Become a Man.

I'd been casting around trying to find something to do, when I heard of an opportunity to work at a new multi-racial school in a very poor African country called Botswana. Maru-a-Pula (literally 'Clouds of Rain') was only four or five years old, and the teachers had a small group of volunteer assistants who might be asked to do anything from building new classrooms to washing-up. They were known as 'teacher aids', and were paid a salary of around £20 a month.

It sounded a lot more exciting than driving round Europe in a van, which is what most of my contemporaries seemed to be planning. And it was in the Third World! No longer would I just be looking at photos of starving black children in the papers: at last I'd be out there *doing* something.

I found Botswana on the map. It was a great big chunk of Africa, bang in the middle of the south, most of which seemed to be the Kalahari Desert. It had a capital called Gaborone, interesting-sounding place names like Rakops, Kang, and Lephepe, and a vast marshy area called the Okavango Swamps. To the north-east lay Rhodesia – in the middle of a war of liberation; to the north, the Caprivi Strip and Angola; to the west, South-West Africa, Namibia as it was to become; to the south and east, South Africa, the border defined by the great grey-green, greasy Limpopo. What more could I want?

So, shortly after Christmas, I found myself being driven by my mother and father down a snowy motorway to Heathrow. Twelve hours later I was in Johannesburg, in the middle of summer. And then I was being met at the dusty little Gaborone airstrip by two of the other teacher aids: a plump, pretty girl of eighteen from Bradford called Nina, and a tall lean American with a beard whose name was Greg.

We drove through the tiny capital to the school. Until

1966, Botswana had been the Protectorate of Bechuanaland, and when the British had left, they'd laid out a 1960s town-planner's dream of a city. Right in the centre was a gravel pedestrian mall, with young trees, stone bollards and ample parking; radiating off from this a rippling series of circular roads that could be extended indefinitely. So far the development was limited: there were two roundabouts, one four-way stop, and a set of traffic lights. Maru-a-Pula was on the edge of town, at the point where the tarmac road became red-brown dirt, and the bungalows gave way to the endless plain of low trees, bushes, and knee-high grass that I soon learnt to call 'the bush'.

There were three more teacher aids: another American with shoulder-length hair and a disdainful expression called Matt, a skinny Indian girl from Johannesburg called Jitika, and a large-boned, white-faced English graduate from York called Sam, who had round wire glasses and was generally to be found carrying the bulky purple and grey paperback edition of Blake's *Complete Poems*. Apart from Nina, who like me was eighteen and a new arrival, they were all in their early twenties and had been there two terms. There was a certain back-history that neither Nina nor I were privy to: a lot of talk about an ex-teacher aid called Jodie; and then the tragic story of Greg's younger brother John who'd gone home from his stint at Maru-a-Pula to be killed in a car-crash. He'd loved Botswana so much they had flown his ashes out to be scattered on the nearby hills.

The school had been the idea of the newly independent Botswana Government. But the driving force on the ground was a white South African called Deane Yates. He'd been headmaster of St John's, South Africa's all-white equivalent of Eton or Winchester, before chucking it all in to come down to Gaborone with his wife Dot and a couple of tents to start Maru-a-Pula from scratch.

Deane – or DY as he was known – was the ultimate 'muscular Christian': a burly, bald-headed man with great bushy eyebrows, who strode around in a khaki safari suit supervising every aspect of his creation. Dot was contrastingly thin, with short dark curls, a cut-glass colonial English accent, and a question-mark on her brow that told of her permanent concern for all living things, most particularly DY.

Round him, DY had gathered a mixed bag of teachers: there was Tom, who had a stammer and taught English; Mike, who had one leg and taught geography; Sandy, who had one arm and taught science. Sandy had never quite accepted that he'd lost his arm, and was by far the most active member of staff. It was Sandy who was building the school swimming pool, Sandy who would be first to volunteer to drive the school truck, Sandy who would be found cutting wood on the electric woodsaw, the stump of his other arm tied by a bandage to the handle of the machine.

Then there was Alan, who was the BBC's Botswana stringer and really wanted to be a full-time journalist; Philip Walker, reluctant teacher of physics, whose passion in life was classical music, whose flat was open to teacher aids at all hours; and George, the millionaire American retired headmaster, who'd built his own comfortable bungalow on the edge of campus, and only taught two terms out of three, so that he could spend the American summer fishing in Maine.

Bar George, they were all white South Africans, all to some extent escaping from the extraordinary political experiment being conducted just twenty miles away over the border. It was 1977, the year after the school-children of Soweto had first risen up against the white regime.

The day I arrived the kids – true to the cliché – all looked the same; as they tore round campus, emerged shouting and screaming from the dining-cum-assembly hall. Half of them had English names, half of them unpronounceable African names, often with lovely meanings, things like 'This is the child God sent us' or 'He is the hope of the village'. My favourite was Morulagane, which meant 'Oh god not another boy'.

Seretse Khama, the President of Botswana, had set up his brave new Republic with four guiding principles: Non-Racialism, Self-Reliance, Social Harmony and Development. He himself had married a white Englishwoman, and was about as decent a leader as you could find anywhere in the world. The whole country had a brand new and optimistic feel about it, as if anything were possible – something of a contrast to what I'd left behind in England. Young black guys would smile and shake your hand in the street; and if you bothered to learn the traditional Tswana greeting exchange ('Dumêla, rra' – 'Dumêla, rra' – 'A o tsogile, rra?' – 'Ke tsogile sentlê, a o tsogile, rra?' – 'Ke tsogile sentlê', and so on: it took about ten minutes, even to buy a loaf of bread) you'd be treated like a long-lost brother.

The school mirrored the country, with the same four noble principles. Non-Racialism was not the same as multi-racialism. This was not a school where a number of races mixed, but a school where race was ignored. In practice, this sometimes proved difficult, and DY would often say about this or that incident that he wasn't prepared to 'bend over blackwards'.

Self-Reliance meant that the kids and teachers did all their own washing-up and cleaning. There were a variety of community service projects that took care of Social Harmony and Development. Perhaps the best of these was the trip to the little village of Gabane, twenty kilometres or so to the west of Gaborone, in the lee of a range of low and beautiful hills. There were people here who were quite literally starving. Once a week a teacher, a couple of teacher aids and twenty or thirty kids would drive the school truck to the back of the Gaborone Holiday Inn and pick up a huge aluminium cooking pot full of left-over steaks, pork chops and so on, over which the cooks had poured boiling water. This mess of pottage would then be driven (usually at maniac speed by the one-armed Sandy) out over the bumpy dirt road to Gabane, where it would be handed out to 'the destitutes', together with small packets of sugar and dried milk. This they would live on for a week. It was the closest I ever got to that childhood dream of giving the scraps on your plate to the starving Third World. Most of the patrons of the Holiday Inn were South Africans who came over for the gambling and prostitution, both banned in their own country.

As teacher aids we had many other duties. Washing-up, serving lunch, driving into 'Gabs' to get the mail; but above all, forming a link between the – mostly black – pupils and the entirely white staff.

In a mixed school where some of the 'kids' were older than us, this too had its potential problems. A week or so after our arrival, DY called us into his study and told us that on no account were we to get involved in emotional relationships with the students. 'Just keep it physical,' said Greg, as we emerged, laughing, into the sunshine. DY had also taken chalk to blackboard and pointed out the appallingly high local rates of gonorrhoea and syphilis. 70% of women between the ages of eighteen and twenty-five had gonorrhoea, 45% syphilis. We had been warned.

The temptations, however, were strong. Sitting in the evening with Sam or Greg on the terrace of the President Hotel, having a beer and looking out over the Mall, listening to the crickets and feeling the warmth of the African night on your skin, you'd always be approached by prostitutes. And these were not raddled old whores, but beautiful provocative girls in their teens, girls who thought that being a tart in town was something far more glamorous than life back in the bush. 'A year ago I was just a simple village girl,' one of them told me once, as she sat with us, stroking her long crimson-varnished fingers down the sleeves of her white angora sweater.

Being eighteen, with only one brief experience of sex, I

managed to stay clear. Sam, who was twenty-four and the
other side of three years at York University, couldn't help
but give in. One night, when we were leaving the President,
and four or five of these girls were sitting giggling on an
armchair, offering themselves in a Dutch auction ('five pula
for the night,' 'OK, three pula,' 'OK, two pula,' and so on)
Sam took one home. He emerged the next morning to say
that he'd had the most wonderful night of his life. These
African girls made you feel like the centre of the universe. A
week later he staggered into the bathroom, white pus pouring
from his genitals. Even Dr Bhoola (M.D. Cairo) the local VD
wizard, couldn't cure him, and in the end he had to be flown
back to England for treatment.

My heart, meanwhile, had settled on one of the students.
Sophie was having a term out in the middle of her A-level
year, so strictly speaking she wasn't a student, and I
reckoned this got me out of DY's strictures. I met her at the
opening of the school swimming pool, which we teacher
aids had been assiduously painting all January. It was a
warm February evening and her black skin and white smile
were set off perfectly by a yellow jumpsuit – I thought she
was wonderful.

For a month or so we met, and talked, and had a very
innocent courtship, culminating in a few kisses behind a
thorn tree on the school playing field. Being eighteen and
romantic, I wondered what it would be like to marry her, to
take beautiful black Sophie back to my parents in green cold
England; to show her my favourite landscapes, the windy
cliffs of North Cornwall, the long seal-strewn spit of sand at
Blakeney in Norfolk.

I was as happy as I'd ever been. For five years I'd been
locked up in an English public school – indoors at 6.15, bed
by 10.30 – and now I was suddenly free. I could drink, I
could smoke, I could drive the teacher aids' moped dangerously along the dirt roads, skidding in clouds of dust, taking
turns off and roaring (in so far as a Honda 50 can roar) down

narrow cattle tracks, parking up under a tree to lie and eat the succulent *marula* fruits that were scattered everywhere at that time of year.

At school, I'd done an A-level in Art, and with the Honda at my disposal I became the Van Gogh of Gabane and the surrounding villages. As soon as the lunch-time washing-up session was over, I'd grab my rattling steed and be off. On the far side of Gabane I'd find a suitable subject: a twisted tree, a rocky hill, a river where half-naked herdboys brought cattle – their cow-bells ding-dinging from far away – to drink. I'd sit in the shade of a tree with my watercolours. Within a few minutes, I'd be surrounded by a silent crowd of little black children. And if you turned to them and spoke, they'd cover their mouths with their hands and giggle, or run off shrieking.

Sometimes, on my way back to town, I'd stop at the village shebeen, which was no more than someone's home, three or four round thatched mud huts surrounded by a dirt compound. The men would sit to one side in the shade drinking and talking while the women did all the work. There were two types of beer, the thick white yoghurt-like *chibuku*, or a thin cidery drink made from roots, called *kgadi*. For a couple of pula you could buy a round of drinks and become the most popular man in the village.

In the evenings I would climb up onto the warm flat concrete roof of the boys' boarding house and try to paint the sunset. The languid colour-changes of England are hard enough to catch; in Botswana it was an impossible exercise: vivid reds and yellows and oranges and greens and purples appearing and vanishing before you could mix the paint, let alone get it on the paper.

One evening one of the students, a coloured* girl from

---

* In England 'coloured' is virtually synonomous with 'black'. In South Africa it has a specific meaning. 'Coloured' was the word used by the ethnic categorists of apartheid to define the large group of people of mixed race, who live mainly in the Cape. The 'coloureds'

Jo'burg called Beverley, came scrambling up onto the roof next to me. 'Mark,' she said, 'd'you think you could teach me how to paint like this?'

And so I started a little art class, in an empty workman's prefab on the edge of campus. DY couldn't offer me a lot of money to get it going, so we began with twenty pieces of hardboard, twenty pencils, a handful of rubbers, a box of drawing pins and a supply of paper offcuts that we got free from the local printing works.

Having been bored to tears at school being made to draw blocks of wood, rusting ploughshares and so on, I decided we'd dive straight in at the deep end with life drawing. One kid would be a model, and the other twenty or so would sit around on hard chairs and try and capture likeness, with varying degrees of success.

It was fun being in the position of drawing master all of a sudden. And I had a bit of luck. One of the biggest trouble-makers in the school, a sixteen year old from a wealthy but broken home, suddenly became my most devoted pupil. Bennett had been smashing up desks and causing mayhem; now he was staying later than all the others, quizzing me earnestly about cross-hatching techniques.

DY was so pleased with Bennett's transformation that he gave me some more money and I was able to splash out and buy some powder paints. The monochrome life-drawing sessions were supplemented by colourful landscape exercises; and in the late afternoon cool the faithful would troop

---

have a rich mixture of bloods, being descendants of the first Dutch settlers; the now-extinct original inhabitants of South Africa – the Khoi-Khoi (Hottentots) and Basarwa (Bushmen); the imported Malay slaves; as well as the various black races.

With apartheid gone, 'coloured' has begun – to some – to have offensive implications, and yet no new word has been coined to describe this large and specific group of mixed-race South Africans. 'So-called coloured' is the nearest anyone has come to it, and most people, 'coloureds' included, still use 'coloured' colloquially. For simplicity's sake, I have followed their example, leaving the inverted commas implied rather than printed.

out to the playing field to experiment with warm ochres and cold blues in the slanting shadowy sunshine.

George, the retired American headmaster, had taken me under his wing. We'd developed one of those close school-teacher-protégé friendships. George offered gin and tonic on his verandah, a record player, the guest flat in his bungalow; and what did I offer? ... youth, a companion for endless games of backgammon, someone to listen as he sat, yarning about the past at the centre of a pungent cloud of pipesmoke, occasionally looking up to bellow at Prufrock, Shakespeare and Wordsworth, his three cats.

I moved my Form One English classes down to George's. In the morning, while he was out teaching Form Four, I would sit in his garden under the thorn tree and take my six little girls through verbs and nouns and adjectives and adverbs. I had no control over them, and more often than not they would end up dancing around me, hands in the air, shrieking with laughter and singing 'Markwe, Markwe!'

In the holidays I took off from Maru-a-Pula and travelled. With a school-friend, I drove from Johannesburg round the beautiful eastern Transvaal and up into Swaziland. We saw the spectacular Blyde River Canyon, climbed the precipitous dirt road to Piggs Peak, bought little soapstone Swazi carvings, made the most of the six course breakfasts on offer in even the smallest guest houses. The topic of conversation with landladies was always, 'Dan't you farnd our cantry beaudiful?' Any attempt to raise the subject of apartheid would be met by silence, or at best, 'There's nah way, kemming from aht-saard, thit you kin understand the complixities of this cantry.'

Then I headed off on my own, hitch-hiking, and saw a different South Africa. A black lorry driver took me home and I realised that for every sweet little European-style town up on the hill there was a not-so-sweet corrugated-iron 'township' tucked out of sight in the valley.

On the beach at Jeffrey's Bay I was accosted by a born-again Dutch Reformed Church evangelical – a very strange hybrid indeed. When I asked him how he squared his evangelism with the Reformed Church idea that blacks were descended from Cain, whites from Abel, and blacks were thus *supposed* to be the inferior race, he said, 'Look men, you must understand that I'd be quart hippy to kneel along-sard a bleck at communion – but there's nah way he's mah equal.'

In another town on the Garden Route – that famously beautiful stretch of mountainous Indian Ocean coast between Port Elizabeth and George – I felt so homesick that I found myself following the sound of churchbells into an all-white Evensong. As I left, having taken communion, and shaken hands with the vicar at the porch, I was overtaken by a little old lady who asked me if I was all right. With my knapsack and tousled hair I must have been more conspicuous than I'd realised. I ended up staying with her and her husband for a week. They lived in Restful Road, in a white retirement complex called Leisure Island, and they looked after me like a son (their own son was away in the South African army) feeding me with huge steaks and fresh guavas from their garden wall. But with them too, as soon as we got onto politics, this terrible self-justifying racism would emerge. Before, such attitudes had just made me intellectually angry; now, with black friends back in Botswana, they upset me more deeply.

In September I flew back to go to university. I had a hope that I might return, when I'd finished my degree, maybe to teach again, maybe . . . But of course I was soon into an exciting new world of amateur theatricals and sudden enthusiasms for obscure medieval poets, and Africa was a string of stories with which to bore prospective girlfriends. I left college, got a job in advertising, life raced on.

Occasionally I'd encounter people from that time. Primrose, one of my favourite kids, called me up in London and we went to see *Daisy Pulls It Off*. It was strange, taking an old friend to the theatre, and then realising you're being stared at because you're white and she's black. Then Sophie appeared out of the blue, engaged to a friend of my cousin's fianceé, of all links, and finishing a law postgrad at Kent University. We had dinner at an Italian restaurant in Clapham, and she told me how she was hoping to go back and set up a home for battered wives in the middle of a Gaborone slum that hadn't even existed in 1977. I bumped into Nina again. She'd been to visit Greg in the States, and had been shocked to find him sharing his flat and life with another man (she'd always had a soft spot for Greg). We had a reunion supper with the white-faced Sam, who was on his fifth or sixth Ph.D and about to marry an Argentinian. But apart from that, it all just remained a happy and intriguing memory.

And then, fifteen years later, I had a dream. It was one of those intense dreams, that linger sweetly with you as you surface. I'd fallen asleep on the London Underground and woken up in Africa. AFRICA was what the black and red station sign said, and when I emerged from the escalator I was in Botswana . . . the sun was hot, for some reason I was wearing a riding hat, and I was being led around those long-forgotten brick and concrete classrooms by two little girls from my English class . . . they weren't any larger physically, but in some strange way they'd grown up . . .

It was all quite a contrast to what I was waking up to. Another grey late-September day in London. Another day when I would have to sit down at my Amstrad and churn out a brochure for a new type of computer system, or at best a 'humorous' article for *Punch*. Another day of drinking too much coffee and being driven insane by car alarms going off endlessly in the street outside. And then in the afternoon I would cycle wearily up the hill to the cinema I managed part-time, and worry about mislaid bookings and ice-cream deliveries, and whether or not we could get through an evening without the ladies' toilet overflowing.

I reached over and woke Sarah. As we sat up together drinking tea I told her about my dream, launched into a couple of African memories. 'Well, why don't you write about *that*?' she said. 'Why don't you try and go back there and see how it's changed?'

The idea moved with remarkable speed. South Africa – 'The New South Africa' indeed – was in the news. By Christmas I had a commission for a book. My plan: to land in Cape Town and drive up the coast and across to Botswana, taking in the places I'd hitched last time, and seeing those I hadn't but had always fantasised about – like Coffee Bay on the Wild Coast of the Transkei, which a hippy I'd met at a deserted crossroads in the Karoo had told me was the most beautiful beach in the world. In my imagination, it was a long curve of coral pink, reached by an empty dirt road across sunlit hills.

As soon as I told my friends what I was doing, where I was going, everybody seemed to have an angle on it. Peter, an actor pal who worked at the cinema, told me I was making a grave mistake. 'I wouldn't go there at all. I certainly wouldn't act there. While the black leaders are telling us not to go, I don't think we should go.' 'Don't be too po-faced about it,' said a barrister friend. 'For god's sake, all these white liberals sitting round not drinking South African wine . . . you've *been* there, you can say what you like.'

With my contract came other excitements. Features editors who'd previously not returned my calls suddenly changed their tune. The travel editor of *The Times* felt sure she'd have room for a couple of pieces; the *Daily Mail* could certainly use something.

With newspaper offers under my belt, I entered the wonderful world of freebies – before I knew it I had a free flight and (it seemed from the letter) the offer of a free hire car for three months.

I drove down to an obscure part of Richmond and found the South African Tourist Board. 'Ah think you'll farnd,' said the white PR officer, 'that whin you git there, that nah, in Seth Effrika, the wyatt Seth Effrikans are ez aware of the racial problems as inyone in the world.'

Things had definitely changed, she told me. Blacks could live anywhere now. People of different races were mixing and getting to know each other. 'If you hitch-hiked,' she said, 'you might meet some black guys. They might take you into their homes, that might be virry interesting.'

'I'd read,' I said, 'of some paradoxes in this New South Africa. Like some of these liberal whites who've been campaigning for the abolition of segregated beaches but don't like the actual reality of having black people on their part of the beach.'

'Well that's true. But it's hardly surprising. In Cape Town, on New Year's Day, the blacks are bringing live sheep and goats down and sacrificing them on the beach.'

I laughed. 'And the liberals don't like that?'

'Well, you'd object, wouldn't you? Imagine doing that in Brighton, or Cannes. It wouldn't happen.'

Then she said something I hadn't heard for fifteen years. 'We have a class system, really – just like you. It's just there are more blacks in the lower classes.'

In South Africa itself things were hotting up. The Right wing Conservative Party had won a by-election at Potchefstroom and President De Klerk had responded by calling for a referendum on whether or not South Africa should continue to move down the road to reform. It was seen as an agile political move. Ever since his famous speech of 2 February 1990, when he'd first announced the dismantling of apartheid, the main Nationalist Party had been losing ground to the breakaway Conservatives, led by an ex-Nationalist, Dr

Andreis Treurnicht. Now De Klerk was calling Treurnicht's bluff. The message was going out to the all-white voters: vote 'No' and South Africa descends into chaos – international sanctions will be reimposed, the economy will go even further down the tubes. Vote 'Yes' and we move forward to the New South Africa.

Glued to the TV, I watched with relief as the result crystallised from victory to De Klerk, to a 60% 'mandate', to a 68% 'landslide'. Had it been 'No' the ANC had threatened anarchy; some commentators had even speculated darkly about 'civil war'. It was a traveller I wanted to be, not a war correspondent.

2

THE NEW SOUTH AFRICA

Now I was circling over Cape Town. The sky was blue, the
sun glinted on the South Atlantic. Through the window to
my left was the magnificent silhouette of Table Mountain:
the sliced-off flat top, the peaks of 'the Twelve Apostles'
running down towards Cape Point. And there, clustering up
the mountain's skirts and down to the sea, the pretty white
buildings and green trees of the Mother City herself – in
1977 exclusively the preserve of whites; now, in 1992 ...
who knew?

One thing hadn't changed. Out here by the airport, stretching for mile upon mile below us were the tiny houses and
shacks of the black townships. I'd never flown into Cape
Town before, so I'd not seen this particular one. But I
recognised the pattern: the regimented rows of corrugated
iron roofs, the smoke rising from fires, the dirt streets, the
swarms of little figures: men, women, children, goats, don-
keys, dogs ... pushed out well away from the privileged
gaze of the whites.

I left the plane and strode out across the tarmac, eyes
skinned for lingering remnants of apartheid. I was all set for a
bullfrog-necked Afrikaner to give me a hard time in immigration. But the queue moved rapidly, and the Passport Control
Officer was bearded and friendly. 'Enjoy your holiday,' he
said mildly, stamping me in for four months without fuss.

My rule was that wherever possible I was going to take the low-budget option. I loaded my cases onto a trolley and headed off past a row of waiting taxis to the bus stop. But there was no bus for an hour and a half. Oh sod it, I thought, heading back to the rank, I'll take the low-budget option tomorrow. With the exchange rate at five rand to the pound I could afford to splash out a little.

My cab driver was tall and craggily good looking. He was very soft-spoken, and said 'sir' after everything. I couldn't work out whether he was white and tanned, or coloured. No, I could hardly ask him what 'colour' he was. But here at least was my first subject: doubtless, if I probed him in the right way, I could find out what the coloured (or was it the white?) community thought of the recent changes, the lifting of apartheid, the referendum.

'Where are you from?' I began.

'I came down here from Durban a year ago, sir.'

'Durban?'

'Yes, sir. It's a lovely town, sir.'

'So why did you come?'

'I came to be with this girl, sir.'

'Right.'

'Only she's changed totally. We went out for a year eight years ago, in Natal. And then last year she called and I gave up everything to come down here and she's changed.'

'But you're still together?'

'We split up. She wants me back now, keeps phoning me and crying. But when we were together she did some terrible things – so it's no good, I'm not going back to her.'

I tried to make reassuring noises. 'Well,' I said, 'if she's wanting you back now, you know, she's probably just being sentimental. If it didn't work out at the time, it didn't work out.'

'Hm.' He sighed, deeply. 'So where are you going in Cape Town?'

'Greenmarket Square,' I said. And as soon as I saw it I

knew that I'd made the right decision. There were cobbles, and shady trees, and market stalls. Shops with awnings, a church, the long low verandah of a coffee bar. A Rastaman with a guitar sang 'Don't you worreh – 'bout a thing . . .' Onlookers clapped. The cab nosed through the multi-racial crowd of shoppers.

The foyer of the Tudor Hotel was reassuringly shabby. Beaten-up armchairs, a worn-out carpet, a caged parrot which wolf-whistled as you entered. A large black lady checked me in, and I rattled up to the third floor in one of those lifts that takes two people at a pinch and looks as if it might break down at any moment. I had a bath and phoned Sarah in London. She sounded alarmingly close.

'Hi,' I said. 'Just to let you know I've arrived.'

'You sound as if you're just down the road.'

Ten minutes later I put the phone down with a lurch in my heart. She wasn't just down the road, and I was on my own on the shiny pink counterpane of a double bed six thousand miles away. I wasn't going to see her for three months. I'd just have to put her out of my mind.

I went back down to the square. It was only 3 p.m., but the market was already packing up. Keen observer of the New South Africa, I noticed no signs of segregation. The stallholders were white, black, Indian, coloured; you could have picked any of them up and dropped them down in Camden Lock no questions asked. There was a white Rasta, a girl with a ring through her nose, a couple of rather tired-looking punks.

I stopped at a stall where a pretty Indian girl was selling sunglasses. I hardly ever wear sunglasses, but hungry for conversation I bought a pair. Anyway they were only twenty rand. With the magic exchange rate, what was that? Four quid.

I bought a copy of the *Cape Times* and headed over to the coffee shop verandah; joined the groups of (now here they were exclusively white) weekenders sipping

beers and cappuccinos, eating open sandwiches and cakes.
This was more like it! In London, my co-manager would
just be unlocking that smelly little cinema office ... I
sipped my beer and looked down at my sun-dappled
paper. On the front page was a huge colour picture showing
row upon row of portable toilets standing in a field. TOILET
TOWN ran the headline. A FAMOUS LANDMARK OF NATIONALIST
MISRULE.

> Dotted across South Africa's landscape are
> thousands of unwanted and unused portable toilets
> valued at R15 million, paid for by the Department of
> Development Aid. These sanitary sentinels were
> photographed in a barren stretch of the Transvaal.
>   The portable toilets have been scattered in rural
> areas by the Department of Development Aid. One
> allegation from the Pickard Report which police are
> investigating is that two officials of the Department
> of Development Aid designed a glass-fibre toilet and
> patented it. Specifications for tenders for the
> purchase of about R2 million worth of toilets for the
> SA Development Trust and the homeland of Lebowa
> were prepared in such a way that only a firm they
> owned could meet the requirements ... a town was
> built with toilets, streets, a secondary school, a
> primary school, a reservoir and a 20-bed clinic at a
> cost of R7 million. It is a town which no-one wants
> or has ever occupied.

There was a shout. On the steps of the verandah a scruffy
coloured man was being barred entry by an impeccably
turned-out coloured headwaiter. 'We're all fighting for our
rights,' he shouted. 'So I'm fighting for mine!' The young
white couple sipping lager at the table by the steps bantered
good-naturedly with him as he backed away.

A chubby black Harpo Marx in a stained green boiler suit
stumbled across the square. Reaching the edge of the veran-

dah he lurched up to a table where a couple of elderly white men were drinking tea and talking in Afrikaans. The larger of the two got to his feet, leant over, gave him a coin. He took it and smiled. Just as the old man sat down again, Harpo shouted again, louder. 'Oh go *away!*' barked the old man, with a tone of command in his voice that you'd never hear in England. The black guy smiled and mooched off, to dance around the now-empty square slapping hands with the other ten or so blacks and coloureds sitting around on dustbins, a bench, the cobbles.

I wandered down narrow Longmarket Street to Adderley Street, where a tour bus was about to depart. Somewhat aimlessly, I climbed aboard, and up to the open top deck, which had been colonised by a drunken group of white teenagers with guitars. 'Wild Thing!' they sang, drowning out the tinny voice of the guide, a sulky blonde twenty-something who remained downstairs. You couldn't miss the Castle, built by Jan Van Riebeeck, the founder of Cape Town and White South Africa, or the massive brown stone Anglican Cathedral, episcopal seat of Archbishop Desmond Tutu, but most of the rest was lost in inebriated shrieks of hilarity. Leaving the high-rise centre, we ground up the hill through the little white houses of the Malay Quarter, then down towards the glinting Atlantic surf, crashing in over the rocks at Greenpoint. 'And in the distance,' came the bored, disembodied voice from the loudspeaker, 'you'll see Robben Island, where Nelson Mandela was imprisoned for thirty years.'

At the Docks I got off. Beyond a swish shopping mall full of uniformed security guards and designer chocolates, there was a one rand ferry, rowed by a tall, silent black guy, which carried the all-white punters across a twenty yard stretch of the dock basin to Bertie's Landing. Stripped pine steps led up from a jetty to an open-air bar, where beer and oysters were on sale, and couples sat on benches watching the setting sun reflected in the mirror of the harbour below. The place was packed, and apart from two blacks collecting glasses, there wasn't a dark face in sight. Even the barmen were white, muscly young studs in shorts and T-shirts.

Up further steps were a trio of stripped-pine pleasure decks, two enclosed, one open to the stars. In the first, a rock band was wading through hits from the '60s and '70s. The lead singer looked like Noel Edmonds, *circa* 1973, and the other two had similar bouffant Bee Gee haircuts. The only difference was that they weren't young. They were mid-forties, the Last Survivors of Rock, wowing an ecstatic young audience on the tip of Africa.

'Are ya riddy?' shouted Noel, tossing back his mane of hair. 'Yeah! Yah! Yiss!' returned the crowd. A theatrical twang. Then: 'I can't git no – der-der der-der – Sitisfiction!'

'There's more tillent outsaide than in,' said a plump blonde to her friend, as they marched past. I ordered a Castle beer and sat up by the bar. 'Dan't you hate beer?' said a thin-faced girl buying a fistful of Lions. 'You spind half your day in the toilit.'

The kids were sure having a good time. At every table they swayed back and forth, joining in the familiar choruses. 'Hey Jude . . . Judy Judy Judy . . . he-ey Jude . . .'

A black cleaner was endeavouring to keep the floor swept. None of your cockney 'Mind yer backs' for him. Eyes lowered, he was dodging among the be-shorted jocks as best he could, every now and then getting his little pile of rubbish and fag-ends kicked to one side by a careless white foot. His English counterpart would have been up in arms. He just meekly reassembled the rubbish and pushed on.

The Base, by contrast, could have been anywhere. There were blacks, whites, browns – and that familiar aura of inebriated boredom common to nightclubs the world over. On the dance floor people bopped; by the billiard table they played billiards; at tables covered with fag-ends and pools of beer they stared blankly into space. A white four-eyes in his forties had his arm slumped round a pretty young black girl with beaded hair; he looked drunk, she just looked tired. On a bench in a dark corner, a coloured man was curled up asleep, his mouth hanging open, a thread of spittle swinging from it like a metronome. At least I thought he was coloured; in the flashing ultra-violet light it was hard to tell.

Slumped in a corner with a can of Castle, I thought not so much of the cruelty, but of the absurdity of the system that had been in place in this country until February 1990. At Maru-a-Pula there'd been a little girl called Marjorie who was whiter than I am. She had curly brown hair, freckles and buck teeth. She was from Cape Town, and was classified as a coloured. Trying to divide people up into groups on the basis of racial characteristics had made for ridiculous logistical problems. At one stage there was the famous 'pencil test', where Civil Service officials would run a pencil through a child's hair: if it was sufficiently crinkly, they were deemed coloured. If you look at the records, you can find statistics of coloured people who applied to become 'white' (462 successful applications in 1982-3); Indians who applied to become 'Malay' (15); even whites who applied to become 'Indian' (3).

The next morning was just as sunny and beautiful. This was unusually good weather for May, the coloured lady at the hotel Reception told me. I should make the most of it, before winter finally arrived.

It was 10.30. I walked up to the Anglican Cathedral, hoping to catch a glimpse of Desmond Tutu. But the Archbishop was away, and the 9.15 service had just ended.

Groups of church-goers mingled on the steps: all colours. Black and white priests smiled and shook hands. A notice invited the congregation to 'Please join us for a cup of tea in the Crypt after Parish Eucharist.' I followed a stooping coloured man down stone steps and found myself in a room that was a mix of well-heeled whites, and coloureds of all varieties; ranging from a smartly turned-out family at the centre table to the ragged man ahead of me in the tea-queue who smelt strongly of stale urine. In the kitchen motherly looking white women rushed around among urns and chopping boards, rewashing cups, pouring tea, making sandwiches.

Sitting down with my tea I was joined by a man no darker than me, but if he was white he was down on his luck. He looked like the travellers I used to talk to when I had a stall in the market in Covent Garden. A face worn out with poverty and failure, eyes nonetheless bright with a mad, unputdownable gleam of hope.

'I need some money for a shower,' he said. I gave him twenty cents. He thanked me, and approached a foursome of whites. After a few remonstrations, one of the women pointed firmly at a black priest who was holding court over the far side of the room. He returned briskly to me.

'Look men, can you help me out? I need a shower. It costs two rand seventy. I've got seventy.' The logic was inescapable; I gave him two rand.

'Thank you,' he said, with a broad smile. He was missing a couple of teeth.

'Will you spend it on a shower, really?' I asked.

'Oh yes.' He was serious. 'I need to get clean.'

In England I'd have got to my feet and left him; but since he'd sat down beside me, and I was alone, and I'd travelled all this distance to immerse myself in this strange society, I decided to ask him the direct question:

'So why are you on the streets?'

'I'll be honest with you,' he replied. 'I went to jail.'

'For?'

'Drugs. Two and a half years.'

'For what – dealing?'

'No, I had some marijuana on me.'

'Two and a half years for *possession*?'

He nodded slowly. 'I will pull myself up again.'

'D'you ever spend this sort of money on drink?'

'I'll be honest with you – yes.' He smiled his gaptoothed smile. 'In the evening.'

'Well – you've got to have a drink in the evening.'

'Yes!' He nodded eagerly. 'Last night I was down at the Waterfront, and this young couple, you know, very nice, took me into the bar with them, bought me loads of beer. I was there all evening. But I kept one back,' he winked, caricature-style, 'for the morning.'

His name was Trevor, and he had two grown-up sons. One was an executive in a factory in Jo'burg that made lifts. The other was a travelling salesman.

'So d'you see them?'

'Sometimes. But I don't want them to know what their father's come to.' He gestured at himself. 'Like this.'

'You have a wife?'

'No. She died. In a car-crash. And the little one died. And the two boys and me were OK. I was driving.'

'I'm sorry.'

'This was in 1976. 1976,' he repeated slowly.

'So did you get into drugs after that?'

He nodded, but didn't smile. 'Yes.'

I took a cab to the beach. My driver was enormous and black. Right! I thought. The other side of the coin.

'I'm from England,' I began chattily, as we drew off. 'It's supposed to be the beginning of your winter, but it's beautifully warm.'

'Yes sir,' he replied. 'Winter.' There was a long pause. I wondered whether I should just dive in and ask him whether apartheid really was on the way out; or merely cosmetic.

'The people of Cape Town are very friendly, sir,' he volunteered suddenly. 'So you needn't worry, you'll have a good holiday.'

'It's a beautiful place.'

'It is. Beautiful.'

'And better now they've scrapped all the laws?'

'Yes. It is better. Some people still have a problem with attitude, but it is much better.'

'But it must make a difference now that things like the pass laws have gone?'

'Yes. But attitude is more important. We can all get along, if there's the right attitude. You know, the blacks are very different. They think in a different way. The coloureds and the whites, the way they think is very much the same. But the blacks, they want to have too many children, and come in from where they live and take all the jobs in the towns . . .'

I'd taken off my sunglasses, and no, I wasn't hallucinating – he was black. In skin colour, at any rate. A black 'coloured'.

'Very beautiful,' I said, as his little rant came to an end and we came down the edge of the mountain on a sweeping curve of road lined with palm and fir trees towards the white sand and blue sea below.

He dropped me at Camps Bay. I set off down the pavement towards the beach.

'It's a beautiful day,' said a shortish, rather plump man walking just behind me. He was wearing a grey T-shirt which said CANADIAN, and large crimson-framed glasses. He had jet black hair and olive skin, and I wondered what *he* was: coloured, Indian, or even, after my recent encounter – black.

'Yes,' I replied, realising as we talked just how much I'd been aching to have a proper conversation. His name was David, and he was an expert at spotting tourists.

'Was I that obvious?'

'Oh *yes*.'

He loved London. Had lived there for three years. Had cousins in Kentish Town. After London, he'd moved back to Jo'burg. But he'd got sick of that and gone to Durban. But Durban was 'dridful' so he'd moved to Cape Town. At first he'd rented out at Sea Point, which was 'faine'; the only problem was his flatmate. 'He's very different from me, doesn't like non-smokers, and his parents are *always* round there.' So now he was moving out here, to Camps Bay. It was the nicest suburb of Cape Town, and he'd just had a stroke of luck; found a place that was absolutely *perfect*.

'I can't believe it. There's some girl who's never there, it's got three bedrooms, and it's only 335 rand a month. The maid costs me seven rand a day. I said to the landlord, "What does she breathe? Oxygen?"' He laughed. 'No, it's incredible. My maid at the moment costs me twenty-five rand a day.'

His smile rippled away from sharp white teeth. We didn't mention the fact that he was gay and I was straight, but that was soon taken as read between us. Sooner or later I would have to drop the bombshell that I had a girlfriend.

He was full of faintly proprietorial advice. Greenmarket Square was nice, but central Cape Town was boring, particularly at night. Sea Point was much livelier. I should seriously consider moving out there. And if I'd taken a cab to get out here, I was insane. Those things cost an arm and a leg. The only way to travel was by African taxi. 'I'll point one out to you. They're like minibuses. If you see a white Kombi full of blacks you just wave at it and it'll stop. What did you pay to get out here?'

'Twenty rand.'

'You're crazy. An African taxi'll take you to the centre for one rand.'

We'd reached the middle of the bay. To our left was a row of little restaurants and shops. Behind them, among lush green trees, pretty white houses climbed the slopes of Table Mountain, which towered craggy and green above. To our right, a row of palm trees and a strip of grass divided the road from the long sandy beach beyond. A sprinkling of bodies basted in the midday sun; here and there people played frisbee or beach tennis; beyond, the surf crashed invitingly.

Right by us was a café with white tables and parasols. I

reckoned I could risk a beer without committing myself to a long-term relationship. Whites in shorts and T-shirts wandered past. On the far side of the road, in dark shabby clothes, sat blacks waiting for taxis and buses into town.

'Is that liver?' asked David, as my 'Bay Salad' arrived. 'I'm Jewish. I only ever eat chopped liver.'

So he was *Jewish*. White, in other words. Even the Nationalists had never been stupid enough to make the Jews 'black'. I told him about my taxi driver.

'Well, yes, the coloured people do have a bit of a chip on their shoulder — they're neither one thing nor the other.'

Eventually I told him what I was doing. 'Well, Mark,' he said. 'I've got one piece of advice for you. Keep an open mind. So many of these journalists from overseas, they come out here and they already know what they think. All they're interested in is, you know, what people earn, where they live, and so on. What's really going on is something else.'

'What is really going on?'

'Keep an open mind, travel around, you'll find out.'

'So what do you think — of the New South Africa?'

'To be honest, I think it's a load of shit.' David laughed loudly, exposing his teeth. 'We have a saying here: "You can take the African out of the bush, but you can never take the bush out of the African." I tell you what I think. I think we're heading for a revolution. No, I think that's the way it's got to go. They're opening the floodgates too fast.'

A couple of teenage white girls were strolling past. One of them was cradling a baby lamb, which she was feeding with a plastic milk bottle.

'Can ah see?' asked David, turning in his chair.

'It's a reject,' said the girl, stroking the little woolly white face. 'Its mother rejictid it.' She looked lovingly at it, as David reached up and gave it a camp stroke.

'To be honest with you,' he said, turning back, 'I'm fed up with South Africa. I'd like to get out. Go to England, or America. All this politics gets me down. You know, every day there's something new in the papers.' He gestured at his paper. 'Yesterday it's death squads, today it's Government corruption, and that's all people talk about, *all* the next day. And if there's a black Government, it'll be twice as bad.'

'Why's that?'

'Don't be naive. Look at Zimbabwe. Mozambique. Lourenco Marques used to be a beautiful place. Now it's a mess. Falling apart. No, I'd like to go and live in England. There's something special about England. They say you haven't seen the world until you've seen England, and I think that's true. Everything around you is so old.'

'What about the climate?'

'I don't mind the cold. You know, you buy a nice coat, you have central heating, I like it. I'll tell you one thing that's wonderful in England – your public transport.'

'Seriously?'

'Public transport is non-existent over here. There's nothing like the Tube.'

No, I thought, looking out through the gently waving palm trees at the blue sea, there was certainly nothing like the Tube.

Out on the desegregated sweep of sand, the New South Africa seemed to be more or less in place. Though there were more whites than blacks about, and though the blacks seemed to have chosen, by and large, to sit fully dressed under the palm trees, while the whites lay bronzing in the sun, it was at least possible for a black to wander down and dip his toe in the sea, something that would have been illegal only three years before.

By six o'clock the sun was setting. A group of black teenagers played frisbee by the surf. A young white guy with glasses joined in. 'Yes sir!' shouted one of the blacks, holding up his hand, as the white held the frisbee. 'Sir! Sir!' shouted another. The game went on, until one of them misthrew and the frisbee landed in the sea. 'You go in,' said the white, 'you've got bare feet. Quickly.'

'No way, sir!' laughed the black. 'No way, there's sharks in there. No way!'

Eventually the white waded in to retrieve it. 'Thank you, sir,' said the black.

I followed David's advice and took an African taxi back to town. A battered white Kombi driven by a little Indian man with a round embroidered tarboosh. Next to him on the front seat were two plump young coloured girls. He drove slowly, hooting at likely-looking blacks and coloureds. A coloured man in a brown suit and battered hat waved, and he stopped abruptly.

On the beach that afternoon I'd decided that I needed to loosen up a bit. Be as easy going as David. Strike up conversations, not just with taxi-drivers and people who approached me, but with total strangers. So:

'I'm from England,' I said now.

'England . . .' said the man in the hat.

'It's a long way away.'

'Long way away,' he repeated, nodding. There was a long pause. 'It's beautiful, the Cape, don't you think?' he said eventually. The minibus rattled along the coast road, lurching to a halt every now and then to pick up another passenger. NAMIBIA GIRL IS MISS UNIVERSE said the newspaper boards on the lamp-posts. One still had a tattered VOTE YES poster. A bus shelter was graffitoed SHE SMELLS SEWERAGE BY THE SEA SHORE.

The taxi was choc-a-block with people. I was squashed against the window by a huge black woman with four shopping bags.

'It's full now,' I said, nodding at the man in the hat.

'No,' he smiled. 'It's never full. They keep on filling it. It's a racket. Very dangerous, driving overloaded.'

'He must make a fair bit of money.'

'Yes – it's a business. But dangerous. They have trouble

with the other taxis. Men can come to them with knives, guns.'

On the Monday morning I woke in my hotel double bed feeling low and lonely. But tea and haddock and an irritating pair of German tourists comparing their maps at the breakfast table next to me did the trick. I clunked back upstairs in the lift having decided that I would at least see about the car hire offer. If it was solid – well, I'd take it. What the hell! I'd hitched last time, and I was thirty-three. The thought of taking an African taxi out to the Cape Town suburbs, standing on the roadside for hours with my thumb out was too depressing.

At best, I'd expected a little hatchback, perhaps something like the battered Renault 5 I drove at home. But once we'd signed the forms and Sherri had told me that she expected me back on or before 8 August, I was shown through to a car bigger than anything I'd ever driven before. A great white gleaming beast of a machine: a Toyota Corolla, emblazoned down both sides with large blue letters reading DOLPHIN HIRE CARS – FOR THE BEST FLIP'N SERVICE. Underneath, by phone and fax numbers, two blue dolphins romped in a sportive circle.

I climbed in and drove off nervously, quite sure that I would crash it and lose my R900 insurance excess before the afternoon was out. I turned right, and in no time at all found myself gliding down into Camps Bay. What a difference a car made! In my sunglasses and CAMPS BAY baseball cap, I was starting to feel like a white Seth Effrikan. What would people think I was, I thought, as I clunked the big door to and strode off confidently towards the beach. A rep? A company director?

The newspapers were full of further revelations of Government corruption. The crisis debate was in Parliament that night. President De Klerk and Dr Viljoen, the Minister for Development Aid, were going to be arraigned by the double-headed Opposition: on the left, the party of Helen Suzman, of Cape Town and Jo'burg liberals – the Democratic Party; on the right, the party that had campaigned for a 'No' vote in the referendum, of hard-bitten Transvaal and Orange Free State Afrikaners – the Conservative Party. There might, it had been suggested, even be resignations.

So after supper I put on my suit and strolled down silent Longmarket and deserted Adderley Street. The whites lived in the suburbs, the coloureds had been moved out to the townships; the street-life you take for granted in a European city was non-existent. Beyond lay The Gardens, a park through which ran a paved avenue of little oak trees, now turning brown and dropping their leaves. Over dark green railings and a lawn scattered with palm trees stood an elegant white and maroon building, lit from the side with pale pink light. This was surely Parliament.

I walked through tall wrought-iron gates and past a sentry box, unchallenged. Inside, white men in suits hurried across the tarmac and up a flight of stone steps. The debate, one of them told me, was at eight. My luck was in: it was two minutes to. I went up the steps, straight past two more security checks and into the packed public gallery.

In 1966, Hendrik Verwoerd, 'the architect of apartheid', President of South Africa from 1958, had been assassinated in Parliament. A 'lunatic' white gunman had stabbed him in this very hall. It seemed incredible that I'd just been able to saunter in like that. It was like attending a university debate, not a crisis meeting of the Parliament of one of the most heavily policed countries in the world.

Like Westminster, the seats were bottle green. Unlike Westminster, they were not in long rows, but divided into two-person units, with little dark polished wooden desks. And there was the familiar bald head of De Klerk, out in front on his own, directly below me. As I bent to sit, he looked up, gave me a broad smile and a little wave. Had my fame travelled so far already? No, looking down, a brass plaque told me I was just above the box containing the Staat President's wife. As the debate began, a black man in a beige suit took the empty seat to my left. As far as I could see, he was the only non-white in the public gallery.

The debate was in Afrikaans. So much for my eager following of the issues. The first speaker, grey-haired and bespectacled, from the Government benches, rattled on for a while, the other MPs behaving much as they do in Westminster. There were cries of 'Hur! Hur!' and occasional laughter. A late arrival marched in, pushed onto the back bench, beamed round at his pals.

At the far end, squashed into narrow pews behind a pillar, were rows of Indian and coloured men and women. Were they members of the controversial tricameral Coloured and Indian Parliament that President Botha had set up in 1984, or were they outsiders? It wasn't clear – but whatever, this was an all-white debate at which they were merely observers.

It was the Opposition's turn. A puce-headed (from where I sat the back of his bald head was all I could see) Conservative started getting very worked up indeed. The place erupted into laughter. MPs and galleries, whites and Indians and coloureds, all were – literally – rolling in the aisles. Only I and the black man next to me remained silent. Whether he too didn't understand Afrikaans, or whether he didn't find the subject under discussion (Government corruption involving billions of mis-spent rands) amusing, I didn't know.

Out in front, De Klerk smiled, reached into his pocket, pulled out a packet of peppermints, slipped one into his mouth.

The comedian sat down and another Opposition member was called, this time from the Democrats. I couldn't see him, but as soon as he started speaking, I recognised that fruity voice. It was Peter, an MP I'd met in London shortly before

I'd left. It was a good speech, all the better for being the first one in English.

'The officials', Peter boomed, 'who have stolen the millions must be pursued through the courts . . . the Government heads must resign . . . in any normal democracy. . . but then this is no normal democracy, sir . . . the Pickard Report reveals a litany of failure . . . annually he exposes corruption . . . the National Party and corruption are old friends . . . the National Party has lost its grip on government . . . we are left with a gang of wimps . . .'

Looking across at the hard-faced members opposite, I wondered whether this was the entirely appropriate epithet. De Klerk had now moved on to a chocolate bar. He turned to the two MPs directly behind him, offered them a slab each.

'Fifty million rands' worth of toilets', Peter continued, 'were left scattered across the veldt . . .'

'A monument to the National Party!' shouted someone.

We were back to the Nationalists and Afrikaans. The word 'toilet' was frequently repeated. Faced with laughter, the promising young party member switched to English. 'Those that laugh and smile along there,' he shouted in his thick Afrikaans accent, 'should remember that *we*, the National Party, unearthed this. *We* took out the corruption. If the Devil came down here today, to see who was on the side of the corruption and who was not,' he paused magnificently, 'he'd be very pleased,' he concluded.

Hm . . .

Back at the hotel I picked up my list of contacts. It was time to take the plunge. But at 9.30 p.m., Susan, who'd been described as 'a successful journalist turned radical activist', didn't sound too keen to talk to me.

'I'm so *weary* of this,' came her thin voice down the phone. 'A lot of us are weary of these questions about apartheid.'

As far as Susan was concerned all journalists came to

South Africa and then went back and wrote the same thing: that all the whites were bad, and all the blacks were good. It was just so easy to apply stereotypes. 'And I do not want to be stereotyped as the classic white liberal.'

I told her I was trying to view things with an open mind.

'You say that,' she countered, 'but of course you've got your own agenda.'

'Well, I'm trying not to have any agenda. I'm trying to be non-judgemental, just describe what I come across.'

'I have this friend,' Susan replied, 'who's an old friend, he now writes for the *New York Times*.' She sighed, deeply. 'He was over here the other day, and we had dinner and I told him – in a private capacity – about the taxi wars. The next thing I knew I was on the front page of the *New York Times*, quoted, in an article about the taxi wars. After that I made a vow never to talk to another overseas writer or journalist again.'

I hadn't a clue what the taxi wars were, but I talked on. Here was a woman with a dazzling grasp of the issues. She spoke like a machine gun. It was all I could do to bluff some vague answers to her questions, feeling incredibly grateful that I'd spent that month in the British Museum mugging up on South African history and politics.

'OK,' she said, eventually. 'You've put up all the arguments I'd have put up in your situation. It's been good talking to you. I've got a lot off my chest.'

We set up a lunch date, and I rolled across the counterpane wondering what age she was, what she looked like. I had a vision of a thin-faced woman with light brown hair, attractive in an emaciated kind of way, a smoker with trembling hands, brilliant but neurotic.

Saul wore blue-framed glasses, and though his bushy hair was entirely grey, looked to be in his late thirties. He was apologetic that he wasn't an 'authentic South African'. 'I've only been here eighteen months, so I'm probably not much use to you.'

Having said which, he launched into the kind of analysis you can only get from an outsider.

'You can observe the economic divisions by seeing where people shop. You see a coloured person might earn 12–1800 rand a month. A black 3–800 rand a month. Whereas a white can earn anything from 2,500 to 10,000 rand a month. Or more.' (A month: that was £240–£360 coloured; £60–£160 black; £500–£2,000 white.)

I could see it all on a Saturday morning, he said. The OK Bazaar was where the coloured people shopped. 'Listen to them talk – they're very entertaining.' Then I should go down to the Parade, which was this big open air market by City Hall. That was the blacks' big weekly shopping-cum-social. The whites I would find in Woolworths. 'Which is not at all like your English Woolworths,' he laughed. 'Very smart.'

He dissected Cape Town for me. It was essentially an English city, but since 1948, when the Nationalists had been in power, Afrikaners had moved back. I could find them in suburbs like Belleville or Durbanville. Then there was the crowd that hung around Greenmarket Square – trendy, artistic, Afrikaans and English, completely apolitical, couldn't care less what went on. The Malay Quarter, up on the hill above Seapoint, was worth a visit. They were the only non-whites who'd escaped being forcibly removed to townships under the Group Areas Act. Of course I knew all about the famous District Six, the old coloured area. But that was worth seeing. After it had been bulldozed in 1966, and the coloureds moved out to the sandflats of Mitchell's Plain, nobody had dared build there, so it was just wasteland, on a prime site bang in the middle of the city. But what I really needed to do was get out to the Cape Flats, where the blacks lived. 'But don't go there till you've seen the rich areas, otherwise it won't hit you, you'll just think: Oh, this is just another African shanty town.'

'How do I get out there? I can't just drive in, can I?'

'No. You need to get someone to take you, a white who works out there, a doctor or an engineer or something. Better still, a black.'

We walked back to his office, and for the first time since I'd been in Africa, at the entrance, stopped to talk properly to a black person.

'This is Patricia,' said Saul, introducing me to a large lady with mop and pail. 'She's a great activist.'

Patricia put down her mop, gave me a huge grin, and grasped my hand with a complicated double handshake.

'That's the African handshake,' Saul said, smiling at my confusion. Patricia was laughing, that full-bellied, deep-throated African laugh. 'I'd better try it again,' I said, 'Get it right.' 'Like *this*,' said Patricia, following an ordinary hand-shake with a second, more intimate, upward clench. 'Right!' I said, 'I think I've cracked it.' We repeated it, Patricia shaking her head from side to side and laughing.

'I had an Israeli friend who came out here,' said Saul, as we said goodbye on the road outside, 'who said that he thought Israel was like a divorce, but South Africa was more like a marriage.'

Jenny was a member of the Black Sash, the women-only civil rights movement that had been founded in 1956 to fight the Separate Representation of Voters Act, which had removed coloured voters from the common roll, placing them on a separate list with the right only to elect four white MPs. On their protest marches and vigils the women had worn black ribbons to symbolise the death – as they saw it – of the South African constitution. As apartheid worsened they'd con-tinued to protest, to no avail on the issue of voting – in 1969 coloured people had lost their right even to be represented by white MPs – but with considerable success in other areas.

She lived with her husband in a cul-de-sac of modern houses on the edge of the seaside suburb of Muizenberg. From the outside, it looked much like a suburban close anywhere. But inside, through huge picture windows, the garden ran down to a small lake; a rowing boat was tied to a little jetty; the magnificent, ever-present mountain loomed behind.

She was in her late fifties, slim, with short dark hair. 'To me,' she said, 'the whole key to everything is education. And when the Soweto riots started in the schools, that said it all. Look, they don't get the textbooks, they're not delivered. I'll tell you a story. A friend of mine went to a black school, he went to teach *Macbeth*, and he found himself in a class of a hundred children, with a teacher who barely spoke English, and one book. So you can imagine, the pupils' grasp of the subject was not as hot as hell.

'There are fifteen departments of education in this country. Fifteen, hey! There's one for whites, and one for blacks, and one for coloureds – in each of the four provinces. Then there's Boputhatswana and Kwazulu and Ciskei, which are supposed to be independent countries, but if you think they're paying for their own education that's too silly . . .' She laughed. 'When you think how much duplication there is, how many top guys, all doing the same work . . . and then they're all sitting separate exam papers, and black results are always late, the papers are always lost, so that sometimes the results come after the start of the university term. How can you get a place at university, if you haven't got your matric results till then? The whole Department of Education and Training is disgusting, what they've done is criminal . . .'

We talked of other apartheid injustices, which she and her fellow Black Sashers had protested against: the Group Areas Act, for example, which had forced specific race groups to live in specific government-designated areas; the pass laws, which had prevented blacks and coloureds from even *moving* through white areas. 'Men were being charged with harbouring their wives. Harbouring your wife, hey!'

'And what d'you think's going to happen now?' I asked.

She shrugged and looked out at the view. 'Something will come of it. It may be a good something.'

'But you must feel it's extraordinary what's happened over the last couple of years ... and now, after the referendum ...'

'Look, everybody is aware that what's happening is incredible, but we don't know how it will turn out. You come from England, which is so safe, so predictable – everyone knows where they're going, what's going to happen. But, you know, the people who work for the Government here, they have no idea what their pension's going to be like in ten years' time, whether they'll have a pension at all.

'But I laughed about a comment I heard the other day in the queue in the post office. This paunchy bloke was going on about what terrible corruption there was in the post office, and how I must never put my money in an envelope as the post office is rotten from top to bottom – and he ended by saying: "I reckon it'll take the ANC ten years to get as bad as this."'

On my way out, she took me into her garage and showed me a pile of her redundant Black Sash protest boards: 3ft square with slogans like 1976–1991: PROMISES BUT NO PROGRESS. 'Of course, standing in a group was banned. You could only stand on your own with a poster. So you'd be there, up on your own, at traffic intersections. And then the changes started happening, and it all went very quickly. There was a time when you'd be standing up there protesting with your poster in the morning – here, you see,' she picked up a placard that said FREE MANDELA, 'and by the afternoon he'd be free, so that one was no longer relevant. Here's another one, GROUP AREAS MUST GO. That's another one that lost significance.'

She turned over another, which read NO EDUCATION WITH-

OUT BOOKS. 'You see, that one's still relevant. I tell you, some of the things these people'd say to you when you were standing up by the robots* with your poster: "Lady, your family are hungry. You should be in the kitchen."' She laughed, and showed me out into the sunset.

* traffic-lights

3

MEET 'N EAT

On my great teenage hitch-hike I'd stayed in Cape Town with an old couple called Lucy and Ernest. They'd lived, not in the centre, but in a suburb twenty kilometres out on the Indian Ocean side of the peninsula, a little seaside bay called Fish Hoek. That time, all I'd seen of Cape Town had been the train into Adderley Street Station, the view from the top of Table Mountain, a large crayfish I'd had for lunch, and the flowermarket.

Now, sick of hotel breakfasts and the wolf-whistling Tudor parrot, I phoned her. Her voice was quavering but enthusiastic. I must come out and stay and make her home my base. For as long as I liked.

'You 'ave a 'uge phone bill,' said the coloured lady at reception. 648R. It took me a second or two to click what that meant: 648 ÷ 5 was £120. For three short phone calls to Sarah in England! The rest of the bill – a room for five nights, laundry, meals, beers – was 610R. Nobody had warned me that South African hotels charge out their international calls at three times the already exorbitant going rate. From now on it was going to have to be letters only.

I retrieved my big white car from the multi-storey car park and headed out on the freeway that runs round the east of the mountain, swooping over the white suburbs of Rosebank and Rondebosch and Newlands and Kenilworth and Claremont, past the Rhodes Memorial and the university, and on down through woods and a nature reserve to Muizenberg. On a long concrete embankment a graffito read: I WAS AN ANGLICAN UNTIL I PUT TU AND TU TOGETHER.

From Muizenberg, the road clung to the seashore, the mountain rising steeply to the right. Round a point was the little sandy bay of Fish Hoek. Lucy's house was on the steep slope of the next spur. I had no recollection of it at all; but seeing Lucy, I instantly remembered her, though she'd shrunk from an active seventy-four to a stooped eighty-nine.

'Come in, Mark, come in. It's lovely to see you again. Now what do you feel like? A cup of tea. Or coffee perhaps?'

The hall was full of framed photographs of her family. Her deceased husband, her two sons, her daughter, their children at various ages and stages. She showed me upstairs. My room was at this end of the house, and at *this* end she had a friend, Tania, who stayed with her, 'in a self-contained way, you understand. She has her own kitchen and this is her bathroom you'll be sharing. Now you'll want to unpack and then we might have something to eat. There's no hurry, come down when it suits you.'

The whole thing reminded me very strongly of visiting my own grandmother, who had died the previous autumn. The kitchen had the same slightly deserted feel, a place that gets used on special occasions and is otherwise dived into for soup and toast and tea.

Tonight was a special occasion. Lucy had cooked me a little supper, 'nothing elaborate, you understand', which I carried into the living room on a tray. Up one end, by a dresser, the mahogany table had been laid for two. There was a lace cloth, a fruitbowl, a cheeseboard and biscuits, a jug of water and a dish of tomatoes.

'This is our only course,' said Lucy. 'What you see on the table is everything there is. I have no servant, you see. We did have a maid full time, and then when Ernest died she kept a room here and worked around town for three days a week – but then I had to let her go,' she smiled, 'for reasons I don't have to go into, you understand. Now will you have a drink – I shan't – but there's wine in the fridge if you'd like.'

I did like. Having prepared myself for an entirely teetotal evening it was a relief to find a third of a frosted bottle of *vin de table* nestled up to a carton of milk.

With shaking hands, Lucy dished out the stew and vegetables, and we got talking: about the intervening fifteen years; about what I was trying to do now.

'You see things very differently when you're eighteen,' I said.

'Yes, and now you're more grown up and in the world. Although physically you look the same. To me.' She smiled. 'Now,' she went on, after a few moments, 'if you want to talk to anyone about the racial problems, you should talk to my son Donald. He spent three years trying to get the ANC and the Government to talk to each other. He laid the groundwork for what's happening now. And he was instrumental in getting Nelson Mandela out of jail.'

'Was he?'

'Oh yes. Donald used to visit him in prison. He thinks very highly of him.'

'He's a great man.'

'Yes, I think he *is* a decent man. But he's old now. I wonder whether or not he'll be able to stand up to it all.'

'What do you think's going to happen?' I said – or rather shouted, for she was a little deaf.

'Well, we're all very hopeful, although of course it's chaos at the moment.' She smiled sweetly. 'But what government isn't in chaos?'

Our plates were empty. 'Now there's some more in here for you to finish up – I shan't have any, I'll have a tomato – but you will? Of course,' she went on, when my plate was full, 'now they're giving the Africans degrees, a lot of overseas money goes into it. But they don't all *want* degrees, it's the education at the earlier level that they want. They can't all be university teachers. We need carpenters, and plumbers, and electricians, and those sorts of skills.'

She paused for a moment; reached out to take a second tomato from the bowl.

'But I don't worry too much because this country's very church-going. Twelve o'clock the bell rings in Fish Hoek and they're all in church. They're a very serious-minded people, the South Africans. Of course, we've got a black Archbishop now.'

'Tutu.'

'Yes.' Her face told me that she wasn't entirely sold on the idea of a black Archbishop. 'Still, our parson here in Fish Hoek thinks very well of him.'

'Of course,' she went on, 'Fish Hoek is getting very big now. When we first moved here it was like a village. But now it's a very popular place to live, from the point of view of safety. You see, it's well away from the townships. I wish it were smaller. Still, what place isn't large these days?'

After supper, we washed up together and took our coffee through to the living room. 'Now I'll just introduce you to the family, and then I shall go to bed. You must make yourself at home. There's an electric fire there, if you're cold.'

She took me through the framed photos on the piano. This was Donald, the lawyer, with the glasses. And this was Simon, her second son, the engineer. And this was Judith, her daughter, who lived in England. 'Of course, after Ernest died, I couldn't live here alone, so we divided the house into three slices. Upstairs I have my friend Tania – I'll introduce you tomorrow. Downstairs is an old couple. But they've managed to get themselves into an old soldiers' home, MOTHS. I don't think you have that over in England, the Memorable Order of Tin Hats. And their place is being taken, next week, by two actors, would you believe! Members of the CTAP, now let me get this right, the Cape Town Acting –

oh, I can't remember! Anyway they're moving in. She with magnificent flame-red hair; he the gloomy type. You know what I mean?' She chuckled with delight at the prospect.

After Lucy had gone to bed I sat alone for a while by the bar fire, collecting my thoughts, gazing out over the glimmering lights of the bay. It was nice to be in a private home, with the clock ticking and flowers on the table.

In the morning Lucy showed me how to make toast. 'Now you want to take the toaster and put it down on the chair. Otherwise it throws the toast out, you see, and then I'm on my knees, scrabbling under the bookcase for it.'

The doorbell rang. Through the hallway I glimpsed a tall, stooping, black man.

'Not today, Johnson,' I heard Lucy say. 'Perhaps you can come back on Monday.'

There were protestations.

'No, Johnson. Come back on Monday and we'll have another go at that bed.'

More protestations.

'Tania!' Lucy called. 'Can you come and translate, dear. I think he's speaking Afrikaans.'

There was a clip-clop on the stairs, and Tania appeared – a thin wisp of a woman in a cream cardigan. The two old ladies stood silhouetted in the doorway, Johnson head and shoulders above them.

'He wants some money,' said Tania.

'No, no money, he never gets money. He'll get some food. Mark,' she called, coming through. 'Could you be a dear and cut two slices of that bread and butter there.' She reappeared with the kettle and made some coffee at the table. 'That's Johnson, our disreputable gardener who speaks no known language. My family are always telling me to get rid of him, but you can't, can you?

*

It was my lunch date with Susan. I spent the morning boning up on the news in preparation. Government corruption had taken a back seat. CODESA 2, the second session of the Council for a Democratic South Africa had just begun, and the excitement was tangible. For the first time for years, for *ever*, almost all of South Africa's myriad political groups were sitting round the same table. Not just the blacks and whites, the Nationalist Government and its old enemy the African National Congress, but the Communists, the leaders of the 'homelands', the Zulu party Inkatha . . . all with the aim of settling differences and coming up with some formula for a transitional government to pave the way for black majority rule.

Susan's house was opposite the university. I'd imagined a little two up, two down and a slightly harassed woman in her late twenties. But 15 Eland Road was a big house with a big garden and a smart modern office to one side. I was met by a secretary. And when Susan emerged, she was in her mid thirties, blonde and confident, dressed for business in a blue jacket and round red-framed glasses, with a flickering smile that spoke of a sense of humour.

She was in a bit of a hurry. We could do an hour's lunch and then she had to shoot off to pick up her son from school. We walked briskly up to the Baxter Theatre on campus; queued in a canteen; loaded up some trays with food; paused for a moment to say hello to her husband Obie, a professor of economics, who was sharing a table with a professor of sociology.

Face to face, Susan spoke even faster than she had on the phone. Ideas, definitions, paradoxes, anecdotes raced out of her. It was a major achievement to eat my pot roast, look intelligent, and make notes of just the headings of the subjects she covered: Minorities. Cultural differences. Ethnicity. Democracy. Dispossession. Partition. The Afrikaner. The English. The homelands. We sped through them all. Susan not only had every detail of The Problem at her fingertips, she was actively involved in solutions. She was on this committee at CODESA, working for that NGO (Non-Governmental Organisation); she was in the Black Sash; she was writing this pamphlet and that report; there were numerous other areas she wasn't at liberty to talk about; she was working on projects in the Cape Flats townships, Crossroads in particular – and god, there were numerous problems *there*. For a start a *huge* language problem that necessitated three way translations in Xhosa, Afrikaans and English. 'Someone speaks for half an hour, it's translated twice, and then the answer is "no".' She laughed. 'Just "no".'

It was time to go. Susan was sorry, but she had a very busy afternoon, and she had to go and pick up her son James from school. Perhaps I'd like to come with her, and we could continue talking in the car?

Leaving the university, she did a rapid U-turn in the main road. 'This is strictly illegal,' she smiled. 'But when you've got used to harbouring black people in your house, a minor traffic infringement seems like nothing.'

We rushed on, zipping through the traffic to the suburb where there was a decent multi racial primary school. We moved on from education to jobs, housing, urbanisation, settling finally on AIDS, which Susan saw as potentially one of South Africa's greatest problems.

'Is it a cliché,' I asked, 'that certain types of African men, you know, have a promiscuous lifestyle which . . .' I tailed off into the silence, wondering whether I'd hit a politically incorrect nerve. 'Is that true?'

'It's absolutely true. It's an absolute norm.'

'And the women, these stories you hear of women being abandoned and not being able to get maintenance . . .'

'The standard unit, in most African townships in Cape Town, is a woman and her children. That is the unit.'

'And the men sort of . . .?'

'Dart around. Yes.'

'And is that just to do with the break-up of tribal culture, or is it something that's always gone on?'

'It's central to social disintegration. But it's so *difficult* to make generalisations about South Africa. I know a hell of a lot of stable families.' We had turned off the main road into a little suburban side street. The car slowed, the engine quietened. Susan found a parking space and backed in. 'The amazing thing is . . .' she broke off. Her brisk businesslike tone had given way to something altogether more emotional. She met my eye. 'I don't know if you've read any Scott Peck?' I shook my head. 'I read a lot of Scott Peck, and I've got enough experience of the world to be *totally cynical*. And my big battle in life, Mark, is against cynicism.'

'Right,' I said quietly.

'People, and their motives, and why they do things. That's why I read so much of Scott Peck, he's the best hedge against cynicism one could ever wish for. And what he says is not: I'm always amazed there's so much evil in the world, but *how much good there still is* – which is quite a good point. And that's always a feeling I get when I go into the townships. What really amazes me is that so many families are actually still having it together. And so many women are still slaving day in and out in very menial jobs to give their children the basic chance of an education – I mean these are the amazing things.'

She switched off the ignition, and laughed. 'Now maybe when I've finished with all these clichés I'll find my little boy.'

Two large black women with white caps on were walking past with dancing little black children attached to their right hands.

'Now this,' Susan said, 'five years ago, you would not have seen in South Africa. A whole lot of little black children, whose mothers are obviously nannies, going home from school in this white area.'

We walked round the corner, through the school gates,

into the playground. It was a bright, blowy afternoon. Brown leaves spun through the air. Blue-green Table Mountain loomed magnificently behind. James was nowhere to be found.

Susan approached a little black girl. It was clearly a delight that she could do so. 'Hello Blossom, how are you today?' she asked.

'OK.' Blossom fingered her lip.

'Have you seen James anywhere?'

'No.'

Eventually we found him, playing a board game on a classroom floor with two friends. One white and blonde haired, the other black. You couldn't have got a prettier picture of multi-racialism on the front of a brochure.

Driving off, Susan waved at another Mum. 'That's Judy Davis. Another Black Sash lady. Hi, Judy!' she yelled. 'It's all a great Mafia in Cape Town,' she laughed.

We raced back to the office, James and his friend gabbling in the back, Susan and I now discussing the Equity ban and cultural boycotts. 'I was completely opposed to those kinds of sanctions,' Susan was saying, 'because they cut people off from good ideas, from the politics of the outside world – '

She tailed off. James and his friend were making so much noise in the back I could hardly hear her.

'OK kids,' I said. 'Now we're going to play a little game. I bet you can't stay completely quiet for one minute. Right,' I said to Susan. 'You've got a minute to tell me about harbouring black people in your house.'

'Oh there's various examples. When they were bulldozing Crossroads, Obie said what we can do is get a family to live with us, and so we did: we got a family in, who then lived with us for six months and remained quite close to us ever since. Father still comes and gardens for us once a week. All that caused all hell and uproar. My husband was charged under the Group Areas Act, and all sorts of things.'

'They found the family in your house?'

'We took them in because their home was being demolished, because they'd been deemed to be illegally squatting. The only way they could get us was to charge us under the Group Areas Act, which is what they did.'

'This was the police?'

'Yah, yah. Because they had complaints from everybody in the area as well ...' She broke off to wave at a man crossing the road. 'He's a city councillor,' she said, as Jamie and his friend erupted in the back.

'You seem to know just about everybody,' I shouted.

'Just about, I tell you. I span the entire spectrum, and I'm very active in politics in a whole range of areas, so I know one hell of a lot of people ...'

Back at her house-cum-office, she shooed the boys into the garden, and turned to shake my hand. 'I hope that was useful, Mark. I can't imagine it was. You'd have to stay here six years to even *begin* to work out this country.'

Saul had invited me to supper. He lived with his wife Melanie in a stripped pine flat in Oranjezicht, a district of pretty little white cottages right under the mountain. Like Saul, she was an artist.

'By black standards,' said Melanie, 'yes, we are rich. But we're not rich.'

'Look at our old fridge,' said Saul, 'you can tell we're not rich.'

We talked about the South Africans and the English. I explained how some people had said I shouldn't even come out at all until there was a black government.

'Well, that's ridiculous,' said Melanie. 'I mean you're born in a place. I didn't say I wanted apartheid. I'm just someone who lives here.'

After she'd gone to bed I sat with Saul, drinking wine and talking. He mentioned another 'interesting woman' I should go and see.

'They all seem to be women in Cape Town,' I said. 'Where are all the interesting men?'

He laughed. 'They don't exist. You've got to see the sort of typical South African man. I can't think of a word for them – you know, they drink, they chase women. I can think of ten amazing women in this town that I respect. I can't give you the name of one man. And these women can't find men. They're single, or divorced. Some of them are dykes.'

The cold front had arrived. Fat raindrops splashed on my bedroom window. As I went downstairs to make some tea, Tania popped her head round the door of her little flatlet: 'Mark,' she said, 'you must be careful. When you drive out of here, don't stop for anyone. If you see an accident in the road, don't stop, drive on till you get to a phone and report it from there. You get these gangs of six, one of them lies down in the road, and the other five hide in the bushes, and then they get rid of the driver and steal the car.

'And don't pick up any hitch-hikers. Of any colour. White men do these things too. My daughter says I worry too much, but I listen to the radio and I watch the television and I know what's going on – and we wouldn't want anything to happen to you, Mark.'

At lunch-time I drove Lucy down to the Meet 'n Eat. This was a cheap lunch run by the local church, that had originally been set up so that whites and coloureds could meet each other ('n eat) in a social context.

But pushing through the double door into the church hall, the first thing you noticed was that – with the exception of two smartly dressed coloured women in hats at a table by themselves – the place was packed with elderly whites.

'Is he your grandson?' shouted the fifty-something brassy blonde from behind the tea urn.

'No,' said Lucy sweetly.

'So where d'you pick him up then? Now we know what you get up to.' She laughed and gave me a stage wink.

There were only a couple of places left in the crowded hall. So we joined Mavis and Eileen. Introductions were made, hands were shaken. Eileen was from 'Rhodesia'. 'A lot of the people in Fish Hoek are from Rhodesia,' Lucy said.

Eileen had left after UDI. 'It was such a wonderful place in the old days. The coloured people were very different from the coloured people here.'

'How d'you mean?'

'They were more polite. They had respect. They used to call us "friend". Every week they used to bring us carnations, and we used to keep a present for them. That was very important, you had to do that. There was a mutual respect between us.'

'And what's the difference with the coloured people here now?'

'They're bitter,' said Eileen. Mavis nodded and echoed: 'Bitter.'

We escaped onto the subject of England. Eileen had relatives in Whitstable. She thought London was a wonderful place. Very exciting. 'I was in a café there, underground, when I saw my first black man with a white girl. It was very shocking. You understand it's very shocking for our generation to see that.'

'Why?'

'It's hard for us to accept. You can put him right on the politics, can't you Lucy? No,' Eileen went on, 'the English don't understand. I was up in Sunderland – that's a very liberal place – having supper, and this one woman was really trying to needle me. She kept saying, "Oh, so what d'you think of the wonderful Mrs Mandela?" So finally I said: "Mrs Mandela isn't wonderful. Look, she had four young boys in her house, in a room full of big black men, and they were set on and one was killed. That's your wonderful Mrs Mandela for you."'

'But Nelson Mandela, you must accept that he's a great man,' I said.

Somewhat reluctantly, they agreed. Eileen shook her head from side to side, confused. 'I think it's a terrible shame,' she said finally. 'They organised it all wrong.'

Before supper, as the sun was setting, I went for a stroll on the beach. The long strip of sand was full of white couples walking their dogs, most dressed in a way you'd never see now in England. Sturdy shoes with knee-length khaki or pale blue socks, matching shorts.

I sat on the cold sand and looked out at the horizon. Across the vast bite of False Bay, above the blue-black line of the sea, the Hottentot Holland mountains rose like a sharply defined bank of low cloud. I felt excited, looking at them, thinking that next week I would be driving up through them, on beyond the peninsula into the real Africa beyond. *Africa!*

As I walked back through the gloaming, up the long flight of steps up the hillside, each house with its ostentatious burglar alarm sign, its elaborate 'burglar bars' on every window, I got a dreadful sense of unease. Of all these whites down here, quietly terrified of the blacks over the mountains, the thousands and thousands who were pouring down each week from the Transkei and the Ciskei, because subsistence in the townships was better than starvation in the home-lands. In the old days, the Group Areas Act and the pass laws had stopped them coming. Now there was nothing anybody could do, except grumble and put up ever more elaborate security devices.

It was Saturday. The day of the socio-economically divided shopping spree. The Parade was a huge area of open tarmac, with the City Hall on one side, and the bus station and the flyover leading up to the N2 freeway on the other. The black and coloured crowds milled among row upon row of stalls selling clothes, training shoes (*takkies*, as the South Africans call them), jewellery, lengths of cloth, neatly laid out secondhand books. Moving among them were entrepreneurial free spirits with, say, just three pairs of fluorescent green socks hanging from a stick, or a single battered-looking radio. 'One rand! One rand!' they shouted.

Over by the bus station a large crowd was gathered round a mobile platform. A little coloured boy, no older than ten, was singing gospel songs, backed by two teenage girls in glasses.

'Raise your arms,' shouted the impeccably suited coloured man at the microphone. 'Raise your arms if you want the cassette, and we come to you. Ten rand only.'

'Let the Holy Spirit come and take control,' came the angel voice of the boy. 'Hold me in your darling arms and – '

'This is now the green cassette. This is ten rand only.'

'All your cares and troubles – '

'Raise your hands if you want the cassette! We come to you!'

'Jee-eesus! Jee-eesus!' The boy knew all the moves, as he cocked his head cutely, then swung his small arms oh-so-slowly down to conclude.

A coloured woman, with tears in her eyes, ran forward from the crowd and put coins in a wooden collection box. Others followed. The boy bowed, a weary look in his hard little eyes, and was swept into the embrace of mothers and sisters at the back.

Then he was at the side of the platform, being chatted to by a very strange-looking character: black, bald, with just two frizzes of hair on each side of his head, he wore bright red lipstick and a camp adoring smile. To the waist, he was just a big balding black queen. But below, in his wheelchair, his legs were the legs of an Ethiopian child, shrivelled to an inch and half thick.

Saturday night. Time, surely, for some South African culture. I bought myself a ticket for a show called *Jo'burg Follies 3*.

The Theatre on the Bay was sleek and white and modern, with a foyer full of sleek and white and modern South Africans, gearing themselves up for an evening of live – and more important – home-grown entertainment.

The lights went down, the shrill cacophony of Seth Effrikan voices hushed, a spotlight came up on a fragile-looking blond pianist in a green velvet jacket. His name was Kevin Feather, and in a voice camper than several rows of tents he told us that: 'We're going to slay some sacred cows this evening.'

From his first mock-missed piano chord, and the stagey entry of his three white co-satirists, Malcolm, Jonathan and Odile, the audience loved it. The first cow was Winnie Mandela (Odile blacked-up): 'If there's a wrong way to do it . . . no–bo–dee does it like WINNIE! . . . If there's a right way to be a *shmuck* – you didn't know I was Jewish did you? – if there's a wrong way to dele*gate*, a new place to put on *weight*, nobody does it like WIN-NEEEE!'

One subject attracted the particular odium of the team. 'Rap,' cooed Kev, as they launched into their spoof. 'Somehow one just can't resist the temptation to put a "c" in front of it.'

'So what does every South African do between 5.30 and 7.30 every evening of their lives?' cried Malcolm. 'Yes! They watch soap operas!' So we had *The Golden Girls*, and then, as night follows day, the rest of the international stars; the international stars who had visited South Africa, that is.

Dolly Parton's breasts were 'ninety-five – and that's not centimetres'. Tina Turner was Malcolm, kitted out with a pair of enormous black lips that got indisputably the biggest laugh of the evening. And then, of course, Rod Stewart, whose lyrics were so polished I have to quote them in full:

> I am wailing
> I – am – wailing
> With a voice that's cracked as well.

Laryngitis,
Like I've had flu
Since I was ten.

I am randy,
Very randy,
But I always go for blondes.
I've had Rachel, Britt and Kelly,
But I turned down Elton John.

And my hairstyle,
Oh my hairstyle,
Always makes my girlfriends blush.
'Cos it looks like
A cross between a
Hedgehog and a – lavatory brush.

At the Nico Malan Opera House on the Foreshore, they were pushing to get into the Rocky Horror Show last night party. DRESS COMPULSORY: ROCKY HORROR, said the poster, and I felt a bit out of place, not having thought to bring my Rocky Horror gear with me from London. The best I could manage was black jeans, a striped blue and white shirt (collar turned up), and my blue blazer (collar turned up). Oh well, everybody else was so busy looking in the mirror they barely noticed.

They'd gone to town. Most of the women were wearing black lace bras, glittery or satin hotpants and fishnet stockings. The more demure had high-necked white satin shirts with black bow-ties. Men wore bow-ties, tails, skirts, fishnets. A fat middle-aged guy in a ra-ra skirt and fishnet top clung rather hopelessly to his fat middle-aged wife. I seemed to be the only one in the crowd not in lipstick and mascara.

We got the backs of our hands (one girl her naked buttock) stamped with a red-lips stamp, were given a small glass of red-dyed tequila ('just a little haemoglobin for you, ha ha ha') and were up a broad flight of stairs, past a video camera and screen, to the throng.

Castle in hand, I got talking to Mary, a – curvaceous was the only word for her – blonde who was sitting on a table in black lace waiting for the music to start. She was out on the town with her friend Ulrike, who was chewing gum and 'disparate for a ciggy'. Mary had wangled two haemoglobins at the door and was clearly a little pissed already.

Having got Ulrike her ciggy, I sat on the edge of the table while Mary made me up. 'Look up, that's it, don't blink.' Eight days away from Sarah the smell of her hair and perfume and skin as she bent over me was almost too much. 'That's better,' she said, in a motherly fashion, rubbing a damp finger on the corner of my lips.

A coloured guy came over – almost the only non-white in the place. He was wearing a cream jumpsuit open to the waist, revealing a lean and chiselled brown body. His hair was tousled, unwashed, shoulder-length. When he smiled his teeth were brown, two were missing; he had a rough, musty smell.

He nodded to me, smiled a little nervously when I shook his hand. Moving from one foot to the other, he chatted with the girls. After he'd gone, our conversation took a turn away from the 'What part of Cape Town d'you live in?' level, as Mary confessed she had 'a lust thing' for this guy.

'So are you going to go out with him?' I asked.

'I couldn't. You don't understand, but I just couldn't. It wouldn't have any future.'

'Would your parents object?'

'Exactly – that's the problem. Plus, you know, I live in one part of Cape Town – '

' – and he lives on Mitchell's Plain.'

'Just about that kind of thing.'

'If you really liked him though, would you let your parents stand in the way?'

'I care about what my parents think, that's the thing. I do care about what they think.'

They went off to dance, and I wandered round the fabulous youth. Here and there were older people, recognisable only to each other: the sad eternal swingers. There were the usual ridiculously drunk young men trying to make it with impossibly pretty young women.

There was a hush, and a fire-eater was up on the stage above the disco floor. It was Mary's coloured guy! He swayed and shimmied, passed a burning torch up and around his body in a series of breathtaking whirls, then plunged the flame deep into his throat. 'Whew!' he muttered, grinning, wiping his brow, as the place erupted into applause.

Some more coloured guys came on, took up positions at their instruments. Mary's lust object was not just a fire-eater, he was the leader of the band. 'Are you ready to party?' he shouted. 'Well, stay with us then.' He shot a long look at Mary, who was flapping around on the dance floor beneath him, doubtless several tequilas the worse for wear.

They moved into a rap number, and the (almost) all-white dance floor went crazy. I wondered what Kevin Feather would have made of the scene.

The following evening Lucy's younger son Simon took us out for supper. He was in his fifties, a stocky man with a few strands of hair pasted to the side of his bald head, and fierce bushy eyebrows. We drove down into central Fish Hoek, carefully unloaded Lucy from the car, proceeded slowly down an empty shopping mall. In the presence of her considerate offspring Lucy seemed to have become ten years older.

The steak ranch was colourfully upbeat and modern. A trendy white waiter emerged from behind a jungle of shiny green foliage, looked at this strangely assorted threesome and said: 'Hi folks! So what can I get you to drink?'

'What would you like, Mark?' Simon asked.

'Erm – I'll have a beer,' I said.

'Right, one beer – and you sir?'

'Hold on there!' said Simon. 'Are you able to serve him a beer? I thought drinking was illegal in this borough.'

'Yes, sir – well, we do serve beer in this restaurant.'

'I'm sorry,' said Simon, his face darkening – or rather, crimsoning, 'I'm sorry, Mark, I'm going to have to make an issue out of this. You mean you serve alcohol in this restaurant?'

'Look, sir. I only work here, OK.'

Simon nodded slowly, lips pursed. 'Could you get the manager for me please? This is outrageous,' he added to me, as the waiter hurried off. 'No, what we have here is a very serious issue. This place, Fish Hoek, is a dry borough. It's been dry for a very long time, hasn't it, Mother?'

'There's a history behind it,' said Lucy. 'The sailors from Simonstown used to come down here and get drunk, you see, and fight in the street, and so forth.'

'The place was full of drunken layabouts,' said Simon. 'You see it in Kalk Bay now, just up the road, people just lying about on the streets. In our suburb, my daughter can't even walk to the corner without the fear of being attacked.'

The manager had appeared.

'Hi,' he grooved. 'I understand there's a problem.'

'Yes,' said Simon, and laid in.

'Yes, it *is* illegal, sir, yes, but this *is* a service that I provide to my customers.' On the defensive, he kept repeating this phrase, like a mantra. 'Yes sir, I take your point, but I *am* providing a service to my customers, sir.'

'OK,' said Simon finally. 'You've answered my question, fine, and I must accept that, we don't have to go on arguing about it, we'd like to get on with our meal now. So what would you like to drink, Mark?'

'Erm – a coca-cola would be fine.'

'And to eat, sir?' asked the manager.

'Mark?'

'What are *you* having?'

With our steaks in front of us, Simon explained that,

politically speaking, he was a radical. But I mustn't, like so many people from overseas, be naive about black people. For example, I mustn't underestimate how every African was still affected, deeply, by the witch-doctor. Or the *tokoloshe*, the evil spirit that Africans believed haunts the floor of their huts, so that they build their beds high up off the ground. 'If you asked that waitress over there', he said, leaning towards me, 'whether or not she believes in the *tokoloshe* she wouldn't even stand here, she'd be off.' He laughed.

He told me the famous story of the Xhosa girl Nongqawuse. In 1837, when the Xhosa tribe were thoroughly tired of being pushed around by the British (they'd fought nine frontier wars in a hundred years) a teenage Xhosa girl called Nongqa-wuse had had a vision. If the Xhosa slaughtered all their cattle and burnt all their crops on a particular day, their ancestral spirits would rise up from their graves to take revenge on the whites, who would all be driven by a great wind into the sea. After consultations with witch-doctors, the Xhosa duly slaughtered their cattle and burnt their crops, and on the particular day . . . nothing happened. Indeed, the self-inflicted wound marked the beginning of the end of Xhosa power. Tens of thousands of Xhosa died; thousands more were forced into servitude on white farms.

'Now this was only a hundred and forty years ago,' said Simon. 'A hundred and forty years is not a long time.'

He was particularly concerned about the university, where his daughter was a student. The place had changed in recent years. With the increasing numbers of black students, the boundaries of what was acceptable had been moved, they were closer now to township boundaries. So much so that they'd had to introduce a university police force – called Campus Control. 'But very few people on campus will tell you this. They take a soft line. They don't want to accept the truth, which is that it is the black students who are behind this.' He told me of black-on-black intimidation. Of an organisation within the black student body which prevented the majority of black students from joining any societies within the university. 'They weren't even able to join the student rep councils in their halls.' And if anyone dared stand up against this, they risked being killed. 'No, not just rejected or intimidated, but stabbed. You don't believe me, do you? But this is true. One of the students was stabbed to death with a screwdriver.

'These are township standards. Because I can tell you these standards didn't exist at the university a few years ago. You know, almost any African in Cape Town carries a screwdriver with them. They're allowed to carry that, that's their weapon. Last night I went up to campus at one o'clock to pick up my daughter from a student dance, and there were two guys, lurking there in the shadows, and they didn't look as if they were up to any good . . .'

'Black guys?'

'Black guys, yes. So I went round the corner, and luckily there was one of these Campus Control guys there, so I reported the situation, and he came round and asked their names, and then back over the walkie-talkie came: "OK, this guy works here, but he's a well-known troublemaker: arrest him."'

'He's a teacher?'

'No, no, he's probably a cleaner or something, but he works there.' Simon shook his head angrily. 'The university workers had a strike last year. The university's reaction was very poor. Look, the violence got so bad the workers threw petrol on a lecturer – lit him. Now these people have never really been punished. The Principal is weak, it's easier for him not to take the strong line. Now I know you might debate as to what the strong line is – but I'll tell you what I think. Tomorrow morning I'm going to phone the police, and lay a charge against this restaurant. If they don't act on it, fine. But I shall lay a charge: now that, in my opinion, is the strong line.'

Back at Lucy's house, seated round a tray of decaffeinated

coffee, Simon mellowed. His face took on different, softer lines, and he waxed lyrical.

'This should be one of your themes, Mark. The Cape is one of the most beautiful places in the world. There's the mountainside, the scenery is very nice. Once you're out of the Cape the countryside is harsh. The Karoo, the Little Karoo, these are almost desert areas. The Cape is an enclave – absolutely. You know, the definition of a person who works in Jo'burg is someone who wants to live in Cape Town.' He chuckled. 'This is one of the floral capitals of the world. There are remnants of botanical species here that missed the Ice Age. There are more varieties of flowers on Table Mountain than in the whole of the British Isles. This is a unique place.

'A question you should ask, when you meet people, is this: "Why don't you leave South Africa?" At every stage in the last ten years you'd get a different answer from the same person. In 1984, they'd have said: "There isn't a country that offers anything better." Then there was the upsurge of urban violence. We live within sight of a major hospital. At the height of the disturbances, ambulances were going past almost constantly. You couldn't walk down the road without a black person giving you a scowl.

'On the 16th July 1986 the story was: this is the tenth anniversary of Soweto. This is the day they're going to murder all the whites. I was away in England that week – but I was worried, I can tell you. Finally, it was just another scare story – but it was very significant to a lot of people.

'A large number of people said at the time that when they felt sufficiently threatened to buy a firearm, they'd leave in preference. But then things got worse and they bought that firearm. They've been through times they've found very, very scary.

'At the end of the day, the thing you have to bear in mind is that the memory of the public is six months. At that time – the time of the State of Emergency – all municipal vehicles had a wire screen over their windscreen. Things are much more relaxed again now. There's a good feeling in the air. Look, this is a nice place to live. You think of living in some cruddy place in England. At the moment nobody is thinking of leaving. What a nice place, eh? The point is, if you're one hundred yards away from danger it doesn't frighten you. In the university no young girl would walk from the top of the campus to the main road. That's sad, hey? But if it doesn't happen in your road . . .'

The Jacobsons were being very kind to me. The next day I was taken out to lunch by Lucy's elder son, Donald, the lawyer who'd helped free Nelson Mandela. He'd told me to meet him at a restaurant on the Waterfront, just the other side of the Docks from Bertie's Landing.

It was another beautifully sunny day. I sat, at a starched white tablecloth, sipping an uncontroversial orange juice, gazing through a long row of sliding French doors at coloured workers in orange boiler suits unloading a grey frigate called SAS Somerset.

Ten minutes later Donald bustled in. There *was* a family resemblance – the same bald head and wispy corona of hair – but his face was thinner, he wore thick black glasses, an ironic smile played around his lips.

What was I drinking? Orange juice. Weren't we going to have some wine? He ordered a bottle of white.

His angle on South Africa was rather different from his brother's.

'The only parallel situation in the post-war world is Nazi Germany,' he said. 'And what's going on at the moment is incredible. Our leaders are criminals. And we're letting them off. There's not going to be a Nuremberg Trial, there's not even going to be any remorse. It's as if Hitler's coming out of his bunker saying: "OK folks, we made a mistake." This is the incredible thing. They're not saying what they've done was wrong, they're saying it has to be abandoned because it's impractical. So Hitler's coming out of the bunker saying to the Jews: "Sorry guys, it's impractical gassing you lot, it's got to be abandoned."'

'It does seem as if the blacks have an incredible capacity to forgive.'

'It is incredible. Quite incredible. Look – just in the small way that the injustices of the regime affected me – *I* don't feel ready to forgive. Not at all. No, I think the question will be asked, in the white community, in years to come, as it was in Germany: "Where were you Daddy, when there was apartheid? What did you do?"'

Our waiter was hovering. He was young and white. Donald was going to have the kingklip. Hadn't I heard of kingklip? It was a South African fish I should definitely try.

'But I think', Donald went on, as we returned to our wine and crumbling bread and pleasant view of the sunlit harbour beyond, 'that when you have a situation like this, and a fundamental injustice has been practised on a people over a substantial period of time, it has to come out somewhere. The modern state of Israel, for example, is quite a frightening place. And what you see in groups like the PAC and AZAPO is some measure of the anger that is felt in some sections.'

With the arrival of the kingklip, the conversation took a turn away from politics, through the problem of 50% black unemployment, to the spiralling violence.

'I was talking to your brother last night,' I said. 'He was saying that most whites now own a firearm of some kind.'

'Well *I* don't.' Donald laughed. 'But yes, everyone in South Africa now has a burglary story. I mean, until recently I would never even have dreamt of owning a gun. But then we were burgled, and I found myself going down to a shop on Church Street and finding out about buying a gun – not that I had any idea how to use it. And while I was there, I noticed these containers of CS gas on the counter, and so I asked about them: "Is that Riot Gas?" And the guy said it was. So I bought two canisters of this stuff, and then when

I'd bought it I went back in there and I said: "OK, so how much of this stuff do I use?" And this guy, this big burly guy surrounded by all these guns and so on, said: "That dipinds."' Donald slipped into thick Afrikaans. '"That dipinds on how pizzed off you are. If you're just a liddle pizzed off, you use just a liddle bit, but if you're really pizzed off, you use the whole lot."'

We laughed.

'So you bought them?'

'I have to say I bought them. But I gave one to my wife and one to my daughter. So now I rely on them to look after me.' He laughed again. I thought I'd put Simon's question to him.

'Was there ever a time you were tempted to leave?'

'Yes. There was a period when things were very bad and we considered moving to Canada. But I went out to Vancouver, and looked around, and I thought: What would there be for me here? What would I get worked up about? And I decided it would be the Alaska oil pipeline and that would be that. So I decided to stay. I love this country.'

A wintry fog had descended on the motorway and airport. Feeling like Philip Marlowe, I parked the Dolphin by Domestic Terminals with my headlights on and waited.

At last I was 'going into the townships'. The famous Cape Flats — Khayelitsha, Guguletu, KTC, Crossroads. I had a rendezvous with a man who had been on Robben Island for ten years, was a member of the far-left Pan Africanist Congress (PAC), one of whose slogans was 'one settler, one bullet'. He was a friend of Susan's.

Danile appeared through the mist, prompt, at ten o'clock. He was big, burly, courteous, and a little reserved. In his late forties, I guessed. I remembered my African handshake. 'So you know that?' he said, and smiled.

He was driving a cream Mercedes, which he suggested I follow. We headed back along the motorway, turned down a slip road, then *bump* off the tarmac . . . and into a different world.

I'd been in a township before. I'd had a drink and a meal with the family of a black lorry driver who'd picked me up hitching all those years before. But that had just been a little group of corrugated iron huts on the side of a hillside. Nothing on this scale.

It stretched for mile upon mile upon mile. Little rows of tiny breezeblock dwellings with corrugated iron roofs, pushed up close to each other on a criss-crossing network of atrocious dirt roads. The place was awash with litter: old cans, paper, torn-up boxes; but most of all, strand upon strand of torn polythene, as if all the plastic bags in the world had been ripped up and left to sink into the sand.

Hungry looking dogs roamed aimlessly. Here and there, a goat, untethered, nibbled at a forlorn clump of grass. And everywhere – people. Women walking along the roadside with buckets or Persil containers balanced on their heads. Some were wrapped in African shawls and head-dresses, some were bareheaded, in Western T-shirts and jeans. Some had babies on their backs, some held small children. Men walked purposefully, men hung around aimlessly, men hammered away erecting shacks. WE DEMAND HOUSE NOT TOILETS said a graffito on a wall.

We had come to Danile's mother's place. She was out; I left the Dolphin round the back and we headed off together in the Merc, at a stately pace along the bumpy dirt road.

There were three types of township area, Danile explained. There were the fully serviced, or 'core' houses, which people could now buy from the Government. These were the ones that were round us now: they had two rooms, a bedroom and a living room, an outside toilet, and, possibly, a bath- room. Moving down a grade, there was 'site and service', where the Government erected a toilet and a tap on a small – say fifteen metres by fifteen metres – plot of land, and people could build their own houses. Finally, there were the shacks, unserviced – that is, without sewerage or water – which were put up willy-nilly on any free stretch of land by the new arrivals.

'So what do they do for sanitation?'

Danile was blunt. 'The only thing that is provided is a communal tap and a weekly picking up of buckets. The toilet situation is buckets at the back of these shacks.'

The new arrivals, he said, were pouring in at the rate of several thousand a week. Originally there had just been Crossroads. That had been bulldozed by the Government, and rebuilt by the residents, and bulldozed by the Government again. But after the pass laws had been relaxed in 1981, more and more blacks had arrived, lured from the homelands of Transkei and Ciskei by the prospect of work in Cape Town. At first, the Government had tried putting them on buses and trains back home. But still they persisted. Now the shack city was mushrooming out of all proportion.

'You see the sort of thing?' Danile gestured out of the window. We had rumbled out of the (relatively) ordered core house district and were now among the shacks, idiosyncratic one-roomed dwellings that had clearly been put together out of anything the people could lay their hands on: bits of old hoarding, broken plywood, corrugated iron, plastic sheeting – all colours, all shapes, all sizes.

'Where do they get the materials from?' I asked.

For the first time Danile laughed out loud, a rich deep-throated African laugh.

'I don't know how to describe it, all this junk, where they pick it up. All I can tell you is, someone would be working in a certain factory, and maybe it's a demolishing company, so whenever he lays his hands on this type of material he brings it to this area and sells it.'

'And how do these people make the money to buy it?'

'Aha,' Danile chuckled. 'That is a beautiful question, Mark. That – is – a – *beautiful* question. What is happening here is people are doing anything to keep their lives going. Look!'

He pointed at a man walking purposefully along with a box of loaves on his head. 'This guy is carrying bread. He is going to sell that bread.'

'Did he make it himself?'

'No, no, he bought it from the correct bakery. Lorries of the correct bakery will be coming round the township. Then he will sell it on. Everything is being sold. When I say everything, I literally mean, *everything*. You see that woman there,' he pointed at a woman sitting by the roadside in the dirt with a few oranges and apples, some bottles of shampoo arranged on top of a small wooden crate. 'That is an unofficial shop – called a spaze shop. Unemployment is very high in these areas, but people survive. Also, the bonds of their culture keep the people together. They share out the little pieces they have.'

We had entered an area called KTC. We drew up outside a larger than average dwelling with a bright red door. It was a crèche, and there to greet me was Oliver Memane, the founder of Crossroads.

Crossroads. One of those 'as seen on TV' places – like Beirut, or El Salvador. The average Western viewer, sitting in their armchair with their cocoa watching *News at Ten*, has no idea of the surroundings, the context, the issues . . . they just know the name, and the terrifyingly incomprehensible footage of people running wild. And here I was meeting the founder, a lean man in his fifties, wearing an ill-fitting brown suit, a red shirt with large collars, and a brown tie. He was keen to talk into my tape-recorder.

'My name is Oliver Memane,' he blurted out at speed. 'I am founder of Crossroads. We started Crossroads 1975 and we argue with the Government with the influx control up till '83. We leave Crossroads in '83, we go start KTC. I'm now one of the delegation to build new houses in Crossroads. We're working with the Minister, Dr Koornhof. I live KTC, and that big fight coming in '86, we are coming here and opening crèche. We've got a school here, but the Government

will not build the crèches. We've got two centres here. We're
looking after 200 kids. I'm Chairman of the Interim Committee of Squatter, Western Cape.'

With the tape recorder off, Mr Memane relaxed and
courteously escorted me round the crèche. For ten minutes I
was back in Botswana, out at the squatter camp on the edge
of Gaborone where we used to go and teach the kids English.
The same little black faces, the same broad white smiles, the
same rows of bright eyes, the same shrieking excitement at
having a photo taken. In the background large women in
shawls smiled and nodded, politely came forward to shake
my hand, seemed ridiculously thrilled that I'd mastered the
African handshake.

I knew there had been trouble in Crossroads in 1986; but I
hadn't properly understood why. As we drove on, Danile
explained. 'Yes, four or five years ago, there was a big fight
here. A heavy one. We were running up and down here
picking up dead bodies. You know what the State did? They
put up barbed wire.' He shook his head and laughed.
'Really,' he went on, 'what happened was, the State started
the fight. They introduced community councillors, who were
controlled by a Government budget. Six councillors were
chosen out of the twenty who were there previously. But
one of the most powerful guys was not chosen. And so they
fought. They fought and they fought until they were tired.
The State could have intervened. But instead they fanned
the flames. With these *kitsconstabels*.'

'Kits . . .?'

'The policemen they use are called *kitsconstabels*. "Kit-"
stands for 'instant' police. They get fourteen days' training.
After fourteen days they are put into the township.'

'But they're from the area?'

'No, they're just picked up anywhere. Unemployment in
this country is so high that the opportunity of being a police
– people will jump for it. And as a result that created
confusion, chaos – very bad chaos – because these people

were not trained. The only thing they were trained in was how to shoot. And as a result they were misusing the guns. I mean,' Danile waved out of the window at a man sitting on a stack of boxes staring moodily across the road, 'you take this guy here. He stays in that shack. He becomes a *kitsconstabel*. He comes back with this loaded rifle, sleeps with this loaded rifle. The next thing, he has a quarrel with his neighbour, or with his wife. He jumps for the gun; he uses it.'

He paused; a long, heavy pause.

'Suicide,' he shook his head. 'In black communities, in terms of percentage, it was very low. But after that period it went up. It shot up because these guns were just free. And the State didn't care what happened to these guns.'

'So they just handed them out?'

'They were just handing them out! Today, if you ask me what happened to those guns, I'd say: the black-on-black violence is based on those guns. What happened to those guns? They never went back to the State.'

As we drove on in the big cream Mercedes, Danile waved out of the window, here, there and everywhere. People knew him, and judging by the looks on their faces, were in some awe of him. He'd gesture at a school. 'That I built,' he'd say, and we'd sail on.

I asked him where he got the money to build these places. He turned from the wheel and gave me a long look. 'That is a question,' he said. 'That, Mark, is a question. I can say wholeheartedly, in the whole of the Western Cape, our NGO is the only one,' he held up a finger, 'the only one controlled by the people in the townships. Its trustees' board comes from the township, its directors, its employees and so on. But if you were to take any other one, they are white controlled, so it is easy for them to get overseas funding. Easy for them because of their whiteness.'

'Which irritates you?'

'It irritates, it irritates. I've been in London. I've been with some of these charities. I stayed with them a whole week, discussing ways and means of funding our projects. Then they came all the way down here, last year, only to tell us they're unable to fund us because their budget has been overused or some such thing. But the fact of the matter is, they funded a white project that was established only a year ago. But because it was white . . .' He shook his head again. 'The overseas people', he continued, 'have a tendency, if white faces show up in their countries, to talk about black development, they'll say "Have this stuff!" But that money is not flowing through, because it pays salaries of these development people; heavy salaries, cars and so on.' He thumped the dashboard of his Mercedes. 'This car – is my own personal car. I bought it in 1973, I've been using it ever since. In the agencies it is not like that. It is the car of the company. They are paid huge salaries.'

He pulled up onto a patch of dirt. In front of a core house, a big black guy leant against his front fence. He looked alarmed to see the Mercedes, and me, Whitey, looking out at him. But as soon as Danile emerged from the driver's side, this alarm turned to grins and shouts of welcome. They embraced and re-embraced each other in the sunshine.

I was introduced, with the double handshake and much laughter. This was Patrick, who'd spent twenty years of his life on Robben Island. He had a broad, flat face, and jet black skin. He was laughing now, but in the blue, red and yellow rheum of his eyes you could see weariness. They stood, bantering, part in English, part in Xhosa, shaking their heads and talking about the latest news of 'this Government, this good Government'.

'You know, Mark,' Danile said, turning to me after one particularly loud exchange of laughter, 'in the City Council, they are debating about whether to spend fifteen thousand rand on gold badges to mark long service. Fifteen thousand rand! When that money is so desperately needed here.'

When we drove on, I asked Danile about Robben Island.

His time in prison had started in 1974, when Mozambique had been liberated, and he'd been involved in a pro-FRE-LIMO march. 'Out of that situation I got detained. The Terrorist Act was widely interpreted. I got ten years on Robben Island.'

What had it been like?

'Mark, when I told my barrister what the police had done to me, he couldn't accept it. He couldn't accept that these things had actually happened to me.

'Until I went to prison I didn't know a man can stand for three weeks. You just stand there. You fall asleep standing. Because if you don't stand they beat you up.

'It was worse when I attempted to fight back. I've never been beaten up so solid as when I fought back. It was October 1975. I got up in the morning and was taken to the interrogation room. They beat me up. And after some time I got tired and felt like fighting back. Boy! That was a mistake. The biggest mistake I ever made. They beat the hell out of me. I was unconscious for two days. They take the black policemen out of the room. You are beaten up by the white policemen only.'

'One thing', I said eventually, 'that's always struck me, is that you have remarkably little anger about this. A lot of forgiveness. I mean, Patrick, who has spent twenty years on Robben Island, will happily shake my white hand.'

'This is within our upbringing, Mark – within the culture of our upbringing. The way we were brought up as kids. Our value system is that of not hating. I am angry at being put into prison, but in so far as why I was put in – I did it with an open mind, knowing I would go. The people who put me in were purely acting on the desires of politicians. So what would it do for me, if I were to be angry? What would it teach the community that I seek to lead? I can't be angry if I want to focus on the future. But I'm very mindful of the fact that the people who put me in prison are alive, and we are negotiating with them at the moment.'

Finally, we talked about Steve Biko, the founder and leader of the Black Consciousness Movement, who, in September 1977, had been beaten up in his cell and had died naked in the back of a police van, being transferred from Port Elizabeth to Pretoria, a distance of 700 miles. Danile had known Biko.

'To forgive that,' he said, 'that would be difficult for me. I won't lie to you. It was glaring – glaring to everybody – that he was murdered. But the good Government of the day, they even installed back the doctor who was found wanting – he was installed back.' He shook his head again. 'A young man, like Steve, to die so quick.

'My cousin's brother was arrested, he died the same day. He had broken ribs, a broken skull. They said he'd hung himself, but his injuries weren't consistent with hanging. And when the family demanded the weapon, they produced a pantyhose. A pantyhose!'

In his office in Parliament, Peter looked considerably more important than he had done when I had met him in London. He seemed broader, altogether bulkier and more substantial, in his pink pinstripe shirt and bright floral tie. Behind him were rows of big green-bound parliamentary books. I congratulated him on his attack on the Goverment.

'Well,' he said, 'that morning I was at a lunch in Johannesburg at the head office of one of the banks. It was a special lunch and there were about a hundred people there, mainly top business people in Johannesburg, and not one of them that I spoke to about the Pickard Report had anything but anger to express. And they said to me: "Are you taking part in the debate this evening?" And I said "Yes," and each one of them said: "Give 'em hell! Give them absolute hell about it!"' He laughed out loud. 'That also, I think, buoyed me up a bit.'

'This is Anglo-American, people like that?'

'Oh sure. The deputy chairman of Anglo was there, the

Chairman of Premier Milling, the Chairman of oh – it was a special lunch, the top sort of business people of Johannesburg were there.' He nodded at me, looked down for a moment. 'So no, I don't think De Klerk realises the depth of anger. I mean, if he did, I'm sure he would have realised that some symbolic gesture was required. Some political head has to roll, somebody's got to carry the can. But it's not the tradition in this country, as it is in the UK. They're just going to ride this out, brazen it out. But we won't let them, because I mean I've got questions on the order paper for next week wanting to know what they're doing with the fifty million rands' worth of toilets.'

'The thing that amazed me,' I said, 'was that after you'd spoken some younger Nationalist guy got up and said that if someone was in charge of a company worth a hundred million rand, how's he supposed to know what's going on in the lower echelons of that company. Which didn't make sense to me. If you take responsibility for a company, surely you take responsibility for the whole thing.'

'Sure. And if anything goes wrong, and the company goes insolvent, you get fired. Yah.'

'So he was just being brazen?'

'Sure. Oh yes. No, they know that happens in business. But in politics in this country, you just keep your head down and it'll go away. But as I say, we'll keep on referring to it, just to embarrass them, see if they'll do something about it. And also to try and get some of the senior officials. So far, six people only are going to be charged. Six lowly officials! For all that money.'

'And no-one will go to jail?'

'No. Oh, they might for a couple of months. But we let murderers out. Somebody the judge called a beast, a Kwazulu policeman who'd murdered countless people, he was sentenced to twenty-six years, he got let out after five months . . .'

'Because the prisons are full?'

'No, the Minister said it was a *bona fide* computer error. I called out and said "Finger trouble!"' He laughed.

Over the courtyard, in the ten year old coloured section of Parliament, I met Michael Hendrickse, a young MP from a famous coloured family.

For fifty years, his grandfather, the Reverend Hendrickse, had been the minister of a small church that he'd built in the centre of the town of Uitenhage, in the Eastern Cape. One day, under the terms of the Group Areas Act, the Government had declared the area 'white', and the church, being a 'coloured' church, had been destroyed by bulldozers. The Reverend Hendrickse had died, by all accounts heart-broken, eighteen months later.

His son, the Reverend Allan Hendrickse, had been the priest responsible for conducting the deconsecration of the church, which he'd described as 'the saddest ceremony of my life'. Subsequently, in 1976, he was jailed, for sixty days, for 'political activities against the Government'. Nonetheless, when in 1983 President P. W. Botha had proposed a tri-cameral parliament, to include coloureds and Indians, but not blacks, Hendrickse had supported him, and become one of the country's first coloured MPs since pre-apartheid days. 'The great thing in this world', he'd said in an interview at that time, 'is not so much where we stand but the direction in which we are moving.'

Now I was facing *his* son Michael, who sat in a spacious panelled office behind a large wooden desk, wearing a pinstriped suit, pinstriped shirt, white V-necked jersey and sky blue tie. He was my age, maybe younger, with short curly hair, and the plumpish face of the young man who spends more time eating well than going to the gym.

'I don't know what you want me to say,' he said rather nervously. I got the feeling that giving an interview to a journalist, especially a journalist 'from overseas', was some-thing of a novelty for him.

I wanted to get some idea of what it meant to be coloured, I said. Michael then talked, without interruption, for over an hour. For a start, I shouldn't talk about coloureds. They were 'so-called coloureds'; in fact, they were the true South Africans 'because we've got part of everybody in us. This colouredness has been forced on us.'

He took me through South African history from the 'so-called coloured' point of view. The famous Jan Van Riebeeck for example: 'His wife Maria didn't come from Holland, she was an East African. But it doesn't fit in with the myth of the great founder of South Africa. So they've led us to believe in our history books that Maria was the daughter of some rich businessman in Holland somewhere – which is just rubbish.' As for the Afrikaners' Great Trek: 'you must remember it wasn't only white people who were in the Trek. There were so-called coloured guides who were leading these trekkers into their Promised Land, who knew where the water was, where the best grazing land was – those weren't white people.

'And a lot of these prominent white leaders now have some coloured background in them. But they'll always deny it. All these guys like Andreis Treurnicht will deny it.'

Michael became most interesting when he veered off politics to talk about his childhood. The panelled room and neatly tied silk tie receded and you saw in his eyes a different look, the look of an angry small boy.

'In South Africa,' he said, 'there were always two doors, the white and the non-white. Only white people allowed, no dogs allowed – all that stuff. One of my first bad experiences was in a communal play-park for children, out in Uitenhage. We used to go and play there, and then one day, you know, we were chased off. And we just ran. And then we wanted to know, like, "Why?" And they said: "It's for whites only." And we just couldn't understand it, because we were play-ing, all those kids were playing there, up and down on the swings and so on, and all of a sudden the white inspector comes around and chases us off like dogs, and then, I mean

– you can't understand it. So you go to your parents, and they explain, "Look, Michael, it's because you're supposed to be a coloured, and you're not good enough," – and so on. And how wrong that is. And then you have this conflict within yourself: how can people who do this be Christians? On the one hand they say they are God's Chosen People – but the Bible says "Love your neighbour" and you can't understand it, until you realise how bad these people are, how totally immoral they are, and how wrong the whole basis of the apartheid thing was. Then you build up this sense of hate towards white people, generally. Right through, you look at white people and you think: these are the people who killed Steve Biko, these are the people who put the dogs on you, these are the people who kick packets out of old people's hands, these are the people who expect you, when you come down the road, to stop and walk on the gravel so they can walk on the pavement.

'For me, what was a learning experience was when I went to Rhodes University, where I lived in a hostel and came into contact with white people a lot for the first time. A particular friend of mine was from Zimbabwe, and it was just when Mugabe had taken over – he was nationalising, taking away the farms. And this friend hated blacks, like I hated whites. You know, we didn't even greet each other, in the whole first year.

'Anyway, my second year, I don't know what happened, but we started talking. And in the end, by the time we left, after five years, me and John were the biggest of friends, because we could talk to one another. I could understand his fears, and he could understand my aspirations, and a lot of times I could understand the things that they did against his family were wrong. And in the same way he could understand my situation and say, "Michael, you know that is wrong, I didn't know." And that has been the basic problem in South Africa, that we haven't talked enough to each other . . .'

4

HARDEGAT AND *BLANC DE NOIR*

Now I was winding uphill into wine country. I had left the rain behind in Cape Town. To my left and right huge fields of vines stretched golden and russet in the late afternoon sun. No shacks here, just the occasional picturesque white cottage. On the gravel verge of the road, the occasional black: orange boiler suit, woolly hat, bicycle; or perhaps a pair of coloured women with headscarves.

And towering high above this scene, so clear you felt you could almost reach out and touch them, the majestic blue-green peaks of the Hottentot Holland mountains, just a few cotton-wool puffs of cloud passing in stately fashion from left to right . . . way, way up.

A sign said START OF THE WINE ROUTE. And before I knew it I was taking the turning off the main road to the centre of Stellenbosch, home of South Africa's premier Afrikaans university. I slowed to a halt by a village green, surrounded by low white buildings in the classic curvilinear Cape Dutch style.

A row of battered African taxis by a noisy crowd of coloureds reminded me that this wasn't England, that there had to be a 'location' (as the smaller townships are known) somewhere over the hill.

'The one-star Stellenbosch Hotel at 162 Dorp Street has *en suite* baths with all its rooms and deserves a higher grading,' said the more upmarket of my two guide books. (Two is all I'd been able to find, back in London, among the huge piles of guides to Europe and America and the Far East: a down-market backpackers one, which did its best to ignore the thorny subject of politics; and an upmarket sights-to-be-seen and meals-to-be-eaten one, which took a more robust line: 'When you are travelling what you need are facts and practicalities, not polemics. For too long one by-product of the anti-apartheid campaign has been a lack of informed travel guidance to South Africa . . .') Clearly its comments had not gone unnoticed, as the place now had three stars.

There was a swimming pool – strewn with autumn leaves – in the entrance lobby, and a ridiculously obliging black man in burgundy livery, who refused to allow me to carry anything.

I checked into the cheapest room in the hotel, the attic studio, whose *en suite* bathroom had dimensions of 2ft by 3ft. 'You can shower easily,' said the crisply polite white woman who showed me in, 'or have a small bath.' I tried 'a small bath'. If you crouched carefully, and then rotated yourself through ninety degrees in the doubled-up position, you could just about get your knees under water. Leaving only the problem of the shower dripping cold water onto the small of your back.

I poured myself a whisky from the minibar and climbed into bed with my list of contacts. 'Stellenbosch: Henry Richardson. Involved in training and industry. Lovely sense of humour,' read the note I'd made back in England. I took a swig of whisky and phoned.

'Where are you?' boomed the voice from the receiver. 'You're very welcome to come out here whenever you want. My wife's away. There's a bed, and as long as you don't mind doing your own thing, you can stay as long as you like. The last one was an Australian.'

'I've got an appointment at the university at nine. Then I was planning to do the Wine Route.'

'Ah,' came the voice, 'now that's something I'd like to do with you. Why don't you get out here around eleven, and we'll take it from there?'

The flat-topped, off-white concrete buildings of the university were bathed in gorgeous October sunlight. Brown leaves tumbled from the trees onto green lawns. Students wandered past clutching books and files. Friends on bicycles stopped to chat. It was hard to believe it was the end of May in Africa.

Amanda was in her thirties. She sat behind a large neat desk in a cream woollen suit and thick-rimmed black spectacles. Behind her on the wall was a photograph of a group of women holding a banner saying SOUTH AFRICAN WOMEN IN THE STRUGGLE FOR A NON-RACIST NON-SEXIST SOUTH AFRICA. Through a long picture window to our left there was a panoramic view: from the pretty white buildings of Stellenbosch right down to Table Mountain and the sea beyond.

I'd arrived at Stellenbosch at a very interesting time, Amanda told me. A week before, Parliament had tabled a bill to entrench Afrikaans as the language medium of the university. She – and many others – were very angry about this. Afrikaans had been the informal medium forever, but the very fact of its informality meant that if it was better to speak English in class, that was something that could be done. The bill was clearly a desperate political move to position Stellenbosch in the New South Africa; specifically to protect the Afrikaner character of Stellenbosch. 'We see it as exclusive,' she said, in her soft Afrikaner voice. 'It excludes blacks who cannot speak Afrikaans.'

65% of blacks in South Africa could speak Afrikaans; but, of that 65%, a large proportion could only use it as a third language. Amanda couldn't understand how the Government could be so insensitive as to bring in legislation like this at such a time. 'It was a pity you weren't around last night. Some of the students organised a meeting to discuss this. They feel they want to have a protest march.'

First, though, they were going to have a public meeting to raise consciousness, because the majority of the Stellenbosch students were so apathetic. Her husband, who was American, and like herself a political scientist, had done a study on the repression and protest potential amongst Afrikaans students. 'Repression potential is the willingness to repress any type of protest, to even involve police action in repressing marches, strikes, boycotts; and protest potential is the willingness to protest against unconventional political behaviour. And what he found amongst Afrikaans students was that their repression potential is very high: 70%, in some cases as high as 80%, while their protest potential is negligible. They're very conservative and very apathetic.'

'So the students are less radical than the teachers?'

'Absolutely. If you go to SASCO meetings, which is the broad, very liberal progressive student movement, you won't see most of them there. And I don't see them making big noises at this corruption scandal in Government. Not a sound out of them. They also don't read newspapers. I'm the one informing them what's happening in the papers. Oh, they might read the Afrikaans mainstream papers, like *Die Burger* or *Die Beeld*, but they don't read the *Weekly Mail*, or *Die Vrye Weekblad*, the radical alternative press.

'I mean, this past week I've dealt with women's rights, and I had a major uproar in my class because they don't believe that gender discrimination exists. They believe that all people are equal, and if they are discriminated against it's their own fault. And I had a very hard time explaining to them a concept like Affirmative Action. Why you use Affirmative Action to address injustices of the past, to try and make amends for past inequalities. They're vehemently against Affirmative Action, whether it's for race or gender it doesn't matter. They see it as a form of discrimination. They cannot put themselves in the situation of others. They seem quite incapable of doing that.'

I asked her how she'd become radicalised; or had she come from an enlightened Afrikaner family?

'No. I grew up in a very staunch Afrikaner home, and at school I had only the usual Afrikaner nationalist indoctrination. And I never really challenged that until I went to university, when I was very lucky to study in a department that was really liberal. That challenged all the existing beliefs and stereotypes that I had. So my attitudes changed very drastically during that period. And then I taught at the University of the North, that's the black university in the northern Transvaal, which, to me, was a real eye-opener. It was at the beginning of the State of Emergency. The police set up a base on campus and my students were taken out of classes and whipped. And every morning the riot police would be there in their riot gear. These students were just protesting against conditions and the existence of an apartheid society. That was the first time I really experienced what the other side looks like; what it is like to be black in this country – and that changed my attitudes completely.'

There was a light double knock at the door and a blond head containing a pair of piercing blue eyes appeared, made an arrangement, and vanished.

'So has this meant problems in your relationship with your parents?' I asked.

'Oh yes. That, to me, is one of the biggest problems in my own personal life: the fact that my parents are very conservative. My father, for example, still has this problem with the English. He refuses to speak English, because he hasn't forgiven them the Boer War. So when I became fairly liberal, it became more and more difficult to communicate with them. I mean, at points we would have conversations and my father would say "You're a Communist!" and I mean, God forbid, I have never even mentioned any Marxist concepts at all, because I see myself as a liberal. But to them there's no understanding of the differences, because the Government in the past conflated all those things: anything that was opposing Nationalism was *per* definition Communism. So what we have now is a sort of truce. We just don't talk politics when we're together, we just talk about the weather, or family matters.'

'So they look on you as the strayed sheep?'

She smiled, an ironic, gentle smile. 'Yuh. It's a strange phenomenon. But I mean this happens in many families. Families are divided. That guy who just popped his head in here, it might be interesting for you to talk to him. He's the grandson of Hendrik Verwoerd, and he's a lecturer in philosophy, and his wife is a member of the ANC, and he's more or less been kicked out of his family, because how can you be the grandson of Verwoerd and have these very pro-black sentiments? To me, his situation is so amazing, because people label him when they hear the word Verwoerd. So the Left people label him as the grandson of the architect of apartheid, and they don't even want to speak to him, although his political views are just as kosher as any liberal that I know, but he's stereotyped before he's opened his mouth, so he really has a very hard time.'

So we went for a walk down the corridor and I met Wilhelm Verwoerd. Full length, he reminded me of a young Oxbridge figure, in his sleeveless jersey and baggy trousers; and indeed, it turned out that he'd studied at Oxford on a Rhodes Scholarship.

I explained that I was in a rush, having fixed up to do the Wine Route. 'Oh no,' he said, with a smile, 'you must do that, that's all part of Stellenbosch. In any case, I'd like you to meet my wife; she's very involved.'

He invited me to tea at his house the following morning.

Henry Richardson was in his late fifties, tall, with wild white hair and a big nose. He was bent double in the garage of his large detached house, fixing a racing bicycle.

'Here you are at last!' he bellowed. 'Right! I'll just finish doing this and then we'll go. Now what d'you want to do? D'you want to do the whole Wine Route, or shall we just go to one or two places and then have some lunch? I've booked us into my wife's favourite restaurant. She's away – did I mention that?'

'Whatever you think's best,' I replied.

'Right, in that case, we'll just do a couple of places and then we'll have some lunch.'

It was a beautiful day. The vineyards were a blaze of autumn colours: reds and browns and golds and oranges and yellows. Behind stood the magnificent blue-green mountains. We turned off the road and up a long avenue of autumnal trees towards the white curves of a Cape Dutch farmhouse. White cast-iron chairs stood half in, half out of the shade of a huge oak tree.

'Hello, hello, hello!' said Henry genially to the tall well-dressed coloured lady who greeted us. 'We've come to try some of your wines, then we're going to nip off and have some lunch, then we'll come back and buy a case or two. Any chance of sitting outside?'

Unfortunately not. It was winter, so we'd have to go indoors. I thought of the British, shivering outside London cafés in November or March; how if you transported such a day and such a place to England it would be packed, even midweek. We sat down at a long wooden table in an echoing stone room. The coloured lady brought us each a winelist.

'Now I think you'll like this one,' said Henry. 'This is a Chardonnay, very dry, very good. And you must try their Blanc de Noir, and perhaps a Grand Vin Blanc. Then their Riesling's extremely good, and we should have one red; how about a Lanoy?'

We sat and sipped from narrow glasses, each filled to about half an inch; the slight reserve I felt with Henry lessening with each glass.

As we sped off up the drive Henry chuckled, 'That was a

bit naughty. We should really have bought a case or two –
that's how it works. They reckon that after you've tasted four
or five you'll buy a case. But I get my wine from there pretty
regularly, so I don't feel too bad about it.' He nodded at a
little obelisk by the side of the drive. 'There's a plaque there
saying this place was founded by Huguenots who brought
the fine old traditions of wine-making from France. All a
load of mallarkey. They didn't know anything about wine-
making; just a load of petty crooks escaping the law.'

We drove on. It could have been France: vineyards, mountains, a white-cottaged village or two. And the restaurant
Henry was taking me to was called La Petite Ferme, a pretty
little auberge on a hillside, with a spectacular view out over
a long wooded valley. Our table was outside. Pink table-
cloths, pink napkins, white wine, sunshine. It was hard to
believe the Cape Flats were only forty kilometres away.

Henry was English South African, but he'd been out of the
country for thirty years, working in industry. He'd been in
the mines in Zambia for twenty years, then working for a
large sugar company in Somalia, Sri Lanka and Botswana.

'I loved Botswana. I had a wonderful time there. We lived
outside Francistown. I had a friend who had a small aero-
plane, I like to do a bit of flying – no, that was a good time.
It's funny you say you like the people so much, because I
remember the expats out there saying they found it bloody
hard to make friends with the Batswana.'

'But then I was teaching in a school,' I said, 'so it was
probably easier for me.'

'Probably so, probably so.'

By the time our starters had arrived we were onto Government corruption. 'They're all crooks,' Henry said. 'No doubt
about it. They've been in power too long – and that's what's
happened. You know, I used to know a guy, a Hollander,
very bright fellow, used to be in charge of Durban docks, and
I remember he said to me: "For years, here we've been, in
South Africa, terrified of the idea of the Communists taking

over. They've been the great bogeyman, held up for us to be frightened of. And you know, what we've had here has been exactly the same. Centralised government, heavy beauro-cracy, corruption endemic – exactly the same."' Henry laughed.

'So,' I said, after a while, 'd'you think it's all going to work out?'

'Well, I hope it's going to be all right.' He fixed me with a beady eye. 'I *hope*. But I don't know. You know, the African . . . I don't know, I'm not sure how good they are at looking to the future. Zimbabwe's a terrible mess now, a terrible mess.'

'Why's that?'

'Mugabe's just got it wrong.'

'Is he corrupt?'

'No, no – he's not corrupt – he's just got it wrong. You know, I hate to say this, but there are certain parts of Africa . . . the people there . . . they just can't be bothered to think about what's coming up. You know, the soil is fertile, life is easy, they sit around for long enough, a banana will drop into their mouth.'

'So the African is lazy?'

'No, I didn't use that word. Now Mark, I've been all over the world, I'm just telling you what I've seen. In Sri Lanka, for example, it's a very different story. A *very* different story. Of course, they're all killing each other all the time – but they do think about the future. I've got a good friend who was involved in one of these international aid programmes, and he said, you know, about Sri Lanka, things are looking pretty hopeful, we're getting there. And then I asked him about Africa, and he shook his head and said: "Hm . . . Africa."'

I checked out of my attic studio and into Henry's place. It was a largish two-storey house set in a mature garden, with an electric steel gate that slid back at the touch of a remote control, two cars in the driveway, and a formidable array of security devices. Burglar bars of course on every window. Upstairs, just above my room off the landing, was an impregnable iron grille, blocking off the master bedroom.

'It's very safe round here,' Henry said, when I asked if I could leave my car in the road for an hour or so. 'You don't need to worry.'

He had two dogs he clearly doted on. Barney, a Basset hound with long floppy ears and a ridiculous sausage of a body; and Zack, a pugnacious-looking bull terrier. 'Oh you don't need to worry about Zack,' he said, as I backed away from the growling beast. 'He's very excitable, but he doesn't mean any harm. Do you Zack? Do – you – Zacky-Zack?'

Wilhelm and Melanie Verwoerd lived in a modern estate of small bungalows on the far side of the big main road that bypasses Stellenbosch. As I arrived, a coloured man was just leaving, in a battered yellow van.

Wilhelm had changed out of his Oxbridge gear and was resplendent in a sky blue tracksuit and *takkies*. His wife Melanie was a few years younger, mid-twenties, with short ginger-brown hair and pretty, intelligent eyes. She was wearing dungarees. Their little girl ran back and forth on the lawn between them.

Wilhelm made us some tea, and then took the child outside so I could talk to Melanie. She, too, was from a staunch Afrikaner family. And yes, her grandmother was bitter about the English as well. Still wouldn't speak English.

Melanie had joined the ANC after she and Wilhelm had come back from Oxford. 'I came back and I was just so sick and tired of being on the other side. The only way I'd ever known black people was through a servant relationship.'

Now she was on the local ANC executive. Of fifteen members, three were white, two 'so-called coloured', and the rest black.

'So was it just because you went to England that you became radicalised?'

'No, in my third year at Stellenbosch, Wilhelm was away in Holland, where the anti-apartheid thing is very big – much bigger than in England: I mean people will challenge you, which they never do in England – anyway, Wilhelm was sending all this stuff back that we never got in our newspapers: cuttings from English and Dutch newspapers, about what was really going on.

'This was in the high years of the State of Emergency, it was quite dangerous really, I mean you couldn't trust anybody. Later on, we found out that some of my best friends at the university were members of the Security Police. They had one person in every hostel who was an informer, reporting back.'

What about her family? Did her parents know? 'Oh yes, they've accepted it totally. But we've never told Wilhelm's parents, they're members of the Conservative party. In fact,' she smiled, 'Wilhelm joined the ANC a week ago.'

'The problem is that Afrikaners have this culture where they're not supposed to question authority. At Government schools, the history that is being taught is still the history of Afrikaner nationalism, which includes perhaps a paragraph about black politics. You're never taught about the black struggle for liberation, or the Broederbond.* The Government tell you that the Russians are a threat, so this is what you believe.'

Wilhelm had joined us, sat quietly on a sofa to his wife's right. This was the main thing, he agreed, the way whites in South Africa had managed to perpetuate this insulation from what was really going on. 'When Breyten Breytenbach returned here after a period of years, he said that the most unbelievable thing was how the whites had managed to protect themselves from all the pain and suffering around

* The Broederbond, or 'band of brothers', founded in 1918 as a society dedicated to restoring the fortunes and national pride of Afrikaners, became an all-powerful secret Afrikaner society, aggressively pro-apartheid, with enormous influence over key appointments in both Church and State.

them. But if you live here, and you have a job, and a family, you take holidays here – you just don't see it. And if you open yourself to the pain and suffering it just gets unbearable. It's so much easier just to block it out. If you watch South African TV and read mainstream Afrikaans papers, you are drawn into this world where everything is fine: fourteen killed in Soweto is overshadowed by the rugby. And then some, like my father, say: "Look what a mess we're in today. When the real Nats were in control, it was OK."'

He told me about *hardegat*, the Afrikaans idea of being 'hard-assed': prepared to stand up for what you believe in, fight against anybody who criticises you. In the case of the Nationalists, it was allied, Wilhelm said, with a profoundly unrealistic idea, both of South Africa's own strength and security, and of international *realpolitik*. There was a joke about this:

'OK, so in the late 1980s the Cabinet was having a meeting. Malan was still in charge of the Security Forces at that time. So they're sitting there and they're all deliberating what to do about the problems of South Africa. "I've got a solution for our problems," says a minister. "Let's declare war on America. We will lose – and they'll have to solve our problems." P. W. Botha thinks this is a very good idea. "But how shall we get them to fight us?" he says. They're deliberating that, when suddenly Malan puts up an objection. "But what if we *win*?" he says.'

We laughed. 'I mean, that's the problem,' said Wilhelm. Melanie brought in some more tea and a tray of little hot cakes, and I asked them about living with the famous name of Verwoerd.

'It's a very disabling label,' said Melanie, 'a very disabling badge to carry. On the other hand, it makes you explicitly say where you stand. So in that sense it can be very enabling. You can say "I am sorry for what he did". And in the end people accept you because of what *you* do.'

Wilhelm seemed able to be very objective about his

grandfather. He had been, he said, an Afrikaner Nationalist who'd used certain ends to justify some very unacceptable means. His vision had blinded him to what was really happening around him. 'I think the thing that hurt the most', he concluded, 'was what he did about education – Bantu education. That's caused the most long-lasting harm.'

On Sunday morning I came down to find a French carpenter friend of Henry's putting up a shelf in his kitchen. It was a shelf for the TV that Henry's wife didn't want, so he was getting it done while she was away. The deal seemed to be: Giles put up the shelf and then Henry took him and his wife out for Sunday lunch.

Giles was in his late forties, his thin face concealed behind a long grey beard and narrow-rimmed square glasses. His accent was South African until he started drinking, when it veered off to reveal its French origins. His wife Julie was pure Seth Effrikan. She was wearing a fetching shell-suit in bright green with shiny black ankle boots. Green make-up above her eyes enhanced the effect nicely.

We drove off to an Austrian restaurant on the edge of town: Die Kelder, a big, roomy, farmlike sort of place with wooden tables on stone floors and a huge open fireplace. A barrel just inside the door had a board propped on it saying: KARAOKE – SATURDAYS.

Right, I thought. Now I'm going to forget I'm in South Africa. I'm not going to lean forward earnestly and quiz Giles about blacks and whites, the future and the past. I'm just going to go with the flow.

We talked about food. Both Giles and Henry were cooks. Henry told us how easy Chinese cooking was. 'There's really no mystery about it,' he said. 'You soon realise it's just stir-fry this and stir-fry that, chuck in a bit of chicken and away you go.'

We moved on to the subject of snails (which we were eating). How crazy it was, Giles said, that the English thought the French were strange for liking snails, when they were the first to go down to the beach and eat cockles and mussels and any kind of thing. 'It's all the same thing. And pigeon – what's wrong with pigeon?'

And so the conversation progressed. We could have been in the depths of the Auvergne, with a charming Frenchman and his wife, thinking how delightful it was that we could all be friends across barriers of language and culture.

But then, inexorably, the conversation turned to Africa. 'One thing all of us round this table share', said Henry, in a lull between courses, 'is a fondness for Botswana.'

'You were there?' I asked Giles.

'Oh yes.' He'd been up in Kusane, right in the far north, building a game lodge. But the drought. He shook his head. It was terrible up there now.

The trouble was that Africans didn't think ahead. 'These people from overseas, they don't understand the African mentality,' said Giles. 'He doesn't think for the future. Only for today. You don't believe me? I'll give you an example. In Swaziland – now this is a black country – you have two farmers, side by side, with the same-sized plots of land. The white guy will have planted that land so there is every little thing growing there. He will have pipes for irrigation and so on. But next door, the black guy – hey – he will have his hut, and round his hut just enough *mielies* for him, just him and his family – and that's it. He doesn't think ahead.'

Having proved his case beyond all reasonable doubt, Giles sat back. I suggested that these differences might perhaps have something to do with education, training; that in the last century, before their land was taken away from them, blacks had been highly effective farmers. Giles swigged at his *vin rouge* and his accent suddenly became very French.

'These blacks at the border – ' he fumed, 'hey – they take their flippin' time. You wait five minutes on the South African side, and then you have to wait for a bloody hour at the Botswana gate. And what about that Botswana Defence

Force? Hey, those guys! They just set up roadblocks where they feel like.'

'As do the whites,' I said. 'I'm sure if you were black you'd have the same trouble with the South African police.'

'They don't kill people,' Giles riposted angrily. 'There was a Rhodesian missionary doctor went through the border gate with his wife and children, and one of these soldiers just shot him. Shot him dead.'

'In front of his wife and children,' added Julie.

'And he got charged with accidentally letting off his gun. He got let off. And I'll tell you another time: I was in Gabs, OK. I'd gone over there with this *bakkie* full of oranges, and these three black guys started coming at me, playing chicken, so I put on the foot, and *zoom*, I went at them – '

'What were they doing?'

'Oh, they were fooling around – so they had to jump out of the way. And then I went to the garage, and these three niggers – one short, one medium, one tall – came round to me, and they swore at me in their language, and I swore back, because I speak that language, and they said, "Hey, what were you doing round there – trying to kill us?" And I said: "Look, you were playing chicken with me." And one of them, he poked his finger at me like this, right at my nose, almost took my glasses off, and he said, "Don't you do that, you shouldn't do that, that was a pedestrian crossing," or something, and I said, "Well, look, in South Africa, if we have a pedestrian crossing, there is a little green man." And he started coming at me again. And I got fed up with this, so I said, "OK, we're going to the police station right now. Come on, let's go." And the old lady who was there serving the petrol, she was saying "Oh *baas*, don't take them to the police station, because you are white and they are black and if you go there – they'll lock you up and throw away the key."'

He had other stories. Blacks who were incompetent. Blacks who were corrupt. Blacks who'd killed whites. They were stories he insisted on telling me, leaning forward towards me, glasses glinting, stabbing his finger at me to make his point.

'But you're always like that,' said his wife. 'I won't go with him up there, because he gets like that. You're French, and you get like that.'

Henry was trying to bring the conversation back to the weather. The day had brightened, and it was pleasantly sunny outside. 'Shall we go back and have some coffee and ice-cream in the garden?' he suggested.

As we drove out of the restaurant gate, there was an old black man slumped in the driveway against the wall. 'Now what's he doing there?' said Julie. 'He's going to get himself run over – oh *sis*, he's being sick all over himself.' He was: a stream of white vomit poured out of the man's mouth and down his trousers. Julie shook her head. 'These people,' she said. 'I don't know how their constitutions stand up to it. They drink, they're sick, and they just go on living forever and ever. I don't think we would survive for that long.'

Back at Henry's house, the sun was shining. Beyond, the lovely mountains stood clear, their peaks just capped with cloud. The sun streamed down through the vines, through the blue, orange, pink and purple flowers of a South African winter, onto the terrace. Henry emerged with a tray of coffee and ice-cream. The two dogs were going wild, racing madly up and down the garden. 'Zack!' shouted Henry, marching after the bull terrier with a warning finger raised. 'Za-ack!'

Barney was dumping several fluid ounces of saliva on Julie's green shell-suit bottoms. 'He can't help it,' she said fondly, 'he's only an animal. That's the thing about me,' she added, turning to me. 'I hate human beings. You know, animals, they don't do terrible things to each other – '

'They kill each other,' said Henry, 'like a lion murders a wildebeest.'

'OK, but they don't put burning tyres around each other's necks,' said Giles. 'No,' Julie went on, 'when people say, you know, "They're behaving like animals," I get angry, because animals wouldn't behave like that. You know, the animal kingdom goes about things in the right way. It's humans that are so bad.'

5

OF WHALES AND OSTRICHES

The open road stretched ahead. Low fields of vines. Little white Cape Dutch houses dotted here and there on the empty landscape. It was good to be alone in my big white car, speeding along with the radio on, listening to a morning music programme that made Radio Two sound dangerously radical. 'Em-*oh*-tion recollected in tranquilli-tair and Freyinck Sen-ar-trah at hey-ars *moh*-st soulful with the Hollywood Streng Quar-tairt,' came the absurd more-English-than-English voice of the DJ, one Paddy O'Byrne.

I drove down through Somerset West. 'Not particularly interesting, a lot of Poms retire there,' Henry had said. There were red roses on the central reservation, a long street of the now-familiar South African shops and eateries: Pick 'n Pay. Mike's Kitchen. Woolworths. Cashworths! Trueworths!!

I pressed on, back to the coast. To the left a new range of mountains hugged the shore line. Low, green, piney sorts of trees ran down to the sea on the right. But hey, as the Seth Effrikans would say, this wasn't good enough for a travel writer: I was going to have to get myself a book on South African flora and fauna. There were plenty of those tall, flimsy, willow-leaved type of trees, too. What were they?

Gordon's Bay was a steeper version of Camps Bay. One, two, three storey houses, in a variety of idiosyncratic modern designs, climbing up the mountainside. It was another perfect day, but the place was deserted. Sunlit waves crashed against a long stone breakwater. Mainstays twanged in an unoccupied marina. Far, far away across False Bay you could see the tiny flat-topped silhouette of Table Mountain.

I stopped for tea in an empty café and met a man from Staffordshire. Tall, grey-haired and moustachioed, Jerry was a surveyor by trade, and had just bought the place, was doing it up ready for the spring.

He'd come out to the Transvaal on a two month contract, ten years before, and enjoyed it so much he'd stayed. 'I went back home in February this year,' he said, 'and it was funny, for the first time I really felt as if South Africa was home. Of course our climate is wonderful. I've got relatives in Staffordshire who won't talk to me since I've settled out here. But they don't understand. You know, in 1985, I wrote an essay, pointing out the positive sides of being out here. I sent it to Mrs Thatcher and the *Daily Telegraph*, but they didn't print it. That's part of the trouble, they don't want to know.

'I'm not racist at all,' he went on, 'but I can tell you, the coloured people in the Cape don't know how to do a day's work. It's not the same with the blacks. Up in the Transvaal I had ten guys who used to follow me around from job to job. They treat you like a father, and they were good. But down here – I don't know – I can't find the workers. Even with the blacks, you need twice as many guys as you'd need in the UK. As they say out here, nothing's kaffir-proof. You know, before I came out here I used to think the sooner the blacks pushed every bloody white man into the South Atlantic the better. After two months, I thought the sooner the South African Defence force pushes every black into the South Atlantic the better.'

I gulped down my tea and scarpered. Up on the winding coast road I was stuck behind an open lorry full of blacks wearing orange boiler suits and green woolly hats. If you were going to have a South African party, I thought, the dress would be: whites – sunglasses, yellow golfing jersey, pale blue slacks, white shoes; blacks – boiler suit and woolly hat. Everything about them looked downtrodden: even the hurried glance away you got when you, Whitey, met their eyes from behind the wheel of your big expensive car.

To the left, the mountains towered upwards, their green slopes splashed with bright yellow flowers. The road snaked up, then swept down to a spectacular stretch of beach called Koeëlbaai.

I took off my shoes and socks, paced barefoot along the cool wet sand. It was noon. The sun had risen just above the peaks, casting the upper half of the mountain into a deep blue shadow. Further down, ochre sunbeams slanted diagonally through outcrops of tiny looking trees. A misty sea-spray drifted across, smudging the chiaroscuro. On the beach, beyond the surf, the sea was adazzle with a thousand pinpoints of light. It was a fantasy place, such as a million English office workers dream of – and apart from the flock of black cormorant-type birds swooping in and out of the surf, it was entirely empty.

Driving on, I entered a strange lunar landscape, the mountains crumbling into dirty grey shale. Round the headland, the sea had suddenly shifted, lay far out over low rocks to the right. Just beyond the half-horse settlement of Kleinmond, a young black couple had their thumbs out. I stopped. They were headed for Hermanus, 70 kilometres further on down the coast.

'I'm just going up to the next town,' I said, 'Is that OK?'

'Yes.'

They got in, the man in the front, the woman in the back. My first hitch-hikers. And they were black! Eagerly, I struck up a conversation:

'So are you going to Hermanus to work?'

'Yes.'

'D'you live in Kleinmond?'

'Yes.'

'You don't mind if I just drop you at the next town?'

'Yes.'

'I'm English, by the way.'

'Yes.'

'D'you speak English?'

'Yes.'

They were of course Afrikaans-speaking coloureds. 'I – not – English – say – good,' the man volunteered eventually.

I hadn't worked out how I was going to play it. Drive on down the coast to Hermanus ('this one-time fishing village has become a most fashionable resort' said the more upmarket of my two guide books) and from there to the southernmost point of Africa, Cape Agulhas, which I'd missed last time and had even then had a hankering to see. Or swoop north to head east through the 'scenically splendid' mountains of the Langberge . . .

I decided to put the constraints of my last trip in reverse and let my passengers dictate my route. I whisked across the flat green landscape at 150 kilometres an hour. What a machine! My silent new friends looked quite alarmed.

In the windy grey afternoon Hermanus didn't seem up to much. The centre was just a big empty car park, a garage, a bank, a greasy looking FRESH FISH AND TAKEAWAYS. It was 4 p.m. It would be dark at 6, and Cape Agulhas was a further seventy kilometres, on an unsurfaced road my guide book described as 'laborious and tough-going'.

Uncertain what to do, I crossed a small stretch of green grass to a white cottage which offered TEAS AND CAKE. A coloured lady was sitting at a wooden table playing with a white toddler. I asked for some tea, and a young white woman appeared and scooped up the child. She was soft-spoken and extremely pretty, her hair a mass of blonde curls. It was funny: she did have a Seth Effrikan accent, but I realised after I'd been talking to her for a minute or two that I was starting not to register it.

'So where could I stay in Hermanus?' I asked. There were two hotels, she said: the Windsor, which was full of old people and got a lot of tours; or the Marine, which was 'naice but expinsive'; or: 'I have a little cottage which you could stay in for fifty rand.' For a moment, I thought she was inviting me to be a paying guest. I had visions of a cosy supper, a bottle of wine . . . but no, it rapidly emerged that we were talking self-catering.

Well, I wasn't going to make the fabled Agulhas today; it was grey and cold and windy; I had notes to catch up on – I took it. 'It's just beyond the Meat Lover's Den,' she called after me. 'Third of the row – the green door.'

> Just one step out of time
> enter god's eternity
> and I am wholly freed
> from human transiency

said the leather teardrop attached to the front door key. The place was sweet, with a white wood slatted front and a table by a big window overlooking the bay; the perfect spot to bring the love of your life and a stack of good books and hole up for a month or so.

I cleared some shale and a spider out of the bath and lay in the steaming water, watching two columns of ants converge as they marched purposefully from a hole in the skirting board to the boiler and back again. Cape Town, Stellenbosch . . . only a day had passed, but already they seemed so far away. Strange how wrapped up in Cape Town I'd become, how *important* it had all seemed. Now, like London, it was just another city; another city whose intricate web of concerns I had left completely behind.

Just across the road, and I was in a little Cornish cove, the darkening sea swirling around rocks of grey and purple slate, a couple of fishing boats pulled up on a concrete slipway. Far away through the dusk to the left was a mighty curve of sand, with yet another range of mountains looming behind.

It was Monday. I suddenly realised, as I walked back along

the coast through the blustery winter wind, that it was May
Bank Holiday Monday. I wondered what Sarah was up to:
strolling down some cow-parsleyed country lane, lying reading in the long grass of Hampstead Heath. We'd agreed on
our last call that phoning for an expensive two minutes only
made us seem further apart; we would just have to stick it
out with postcards and letters.

It was dark. I stopped at what looked like a beach café, a
rickety wooden building with picnic tables outside. A
couple of beers and a burger and I could roll into bed happy;
well, happyish, anyway.

But inside it was a different story. Pink linen tablecloths,
candles, two uniformed coloured waiters who looked like
slim versions of Tweedledum and Tweedledee. An enormous white girl in a frilly black cocktail dress approached
from behind a candlelit bar.

'Can ah hilp you?'

'Could you do me some supper?'

'One of mah schiffs has just lift,' she said grandly, 'but I'll
see what the other one can manage. Please sit down.'

Tweedledum approached with a menu. The prices were
exorbitant, about double what I'd been paying in Cape Town.
What *was* this place?

The winter wind rattled at the windowpanes. Tweedledum and Tweedledee offered bread from a breadbasket;
poured just a little bit of wine into my glass for me to taste;
replied 'Eet's a plizher, sir,' every time I said 'Thank you.'
Never had the rituals of eating out seemed more
preposterous.

'Is iverything all rart for you? asked the cocktail dress,
reappearing.

'A bit off-season is it, at the moment?'

'We're awaiting the imminent arrarval of the whales. Then
we'll be busy again.'

This, apparently, was what Hermanus was famous for.
Southern Right Whales. They came up from the Antartic at

the start of June to calve and dance around in the bay.
'They're just incridible. Last year we had one which had a
perfictly wyatt pup, and they came down from Cape Town
with TV cameras and this whale held up her wyatt pup as if
she was showing her off just for the cameras. It was qwart
adorable. They're the most wonderful mothers, the whales.'

So it was the wonderful mothers that were responsible for
the prices. The meal ended up costing more than the cottage.

I was glad I'd left the Cape Agulhas road for daylight and
morning. Beyond the Hermanus mountains, the wind
howled across a huge flat peninsula. Sudden showers of rain
splattered the windscreen. Thirty or forty kilometres out of
Hermanus the tarmac stopped, the radio signal broke up,
and the Dolphin and I were alone, skidding along on dirt.

DANGER POINT said a sign. PEARLY BEACH. There was nothing
on the road, nothing off the road, just mile upon mile of low
scrub, a few windbent apologies for trees.

Then, suddenly, I came over the top of a hill and ahead
stretched a vast plain of the most stunning green, as intense
as the green of an English landscape in April. Cows grazed.
A little river, its banks lined with trees, ran away to the left.
The rainclouds had cleared, the sun had come out, and I
found I was enjoying being alone. It was Tuesday. At home
I'd have been making my fifth cup of coffee of the morning,
jumping as the seventeenth car alarm of the day went off in
the street outside; and here I was, racing along in my big
white car, chucking up a sunlit trail of dust, in the middle of
absolutely nowhere.

After an hour or two I came down through a long valley to
the Moravian mission village of Elim; which Time had
passed entirely by.

A cock strutted down the main street – a winding dirt road
lined with thatched and whitewashed cottages. On a green
at the centre stood a big white church. To its left a water-
mill.

Inside the roomy village shop, tins and bottles were stacked up on high shelves like something out of a pre-war photograph. Two coloured shop assistants in overalls stood waiting behind a long polished wooden counter.

'Have you heard the news?' I asked.

'What?'

'The King has abdicated. He is to marry Mrs Simpson.'

There was only one detail to give the lie: a microwave on a shelf by the pie counter.

'Are these fresh?' I asked.

The girls looked at each other and giggled.

'No,' said the taller of them finally.

'When did they come in?'

'Saturday – I think.'

I bought one, and immediately regretted it. It tasted *extremely* stale.

On the far side of the green, outside a long whitewashed hall, a gaggle of kids screeched around in the sunshine. I pointed my camera at them and they lined up grinning. Two or three rows of dark faces and white smiles, just like Khayelitsha. But what a contrast! The streets were not littered with torn plastic, there were no roaming dogs, and the thatched cottages, if not luxurious, were at least proper homes. An old lady leaning on her gate let me peep past the roses winding round her door. There was a fireplace, with a mantelpiece, and a collection of china ornaments you might have found in Somerset. Elim, stuck way out here at the back of beyond, had somehow avoided the dignity-stripping ravages of apartheid.

The landscape continued flat. By the roadside were more of those tall trees whose name I didn't know; they had peeling white trunks like birches, leaves a little like willows . . . and in the next town I came to I was going to buy a book on South African trees.

I was having fun on the dirt road, seeing how fast I could push the Dolphin before it started to skid . . . when suddenly

I came to a T-junction and back onto boring old tarmac. It was the main road south to the end of the continent.

Ever since I'd not visited it all those years before, I'd imagined Cape Agulhas as a mighty and deserted promontory, a more majestic version of Land's End or the White Cliffs of Dover. But it was nothing but a flat rock-strewn shore, Africa just petering out into the sea. Nor was it deserted: in addition to the orange and white striped lighthouse, there was a dreary settlement of bungalows, a craft shop and the Cape Agulhas Superette.

I took the inevitable photo of the plaque that marked the Southernmost Point, then spun the Dolphin round and headed off, north and east. Having missed this chunk of coastline before, and having held such a misconceived vision of it in my head for all these years, I now had an absurd desire to 'do it' properly; to visit every last little dot on the map, to check reality against fantasy.

So half an hour later found me standing alone on a windswept breakwater at Struisbaai, gazing at deserted rows of colourful little fishing boats, watching gusts whisking up whirlpools of sand along the vast curve of beach and dunes beyond. Then I was bouncing along another dirt road to Arniston, which a Cape Town acquaintance had told me I must see: 'It's our Greek-style fishing village.' But that too was empty and windswept, the owners of the flat-topped white houses all doubtless away getting rich enough to own a holiday home.

I turned right, onto the long straight empty road that ran north to the N2. This was better. I was driving at speed towards the distant blue outline of mountains. Here and there, a lone tree stood out, starkly silhouetted against the bright sidelit plain. *Africa!*

In a quiet sidestreet in the little mountain town of Montagu I found a guesthouse called the Acacia Lodge. It looked just the ticket: a pretty wooden-slatted house with a verandah –

or *stoep*, as the South Africans say – out front. After my long drive, I was hoping for some cosy landladyish set-up where I could just crawl into bed and study my guide books.

Reception was dominated by a ripplingly fat man in a pale green poloneck. He was signing in a smart couple with smart suitcases. 'Yes, we do have one room,' he said coolly, giving my grubby jeans a disapproving stare. 'A hundred and ten rand: dinner, bed and breakfast.'

It was too late to go hunting for a hotelier who liked my dress sense, so I checked in. 'Now if you'd like to go upstairs and wash or whatever,' he said, 'and then I suggest you come down and have a cup of coffee or tea and we can tell you what we're all about.'

On the first floor landing, two old ladies were sitting at a table with a lace cloth playing cards. They smiled at me over half-moon spectacles.

My double bed had a pink satin cover. There was a jug of water by the bedside and fruit in a bowl. Above the wash-basin was a photo of a large coloured lady and a notice which read: 'My name is Louise. It is my pleasure to keep your room clean and ensure that there are clean towels and linen. If I can be of assistance, please tell me, or Lindsay or Bernard.'

I thought I'd better do as I'd been told. I washed quickly and went downstairs, to find a tray of tea in a lounge full of old sofas, old books, framed prints of nineteenth century Cape Town scenes. A smart blonde businesslady – fortyish, or so – in a black and white checked suit was flicking through a copy of *Fair Lady*, South Africa's version of *Harpers & Queen*.

We nodded at each other, and I wandered over to the bookshelf, found it was full of books on . . . well, well . . . South African trees. Aha, so those tall ones with willowlike leaves were milkwoods; and the ubiquitously uninteresting ones (I should have known *that*) were gums.

I caught my companion's eye. We smiled. 'Are you here on business or pleasure?' she asked.

'A bit of both,' I replied.

'Same here.'

She was called Angela, and she published brochures and travel guides for the Cape Town Tourist Board. Having spent a miserable six months in my twenties sitting in a rabbit hutch in the Farringdon Road writing brochures for places my company's clients were too mean to send me to, we had something to talk about.

Bernard appeared. He seemed a trifle friendlier. 'Ah, so you two have met. And you've got some tea. Good. Now the way we do things here is we all meet at seven, in here, for a glass of Muscadel, which is something of a local speciality, and then we move through for dinner. So tonight, to start, we have sheep's brains. Then we have a little lemon sorbet. Then we have fish, which is a monkfish in a cream sauce . . .'

'D'you have any alternative to sheep's brains?' I asked, when he'd finished detailing the feast. Bernard laughed. 'No, no, it's all right, we're not really having sheep's brains. It's a smoked trout with cream cheese. Will that be all right? And if you'd like some wine – I suggest you two share a bottle. I'll be making up a mixed table, so I'll put you both on that. And after dinner,' he went on, 'rather than just sitting, I suggest you try the hot springs, they're just up the road. We have costumes – sterilised – that'll fit you. And if you have too much fun, we'll charge you extra.'

He didn't give me a lecherous wink and add 'knowwhaddImean?' But he might just as well have done.

Angela had brought some CapTour brochures. Bernard was very attentive. 'You'll excuse me,' he said, 'if we just talk business for a moment.' 'No, no, that's fine,' I said, going back to the trees. 'No, the person', said Bernard, 'who does a really good Michelin-type guide to South Africa will go straight to the top.'

'Michelin,' Angela queried. 'Has that got anything to do with the tyres?'

'The tyres?'

'Michelin tyres.'

'No, *no*,' Bernard shook his head firmly. 'Entirely separate. No, nothing at all to do with the tyres.'

I sneaked upstairs, had a long hot bath and changed into my suit. When I re-emerged at 7.01 Bernard was dispensing Muscadel to two elderly couples. 'Can I introduce Mark everyone? This is Mark. This is Jenny and Bobby, and Evelyn and Ian.' Ian, thin, dark, ramrod-straight in a blue blazer, had stood up. With his hair brushed into a firm, Brylcreemed parting, he had the look of a retired engine driver *circa* 1962.

Bernard gave me a flute of Muscadel on ice (he was drinking it from a tumbler, I noticed) and I took a seat between Ian and Jenny on a wooden-backed couch. They were on holiday from Cape Town; from Camps Bay, indeed. 'Ah, well,' I said, 'I know Camps Bay. A beautiful place.'

'Yes . . . it is,' Ian replied measuredly, as if he wasn't quite sure how beautiful it was. 'Beautiful.'

Evelyn, with dyed black curls and pursed pink lips, was even less forthcoming.

'Have you been up to the hot springs?' I asked. 'I was thinking of going after supper.'

'Of course they're letting blecks in there now,' Ian said.

'I wouldn't want to swim in there,' his wife added. 'There are so many people in there now, and they're from all these different population groups.'

I reeled quietly. Another couple had joined us. Roger had a bushy white beard, white hair over his collar and ears, a yellow V-necked jersey, and a booming English yacht-club voice. Penelope was thin and Home Counties looking, with a string of pearls and an accent to match.

'*What* did you say your name was?' Roger asked, leaning theatrically towards Evelyn.

'Eve,' she said quietly.

'Oh, Eve. Ha ha ha!' He chuckled loudly. 'That's funny, because we're Adams.'

'Adams . . .?' said Eve.

'No, Adams is our surname. Adams . . . Eve.' His laughter tailed off.

'Oh,' said Eve, blankly.

In England, I thought, they would never have met, let alone drunk Muscadel together.

'You don't have to keep standing, Ian,' said Bernard. 'You're going to be bobbing up and down all evening at this rate.' Ian sat down abruptly. Roger was emerging as the life and soul – indeed the saviour – of the party. He was a wine buff. The conversation turned to Muscadels and Chardonnays and vintages and . . . indeed, the reason Roger and Penelope were here was for their annual stock-up of wine. They lived in the Eastern Cape, and they came every year.

We went through for dinner. Bernard took charge, putting me at the head of a table for six, in the middle of the room, with Eve to my left, and Penny to my right. At the other end, beyond Ian and Roger, now looking like something out of *Death on the Nile* in a spangly blue evening dress, was Angela. 'That's the bottle of wine you two are sharing,' said Bernard. 'I'll put it in the middle.'

'Are you together?' Penny asked.

'No, no,' I replied. 'I'm on my own. I'm from England.'

The formality of the scene had entirely taken away my appetite. Or perhaps I'd been poisoned by that chicken pie from Elim. A huge plateful of smoked fish, stuffed with cream cheese, was put in front of us. I toyed delicately with it. 'Everything all right for you?' said Bernard, leaning right over me. 'Fine, fine,' I murmured nervously.

It was turning out to be a monumentally boring evening. Eve had nothing to say *at all*, and Penelope was trying to join in the conversation at the other end. Eventually she gave up and turned to me: 'I don't want to be personal,' she asked, 'but what are you doing out here on your own?'

I thought of telling her that I was a wealthy young Englishman with a broken heart, but . . . oh what the hell! 'I'm writing a book,' I said. Anything to inject some spice.

'Oh – a book,' she said, 'how *interesting*. On what?' I explained. 'So, are you a journalist, or . . .?'

'Sort of thing.'

'I hate journalists,' she said. 'Particularly English ones. No, I have a reason, because my sister used to be married to one, you've probably heard of him.' She mentioned a famous name. 'An absolute shit. To her. He was. And then they come over here, and write rubbish about this place, and go back home feeling morally superior. I hope you're not going to do that? No, really – it's so boring.'

'I'm trying to keep an open mind,' I said.

Penelope leaned over and grabbed Roger, whose pontifications on the merits and demerits of this or that vintage could be clearly heard above the general babble. 'So you're from *England*,' he bellowed down at me, in that fruitiest of English accents. 'Yes.' 'The English are so bloody insular, that's what I object to. Present company excluded of course. But don't you agree? What a place, what a climate, and so bloody insular.'

You don't tell people you're writing a book, they ignore you. You tell them, they just can't wait to let you have their entire life story. Penelope, who'd cooled me totally during the starters, was now barely able to eat her monkfish so eager was she to tell me about her childhood in Kenya, how she and Roger had had to move from there to the Transvaal; now, finally, to a village in the Eastern Cape.

'So d'you think', I asked, 'you're going to stay here? Or will you move on again?'

'God knows. I don't want to think about the politics of this country. I just try and keep out of it. As soon as we've had our holiday, I shall just slip back into my quiet Eastern Cape existence.' She smiled.

The table was on its sixth bottle of wine, the rest of the

restaurant was empty. Bernard ushered us back through to the lounge for coffee and mints and brandy. 'Got to be up for breakfast,' said someone. 'You know Bernard has fifty-four different varieties of marmalade.' Penelope leant over the edge of her chair. 'To tell you the truth,' she said to me, 'I hate them. Blacks. I just hate them. I'm sorry, but after what the Mau Mau did to my friends in Kenya . . .' Her voice dropped off, as if she'd suddenly remembered I was one of those dreaded journalists, tape-recorder constantly whirring in his head . . .

'So why d'you stay?' I asked, after a few moments. 'Oh, I don't know. Roger likes it here, and where Roger goes, Penny follows. But if he were to die tomorrow, I'd probably go back to England.' She gave me a wan, inebriated smile. 'I don't know. It's so cold, perhaps I wouldn't.'

Roger was ready for bed; where Roger went, Penny followed, albeit lurching a little.

I was left with Angela and the rest of my brandy.

'Having fun?' she asked.

'Amazing people you have out here,' I replied. 'One moment you're just having a normal conversation, and then suddenly, out of nowhere, you get these astonishingly racist remarks. It's like a knife in the chest.'

'Oh, you'll find that everywhere. What amazes me, is how well we all tolerate each other. There are so many different races here. Xhosas and Zulus and – and Indians and whites and – and – so many people co-existing. OK, we have a bit of violence. Here and there. But basically we all respect each other, and live with each other. No really, I'm very optimistic about the future.'

She was less optimistic about personal relationships. 'I'll never marry again,' she said, twenty minutes later, after Bernard had brought us another large brandy each, and we were sitting alone, with only the ticking grandfather clock for company.

*

And then we decided, like two naughty children, to drive up to the hot springs. In England, I had a firm rule with myself. After three drinks, I abandoned the car. Here, now, suddenly, I didn't care. I had drunk too much to drive, but it was the other side of the world, and . . . the roads were completely empty and . . . soon we were stumbling around the grounds of the five star Avalon Springs Hotel, laughing as we tried to find a way into the springs.

'They're closed now,' a black security guard told us, but that wasn't going to stop us . . .

Under a cocktail umbrella by a rippling blue pool, the orange-floodlit crags of the mountain towering behind, I found myself kissing her. A forty year old businesslady from an Agatha Christie movie. 'I shouldn't be doing this,' she said. 'Neither should I,' I replied. 'Why?' 'I've got a girlfriend in London.' 'I've got a boyfriend in Cape Town. I didn't realise you felt like that about me. You were so cool earlier.'

I didn't, really. I was just lonely. And walking hand in hand through the hotel grounds, with my arm round this woman and the night breeze on my cheek made me feel so much better . . .

Driving back, I was already regretting the whole thing. But still, if she offered, despite the embarrassment in the morning, despite Bernard, Sarah, the fact that everyone in the guest house would know – I knew I'd sleep with her. We got to her bedroom, where we opened a bottle of wine she had, sat on the edge of her bed. 'I'd like to,' she said. 'But I couldn't face Caspar tomorrow if I did. Let's go back to the lounge and drink it.' 'OK,' I replied, glad suddenly that I'd been saved from myself, from betraying Sarah, from everything.

We sat by the grandfather clock until half past three; swapping emotional CVs; talking people, relationships, sex, love, everything but politics. In the hallway, I gave her a chaste disappointed-relieved kiss on the cheek. 'Goodnight,' I said, and stumbled up to my shiny pink counterpane. 'If I get up and go to the springs before breakfast I'll come and get you.'

I woke at seven. Had it really happened? It had. Ten minutes of groaning remorse between the sheets was enough, and then I was up and off to the hot springs on my own.

Despite the garish ugliness of the hotel that had been built all around them, they still had a certain magic; with the orange-brown crags of the mountain towering above. I tried the cold pool; then the warm pool; then found a spot in the hot pool where I could lie with my head in the bubbles and let my hangover seep away . . .

I emerged from this nirvana to find a seventy-plus white woman, in a rigid blue bathing suit, lowering herself in beside me.

'Goot morning,' she said, in a strong German accent.

'Good morning,' I replied. We agreed it was a delightful place.

'If you want to go to some really beautiful hot springs,' she said, 'there's a lovely little spot, twenty kilometres up the road at Baden, and if you ask the woman nicely she will let you in. Being an Afrikaner woman, she doesn't want blacks swimming in there, so she's made it into a private club. So you see, the problem is overcome. And since I have been going there all these years, I joined the club. It costs me one rand membership a year,' she concluded, with a horrible little chuckle.

I left the old bigot to the radioactive waters and went back to try Bernard's fifty-four varieties of marmalade. Angela was at the other end of the breakfast table, with Penelope and Roger on the far side. 'Morning, morning, morning!' I said cheerily, taking the seat next to Angela. 'I've just been up to the hot springs. Beautiful!'

I drove on. Last time, hitching in the opposite direction, I'd – inevitably – gone along the busy main N2. Today, I wanted to see what I'd missed, the dry plain behind the mountains that is called the Little Karoo.

It was everything I'd hoped. A straight, fast, empty road over an arid landscape of bush and low scrub-covered hills. The kind of place where you could get out of the car and do primal scream therapy for six hours and nobody would notice; or even pass by. On I sped, an endless carpet of landscape unrolling before me. Lumpy brown hills to Ladismith. Then the silhouette of mountains – surprisingly green mountains – up ahead.

Outside Ladismith, I picked up three black lads, each with his neat carry-all sports bag. I tried to have a conversation and failed. They only spoke Afrikaans. We got as far as: 'Are you going to work in Calitzdorp?' 'No, Oudtshoorn, sir.' And three spotless white grins.

We drove together through steep rocky passes to Calitzdorp, where there was a Wine Route. Up the hill in the winery, the Afrikaner farmer was just going off to collect his wife. He was flushed with drink and friendliness. Maybe when he came back we could talk. Left alone with his sober black assistant I worked my way through a white Muscadel, a port, a dry white, and a second sweet Muscadel. Hm. I gazed out over the sunlit vineyards, half-wishing I had Sarah with me, half-relishing being entirely alone.

Approaching Oudtshoorn I saw my first ostriches. With their big bottoms, long thin necks, and black feather skirts over white feather petticoats, they looked like awkward teenage girls all dressed up for their first big party. There they stand, staring goofily out over the wire fence as you pass. But when you stop the car and jump out to photograph them, they scamper off, bow-legged across the scrub, back to their bedrooms and their Take That CDs.

Oudtshoorn was nothing to write home about: the usual long central street, the usual shops and garages, the dominating white spike of the Dutch Reformed Church. I wondered whether I should visit the nearby Kango Caves ('extraordi-

nary coloured formations of stalactites and stalagmites'), or
an ostrich farm. Ride an ostrich. Do the Tourist Thing. But
the idea of spending a night in Oudtshoorn depressed me
almost as much as the idea of gawping mindlessly at stalactites, so I turned south, up into the Outeniqua mountains,
the spectacular range that separates the Little Karoo from the
sea.

Up and up I climbed, high into the Outeniqua Pass, the
setting sun casting an orange-pink glow on the forest-covered
slopes. It was one of those roads that makes you shiver as
you drive along it: tight curves above suicide plunges, those
signs that warn (helpfully) of the ever-present danger of
boulders dropping and crushing you from above.

Then I was over the top, and there, below me, a sprawl of
white houses against the blue sea, was George, the town that
marks the start of the Garden Route, that beautiful stretch of
mountains, lakes and coastline that had been the focus of
my long-ago hitching trip.

The Outeniqua was certainly a contestant for The Most
Depressing Hotel I Visited in South Africa. Not the winner,
or even in the top three, but a definite finalist. The bed-
spreads were of a floral pattern, old and grey and dirty,
matching old and grey and dirty floral curtains. The carpet
was dusty and crimson, the water that spurted from the
bathtaps brown. The whole room smelt strongly of a mixture
of old cigarette smoke and the air-freshener hotels like this
use to get rid of the smell of old cigarette smoke. There was
no TV, just an ancient bakelite in-wall radio which seemed
to pick up nothing but endless Afrikaans pop stations.

It was 7 p.m. when I climbed into bed with the bottle of
sweet Muscadel I'd bought in Calitzdorp. 9.15 when I put
the light out and fell asleep, not actually in tears, but in
about as low a mood as I'd yet been. In between I did one
sensible thing. I phoned the number Henry from Stellenbosch had given me, of a Latvian baron who lived near
Plettenberg Bay and would be sure, Henry had said, to put

me up for a night or two. 'When you phone him up, just say "Tonk sent me" and see what happens.'

'Er hello,' I said, with some embarrassment, when he came on. 'I've been told to say, "Tonk sent me."'

A loud guffaw from the other end? A 'Check out of that hideous place now and come straight down any friend of Tonk's is a friend of mine.' No. Just a rather muted: 'Fine. Why don't you come to lunch tomorrow.'

Lunch! That wasn't what I wanted. The South African Ascension Day long weekend started tomorrow, and I had an awful sinking feeling that I was going to spend the whole of it in hotels like the Outeniqua, my loneliness set off by the holiday fun everybody else would be having.

Heading out of George the next morning I picked up my first white hitch-hiker, a blond guy in his early twenties. He was called John, and he worked on an ostrich farm just outside Oudtshoorn.

'Oh good,' I said, 'you can tell me all about ostrich farms. I was going to go to one yesterday afternoon but I couldn't face it.'

'We've had quite a lot of journalists through recently,' he said. 'And TV crews. Dutch, German, English, you know, writing about the positive side of South Africa. One Japanese film crew spent a whole week living with one of the black workers, filming how they lived. They're doing a whole series on the black way of life.'

I told him that I, too, was trying to see both sides of things, black and white. But, just driving around, it tended to be the whites you ran into. I explained about my township visits in Cape Town, but how they'd very much been township *visits*.

'Originally I was going to hitch,' I said. 'I sometimes think that if I'd hitched I wouldn't have had this problem.'

'Yeah, well, I wouldn't get a lift with black guys. You get into a car full of black guys you're going to have to be careful you don't lose your wallet and every little thing you're carrying by the time you get out.'

'Have you ever been in a car full of black guys?'

'No,' he replied, a little sheepishly.

Yes, he'd done his army service. Never seen action, though most of his friends had. He'd trained up in South West Africa, what was now Namibia. Then he'd been in intelligence, making videos of township violence, so police could work out who the ring-leaders were.

'So were you in townships when the fighting was going on?'

'Sure.'

'Were you frightened?'

'Yeah, it was pretty scary.' He'd seen people being necklaced. A woman being stoned to death. The press paying the kids money to get things going.

'Is that really true?'

'Sure it's true. That's how they get their footage.'

'But you've never seen a journalist paying someone money to necklace someone, surely?'

'No, but the TV cameras come, all these guys get in a frenzy, and then they go completely wild, they'll do anything.'

We were on the N2 now, driving past Wilderness; then the Knysna lakes, as beautiful as I remembered them, here and there a fishing boat making ripples on the landscape mirror; then into Knysna itself, past that same little church where the old lady had taken me in fifteen years before. I'd meant to stop; have a look around; maybe even try and find Leisure Island, Retirement Road, and my kind protectors. But John was going on to East London, and now he was telling me how much he hated the South African police. I could come back later.

'Look, like in South West Africa we found this group of black guys just smoking grass. That was all they were doing, and we just wanted to leave them alone, but our lieutenant phoned the police and they came over and beat these guys up, just for smoking *dagga* for Christ's sake! They've got too much power. They can do exactly what they like – and they do.'

He was very disillusioned with the politicians also. 'They're all corrupt. I tell you, there's about seven people running this country, that's about it. A lot of young people are really fed up with it. With the corruption, the way all they seem to be interested in is party politics and infighting – rather than addressing the real issues.'

'So if you hate the Government so much,' I asked, 'how did you manage to fight for them?'

'Man, when you're fighting you can't afford to think like that, because you couldn't do it if you did. You can't afford to have conflicts within yourself. You just know that if you don't shoot the other guy, the other guy's going to shoot you – and that's all there is to it.'

The world was a mess, he told me. 'There's wars everywhere. Every little thing is messed up.'

The worst of all, though, were the businessmen. 'I tell you if I got into power those are the guys I'd kick out right away. They're milking this country, man. Taking the money they make out of South Africa and storing it in Swiss bank accounts. I mean, there I am at the ostrich farm, working away for tuppence so that some mother can make a whole pile of money off my back.'

'And you're white,' I said.

'Sure,' he said. 'Sure.'

We'd reached Plettenberg Bay. I dropped John by the roadside, right by what looked to be the Plettenberg Bay township, a mess of shacks and corrugated iron houses running down the hillside from the N2.

'There you are,' said John, with a smile. 'If you want to meet some more of your black friends you can go in there. They won't do you much harm in that little place.'

6

AND FROM THE CASE OF
THE MURDER . . .

In the Baron's drawing room there were books everywhere. Mozart filtered through expensive speaker cones. A log fire crackled in a huge stone fireplace. As I walked in, that sunny before-lunchtime, I got a general impression of well-matched antiques, interesting prints and paintings, substantial flower arrangements in vases. Outside, beyond the white wooden *stoep*, a ragged lawn stretched down past a matching pair of white cottages to a shady tree-lined track. Beyond lay woods and the blue-green Tsitsikama Mountains. It was a shimmering piece of paradise.

The Baron himself came close to living up to the expression 'a great bear of a man'. Tall, with a stomach that billowed out above blue shorts, Alex had a face that was somehow both boyish and exceedingly well lived-in: a twinkle in his bright little eyes, a permanently amused, infuriatingly insouciant, ultimately kind expression on his lips.

He sat – or rather lay – to one side of the fireplace on a huge crimson throne of an armchair, his feet up on a pouffe, everything he needed on two occasional tables to either side: four or five different books, the telephone, the radical *Weekly Mail* and *Die Vrye Weekblad*, the *Spectator*, a tumbler of Chardonnay . . .

His wife Geraldine was something of a contrast: petite and

blonde, a decade or two younger, she'd been running a boutique in Jo'burg before she'd fallen for Alex's patrician charms. She was his second wife; he, her third husband. Later, over lunch, he took her hand fondly and said: 'The first you married for children, the second for sex, the third for love.'

Despite her blonde hair she was Jewish, 'well, half-Jewish – I don't know what I am.' She giggled. Alex, being 'a privileged Cossack' had never experienced prejudice of any kind until he'd been married to her. 'No,' he mused, as if astonished there was such a thing as prejudice in the world, 'I never noticed anti-Semitism before . . . I do now . . . yes, I usually say something if they don't realise.'

Alex and Geraldine had what you might call an active relationship. He talked, she interrupted; she talked, he interrupted; every now and then, in a fit of frustration, she would cry: 'I should never have married you!'

Like all white South Africans, they were keen to put me right on South Africa. The worst people, the very worst, Geraldine said, were the Jo'burg liberals. 'I tell you,' Alex agreed, 'you'll find more racism in the twelve square miles of the northern suburbs of Jo'burg than anywhere.'

'The Afrikaner,' said Geraldine, 'out in the sticks, is basically honest. I'd rather have an Afrikaner than a South African English any day.'

'The English are the worst,' said Alex. 'The bloody colonial English types. They've just stayed out there enjoying the benefits and doing nothing. At least the Afrikaner, however misguided, is doing what he thinks is right.'

'An Afrikaner,' said Geraldine, 'treats his blacks, children, and animals the same. If they do wrong he'll give them a good hiding, he's very paternal, but if they get sick, or need help, he'll look after them.'

'And that's what he thinks is right,' Alex repeated. 'At the end of the week, he can go to church and look his God square in the eye and think he's done the right thing.'

'The expats,' interrupted Geraldine. 'They're actually the worst. The wealthy liberal South African expats. Live in Knightsbridge, say all the right things. Every year, around 15 or 16 December you hear this whirring sound in the distance round here. It's the private planes, coming in from London and Australia and Los Angeles for Christmas. From mid-air, they phone ahead, to Samuel, whose surname they don't even know, to get their gin and tonics ready for them for when they arrive at their houses. They're here for a month and then they go back to Knightsbridge. And if you meet them in London they're terribly liberal. But what happens to all the extra staff they take on over Christmas? What happens to them when they fly back?'

'Are they over there because they're frightened?' I asked.

'They're frightened,' said Alex. 'God they're frightened. They say they're just spending a couple of years in London because they want to live somewhere where there's some culture,' he chuckled his deep chuckle, 'but basically, no, they're terrified.'

We went through to a big stone-flagged kitchen to have some lunch, and I was introduced to Ernestina and Gertrude. Gertrude was a Zulu, Geraldine's 'special maid' who'd followed her down from Jo'burg. 'She just seems to think I'm the person she should work for,' Geraldine told me later. 'So here she is, this Zulu alone in a district full of Xhosas and coloureds.'

Alex opened a fresh bottle of Chardonnay and we settled down to home-made pancakes stuffed with tuna fish in a cheese sauce and talked some more about hypocrisy and liberalism.

'There was a period,' Geraldine said, 'when it was fashionable in the northern suburbs to have a black friend. You know, your token black friend. People would sit through dinner parties ignoring the fact that whoever it was would eat their *gemsquash* with their fingers or didn't turn up on time. But I remember saying to this friend of mine: "Come off it, this person isn't your *friend*. A friend is someone you can phone up in the middle of the night when you're depressed, they're someone who's known you for years and years, who doesn't mind how you are. He's not your friend."'

She was very down on white hypocrisy, Geraldine. Even to the extent of telling stories against herself. 'I remember I was at this lunch party – in Jo'burg this was – and one of the guests, a black man, got struck by lightning. Now I've been trained in mouth to mouth resuscitation, but confronted by this black guy, lying on the ground, frothing at the mouth, I just couldn't bring myself to do it. Me, the little white liberal! I couldn't do it. Isn't that terrible? Luckily he was OK in the end, but isn't that terrible?

'You know when I first arrived here,' she went on, 'I was such a little Jo'burg radical. I ripped the place apart. I went round the whole estate, mending roofs here and fixing leaking taps there. I took all the mattresses out of the house and gave them to the people on the farm, because, you know, how could we sleep on a mattress, and not them – but I don't know, I'm getting less radical. Since I've been here, I've lent the coloured people a lot of money, to do this, to fix that – '

'How much darling?' interposed Alex, with his fond smile, from the head of the table. 'Twenty, thirty?'

'A lot of money. And never once have I had a word of thanks. Never once has anyone suggested they might try and pay me back.'

We had finished lunch, and I wondered whether it was time to make a move, time to go searching for another dingy hotel.

'You will stay,' said Geraldine suddenly.

'No you *must* stay,' said Alex. 'Really. We've got a guest cottage, you can hole up there and write, or go to the beach and surf, or . . .'

So I settled into the guest cottage. It had a large four poster bed, on which floated a soft white eiderdown. There were white curtains and when you were out your dirty laundry vanished, the room tidied itself, and your laundry reappeared, ironed and folded, on the mahogany bedside table.

In the evening, Alex was back in his crimson throne, a whisky at his side, a Brahms piano concerto rippling through the room.

'So what about the township?' I asked. 'D'you think it would be safe for me to go in there?'

'You want to go into the township?' said Geraldine. She turned to Alex and a look passed between them. 'He should meet Majola.'

'Well . . .' said Alex, shrugging.

'No, really, that would be brilliant,' said Geraldine. 'You want something for your book, you come with me tomorrow morning. Majola's like our local shacklord. You know what a shacklord is? I shan't tell you any more.' She looked at her husband and let out a little giggle. 'Alex has only once been into that township.'

'Not true, darling . . .'

'Once!' said Geraldine, holding up a finger and laughing. 'This was just after Mandela was released, and De Klerk made that speech . . . god, what a moment that was: at last you felt, right, they're going to get on with it, whatever's going to happen is going to happen . . . Anyway, you've got Alex here, who's lived for years and years – forever – holed up in this place, surrounded by books, and keeping a real arm's length attitude to the farm. When people have come to him he's been reading. "Go away," he's said,' she giggled again, '"I'm reading." And now all of a sudden he's got this radical young wife, who's come down here from Jo'burg and is redecorating everything and generally going crazy about the place. And there's a march organised. From the township, to protest against whatever – this, that or the other. So up they get, the two of them, at 7 a.m. and they pitch up at the township and there's nobody there. So they wake up the guy who's organising the march. He's fast asleep, but he soon gets up. "Right, yes, the march, yes." And they look around, and there's all these dreamy looking white guys approaching. And they've got all these bowls of water. They're happy-clappies come to wash the feet of their enemy – all these white guys getting down on their knees trying to wash the black guys' feet. And then we're all marching – and Alex, who's never been on a march in his life, is marching into Plettenberg Bay with his banner – it was so funny – and then Alex gets fed up with it and wants to go home. So he hails this police van – the policeman is a friend of his. And the head of the Port Elizabeth ANC, who's also a friend of his, gets in too, and the crowd are going wild because they think this ANC guy is getting taken away by the police again – it was too funny. Those are the things you should write about, Mark. That's South Africa.'

'What you've got to realise,' said Alex a little later, when we'd all drunk a little more, 'is that all our lives out here we've been waiting for the End. You never knew how it was going to happen, and when – but you knew it was going to happen. So there's never been any sense of permanence or planning for the future. You just can't do that. How long are you going to have? Another two years? Another three years? And meanwhile,' he went on, 'you get innured to increasingly higher levels of violence. Originally, if one person got murdered, it made headline news. And then, after Sharpeville, you got used to the idea of forty people being shot; and now, if the level is down to forty a month it seems acceptable. It's like the tide coming in. Each time it goes that little bit further.'

In the morning Geraldine took me to meet Majola. On the way into town I got a running commentary on the houses we passed. '70% of these places are second homes, owned by the richest and most influential fat cats in South Africa. They're mostly lived in for three weeks a year. We'll have to take you along Millionaire's Drive later. The houses are incredibly fancy. A Sardinian villa, a Spanish hacienda, an English mansion, all pushed up against each other – it's absolutely appalling.'

We turned right off the N2 onto a dirt track, bumped past a collection of small factories and warehouses. 'Right,' said Geraldine, 'this is the industrial estate beyond which the citizens of Plettenberg Bay *do not go*. The shanty town.'

And there, stretching right down the steep hillside into the valley below, was the same old sight. The shacks. The half-naked children. The women with Persil tubs on their heads. The dogs. The smoke rising. 'These people came here when they built the big hotel in the bay. But then they didn't go away. Then more and more came. There's absolutely no sanitation here – just one or two taps. It's truly appalling.'

We went down to find Majola. He was standing outside a corrugated iron warehouse, leaning against the windows of a lorry: a tall thin man, with an angry scar high up on his left cheek, and bleary, bloodshot eyes.

He shook hands with Geraldine, and I was introduced as a journalist who wanted to do an interview. Geraldine left and Majola led me to his office. It was round the back of the warehouse, through a room full of small children watching *The Terminator* on video. Flames filled the screen. A woman screamed and ran. None of the kids was over about ten. A few young men at the back of the room sat on hard chairs or leant against a makeshift bar. As I came in with Majola, one of them got to his feet, offered me his chair. 'It's OK,' I said. 'No, no, please, sir,' he insisted. I sat down.

I was called into the next room, which was bare except for a desk and two chairs. 'I am sorry,' Majola said, 'my office is not ready at the moment.' He gestured at a tall cupboard in the corner, stuffed full of a haphazard mess of files and papers.

He gave me permission to switch on my tape recorder and the interview began. I learned that his name was J— Majola.

That he'd arrived in Plett from the Transkei in 1983. That
during the State of Emergency of 1986 he'd been arrested
because he'd associated with the UDF; that he'd been held
in detention for a year. That he was now head of the local
Civic Committee, affiliated to the ANC Western Cape; that
the Civic was negotiating with the Municipality for better
housing, site and serviced, up on the hill. It all sounded
alarmingly familiar.

After about ten minutes, rather tentatively, I did as Geraldine had suggested, and asked if there'd been any violence
in the township.

'Yes,' Majola replied, 'we did have such things. And I
used to be a victim of harassment – for all those things.'

'You used to be a victim of police harassment?' I asked.
Perhaps this was what Geraldine had meant.

'Yah,' said Majola, staring out beyond me with his bloodshot eyes. There was a pause. Then: 'And from the case of
the murder, you see, whereas I was not present in that, you
see, only because I'm the head of the organisation, ANC,
Civic, you see, they then decided to arrest me. Even the day
they arrest me they say: "We are just arresting you because
you are the head of these people."'

'What was this case?' comes my anxious voice onto the
tape. 'Sorry – I don't know about this.'

'There was a case', Majola replies, 'of someone who was,
er – killed by the people. He was trying to be against the
ideas of the people.'

'He was, what – against the squatter camp . . .?'

'He was just against the Civic – and – all those organisations the people are forming for themselves. He used to
side with the organisations that are formed by the
authorities.'

'And so – what – did the people just . . . rise up . . .?'

'So the people were just angry, and then they decided to
kill him.'

                              *

Geraldine was waiting for me at the top of the road. 'So did Majola do the murder?' I asked. 'Of course he did,' she said. 'Him and his henchmen. Come down to the shop and I'll tell you the whole story. I've got to keep an eye on things. I could do more business today and tomorrow than the whole of the rest of the winter.'

So we drove two hundred yards down the hill and into a shopping centre full of well-dressed whiteys and shops called things like Hyperette and Just Biltong. Geraldine's boutique sold fashionable clothes, duvet covers, cushions. We sat in a back room with St Leger and Viney samples on the wall, a cork board covered with clippings from *Vogue* and *Harpers & Queen*. Through in the shop, opera arias played over the CD. Every now and then, Geraldine would jump up to close a sale. Or in a pause in her story you'd hear, 'How's your garden? . . . I remember you were building . . . all your hats, yiss . . . those are virry, virry pretty . . . that's a naice lingth . . . my dear, that's perfect . . .'

'It was just after the release of Nelson Mandela,' Geraldine said, leaning towards me and speaking in a hushed and rapid voice, 'and the place was crazy – it was a very exciting time, a marvellous time. Anyway, the local sort of unofficial township leader was called Walter Dlamini. He was just a totally good man, I mean he had the face of an angel and the attitudes and social commitment of, you know, the most evolved and saintly human beings. He worked as a waiter, at a very fancy hotel down here called The Plettenberg. He'd been in the area for years, he had a wife called Patience, and several chidren, a lot of whom he'd adopted because their circumstances were bad. And whenever people from his village would come to Plettenberg Bay he would look after them, and he'd make sure they got a house, and that their children were OK. If they'd no money, he'd try and land them a job, and if he couldn't land them a job – ' She broke off, and looked me straight in the eye. 'Mark, he was just the most wonderful man that was ever born – he had a caliper on his leg . . . he was just absolutely wonderful.

'Anyway, his cousin, J— Majola, arrived from the Transkei. Walter looked after him, like he looked after everyone else, only more so – because he was his cousin. He sorted him out a house, he sorted him out a job – the guy was just a simple guy, and Walter ran the township in a very – he just organised everybody, he was just good, good, good.

'During about 1983–4, there was a lot of shit in this country – the State of Emergency – and Majola was arrested. He had a pretty grim time in prison, and he came out, I don't know how much later, cross. OK? Radical, cross. Understandably so.

'He'd got involved with the ANC in prison and now he found his cousin Walter sort of a little bit of an *impimpi* almost – '

'An *impimpi*?'

'Too involved with the whites, you know, soft on the whole thing. And so he's not that impressed with Walter any more because Walter's got a bit of a soft attitude, and so – two camps form. The older blacks in the township, guys who've been there a long time, have got jobs, they're with Walter, who's got a slightly more realistic viewpoint. And the younger ones, who are now streaming in from the Ciskei and the Transkei, are with Majola. They're unemployed, they're angry, and he's saying: "Fight! Fight! Fight!" and Walter's going: "Come on, let's negotiate."

'OK next scene is: Nelson Mandela gets released and the whole thing goes absolutely crazy very suddenly. The ANC was coming out of the underground. Mark, it was the most amazing time. It was like the Hobbits, literally, like everyone was suddenly unfurling their ANC banners and wearing T-shirts, millions and millions of people in South Africa wearing these Nelson Mandela T-shirts. It was just marvellous, it was two weeks of – it was extraordinary. And Mr Majola started taking serious charge in the township. To the extent that if he decided that any of the older blacks were informers, *impimpis*, had even been *seen* talking to a whitey, Majola would get them undressed, by his civics, his comrades, and they'd be paraded through the township at night with no clothes on, with all these people *toyi-toyi*-ing behind them.'

'*Toyi-toyi*-ing?'

'You know, the dance they do.' Geraldine got to her feet and boogied across towards the St Leger cuttings, arms to the front at right angles. 'Have you never seen it? It's terrifying. Anyway, the indignity of this was absolutely horrifying, which worried Walter Dlamini immensely. He tried to reason with Majola and say: "Don't turn on your own people." This had all been done in the name of the ANC, and Walter was saying: "If this is the ANC I don't want to be involved with it."

'Anyway, one night, Walter and some of the older men had a meeting in the township. To discuss this. And while they were all there Majola was *toyi-toyi*-ing around the township with his comrades and really causing unbelievable shit. And he went to Walter's house, where he'd lived for years, full of these children that he'd taken in and looked after. And Patience, Walter's wife, came out of the house to see what the noise was, and they grabbed hold of her, all these comrades and Majola, and they said they were going to kill her. One of the kids quickly ran to tell their father what was going on. By this stage Majola and his men had set light to Walter's beloved little house. Walter came back, and there was his wife, in her nightdress, with all these screaming children being threatened by Majola, his house on fire, his car on fire. And there he was, this little crippled man, and they got hold of him and they started to stab him. With Majola stabbing him right in front with the best, with these things called *knipmes*, they're little short knives . . .'

Geraldine shook her head and sighed deeply. Beyond in the shop, the smart Ascension Day weekenders came and

went. 'My dear,' they said, 'you don't have another set like
that, take it.' And over the loudspeakers: '*O mio babbino
caro* . . .'

'Anyway,' Geraldine went on, 'at six o'clock in the morning I got a phone call from the local doctor, who says,
"Listen, there's a huge amount of shit going on in the
township, Walter Dlamini's been stabbed, and we've got
Patience and the children in the middle of town in their
nightdresses, can you help?" "Absolutely." So I came to
town, fetched Patience and the children. My car was surrounded, the police came, thank god, and we managed to get
the last few children in this big Toyota car we've got, and I
took them home; OK, waiting now because Walter had been
taken to Knysna Hospital. So we spent the afternoon waiting
for news, with the children, Patience and me trying to keep
the thing jollied up, waiting for the news . . . and the news
we got was that Walter had died.

'And I just can't, I *cannot tell you* what that was like.
Patience was hysterical. And the children were hysterical.
We had all these elders arrived from the township. The
house, the guest room, the cottage that you're in were full.
Patience was lying on the bed . . . all of a sudden these
people arrived, they were singing and chanting, they were
heartbroken. It was the saddest scene. Mark . . . you just . . .
it was the last . . . one of the great men in the world . . .'

She shook her head again, and sighed, a little too deeply,
I thought, to be entirely convincing as the cynical ex-radical
she'd portrayed herself as earlier.

'Anyway,' she went on eventually, 'to cut a very long story
short, the police went and arrested Majola. Majola was
brought into the cells in Plettenberg Bay. The jail was
marched upon by all the youngsters, threatening to burn it
down. So they moved. The same thing happened again, so
they let him go.

'Then there was Walter's funeral, which was just appalling. Majola now said that Walter couldn't be buried in the

township. Now he makes all the rules. So we arranged for
Walter to be buried in New Horizons, which is the coloured
area. And afterwards there was going to be a party at the
crèche, which is just on the edge of the township. After the
funeral, I dropped Patience and the grannies and the children at the crèche. And I came home. And I said I'd come
back and fetch her at 5 p.m. Alexander had gone for a walk.
It was a very bad time between Alex and I, politically. I'm
much angrier than he is, much more involved than he is,
and he thought I was endangering my own life. I was getting
terribly, terribly involved. My children disapproved, everyone disapproved, and they weren't altogether wrong.

'So I went back to fetch Patience at 5 p.m., and as she was
loading into the car with the grannies and the children, a
busload of Majola's supporters came back. They'd been at a
rally in Knysna, and they started getting out of this bus, and
Majola told them to attack the car. These guys were all
around – Mark, it was the most terrifying moment of my life.
As I drove off, I had the one granny who was just falling out
of the car, I thought she'd just die. Anyway I managed to get
away.

'And the police came to me later and said, "Look Majola's
got a hit-list, and because you harboured the Dlaminis you're
on it, so arm yourself." So Alexander and I went and bought
these 2.2 revolvers and I walked around with a revolver on
me, all the time, for a year. It was lovely.'

Geraldine tried to get Majola convicted, but the authorities
couldn't get a case together. 'Every single person was intimidated. When I went to speak to them they explained that
Walter had died and they all felt very strongly about that,
but they weren't going to lose their own lives being witnesses, so they backed off. And things got worse and worse.
Majola was just treating people in the township like – ' she
shrugged – 'it was unbelievable. I tried to get people from
the ANC down here, but they were so involved with rallies,
they were so involved with ego, that people became second-

ary. It wasn't that important that people were really having a terribly terribly rough time down here.

'In the end, the ANC guy from Port Elizabeth, who's a friend of ours, came down, and went to see Majola. So, obsequious Majola says: Oh no, he absolutely understands, he'll stop this, he'll do this, that, and the other, and just bullshitted this guy about the whole thing.

'The ANC guy leaves, Majola calls a meeting, and says Geraldine Harrison has bought the ANC Eastern Cape with her white cat money, so we'll now be affiliated to ANC Western Cape. Everyone likes Majola now, everything's forgotten, he makes everyone in that township pay him five rand a week, to keep his Civic Committee going . . . I don't know,' she said, peering once more round the door to see that she wasn't missing a sale. 'I fought this battle literally on my own. I got so despondent, with white and black, that I became apolitical. I became wiped out. I thought: What's happening to me? I'm running around like a chicken with its head cut off and nobody cares.'

I left the boutique and wandered down the hill. In a quiet road I found a European churchyard. Tall milkwood trees shifted slowly in the sunny breeze, their strong shadows playing on the lush green grass. Below, the roofs of holiday bungalows dropped away to the blue sea. To the left, over the tree-tops, was the sicklelike curve of the wonderful long beach, the mountains rising up blue-grey behind.

I walked up past a wheelbarrow full of clippings and into the shade of the little brownstone church. At the back, on a wooden table, was an intercession book. 'If you would like us to pray for anyone,' I read, 'please enter their names in this book under the correct month.' December read:

    Anne – nervous breakdown and family problems
    Hayden Roberts – 5 year old with leukaemia

Pat Jackson – cancer
Tony Birdswager – skiiing accident – and a new faith in
    God
Our land – end to violence
Carmen Blackman – to sell farm
Moira Hodge – yuppie flu and Brian Robinson
All holiday trouble on roads
Daisy Jones – for return to old self
End to violence
Ron and Liza Morris – their baby who lived a very short
    while being buried Monday
End to all violence

On Saturday night Geraldine's children wanted to take me
jolling – that Afrikaans word for which there is no easy
translation. 'Partying' is perhaps the nearest, but you don't
need to go to a party to *joll*.

Ben, nineteen, long-haired, at Art School in Cape Town,
had just passed his driving test, so we sped into town in the
brand-new black hatchback Geraldine had given him, with
his younger brother Tom and their friends Daisy and Elaine,
who lived in a cottage on the estate. Ben was talking about
some friend of theirs who had been walking through town
with his girlfriend and they'd got attacked by three black
guys who'd raped her. The police had caught them, and, Ben
said coolly, 'as they haven't been heard of since, the police
probably beat them to death.'

We drove down to a club called the Grapevine. It was in
the basement of the swanky hotel on the beach (where
Walter Dlamini had once worked) and, in the opinion of the
gang, it was *did*. So we hit the Formosa Inn, which was also
did. 'You should have been here last night,' said Tom. 'This
car park was full. It was really great.'

'It doesn't matter if you're black or white,' sang Michael
Jackson from the giant video screen. But there were no
blacks in sight, apart from the barman and the guy collecting
the bottles. Slowly the place filled up. We drank, we danced,

we *jolled*. Right at the end, I was sitting up at the bar as they brought the grilles down. 'I'm really not interested around politics,' said the long-haired dude next to me. 'I'm more interested around girls, and the things that interest me.' He'd been brought up on a farm and his first language was Xhosa. But he wasn't hopeful for South Africa. 'Before there's black majority rule, there's going to be a civil war, I promise you. It's a fact. Because the Right wing aren't going to let them just take over. And when the bullets are flying, I shan't be in a hurry to get on a plane to leave. This is my country. This is where I was born. This is where my friends are. This is where my family are.

'Like I told you, I was brought up on a farm. I spoke Xhosa before I spoke anything else. I know their ways, and they're just not ready to take over.'

His short-haired blond friend was more succinct. 'We'll kill all the niggers before they take over,' he said, laughing, lurching drunkenly away.

Alexander and Geraldine wanted to take me to meet Patience, Walter Dlamini's widow, who'd had to flee for her life to Knysna.

After the murder, they'd had Patience and the children to stay for a year. 'The front lawn was covered in laundry. And then her family came to stay, and then her extended family, and then her cousins. And all the local white do-gooders heard about what had happened, and pitched up with clothes for Patience and the children. So she had too much, and she started selling this stuff off to other people on the estate and in the locations.' Geraldine giggled. 'She had a little secondhand clothes business going. Then she realised that she could buy a fish for eight rand and chop it up into ten slices and fry them in batter and sell them for two rand each. So she had this fried fish business she was operating out of the kitchen. It was a complete nightmare. I didn't

mind, but I've never once had a word of thanks from
Patience. Not one simple "thank you".'

On our way through 'Plett' we took a detour down Millionaire's Drive, the seafront road which had the most elaborate
houses. They had names like Sea Hill, The Alassa, Ukuzola,
Ikwazi, and, as Geraldine had said, they were an exotic mix
of architectural styles.

'I just happen to know that that house over there has eight
bathrooms,' Alex said.

'You notice the liberal-sounding African names,' said
Geraldine.

'That's where Joe Slovo's brother lives,' said Alex. 'You
know who I mean by Joe Slovo? Head of the Communist
Party. Last time I saw him he was sitting on the beach right
there.' Alex chuckled loudly.

By the time we reached Knysna it was pouring with rain.
We slowed down by the sodden little township. 'You can't
just drive in there in your Mercedes, Alexander,' said
Geraldine.

'When the ANC come down here they drive Mercedes,'
Alex replied. 'Let's go and have some lunch and come back
when it's stopped raining.'

So we went to a restaurant on 'the Heads', a pretty little
stripped-pine place with a view of surf crashing on the rocky
headland. Back in Whiteyland we ate chicken and line-fish
of the day and crepes and drank wine and whisky. Then we
returned to plough down a liquid mud track through the
shanty-town to Patience's place.

It was a three-roomed shack. Rain dripped through a hole
in the roof. Patience and a friend and five or six small
children were watching American football on a tiny black
and white portable TV. She was large and motherly and
delighted to see Alexander and Geraldine, welcoming them
in, laughing with that familiar gurgling African laugh.

I went through with her to a little bedroom at the back.
We sat opposite each other on two damp truckle beds and I

asked her for her side of the story. It was the same terrible tale. 'They burnt my house down, they take the car off my husband, they light my husband's *bakkie*, and they burnt my house, *all* of my house, and after that they kill my husband with the *pangas*.'

'And you saw all of this?'

'Yes, I saw them. They do everything in front of my eyes. Yes, sir.'

'And are you frightened of him now – Majola?'

'No, I'm not frightened of them. No, I'm not.'

'But you are angry with them?'

'Yes, I'm very angry. I'm very angry.'

'Because he should go to jail.'

'Yes, but they didn't go to jail. And they do such a lot of waste. My house was six rooms and it was well furnished. Lot of furniture, it was very new.'

'And you stayed for some time with Geraldine and Alex in their house?'

'Yes, they helped me a lot. They took me to the farm and I stay with them for one and a half year, and they are doing everything for me, everything. They gave me everything. They are really very kind, very kind. I don't know what can I do, what can I say, for them. All this material, for this house, Alex gave me. All the furniture, beds, chairs, tables, cupboards, they gave it to me. It's only them who's helped me. No-one in the ANC. And there is other white people – gave me clothes for the children. And they take that girl I've got, eighteen years, they gave me money to send her to school.'

'So you don't feel angry towards the white people?'

'No. I trust them. I trust white people. Really.'

'And not necessarily the other black people?'

'No. Till I die. I'll never never trust black people till I die. Till I die, my friend.'

7

THE FRIENDLY CITY

High above me, on either side, towered tree-smothered crags. Below, the little road wound down into a valley of the wildest vegetation, trees toppling into one another, hung everywhere with great curtains of a lichen that looked like pale green Old Man's Beard. Mist floated across in distinct patches. In the early morning sunshine it was quite magical; and I became, here in the depths of the Tsitsikama Forest, aware of another South Africa I was missing. Hiker's South Africa. One day I would come back and do the six day Otter Trail, the most popular hike in South Africa, which passed down through this forest to unspoilt beaches, deep blue lagoons, a swing bridge over the Storms River . . .

I jammed on the brakes. The signs warning against falling boulders were not just there for fun. A pile of rocks blocked my side of the road. I edged the Dolphin slowly round them. DO NOT FEED THE BABOONS said another sign. I drove carefully on, eyes skinned for boulders, baboons, baboons with boulders . . .

Eventually I came out onto a long straight road, pine trees to the left, milkwoods to the right. Suddenly I saw a sign to Jeffrey's Bay, where I had a serious appointment with Memory.

I'd spent one of the coldest nights of my life in the dunes above Jeffrey's Bay, head on knapsack, shivering inside my windjacket, not having the price of a hotel bed. An old white (surely, I realised now, he would have been a coloured) tramp had slept one dune away from me, had woken me up in the frozen small hours, poking me with his finger and jabbering right into my face. And earlier, at sunset, walking alone across the long empty beach, watching the fiery crimson and purple cloudscape reflected in the wet sheen of the sand, I'd been accosted by that extraordinary Dutch Reformed Church evangelical, who, having told me about the separation of the races as ordained by God, had then urged me to be born again on the beach.

Now I drove down to the seafront. Had it been the Savoy Hotel – with balconies in pink and blue, and a strange triangular roof – where I'd been unable to afford the price of a bed? La Mer Sea Front Accommodation where I'd gone shivering in the morning to eat my way through six courses of a full South African breakfast? I couldn't begin to remember.

Out on the beach, a group of young coloureds were practising their golf swings. A lone white surfer sat on his board on the flat silver-grey sea. I was trying to work out which particular stretch of beach the Christian and I had walked on in that far-distant sunset, which particular dune I'd slept under. No, it was impossible to bring back any of it.

Pacing out over the wet sand, among a litter of cans and seaweed and driftwood and polystyrene chunks, I was struck by the futility of this yearning of mine to relive the past. Why had I wanted to trek all these thousands of miles alone to revisit this dreary beach? What had this expanse of sand got to say to me? Nothing: unless that forever after I should eschew sentimentality, live entirely in the present.

I drove on. Across an empty plain towards yet more mountains. This lot had a row of little white clouds floating in front of them, a finger joint or so above ground level, brightly sidelit by a hidden sun.

All of a sudden I was coming into Port Elizabeth. I passed

a gigantic car park full of new cars, factory buildings, the Easi-Gas works; then I was up onto a raised urban motorway – the M4; then swooping down into a long street of tall stone buildings, turning right up a steep grassy hill edged by pretty black and white houses, a row of stubby palm trees looking rather bedraggled in the rain.

Alex had told me that Port Elizabeth was 'a dump'. All three of my guide books (Alex had given me a new, detailed South African one) described it as 'The Friendly City' before telling me that it was famous for, er, the largest Mercedes car assembly plant in Africa, the beach – the King's Beach – that the British Royal Family had swum from in 1947, and the 169ft Campanile commemorating the arrival of the 1820 British Settlers. Oh yes, and the Horse Memorial, dedicated to the horses killed in the Anglo-Boer War 'which had', said my upmarket guide, 'a particularly moving inscription'.

Cape Town Susan had recommended Mike O' Hanlon as *the* guy to see in PE; he was doing some very interesting work, was closely involved with the ANC. But it wasn't proving that easy. On Tuesday he'd had a workshop; on Wednesday a seminar; now I arrived for our appointment on Thursday to find two white teenage schoolgirls hanging round an empty office. 'Oh, Mike's still at lunch. Sorry,' said one of them, raising her eyebrows theatrically. When he finally appeared, blond and genial, in the company of two radical-looking white females, he was terribly sorry, but he was far too busy for an interview right now. 'But really,' he said, 'I think you need to see the conditions on the ground, in the townships, before you do anything else.' Before I'd had a chance to tell him that I'd already seen the conditions in the townships, that . . . he'd pressed a buzzer on his intercom, and John, a young African guy had appeared.

'This is John,' said Mike, 'he's on the ANC Executive Council here in Port Elizabeth – a very fine young man – he'll show you round.'

John was thirty-three, and had been born, like me, in September. We were almost exactly the same age.

'Are you married?' he asked, as we walked back down the hill towards the Dolphin.

'No – not yet.'

'Still waiting, eh.' He laughed. 'Me too. I'm hanging on till the ANC is in power so I can have the pick of the field.'

He'd done his time on Robben Island. Five years. Indeed, he told me, he'd only had one Christmas at home since 1976. Since 1976! I thought back to all the comfortable Christmases I'd had, year after year . . .

We drove back out down the freeway. 'Take left!' barked John imperiously as we reached a junction. 'Take right!'

We came to Red Location, where people were living in the corrugated iron barracks that the British Army had left behind in 1913. No, that isn't a misprint: *1913*. Three years after the Act of Union had ended South Africa's status as a British colony. They were brown with rust, half falling down, set in a bleak landscape of rubbish-strewn mud.

'These corrugated iron houses', John said matter-of-factly, 'were left to the municipality of the time, with the aim that they were going to service this area, give it sewerage, give it taps, give it toilets – but nothing came. Now you have people living here for ages, without any services whatsoever. Most of this area here is infested with tuberculosis. In fact these are called TB houses, because most of the people are suffering from TB. They were supposed to be treated, but treatment didn't come. Most of the children die at very young stages here.'

We 'took right' and parked up on the mud. 'In one of these houses', John said, as we got out, and a group of ragged little boys ran screaming towards us, 'it is not unusual for an eight-member family to stay. And they will park like sardines, like prison, and go out, in and out. We are lucky if one member of the family works. They share one tap, all these houses.'

Escorted by the dancing little boys, we walked over the mud to meet a group of people whose 'houses' had burnt down a few days before. They were sitting, men, women and children, round an oildrum in which a fire had been lit. The thin drizzle continued to fall.

'Hello Comrades!' shouted John, striding towards them. Everyone seemed to know him. Two emaciated old men in suits – one wearing a porkpie hat – ran up to us. 'Please master,' one kept saying, grabbing my arm. 'Please master, you must come and see over here.'

'Sorry about these men,' John said. 'They're both a bit drunk.' Another younger guy seemed to object to the appearance of Whitey on site, scowling at me from behind his two inebriated associates.

'This is my friend Mark,' said John. Courteously, the women round the fire rose to greet me. There were perhaps eight of them, ranging in age from a teenager in a blue jersey to a toothless old lady in brown headscarf and spectacles.

With our entourage of boys and men we walked through to what John described as 'the disabled area'. Here the barrack huts had been divided into two. We climbed a couple of wooden steps to enter a room that stank of stale urine. It was ten foot by fifteen, decorated with shiny gold wallpaper. 'Five people are living here,' said John. To one side, wrapped in a grubby green blanket on a foam mattress, was a toothless old man with a damaged leg. As we looked in, he sat up, swung himself round, greeted John in Xhosa. I was introduced, he smiled warmly, we did the African handshake.

'Have you got a few minutes?' said the old man after our greeting. 'There are certain issues I would very much like to discuss with you gentlemen. I am on the committee of the . . .'

'Another time, another time,' said John, backing into the daylight. The man grabbed an aluminium crutch, struggled to his feet, followed us out to the steps, still burbling committee-ese. 'It would be very good to discuss these issues with you gentlemen,' he called after us.

We walked back across the mud to the people huddled round the fire. I crouched to take a photograph. The men, women and children arranged themselves in a formal group, standing still like Victorians, one of the drunk old guys with his arm raised in a black power salute. John, grinning in the middle in his trendy blue jacket, was the only modern thing about it.

As we walked back towards my big white expensive car, one of the old men came after us, pulling at my arm. 'Please master,' he said, 'please master, you must do something about this . . .'

'I can't,' I said, turning to him, meeting his eye. 'I'm just visiting, just writing a book, you understand. I can't help you. I'm sorry.'

'All these people', he cried, gesturing round, 'have no houses. Now that you have been here, master, I can hope something will be done. I can hope . . .'

'I'm sorry,' I said, taking his hand. There was no point trying to explain. 'What *will* the council do?' I asked John, as we drove off.

'Nothing will happen,' he replied, in that same matter-of-fact tone. 'And as you see, they have no houses.

'All these people are very solid politically,' he continued, as we drove on down the mud road into a sprawl of shacks called New Brighton. 'Everyone here is a member of the ANC, so there is no trouble.'

The drizzle had stopped. As we proceeded, John kept waving out of the window, shouting 'Hello chaps! Hello chaps!' at groups of people who squinted at DOLPHIN CAR HIRE – FOR THE BEST FLIP'N SERVICE, then recognised John and broke into smiles and waves.

'Everybody seems to know you,' I said.

'Yes, it is difficult sometimes, because they know me and I don't know them.'

'How is that?'

'I've been leading them for a long time. In this area. I'm one of the known people around. I moved from the Youth Movement straight to the United Democratic Front, to the ANC. I've moved through all these stages, so I'm addressing people in big crowds, in stadiums, so they know me.'

We had arrived at an area known as Soweto-by-the-Sea. 'Stop the car,' John said. 'Come and look at this.' He led me down to a narrow gully between the shacks. A half section of grey pipe, maybe two foot across, ran off into the distance.

'Now this pipe here,' he said, 'this pipe is disease-infested. Many children have drowned here, and actually died. Because they thought that it's a place to swim. Next thing they found themselves between rubbish and urine and waste . . .'

'It's just an open sewer?'

'Yuh. This is sewerage water, goes straight to the sea.'

We drove on between the endless shacks. A pig waddled out onto the road and I braked sharply. Behind me, an African taxi skidded to a halt on the mud. 'One pig, holding everything up,' said John, and we laughed.

'Now this area,' he said, 'this is where we hid underground during the State of Emergency. This area was a no-go area. This was a war-zone. The police wouldn't come here. The army wouldn't come here. It was impossible for them to recognise the fire coming from this house or that house or that house . . .'

'Gunfire?'

'Gunfire, yes.'

'You guys were there, ready for them, were you?'

'We were ready for them. Definitely we were ready for them. There was an exchange of fire. Because it was a time of very strong insurrection.' He grinned. 'This is the best area ever.'

'You see this house here,' he said, pointing at a two-roomed brick house. 'I was arrested in this house. It was my underground house, this one.'

'So they came here . . .?'

'They came here and pounced on me. I stayed here for months. They were passing up and down here, without knowing that John was here, and they were searching for me high and low, so when they came here at about 2 a.m., I pretended to be an owner of the house, and said to them, "I'm not John, I'm not John."' He laughed. 'Then they took out a photo, and it was almost over. They looked at the photo – but I had no hair then. So I said, "No, it's not me, it might be one of those who are like me, but not me, definitely." They said, "OK, but we suspect – you come. Some people will identify you." So they took me to the police barracks, so I realised I was now in hell.' He laughed.

'When was that?'

'That was 1986 – 20 November. And that cost me three years. '86 up till '89. Stupid. I could have changed that place. I was about to change it. On that day they were so fortunate.'

'What were they trying to get you for? Just for leading the people?'

'For leading the people, yuh. They believed I was influential.'

We visited a big open street market, where traders huddled under black umbrellas in the drizzle, selling oranges, apples, cooked sheep's heads, bunches of herbs for traditional medicine, fried fish, bread, shampoo, washing powder – you name it. 'Hi chaps! Hi chaps!' shouted John. We called into the headquarters of PEPCO – the Port Elizabeth People's Civic Organisation – which was decorated throughout in ANC colours. We attended a meeting of local activists (broad smiles and handshakes all round) who told me I should write a book on the history of PEPCO. Grinning with pride, John took me inside a burnt-out building that had once been a beerhall. 'These were created by the Government after 1976,' he said, as we stood in the echoing darkness, 'so that the youth should be diverted from struggles against apartheid, to these beerhalls, where they would sit down and play draughts and cards and poison themselves with drinks. During the '80s people identified that most of our people were now dying of this, now beginning to see this as the end-all and the be-all. So these beerhalls were destroyed by fire, all of them. The young black people got angered: they destroyed them by fire.'

A huge colourful mural had been painted on the outside of the ex-beerhall: two large black guys, one in an ANC T-shirt, the other in a red T-shirt with a hammer and sickle inside a black star, stood with their hands raised in a black power salute. The women beside them were half their height, dressed in yellow, their raised fists barely reaching the men's armpits. 'Now recently,' John said, 'in the last three months or so, the residents in this area took over this place, cleaned it and painted this – this is the work of last week. So you can see here, this is the Communist Party, this is the ANC, you can see how all these things reflect exactly what the need of the people is. The need is reflected in this art.'

Driving back down the freeway into town, John explained that he himself no longer lived in the township. 'There's a gradual stream into white areas,' he said. 'Now we call them grey areas. Where the office is, that is a grey area. And there are mixed affairs also, so a few whites who happen to love African girls or coloured girls stay together. That is another part. The sexual part.' He smiled. 'Or the love part.'

Mike O'Hanlon was still too busy to see me. 'I'm terribly sorry about this,' he said charmingly. 'Could you come tomorrow morning early, say 9 o'clock?' 'Sure,' I replied. I checked into a great pink and white wedding-cake of a hotel, with views out over the grassy hill, the docks, and the broad sweep of Algoa Bay beyond. Round the corner was a Mike's Kitchen, a chain I'd noticed in every major town I'd visited. It was clearly part of the South African Experience, and in any case I felt like a burger.

It was cheap and cheerful and full of whites. Couples mostly. A little family at the table to my right: Mum and Dad and two girls in Alice bands and ponytails. And then, suddenly, in the corner, I noticed an astonishing thing: a *black* family, having a meal. A little black girl in red dungarees and her older sister in a long fluffy purple cardigan, a stocky Mum and Dad to either side. And then, lo and behold, *another* group of black people came in. Two guys and a girl. OK, so they were only having puddings – but what the hell! And then the white waitress was bringing a little birthday cake with sparklers. It was the little black girl's birthday and all five of the white waitresses were lined up and singing 'Happy birthday'. 'Happy birthday, dear Noma – Noma – Noma . . .' They burst into giggles trying to pronounce the unfamiliar name. As did the table of black pudding eaters watching. There was general applause. To my right, the young blonde mother watched through the candlelight, tears brimming in her eyes.

Walking back to the hotel I suddenly felt bitterly lonely. So many contrasts in one day and nobody to talk to. I found a public phone box and called Sarah in London. Her answerphone was on. I left the hotel number and a message to call whatever time she got in.

Hearing disco music I followed my nose into the George Hotel. A band called Quest were entertaining a bar full of the ugliest people I'd seen for ages. Tall, loud, lecherous men with bristling moustaches. Short, fat, giggling dumplings of women. Quest themselves were all trying to look like Rod Stewart, with shirts open to the waist, and shoulder-length blond perms. 'It doesn't madder if you're black or white,' they sang. And then: 'Ki-i-iss me, put your tongue around my mow-ow-ow-owth. Don't talk, just ki-i-i-iss.' Great! Just what I needed. I paced back to the wedding cake, lay awake until the small hours listening to the discobeat and waiting for my bedside phone to ring, unable to feel sorry for myself in a warm double bed with a roof over my head.

At 9 a.m. precisely I arrived outside the Human Rights Trust, notepad at the ready. A car was just drawing out of the parking lot. It contained O'Hanlon and John. O'Hanlon smiled like the Cheshire cat, waved, and drove on. 'I'm so sorry,' said his secretary. 'If Mike doesn't write it down in his diary he forgets – he'll be back around eleven if you want to come back.'

I didn't. The O'Hanlon view of The Situation was one I was just going to have to miss. But at the end of the street, on an undistinguished pavement between a car park and the Maverick Spur Steak Ranch, I stumbled upon the famous Horse Memorial. On a stone plinth was a lifesize bronze of a kneeling soldier giving a horse water from a pail. It read:

ERECTED BY PUBLIC SUBSCRIPTION
IN RECOGNITION OF THE SERVICES
OF THE GALLANT ANIMALS
WHICH PERISHED IN THE
ANGLO-BOER WAR 1899–1902

and on the other side:

THE GREATNESS OF A NATION
CONSISTS NOT SO MUCH
IN THE NUMBER OF ITS PEOPLE
OR THE EXTENT OF ITS TERRITORY
AS IN THE EXTENT
AND JUSTICE OF ITS COMPASSION

8

HAPPY SAD LAND

Grahamstown was my first poste restante address. In the restless night I'd had a dream that Sarah had left me. For a shadowy dark-haired man. Over breakfast I had reassured myself. She hadn't phoned because she'd got in too late. Maybe she was out of town. Whatever – I badly wanted to get to Grahamstown and see if there was a letter.

I sped out along the N2, over green-brown countryside dotted with bush. It was 120 kilometres to Grahamstown and if I put my foot down I could be there in an hour. Nor was I stopping for hitch-hikers, however deserving they looked. Sorry guys, not today.

Music blared from the car radio. Then the news. 'And now', said a chirpy Seth Effrikan female, 'a crime story with a difference. Driving from Port Elizabeth to Grahamstown on the N2, Mr John Barnard picked up two hitch-hikers. When he stopped the car to go to the toilet, they assaulted him and stole his money and car keys, and left him by the roadside. But then, overcome with remorse, twenty minutes later they returned, and drove him at high speed to Grahamstown police station where they fled on foot. Mr Barnard is presently recovering in Grahamstown Hospital, and the incident is being investigated, say the police.'

I found the main post office without difficulty. Grahamstown wasn't a large place. Just one long street from the elegant cream and red-tiled buildings of Rhodes University at one end to the industrial estate at the other. Up on the hill behind was the inevitable township, a mess of shacks and dirt tracks against the blue sky. In the centre of town, bookshops, students, a café selling baked potatoes, and at the main crossroads, a splendid English-style cathedral in sienna stone, its tall spire dominating the scene.

Just ahead of me in the post office queue was a short black man in a three piece pinstriped suit and a black bowler hat, with a gold watch chain on his waistcoat. And yes, there was a letter for me. One. From my mother. 'Nothing else?' 'Sorry, sir.' My parents had had a lovely Whitsun weekend in Cornwall, the new laburnums were in full flower, and the weather was 'stunning if slightly too hot'. But what about Sarah?

On Alex and Geraldine's coffee table there had been a book of landscape and portrait photographs of South Africa. They had vivid colours and featured off-beat arrangements of people in quintessentially South African situations, and I'd admired them. It turned out Alex knew the photographer, an Afrikaner called Otto, who taught photography at Rhodes University and lived in Grahamstown. From PE I had phoned him, but, oh dear, he was sorry, he wasn't going to be in Grahamstown this weekend. He was driving out into the bush to take some photos of a game farm that this guy was setting up for upmarket European tourists.

I had mentioned my book and a couple of English newspapers: 'Maybe I could write something about it.' And down the line, Otto had perked up. 'Look, phone me tomorrow between 1 and 2,' he had said.

It was one o'clock now. I phoned. 'You're in Grahamstown already?' he said. 'You'd better come straight over.'

It took me two minutes to find his house. A pretty, white, one-storey building with a green roof, white pillars along a *stoep* and a flight of steps leading down to the street. Rather nervous all of a sudden, I knocked on the glass door. There were heavy footsteps down the hall, and the famous photographer stood before me. He looked like a wild and well-travelled walrus. A dark bushy moustache, narrow – almost Chinese – eyes in a plump, heavily tanned face, a mane of unkempt curly brown hair. He was wearing tight blue jeans and a battered brown leather jacket. Mid-forties, I reckoned.

His wife Chris was in the kitchen making bread. She was tall and thin, with short dark hair, and very welcoming. 'Come in, Mark, sit down, would you like some coffee?' Otto was packing cameras, all set to go. 'So are you going to come to this game farm with us, Mark?' he asked.

'Sure,' I replied.

Two men who didn't know each other, we debated how we'd get there – in one or two cars. 'It'd be silly for you to go in two cars,' said Chris, briskly. 'You must go with Otto.'

'I've never spent such a long time in a car with an Englishman,' Otto said, chuckling. 'We've fought wars against each other . . .'

He went off to pick up Christine. 'You wanted to talk to some students. Christine is one of my students. Postgrad. This is her stuff here.' He pointed out a highly coloured etching on the wall. It was of Camps Bay. The beach, the line of palm trees, Table Mountain . . . oh, I knew it well. 'There's some more of her stuff in the other room. Not bad, is it?'

I sat on the *stoep* in the sunshine. Otto returned with Christine, who was in her early twenties, with a sliced-short mop of blonde hair and big blue eyes. 'This is my girlfriend Christine,' he said. She smiled, blushed slightly, and gave him a sideways glance. 'Hi,' she said, rather coolly.

We packed the car and set off, the luggage and I on the back seat, Otto driving, Christine in the front with Jono, Otto's eight year old son, on her knee. Otto continued his gentle tease. 'Let's put on some English music,' he said, 'make our guest feel at home.' He put on a Herman's Hermits tape, and we sped back along the N2, Christine and Otto and Jono singing along in the front, me silent and English and faintly embarrassed in the back.

After ten kilometres or so we turned right onto dirt. 'Oh shit,' said Otto, looking up at the sky, which was clouding over fast. 'This is not the weather we want. First time it's rained for twenty-five years and I have to shoot a bloody game lodge.'

We were right out in the bush now, bumping along a narrow dusty road. The low hills to either side were studded with magnificent cactus-like plants, eight to ten feet tall, bursting into bright orange flames of flower at their heads. 'What are those orange things?' I asked.

'Aloes,' said Christine. 'They're beautiful, hey?'

We arrived at a perimeter fence. 'Open that gate, my boy,' said Otto to his son. 'In the New South Africa little boys have got to learn how to open gates.'

At the manager's farm, a leopard snoozed in the sun. 'He puts them in there when they first arrive,' said Otto. 'Eventually he's going to have herds of bontiebok and springbok and several leopards in the wild. If this place is going to make money it's going to be from hunting rather than viewing. There's no way a little place like this can compete with the big reserves on the edge of the Kruger, Mala Mala or whatever. He wants to charge a thousand rand a night. He's poured millions into it, millions. But I don't know,' he shook his head, 'I don't know that it'll work.'

We drove down to 'the lodge'. It was not a lodge at all, but a great oval compound of thatched white buildings around the obligatory blue oblong of pool. A lounge led through to a dining room, to a kitchen, to a paved barbecue (or *braai*, as the South Africans call it) area. At one end of the pool was a wooden horseshoe bar, under a protective 'V' of thatch. A black guy called Lucky was on hand to help us unload our baggage. He was all smiles and helpfulness.

Otto was looking upwards. 'Can't do photos of a game lodge in this weather. These fancy European tourists don't want to see grey skies. We'll have to do some indoor shots.' He turned to me. 'You don't mind modelling, do you Mark? Be in a couple of South African tourist brochures. You've got something a bit smarter than that?'

Soon, Christine and I – now resplendent in my blue jacket – were sitting on the couch by a blazing fire, posing as the perfect couple enjoying their pre-prandial glass of wine. It was clear that Christine found me about as attractive as a cup of cold sick, but I kept smiling, wondering what the hell I was doing in this game lodge in the middle of nowhere, with this crazed walrus of an Afrikaner barking instructions from one corner of the room, wondering whether I still had a girlfriend . . .

'You want me just to stay sitting here?' I asked, as Christine hurried off to change outfits.

'You just sit there, Englander,' said Otto, draining his tumbler with a smile. 'Have some more wine . . . think about Africa . . . the happy, the happy sad land . . . and beyond . . .'

We progressed from the lounge to the *braai*place. On Otto's instructions, Lucky had built two magnificent fires, one at each end of the big wooden table. Christine and I sat facing each other, while Otto took long, long exposure photos, darting around us in the darkness like a magician, a burst of flash here, a stoking of the fires there.

'Is it OK if we talk?' I asked.

'Sure, sure,' said Otto. 'It's a forty-five second exposure. Just don't move too much.'

When we'd finished, Jono was packed off to bed and we had a *braai*. Goodness! The first *braaivleis* I'd had since I'd been back in Africa. Huge chops and *boerewors* sizzled on the grill above the fire. Christine appeared from the kitchen with an elaborate salad. We ate and drank and drank on.

'This is reelly *lekker*, hey . . .'

'Yiss.'

'What's that . . . *lekker*?'

'*Lekker* . . .' they looked at each other and laughed. 'It means, reelly naice,' said Christine, 'reelly beautiful . . . reelly . . .'

'*Lekker*,' said Otto. 'So are you enjoying yourself out here, Mark?' he asked, as we sat, tumblers of whisky in hand, relaxed with each other at last.

'Yuh, yuh . . . most of the time. It's lonely sometimes, you know. Lonely without people, lonely with people.'

'You should loosen up, Mark. You know why I took you on this weekend . . . because I felt sorry for you. No, really, when I saw you standing outside my front door in your blue jeans, hey . . .' Otto pursed his lips, shook his head, and gurgled to himself. 'No, you've got to be a bit more . . . hey . . . you've just got to ask for what you want, go for it a bit more . . . oh don't you roll your eyes at me, little eye roller.' This last to Christine, sitting right up next to him, flushed pink in the firelight.

'Don't you think she's got beautiful eyes, Mark?'

I smiled.

'Come on! Don't be so English – say what you think!'

'Yes,' I said quietly. 'She has got beautiful eyes.'

'She just rolls those eyes at me,' said Otto, as Christine blushed like a schoolgirl. He leaned forward and kissed her on her golden hair. 'So many women, so little time,' he chuckled.

'D'you call the whole of Africa the Happy Sad Land, or just South Africa?' I asked.

'South Africa, Botswana, Namibia . . . all the southern bit. I also call it the Big South Land. You know what I love about this country, there's just so many contrasts. That's what makes it so great to be here. Europe . . . Europe's boring. So predictable. I can take you for a two minute drive in Grahamstown, from the big English cathedral at the centre, out down the main street and up the hill to the shacks where people are literally *starving*. Two minutes, that's all it takes.'

We sat in silence by the fire.

'I've calmed down now,' Otto said, 'but a few years ago I'd have been up to something crazy by this stage of the evening. I'd have been driving the jeep up into the hills or something.'

Ten minutes later he was driving the jeep up into the hills. He had a big torch that he kept swinging in drunken swerves round the bush. 'We're making so much noise, any game there is in this park isn't going to hang around,' shouted Christine against the screaming grind of the engine and the rattle of jumping stones.

'Hey porky!' yelled Otto, catching a porcupine in his torch beam. 'Bigger than you'd think, hey?' It was about eighteen inches to two feet long, eyes bright with alarm at this crazed vehicle-load of unnatural creatures.

'Four wheel drive now I think!' Otto hit a track that felt as if it was forty-five degrees to the vertical. 'Rabbit!' he shouted suddenly, catching a bunny in his beam. We drove on, the last of the Big Game Hunters, lurching up the broken-rock strewn road.

Back at base a calmer mood prevailed. 'Hey, leave us alone now, would you?' said Otto. I scuttled off gratefully to bed.

To wake with a throbbing head. The cloud had cleared and the pool glinted in the bright morning sunshine. Otto had gone out early in the landrover to take some shots of the other lodges. Christine was in the kitchen making *rooibos* tea, no longer the firelit beauty of last night, merely an unexceptional-looking young woman with a South African accent. The awkwardness between us had returned.

We were just sitting down to breakfast when Chris turned up, with Otto's other son, Donald. In my hungover state her voice seemed piercingly loud, as she briskly took command, started unloading plastic containers full of food into the fridge and cupboards.

Kitchen clear, Chris and Christine sat and drank coffee on mock wrought-iron white chairs by the pool, chatting away as if they'd been friends since childhood: Chris this, Christine that. Chris had just come back from a month-long cookery course in Italy. 'And I think, Christine, that what the children in Europe take for granted, is the *age* of everything. They just don't know how lucky they are.'

Otto returned, and we headed off *en famille* in the land-rover. I wasn't at ease. Chris's voice seemed painfully loud. The bright sunshine on the bush, the blue sky, even the startling orange of the tall aloes . . . it all just depressed me. Even the game we stopped to look at . . . the little herds of bontiebok, blessbok, springbok . . . here and there a blue-bottomed monkey darting up a tree, a pair of baboons . . . I just couldn't get into it at all.

'I don't know what you're going to make of this place, Mark,' said Otto, as we drove on dirt towards the *pièce de résistance* of the embryonic reserve, the private hotel and conference centre. It was a pink Tuscan-style house that looked as if it had been dropped, gardens and all, into the barren Eastern Cape bush around it. There were white Italianate balconies. Huge terracotta vases. A formal herb garden. Slim, dark green cypresses in pots. Down in front of the house, an old black guy in a blue boiler suit was meticulously weeding the lawn by the pool.

The manageress, an early forty-something with startling pink lipstick and cropped ash-blonde hair, greeted us in the pillared porch. 'Hello,' she said, 'Ahm Chris.'

While Otto set up his cameras, the first Chris, Christine and I nosed our way round the house. 'This is completely over the top,' yelled Chris, of a room which had two four-poster beds hung with heavy Victorian-style floral draperies. 'And look at *this*,' she shouted, at the huge bed in the master suite. 'Now that must be what they call a king saize, mustn't it?' Christine had pulled off the eiderdown: it was two broad single beds pushed together. 'Oh,' said Chris, disappointed. 'Well I suppose you could cuddle across.'

'At a thousand rand a night!' said Christine.

'Who sleeps in the crack?' said Chris.

'The dog,' said Christine.

'No,' said Chris, 'this is virry Italian. Wouldn't you say so, Mark? Virry Italian, I think, the whole place.'

Christine had to go off and change into a nightdress. She was posing for Otto in the master suite. The little boys played by the pool. Chris went into the kitchen to borrow a bottle opener and made instant friends with the other Chris. 'Well, Chris,' said Chris, 'I think you've got a hells of a job here.' 'Yiss, Chris,' Chris replied. 'Well, Chris,' Chris concluded, 'I think it's going to be virry hard work, but virry rewarding. She's a single parent mother,' she said, returning. 'I think it's a good job for her. She'll be kept virry busy, and she won't have time to worry about her social life.'

Eventually Otto was finished. We clattered off in the landrover. The black gardener was still weeding the lawn. 'He must be stoned,' said Christine. 'He's been weeding that exact same patch for five hours.' At my request, they dropped me off a couple of miles away from the lodge. Walking back alone through the late afternoon sunshine I recovered my mood. In the silence, the exquisite springbok and bontiebok appeared from nowhere, moved at their own pace through the bush, not running helter-skelter away from the din of the landrover. It seemed a shame that they were being bred merely to be slaughtered by wealthy Europeans.

When I reached the lodge, Otto was sitting silently by the pool with a beer, watching the sunset. It was my first really African sunset, the sky still and clear above the bush, livid yellow turning to brilliant orange, then as the upper sky darkened to a rich blue, a deep crimson blush was thrown up, hung in the air, vanished again. There wasn't a cloud in sight.

There was a small row about what we were having for supper. Chris had brought pasta. But Otto wanted to do a venison *pondokkie*, which was a special Afrikaner stew, cooked in a cast-iron pot over the fire. 'Mark's never had a *pondokkie*,' he said. Eventually, a compromise was arrived at. We would have both: the pasta at seven-thirty, the *pondokkie* at nine.

But by nine, Otto, who'd moved on from beer to brown sherry to wine, was so tired and drunk that he was slurring his words. His wife leant over him, arms thrown loosely around his neck. 'Would you do the *pondokkie*,' he murmured, 'I've lost interest.' So Christine cut up the venison, and Chris leant over the fire and cooked it.

'She talks like a kaffir,' Otto chuckled to himself. 'You know, Mark, loud – that's how they talk. Like Chris.'

She came over. 'We were just saying you talk like a kaffir,' Otto repeated. His wife looked at him in a resigned, loving sort of way, knelt down, put her arms around him. 'The older I get,' Otto said, looking over at me and Christine, who was briskly chopping up salad, 'the more I appreciate her.'

'So Mark,' he mumbled, as we sat, post-*pondokkie* with our whiskies, 'are we going to see you again? And if not,' he looked across at me with glazed eyes, 'goodbye.' He nodded to himself. 'Goodbye. You must listen to what I said, though: you've got to go for it more. That's what you've got to do.'

I decided to leave Grahamstown by doing Otto's two minute drive. It took me ninety seconds, cruising slowly down the main street, past the university bookstore, the post office, Church Square, the Grand Hotel, sundry garages, bottle stores, laundries, the industrial estate, the cemetery, and then suddenly – bump onto dirt and into the familiar township landscape: little corrugated iron and brick serviced houses to start with; on up the hill to shackland. Goats, mangy dogs, hens, colourfully-dressed women doing their laundry around a single tap: here it all was again. And I wondered what it would be like living here, day in, day out, looking down the hill onto the cathedral spire, the neat white houses and lawns below; rather than looking up, feeling white and guilty.

Passing the post office again on my way out I stopped on a whim, asked the lady behind the counter whether she could just double-check the poste restante boxes for me. And yes, there *was* another letter for me, mis-filed under N. It was from Sarah, and – silly mistrustful fool I'd been – it was full of the tenderest expressions of love and affection.

9

THE STRUGGLE FOR LIBERATION

I was driving out of White South Africa now, along an undulating road through thick green bush. I wound down into the Ecca Pass, and then, coming over the top of a rise on the far side, saw ahead and below me a rippling landscape of brown hills, with blue-grey mountains beyond. Perhaps it was just my imagination; but they looked mysterious, forbidding, dark.

This was the Ciskei, ancestral land of the Xhosa tribes, and now one of South Africa's ten 'homelands', where a nominal black Government ruled. As any defender of Verwoerd will tell you, apartheid was not a deliberately evil system designed to oppress the blacks, but a logical solution to the problem of a country that contained so many diverse cultures. The whites would have their bit of South Africa, each of the different races of blacks theirs. So the Xhosas were given the Ciskei and the Transkei; the Zulus, Kwazulu; the Tswanas, Bophuthatswana; the North Sotho, Lebowa, and so on – the only problem was that the Government was absurdly niggardly in handing out the land. Kwazulu, for example, is divided into forty-four separate parcels of territory, criss-crossed by juicy bits of White South Africa that the apartheid practitioners just couldn't bear – when it came to it – to let go.

Like so much of apartheid-in-practice, the homelands

became a preposterous muddle. To pretend that they were
'real', successive Nationalist Governments poured in money
to support leaders who redefined the phrase 'tinpot dictator':
men who were prepared to kid themselves and the world
that they really were in charge of proper little countries.
They built swish modern capitals, surrounded themselves
with well-equipped armies, had 'embassies' in Pretoria that
no other country except South Africa recognised; meanwhile
their 'people' rushed headlong out of the land they'd been
given, to Cape Town and Durban and Jo'burg and anywhere
else that might offer even just the hope of a subsistence
wage.

I was driving in the reverse direction, down over the
sunburnt hills towards the Great Fish River. The Great Fish
River! Famous frontier between blacks and whites. Until
1846, when a vicious British scorched-earth campaign
finally drove the Xhosas back to the Keiskamma River,
twenty-five miles to the east, this had been the much-fought-
over dividing line between westwardly moving blacks and
eastwardly moving whites.

Now, in the drought, far below the tall white roadbridge,
it was no more than a trickle on a bed of red-brown earth.
To celebrate my arrival in both historic and modern-artificial
Black Africa, I stopped the car to pick up a woman and her
three children who were trudging up the dusty verge on the
far side. She looked battered and old, but her kids were no
more than ten or twelve: three laughing little girls who sat
upright and silent on the back seat, and then, when I let
them out at the end of their journey four miles later, jumped
and shrieked and waved as I sped off. A little further on, I
picked up three burly young blacks who were going to Fort
Beaufort. The guy in the front, with a shaved head, looked
distinctly shifty and wouldn't catch my eye. But one of the
guys in the back made me feel confident that I wasn't about
to become one of Cape Town Tania's nightmares or 'a crime
story with a difference'. He had gentle eyes and a broad and

beautiful smile. I explained that I was from England ('from England, oh'); that I was touring ('tow-ring, oh'); that I was headed for Fort Hare ('ah-oh').

'So are you working on a farm out here?' I asked.

'We are staying on a farm. We are not working at present,' he answered politely. I dropped them off in Fort Beaufort, and picked up two teenage schoolgirls, neat in their uniforms, who jumped in the back and sat silent, answered my questions in shy monosyllables, looking at me as if I might suddenly stop the car and announce that I was now going to eat them. They lived in Alice, but went to school every day in Fort Beaufort. There was no public transport, and they were going home. It was 11.15 a.m.

As we came down the hill into Alice, they pointed out Fort Hare University to me: a collection of imposing red-brick and concrete buildings on the hill above the dusty little town. I dropped them off and drove straight there, in past the security barriers with a wave.

Until the formal ending of apartheid in February 1990, Fort Hare was a black university. It was here that many of the leaders of the South African liberation struggle were educated. Mandela and Buthelezi were contemporaries and friends here. Robert Mugabe of Zimbabwe was here, as were many of the major political figures of Uganda, Kenya, and Nigeria.

This was very much an 'on spec' visit. A university professor I had met in Cape Town had given me one name: Petros Mkhize, head of the Student Representative Council.

Petros had a thin, intelligent face and a smile that hovered round his lips as he talked. He was twenty-four, doing postgrad research.

We walked across the red-brick paved campus. Sprinklers played on green lawns. By an artificial waterfall stood three palm trees. The staff centre was an elegant building, a white cube surrounded by square white pillars, a criss-cross wooden verandah running around the first floor. As we queued with our trays in the canteen, it felt strange to be in such a pleasant environment, surrounded by well-dressed prosperous-looking people who were mostly black.

Over lunch this mild, intelligent postgrad revealed the other side of his life. His liberation CV. Though he'd never been on Robben Island, he, too, had been dodging the police for years. Detained for a day in 1985 and then again for five days in 1986. Between 1986 and 1989, he was keen to tell me, he'd been 'one of the most highly sought-after activists'. He'd been able to sleep at home for the first time in December 1990. 'I'm having many different names,' he confided. 'About five names in fact.'

'So Petros Mkhize is one of these names?'

'No,' he chuckled, 'Mkhize is my real name. Really. But in the township I still have another name, a nickname they call me by.'

Fear of the police meant that he'd only been able to tell his friends and associates that he was studying at Fort Hare two years ago. 'Until then, only my family knew where I was. It was too dangerous.'

Yes, he had been – he was – a comrade. But then, he was at pains to point out, 'comrade' was not just a term to describe the youth leaders who'd been involved in school boycotts, school and liquor hall burnings, necklacings and so on. A comrade was anybody who identified with the liberation struggle. 'When Nelson Mandela addresses us, he addresses us "Comrades and friends . . ."'

And had *he* ever been involved – as a township leader – in such things as burnings and necklacings?

I hardly expected him to say 'yes'.

'You have to locate this violence in a particular context,' he replied, 'and I locate it in the context of intense repression. In the period before 2 February 1990, when the Government was using other black people as a means to entrench this repression, the only way for the youth to show its total abhorrence of the Government's policies was to burn down and destroy certain buildings which were symbolic of the Government. Like schools. Beerhalls. Any Government building or Government car. All those things were burnt. Obviously, I cannot condone that and I cannot condemn it. I think I have to approach it in this way, that I understand why people did that, even though I don't condone it.'

As for the Inkatha–ANC violence, he went on, it was Inkatha who had started it – in the hostels on the Reef – and so, 'although there's no doubt that the ANC do sometimes get involved with violence, this is aimed at retaliation, at self-defence.'

Was it a clichéd misrepresentation to say that this black-on-black violence was tribal, I asked. Petros smiled and shrugged: 'Well, I'm a Zulu, and I support the ANC, so yes, I would say that is a misconception.'

What happened on campus? Was everyone a member of the ANC? No, 80% supported the ANC, 20% the PAC. This did cause tensions, yes, 'but finally we all belong within the one camp, in the struggle for liberation. We recognise this.'

The main violence on campus had occurred over protests about the previous administration. That had been an almost entirely white administration, headed by a professor who'd been a leading member of the Broederbond, the secret Afrikaner society that had been responsible for so much of the behind-the-scenes orchestration of apartheid. They'd effectively been running the university on behalf of the Government. But now, with the new university Council and the new black Rector, student-staff relations were not just fine, they were excellent. 'The Rector describes Fort Hare as a liberated area within South Africa. In fact, a liberated zone from which one can join the educational front of the liberation struggle.'

Before, if there had been any trouble on campus, the university authorities would just call the police, and the activists would be carted off. 'They were not prepared to consult any of us. They were in fact virtual dictators.

Whenever there was a dispute with students they wouldn't solve it through peaceful means, through dialogues and discussions. They would rather ban the SRC, call the police to arrest student leaders, invite in the Security Branch.

'But this new management doesn't do that. We are now members of the university Council, where we have observer status. I sit on the Council as President of SRC. We sit on the Senate. Management, when it has a problem, approaches us. We are happy with that arrangement. Which is why there haven't been any violent confrontations.'

Nosing round the art block, I found Hilary, head of the art department, sitting on a battered swivel chair in a narrow office decorated with clippings from the Arts section of the English *Sunday Times*. He was white, a thick-set guy in his forties, with coarse black hair swept back off his forehead in a quiff. He looked like a retired Mod; albeit a retired Mod with a thick Seth Effrikan accent.

He made me some tea. The kettle was spattered with paint, the milk was on the turn, the sugar was full of coffee-stained lumps. It was just like every art department I'd ever been to.

We'd soon left the problems of Fort Hare (the fact that Bantu education meant that art wasn't really taught to blacks at a primary or secondary level, so the students had virtually to start from scratch when they came to university) and moved on to a discussion about African art. What was it? Why did they bother to teach the Western European tradition? Why not connect straight to, say, the Chinese, or the Indians?

When Hilary had been at art school (at Rhodes) he'd been taught 'all that sort of Ben Nicholson non-representational stuff'. Then an English painter called Bradshaw had come out and become professor of fine art, and got him involved in painting. So Hilary had become a painter. He particularly liked Hogarth, Rowlandson, Gillray: 'that sort of stuff — figures doing things in landscapes.'

His figures and landscapes were local. He was painting subjects from the Xhosa oral tradition, which was incredibly rich. A big painting he'd done recently was called 'The Death of Hintsa' — about the British Colonel Harry Smith's betrayal and killing of the Xhosa chief Hintsa, during the Sixth Frontier War of 1835, a story that was very important to the Xhosas.

'I don't have a problem with not being African enough,' Hilary said, in answer to a dig of mine about him not being black. 'I am an African. This is where I was born.'

He'd been brought up in Jo'burg, in a typical white working class area. 'You know, the kids played in the street, the garage was the goalposts, that sort of thing.' To this day he was a mad soccer fan; followed English football; had his English team. Then, of course, there were the emerging South African football teams: the Mamelodi Sundowns, the Kaiser Chiefs, the Orlando Pirates. 'The South African team's going to play Cameroon one of these days,' he told me. 'Then there'll be fireworks.'

He showed me round. I admired some tall wood carvings of tortured, semi-abstract figures. They were by a very talented student called Phinneas, Hilary said. 'I'll have to get him out of the video room. They're watching Kenneth Clarke, you know, *Civilisation*.'

Phinneas was quiet, intense, with a nervous laugh. He had a face that switched in a second from a broad white smile to a troubled frown. He ended every sentence in 'yes'; pronounced softly, 'ye-es'.

His sculptures were all part of a group, he told me. Ye-es. Entitled 'The Road to a New South Africa'. Ye-es. A tall figure, bent double, chewing its own feet, was called 'CODESA'. 'You see,' said Phinneas, 'to me, CODESA is just the mental exercise of individuals . . . . it's just power games.

But there's no achievement. You see, if things don't go right, you force yourself into a position, ye-es.'

Another horribly pained figure had a bird-like animal growing at its waist. 'What's this?' I asked. Phinneas broke into his nervous smile, looked at Hilary and then back at me. 'That is an animal, ye-es,' he said. 'What sort of an animal?' 'It is no sort of animal, it comes from the conscious mind; but you see, the confusion, the pain of apartheid, I believe is felt by all the animals as well as humans ... birds ... even cockroaches and flies are feeling this same pain.'

Phinneas believed in reincarnation, it emerged. Hilary, looking like a football coach with David Icke on his hands, stood in the background, chuckling and shaking his head. Phinneas was elaborating on his beliefs, talking about 'the life of nine months'.

'You mean, life in the womb?'

'Ye-es. I believe that in the womb people are going to school and playing games and having all kinds of times with each other.'

'But you're alone in the womb, surely?'

'No, but the soul, the souls are meeting, somewhere, going to school, playing with each other, and so many things, ye-es. I personally believe that I was not born this time for the first time, you see. I believe that I was born somewhere else, and as a result, most of the things which I'm exposed to, I'm not surprised. In actual fact, there's nothing which puzzles me at all, nothing at all. I look at a tree, but I cannot waste my time looking at a tree, because I feel for long familiar with that, before in fact I was born here now in South Africa, as a black man, ye-es.'

'So you could have been a white man?'

'Exactly, ye-es. I personally believe that for the first time I was born in England, as a white man. And from there, I went to America. And then, from America, came straight away here. Ye-es.' He laughed; as did Hilary.

A large, I might say enormous, woman in a flowing green

dress came into the studio. Oh gawd, I thought, just as I'm getting to talk to some black people at last, here comes another white liberal. Her name was Rosie, and she had a pretty face under a pre-Raphaelite mass of brown curls. From the softness of her skin I guessed she was mid-twenties.

She taught art history, and Hilary was clearly keen that I should talk to her, so we left Phinneas and I followed her through to a cluttered little office, piled high with art books. We discussed art history for a while, then she said, 'So where are you staying tonight? You can come and spend the night with me and my boyfriend if you like. We live up in the mountains, in Hogsback.'

I said goodbye to Hilary, who was now standing in the sunny courtyard engaged in a deep conversation with Phinneas. He had stopped laughing. 'I was just talking to Phinneas about reincarnation,' he said. 'It's interesting what he says, because, you know, he's right in a certain way. I mean, I know I was on a certain road in the 1920s; it's way out in the Ciskei, in the bush, but I *know* I've been on it before.'

Rosie and I drove out of Alice and off in the gloaming across the dusty plain of Ciskei, which was dotted here, there and everywhere – this being a homeland – with *rondawels*. No fenced off white farms here. Smoke drifted upwards from bright little fires.

Ahead of us loomed the mighty fir-covered slopes of the mountains. Above the tree-line, the peaks glowed orange-pink in the sunset afterglow.

'It's beautiful,' I said.

'I'm glad you think so. I love living up here. That mountain there', Rosie pointed to one with a strange, hollowed out summit, like a volcano, 'the Xhosa call the Enchanter's Mountain.' We wound up and up through the woods, the view down over Ciskei getting ever more spectacular as we climbed.

'D'you know the works of JRR Tolkein?' Rosie asked.

'Sure.'

'This is where he grew up. It's supposed to be the inspiration for *The Lord of the Rings*.' I could well believe it. We had bumped off tar onto a winding dirt road; had Bilbo Baggins appeared through the pinetrunks to left or right it would have been no surprise.

Rosie was revealing herself as a bit of a New Ager. Our talk had turned to astrology, crystals, varieties of herbal tea. By a row of tall milkwoods we turned left up a track to her house. It was cute as anything, a little cottage in the woods that could easily have housed a Hobbit or two.

Rosie's boyfriend Rod, however, was far from Hobbit-like. He was tall and lean, with a thin face and a pronounced black moustache. He was unloading his crimson *bakkie* by the garage. 'Hi Rod!' shouted Rosie; and then, receiving no reply, 'Hello, Rod!' Rod looked coolly across at us and vanished into the house.

With the exception of Princess, the maid, who was doing the washing-up in the tiny kitchen, you could have picked the whole place up and dumped it down in Somerset without a problem. A thatched roof with low beams, a huge stone fireplace, Indian drapes on all the sofas and chairs, three or four cats. In the living room was a large painting of a naked greenish-skinned maiden drowning in a green river that was overhung with lush green trees. Rosie had painted it. She showed me the cluttered room at the side of the house that was her – or rather their, for Rod was also an artist – studio.

'It's terribly untidy,' Rosie said, making a dash to pick up scattered books and newspapers. 'I haven't tidied it for a week.' Rod was in the kitchen, boiling a kettle. Finally Rosie managed to get us introduced. 'Hi,' said Rod, nodding from the corner.

Rosie thought it would be nice if we went out for supper. There was a hotel in the village that was just like an English pub. And then maybe we could go and visit some of their friends; that might be interesting for me. She was just going to brush her teeth and have a wash, then we could go.

'Can't we just go now?' asked Rod.

'I just want to clean my teeth, *OK*.'

Rod and I were left alone. We sat opposite each other in silence, each with a cat on our laps. I stroked mine; he stroked his.

'So – d'you also work at the university?' I asked.

'Yes – I'm in maintenance.' He flashed me a toothy smile; that ended as abruptly as it had begun.

'It's a lovely place you've got here. Hogsback.'

'I hate it. Really, I'd rather live anywhere else. But Rosie likes it, so it's something of a compromise.'

'Right.'

He continued to stroke his cat. 'Hey, mumma cat,' he murmured lovingly to it. 'This is mumma cat,' he said. 'And that's baby cat. There's another cat that pees all over the place that I'm trying to persuade Rosie to get rid of.'

'Right,' I replied, carefully; nervous tension rose off this bloke like steam.

'I heard a good joke at work today,' he said, after a silence. 'There's three types of sex in marriage, OK?' He flashed me the grin again.

'OK.'

'The first stage is house sex. OK, you're in the first six months, and you have sex all over the house, on the armchairs, anywhere.'

'OK.'

'The second stage is bedroom sex. Things have quietened down now. You have sex in the bedroom, preferably with the light off, what with the stretch marks and that.'

'OK.'

'The third stage is passage sex. You know what that is?'

'No.'

'The husband and wife bump into each other in the passage. And they say to each other, "Fuck you!".' He laughed.

I managed a chuckle. Rosie came back, big and beautiful, having cleaned her teeth, brushed her hair and made herself up.

'So can we go now?' asked Rod.

'Yes.'

'Actually, I want to clean *my* teeth.' So we waited while Rod cleaned *his* teeth. Then we were off, bumping down the dirt road in the *bakkie*, me squashed between Rosie and Rod, my legs pushed up against the gearstick.

'Rod's a real South African,' said Rosie.

The Hogsback Inn *was* quite like an English pub. It had a cosy little bar with tables in wooden booths to one side. Apart from two red-faced locals and William, the landlord, there was nobody there.

'Well, it is Monday night, I suppose,' said Rosie.

While I bought a round of whiskies, Rod went off to say hi to the locals. Rosie and I dived back into a conversation about 'modern art' we'd been having earlier. She'd never heard of 'installation', so I'd explained what it was, and we were just getting into a discussion about the validity of artworks that were not actually made by the 'artist', when Rod came back for his whisky.

'Would you like to hear some incest jokes?' he asked.

'No, don't Rod,' said Rosie, 'that's ugly.'

I made an attempt to include Rod in the conversation ('we're talking about this kind of modern art called installation') but he wasn't interested. Eventually he turned away and went back to the two locals.

Our food arrived. 'Are you two going to stop talking that intellectual cuck and come and have something to eat. Sorry,' he added, giving me an unexpected flash of the smile again, 'but I can't keep up with all this stuff.'

Terrified of saying anything intellectual, I chewed silently on my fish and chips.

'OK, I'm going to tell my incest joke now,' said Rod. 'This girl goes to her father, OK, and she wants five hundred

bucks. So he says: "OK, but you've got to suck my dick."'
Rod looked eagerly from Rosie to me and back again. I
cranked my face into a weary smile. '"But I *can't* do that,"
she says. "If you want five hundred bucks," he says, "you're
going to have to." So anyway, she starts to suck his dick, and
then she says, "Ugh, Dad, your dick really tastes of shit."
"Oh yes," he says, "well your brother was here earlier and
he wanted a car."'

'Agh Rod – that's so *ugly*!' said Rosie, turning away. Rod
laughed matily across at me. Rosie was opening up her bag,
taking out cigarettes. She offered me one. We lit up.

'Agh – Rosie,' said Rod, 'that smoke's blowing right in my
face. Just sit the other side, could you?'

I twisted my lips to blow my own smoke well away from
Rod.

Our ice-cream had arrived. 'You've got more ice-cream
than me,' said Rod to Rosie. 'How come you've got six bits
and I've got four. Well, never mind, I'll take you home and
eat *you* later.'

'So shall we go and visit Mike and Lindsay?' Rosie asked,
as we walked out into the chilly night. 'Would you like to
meet some other people, Mark?'

'I'd like to go home and watch telly and go to bed,' said Rod.

'I'm easy really,' I said.

Back at the house Rod stood in front of her, almost like a
little boy: 'Please don't make me light a fire, Rosie,' he said.

'It's fine,' I said, though it was barely nine o'clock. 'I had
an early start. I must go to bed.'

'I'm not going to get up with you tomorrow, Rod,' Rosie
said. 'I'll drive down with Mark at nine o'clock.'

Rod looked uneasily from one to the other of us. 'Rosie,'
he said finally, 'that's really not acceptable. Who's going to
make my tea?'

Ten minutes later they were sitting side by side on an
Indian drape. 'You look really beautiful tonight, Rosie,' he
said. And then: 'I love you. I don't know why, but I do.'

10

ONE AZANIA, ONE NATION

Coming out of the university gates the following morning, I caught the flash of some long brown legs and a brightly coloured dress. Two girls by the roadside with their thumbs out. I braked sharply. Here were some hitch-hikers I was happy to have.

They were both Fort Hare students. Savita, the tall leggy one, was half Indian and half Xhosa. She sat in the front and fingered her bottom lip and didn't do much talking. Mametsoki, who was shorter, and half-coloured, half-Sotho, was altogether more garrulous. They laughed when I asked them about their race. Savita was clearly embarrassed by the question.

They'd asked for a lift to King William's Town. Once in the car they told me they were really going to East London, to do some shopping. My plans were − naturally − flexible. 'I could take you down there,' I said, 'but I want to stop in King William's Town and visit Steve Biko's grave. And then have a quick look at Bisho. If you don't mind coming with me, I'll take you to East London.'

'That's OK,' they said, after a short over-the-seat consultation. 'We'll come with you.'

'We're not really going shopping,' said Mametsoki, leaning forward from the back, 'just window shopping. I really want to see a movie.'

'Are you skipping school?' I asked.

'No, Wednesday's our day off. The labs get used all day by third years doing practicals.'

'Why go all the way to East London?'

'Alice is boring. There's nothing there.'

I wondered whether it was safe for them, two young women alone, to hitch to East London.

'We do it a lot,' said Mametsoki. 'Although yesterday some people were trying to frighten us, saying we might get raped or murdered.' In the front Savita laughed.

'But you don't hitch back in the dark, I hope,' I said, feeling suddenly paternal.

'Oh no,' Mametsoki replied. Savita shook her head. Daddy wasn't entirely convinced.

As we drove, Mametsoki kept the chatter coming, leaning forward between the seats. I'd told her I was English, and now she wanted to know all about London, and Paris, and Europe. She had such a romantic idea of Paris, she said, from books she'd read, movies she'd seen. One day she was hoping to go there.

'So why d'you stay in London?' she asked, 'if you don't like it so much?'

'Oh, I don't know. I've got a lot of friends there ...'

'Are they all snobs?'

I laughed aloud. 'Why d'you say that?'

'I thought everyone in London was supposed to be a snob.'

'Well, some of them are, yes.'

'Although,' she added sweetly, 'if they're friends of yours, they can't be.' She was a honey, Mametsoki: knew exactly how to get to the heart of the lonely traveller.

I felt duty-bound to ask them about apartheid, though it wasn't a subject any of us wanted to dwell on. Mametsoki wanted to make the point that there were some bad people who were white, and some bad people who were black, but it was people – or rather persons – who caused the violence. 'It isn't races,' she said, 'it's individuals.'

I asked them about necklacing. They both agreed that it was 'very bad', but yes, nonetheless, it was understandable, because of 'the centuries of repression', because black people had become so very frustrated.

'But what I can't understand,' said Mametsoki, 'is how the white people can be so violent, when they've had it so easy. What have they go to fight about, that's what I can't understand.'

Savita, silent in the front, nodded agreement.

'It used to make me so angry I would cry,' Mametsoki went on, 'when the police came onto the buses and searched the bags. They took plastic bags off old ladies and just tore them apart.' She shook her head. 'How could they do that?'

We arrived in King William's Town, which was another South African special built around a long main street of one and two storey banks and shops and take-aways and garages and bottle stores. It was big though, with plenty of cross streets. Finding Biko's grave was going to be a problem.

But as we left town we passed a large cemetery: stone walls, cypresses, headstones. 'Look,' I said, 'a cemetery. We can just go down and see if Biko's in there.'

The two girls were laughing. 'That's the *white* cemetery,' they chorused. Savita was doubled up, shaking her head. From the back, Mametsoki said, 'You see, Mark, even to death . . . even to death.'

We drove on, a kilometre or two, to Bisho, the capital of the Ciskei homeland, which merited upper case letters on the map, but which wasn't – of course – a real town at all, but a 1980s joke, a post-modern absurdity plonked down by politics in the middle of nowhere.

You drive two miles up the road from King William's Town (which is just inside South Africa) and there it is ahead of you, across the dusty scrub: BISHO: a square of administrative offices in pink- and grey-faced concrete; a ceremonial arch; to one side a yellow skyscraper with a startling pale blue plexiglass lift.

And then, beneath all that preposterous splendour, at ground level, was the reality. A shopping mall with all the same old South African shops: Pick 'n Pay, Fish and Chip Take-away, New Look Hair Salon. Half of them were having closing down sales. Mother Tiny T, a young kiddies outfit-ters, was already boarded-up.

The real commerce was being done outside, on the pave-ment, where a row of makeshift African stalls had sprung up. Fruit, shoes, shampoo, medicinal herbs, you name it, in a long line stretching away from the 'town centre' to the car park full of African taxis, where the same old crowds of unemployed Africans sat around in groups, on steps, on the pavement, on walls – presumably wondering how they, too, could get a joke job in this joke town.

Mametsoki and Savita held hands and skipped after me. 'Can I hold your camera?' asked Mametsoki. 'Then they'll think we're tourists.'

'Now I'm seeing it through your eyes,' she said, as I knelt to take a photograph of the yellow skyscraper.

'What are you seeing?'

'It's beautiful,' she said. 'We've never really looked at it before.'

Leaving Bisho we came to a crossroads on the main road.

'Oh,' said Savita, waking up suddenly, 'that's where Biko lived, straight on. He's probably buried in that location.'

So we drove under the railway and up a dirt road into the township, past a cruising yellow police lorry, its windows fortified with thick steel-mesh screens.

'Ugh,' said Mametsoki, 'a hippo. D'you see?' She shook her head. 'They still frighten me, those hippos. They used to come into the township, and just chase us, and shoot.'

It was lucky I had the girls with me. With frequent stops for directions in Xhosa, we found our way through the township and then out down a long dirt road that ran round a dusty hill to a group of corrugated iron sheds by the railway. The black cemetery was beyond that: a patch of dry scrub, the only demarcation being a broken barbed-wire fence. In the hot noon sun we trod carefully through the bone-dry grass, back through the years . . . June 1986 . . . May 1984 . . . September 1979 . . .

Half way down, we found it, a grave a little larger than the others.

BANTU STEVE BIKO
ONE AZANIA ONE NATION

Savita and Mametsoki posed on either side of the headstone while I took a photo. For two minutes their laughter had gone, as they gazed down solemnly at the broken grey pebbles on the grave.

Not 'one settler, one bullet'; but 'one Azania, one nation': from a man who had been picked up on suspicion of distributing inflammatory pamphlets, and then, over the course of three weeks in detention, slowly beaten to death. None of the police involved in the case had ever been punished, or even suspended, nor had there ever been an official admission that Biko was murdered.

As we walked back to the car I asked Mametsoki and Savita what they knew of Biko. He was, they agreed, 'a famous historical figure in the liberation struggle.'

I didn't want the day just to end there, so I offered to buy them lunch in East London. 'You take me somewhere,' I said. 'Anywhere you like.' I had visions of some fancy French restaurant where we could drink cold white wine at a crisp pink tablecloth and live up to Mametsoki's visions of Paris . . . but Savita knew exactly where she wanted to go. To the seafront, to a place called Santa Monica, which served steaks and pizzas, where Tina Turner yelled from an overhead TV screen and the groovy young white waiter said 'Hi folks' and showed us to a booth overlooking the road that ran by the sea wall.

Mametsoki had a banana milk shake and Savita a fruit juice. They didn't drink. They'd only taken drugs twice. Marijuana. 'The first time I took it,' said Mametsoki, breaking into that easy laughter, 'I was so scared I thought I'd jump out of the window or something. Is London full of drug addicts?'

'It's not *full* of drug addicts, Mametsoki.'

'I thought it was full of drug addicts and people having orgies [she pronounced it or*g*ies, with a hard "g"] and all that kind of thing.'

'What about the snobs? Where do they fit in?'

She laughed.

'Where d'you get these ideas from?' I asked.

'From books, you know, and films.'

'No, I don't think there are many orgies these days. What with AIDS and so on.'

So we talked about AIDS. They'd run a test at Fort Hare, and twenty-two people on campus had tested HIV positive. 'But I don't know who they tested,' said Mametsoki, 'because they didn't test me.'

Our pizzas arrived and the conversation moved from AIDS to sex to relationships to marriage to divorce. Both had divorced parents. 'It's partly because they have too much money,' said Mametsoki, 'and also, in the old days, there was polygamy, and now some of the men want to practise it when it isn't there any more, so they end up having a girlfriend, and then getting divorced, and then marrying the girlfriend, and so on.

'Men are so *weak*,' she went on. 'They just can't resist temptation. Poor little men,' she laughed. 'I don't think there's a man in the world who could be faithful.'

Savita nodded. Mametsoki didn't take betrayal lightly. She approved – with a new glint in her eye – of vengeance. 'Yes, yes,' she cried, 'they *should* be revenged. I like the kind of woman who goes through men.' She dropped her eyes. 'I don't want to be like that myself – but I can watch and have a secret admiration for them, because they give back to men what men do to us.'

I laughed. 'It's *true*,' she said, smiling across at me.

Their film started at 2.30. I paid up, we walked out onto the promenade, persuaded a black ice-cream seller with a very shaky hand to take a photo of us, sitting together on the seawall in the sunny afternoon breeze.

'What famous actors and actresses do you know in London?' Mametsoki asked, as I drove them through the traffic to the cinema.

'Well, let's think,' I said. 'I knew Emma Thompson at university.' They hadn't heard of her. 'And Stephen Fry, he's a big comedy actor in England.' No, they'd never heard of him. 'Kenneth Branagh?' I asked (not that I'd ever met him). 'No,' they said. I laughed. London seemed a long way away.

There was a choice of two movies: *Bloodfest II* and *House Party*. 'I don't think *Bloodfest* sounds very nice,' said Mametsoki. With a shrug they bought two tickets for *House Party* 'Or is it three?' asked Mametsoki, flirtatious to the last.

'I've got to get on to the Transkei.'

'If we didn't have school we'd come with you. Don't forget us, will you,' she said, as I kissed them both goodbye.

'I shan't,' I said, stumbling out of the foyer into the sunshine.

East London, East London. I'm sure there was lots to see in East London. Rich and poor. Squalid townships and splendid white residences by the sea. Museums and maybe even a horse memorial. But in my present mood, I couldn't face it. I didn't want to check in to one of the dreary hotels on the seafront and trudge off dutifully to the Tourist Information Centre. I wanted to get on, away from sweet Mametsoki and her beautiful friend; before I became the man who sat on the cinema steps and asked them to give up school and come with me.

I put my foot down and headed out of town on the freeway. To my right, pretty old houses on wooded crags – I'd no need to ask what colour their inhabitants were. Ahead, the open road.

Moorland. Low hills. Then, over to the right, the undulating brown landscape fell away to the distant blue of the sea. I passed circular white *rondawels* with dark thatched roofs; rugger posts in the middle of a field of sheep. On a ridge up ahead the gums made a dark green-black silhouette against the clear blue wash of the sky: the narrowness of the trunks and the tiny leaves making for particularly intricate and lovely detail.

Over the top of a rise the road curved away to the left. Ahead was a sweep of blue hills ... the Transkei ... the biggest and oldest of the homelands, with a real border post where I had to show my passport, and a six rand fee for a two-week entry permit. Just the other side of the barriers a big green sign read: WELCOME. FEEL FREE. TOUR TRANSKEI.

The difference was tangible. Pale blue huts spread out loosely on the tops of hills, not bunched-up, not hidden away out of sight. I wound on, past signs to Haga-Haga, Quko, Komga, until around four I arrived at Butterworth. At the petrol station, nobody jumped to fill my car. Everything was slower, noisier. The streets were awash with black faces, the shops were tattier, there was no dominating Dutch Reformed Church spire.

It was sixty-five kilometres to Wavecrest, which Otto had told me was a wonderful place to stay. Everyone had said the dirt roads out to the Wild Coast were atrocious. Already the sky was turning orange. Oh what the hell! I decided to feel free and go for it.

The road was rough with jagged, jutting stones. I pressed on, slowing frequently for goats and cows who had no interest at all in getting out of Whitey's way; staring moodily at me as I slowed to walking pace, manoeuvred the Dolphin carefully round them. Behind me, my arrogant dust cloud was lit orange, then pink, by the sinking sun.

The road got worse and worse; the landscape better and better. Lovely low hills scattered with huts. Here and there you could see a fire glowing through a doorway. Groups of children stood by the roadside, sometimes staring, sometimes grinning and waving.

In the rear-view mirror, the crimson sun set through the dust. I drove on, praying that I wouldn't get a puncture, wondering if I was still on the right road, as I came down in the darkness to an empty little valley with a cracked paving-stone bridge just wide enough to take one car; as I revved and roared in first and second gear to mount the dirt humps and dry gullies that passed for 'road' on the other side.

Eventually, just as I was giving up hope and preparing to turn back, I came up a hill and there ahead of me was a sign: WAVECREST. Miraculously, the road improved. And I could smell and sense the sea.

Below the hotel, a steep green lawn fell away to the still water of a river estuary at low tide. On the far side, beyond a fat spit of sand, a great semi-circular sweep of surf receded to the dark horizon. Inland, upriver, were the shadows of mysterious looking woods. Picked out by the moonlight a tall black and white bird . . . a crane? a heron? . . . stood on one leg, stock still in the centre of the river, its reflection rippling away beneath it.

The only thing spoiling it was the hotel: a cluster of twenty or thirty thatched *rondawels* around a run-down looking central building. There was a bar with big picture windows, leading out onto a wooden verandah with steps down to the lawn.

The place seemed deserted. Eventually I found a young guy with a New Zealand accent – Scott by name – and checked in. To *rondawel* no. 13, in the front row, where you could lie on your double bed with your head on your hands and get an uninterrupted view of paradise panorama.

I was exhausted. In the bar I avoided a bespectacled man

with a frazzled goatee beard and a very elderly woman who had to be his mother; listened with the heightened irritation of the dog-tired as he was unnecessarily rude to the plump black waitress at dinner ('Nah, you've brought this one with the cork in. Please take the cork *out*.'); and rolled into my double bed at 8.30, wishing I had someone beside me to share the rewards of being good all my life and ending up in heaven.

I woke at six, to draw back the curtains and watch a huge crimson sun moving slowly away from its perfect reflection in the river, the magical crescent of surf beyond.

It was a beautiful day so I decided to try my luck in the waves with the paddleski. This Serious Leisure Item was bright yellow, with the words WAVE RAVE emblazoned across it in fluorescent blue. It was shaped like a surfboard, with three stabilising fins beneath, and velcro straps to put around your waist and feet above. 'I should keep your feet dangling over the edge until you get used to it,' said Scott, cheerily.

I strapped myself on and paddled down river, wobbling nervously. It didn't feel at *all* stable, and I'd soon taken Scott's advice.

The tide-rip was stronger than I'd expected, and I was rapidly out of the river, in the thick of the surf, a shoaly looking line of low rocks a mere twenty yards or so to my right. I paddled keenly away towards the beach, but the rip pulled me ever closer to the rocks. Right, I thought, I won't panic, I'll turn, catch a wave, and be swept back in to shore.

And here it was that I came closest to being sent home in a box. Not necklaced by a gang of angry comrades in a township; not taken out in a cul-de-sac by one of Eugene Terreblanche's hooded henchmen; not even in a run-of-the-mill car crash: but predictably, in utterly trivial and unforeseen circumstances.

The wave I'd chosen flipped me over like a kipper. I was upside down below the board, gulping salt water, trying desperately to undo the velcro strap that was holding me under. I couldn't even *find* it, let alone undo it. Another wave biffed me, and I choked down a further lungful of sea. You can drown in two inches of water, I heard my mother saying, as I jerked furiously, trying to flip myself back. No deal. Oh Christ, I thought, as another wave thwacked me sideways, and I inhaled another pint, this is it, this is finally it, I'm going to die strapped to a WAVE RAVE out of my depth in the Wild Coast surf.

Just as my lost life started to flash before me – home, my family, my beautiful Sarah – a miracle happened. I felt sand under my feet. Not asking why, I reared up like Samson, the WAVE RAVE firmly strapped to my back. I gasped for one gulp of God's fresh air and fell over again, face down in the water, the RAVE on top of me. Oh shit, I thought, taking in another bucketful of ocean, this is your punishment for never bothering to get fit. Death. Oh Christ, how absurd, this is it, this is finally it . . .

God only knows how I eventually got upright – enough at any rate to tear back the killer velcro that was binding me to the board . . . but there I was, standing shaking like an alcoholic at a tea party in what I realised now was a mere eighteen inches of surf. What had happened? I'd been over there by the rocks. Some crazy current had swept me sideways onto a sandbank. Gee, that had been close.

Back at the hotel I phoned Sarah in London. She was at work, and didn't seem to be able to take me seriously. 'But have you been in any really *dangerous* situations?' she asked eagerly. 'Yes, yes,' I burbled, 'I just have been – I just . . .' It was impossible to explain. On the crackly Transkei line she sounded a million miles away.

The bar was empty that evening. Keen to reacquaint myself with the manifold delights of being alive I ordered a dry sherry and got into conversation with Scott. 'I imagine it's pretty busy in the summer,' I said, savouring the pleasure even of a conversation as boring as this.

'Whew!' he replied, in fluent Kiwi. 'You wouldn't believe

it. I'm fully booked for Christmas already. Already got a waiting list, in fact. No, it's great here in the summer. The place is packed with people. We do inflatable rides up the coast, take people out in the plane, and the women . . .' His lips went into overdrive, as he made a noise that was as close to *Woo-argh!* as I'd ever heard. 'The women . . .' he repeated, shaking his head, gesturing out at the empty lawn, conjuring up a sultry summer's night, fifty nymphomaniacs in bikinis lying around with cocktails just waiting to be ravished by a passing stud.

The next morning it was raining. I decided to push on. I wanted to have a look at Mazeppa Bay, which was a mere twenty kilometres up the coast, but would need a journey inland and out again of at least fifty. From there I could head back inland to Willowvale, sneak up dirt roads over the Bashee River, spend the night at The Haven, before driving down finally . . . and I wanted a perfect sunny day for this blind date with fantasy . . . to Coffee Bay.

I drove on across a gently rolling landscape. On the radio they were talking about the ANC Mass Action planned for the anniversary of the 1976 Soweto riots, on 16 June, just four days away. Inkatha had demanded a police presence in Pietermaritzburg. Political observers generally were concerned that this year's 16 June might turn out to be etc, etc, etc . . .

I passed a woman in tribal dress, her face whitened with clay, and felt relieved that I'd be away from South Africa, from any trouble, feeling free in the Transkei. I flicked up the radio dial, got an instrumental version of 'Imagine', and nearly crashed into a large black cow as I rounded a corner singing along.

A few miles further and I was in such a good mood I stopped to pick up a middle-aged guy in a brown pinstripe suit and Homburg hat. He was accompanied by a young woman whose relationship to him was not entirely clear. She jumped in the back; he, gleefully, in the front.

'Yes *baas*! Yes *baas*!' he cried enthusiastically. 'Butterworth!'

'I'm going to Mazeppa Bay. Not all the way to Butterworth, I'm afraid.'

'Butterworth!' he repeated.

'Mazeppa Bay is where I'm going. I'll have to drop you at the turning.'

'Butterworth!'

'I'm going to Mazeppa Bay. Maz-eppa Bay.'

His face fell. 'Oh, Mazeppa Bay.'

'Yes.'

He mused for a bit, then had a bright idea. 'Butterworth!' he said. 'Butterworth! *Then* Mazeppa Bay!'

'Butterworth isn't on the way to Mazeppa Bay.'

He smiled, a broad gap-toothed smile. 'Butterworth!' he repeated. 'Butterworth! *Then* Mazeppa Bay!'

I gave up the struggle. What the hell, I hadn't been that set on Mazeppa Bay.

At this time of the morning the road to Butterworth was lined with people wanting lifts. School-kids, mothers, young men. Every half mile or so another band appeared on the corner, and seeing a black face in the front turned their half-hopeful stuck out thumbs into a wild waving. But this black face had only one concern. 'Butterworth!' he repeated, gesturing forcefully on down the road. We weren't stopping for nobody.

Eventually we got there. I dropped him by the turn-off onto the main N2. 'Mazeppa Bay,' he said, with a broad smile, pointing up the road towards Umtata.

I drove on across drought-dry brown hills. Before I knew it I'd come upon a sign for Coffee Bay. Not only was the road to the coast tar – it was being resurfaced. Trucks and diggers shunted back and forth among red and white barriers and traffic cones. Oh dear, oh dear. This wasn't part of my fantasy at all. And the sky above was even greyer now: great banks of inky English-style cloud.

Beyond the roadworks I stopped for three African ladies who were like ebony versions of those Russian dolls that fit inside each other. One was large, the second larger, the third was so huge she could barely cram in the back. They were all extremely friendly.

'Where you from?' they asked.

'England,' I replied.

'Oh – just now?'

'A month ago.'

'Oh. My name – Patricia,' said the smallest one, who was in front.

'Mark,' I replied.

'Where you going, Mark?'

'Coffee Bay.'

'Coffee Bay,' they repeated to each other. The huge woman in the back said something in Xhosa and they all laughed.

'What did she say?'

'She said you should take her to sleep with you in Coffee Bay.'

I chuckled, as I hoped nonchalantly. The huge woman said something else.

'Now,' said Patricia, 'she says you should stay at Mqanduli and sleep with her there.'

'Really, I'm fine,' I said, a little nervously. These three could have trussed me up like a chicken if they'd wanted to.

We arrived at Mqanduli in silence. 'Here we are!' I said jovially. 'Here you go!' They clambered out with difficulty, laughing at their efforts to get through the doors. I waved goodbye and was greeted by two broad smiles and a scowl.

The landscape was getting hillier and greener now, altogether prettier. Deep wooded valleys and rounded grassy hills. The little road wound between them, pockmarked with holes. Every few miles a cluster of blue and white huts, groups of children grinning and waving by the roadside.

Then glimpses of sea were visible and I was coming down a long hill . . . to Coffee Bay. At the bottom there was a T-junction and two battered signboards. Ocean View Hotel to the left. Lagoon Hotel to the right. I chose Ocean View, and found myself approaching a barrier with a uniformed security guard. I drove through and checked into a low, square, modern building painted an attractive shade of seasick green. The lounge was done out in pink and green, with potted palms, bright lights, cane chairs.

I paced down past empty sun-loungers and a deserted thatched bar area to the beach. It *was* beautiful, but not in the way I'd pictured. The sand was darker, the headlands taller. It was, in fact, just like north Cornwall on a dull day in October. The sky and sea were the same shades of grey and blue. The surf pounded into the black and purple rocks in the same way. The headlands were more rounded than Cornish cliffs, but the view up the coast was much the same. Only the dots of the little blue huts made the difference.

Walking back, I thought I'd check out the Lagoon Hotel. It was boarded up. Voices and laughter came from what had once been a beach-hut area. Somebody had turned one of them into an improvised shebeen. I turned, and was just striding back over the beach when I heard a shout.

'Oya! Oya!' There were two, three, four of them, big black teenagers running after me. Shit, I thought, with the instant reflex of the Western whitey, I've got three hundred rand on me. Was this what was going to happen? On Coffee Bay? Mugged in the rain. That would teach me to have an imagination.

'You want to smoke dope?' said the first of them, catching up with me. He was dressed in truly tattered rags. 'I have good dope.'

'No, really,' I said, marching on, 'I'm fine.'

'Can you give me two rand, sir, for some bread, please.' He jumped along after me. 'Please, just give me two rand, please, sir, two rand, sir, please sir . . .'

I gave him a rand, and he ran off shrieking with excitement. It was the wrong thing to have done. Two others ran up; they each had to have a rand. Three more materialised from nowhere.

'You give our friends money, now they're saying they've got money off you but not us.'

I stopped. 'OK,' I said, 'one rand each. But then – I walk on alone to the hotel. OK?'

It was a long beach. I reached the hotel with an entourage of nine teenagers, each offering a different service: dope, carwash, guided tour of the cliffs . . .

11

SATURDAY NIGHT IN PORT ST JOHNS

I had two or three contacts in Umtata. A couple who ran a mission hospital; a white lawyer friend of Alex's who was – he'd told me – heavily 'in' with Brigadier Holomisa, the ruler of the Transkei; a man who was 'big in forestry', who had a charming wife.

But somehow I'd lost my nerve. I just couldn't bring myself to phone any of them. I couldn't summon up the energy to be interested and appropriate and . . . no, no I just wasn't in the mood for *any* of that.

The sky was blue; the Transkei landscape even lovelier in the sunshine. A couple of boys on a bicycle freewheeled down a hill. Women walked up the roadside with long bales of straw balanced on their heads. Groups of kids played football at makeshift goalposts. A colourfully-dressed young man galloped past on a black horse. In the village centre, Saturday morning meetings were taking place, forty or fifty men sitting talking.

I drove on into the hot, bright, crowded centre of Umtata, stopping for nobody. It was paradoxical: that I felt utterly lonely; yet the last thing I wanted to do was phone anybody. It was like that state you can get into where you know the only thing that'll stop you feeling nervous is to eat, and yet you're too nervous to eat.

To try and break the cycle I stopped the car and opened a

beer; and as soon as I'd had two sips I knew what I wanted to do. I wanted to go back to the sea; to Port St Johns, where the hippies hung out. Alex, Rosie, Otto . . . they'd all said I should see Port St Johns.

The road east was good and fast, and I was moving through spectacular scenery, curving down through the mountainous valley of the Mlengana Pass. Within an hour, I was coming down a long hill, to my left were the rippling blue waters of the Umzimvubu River, tall crumbling white cliffs on the far side . . . I'd arrived.

First Beach was wide and flat and uninteresting. The place looked semi-derelict: tatty hoardings and the blackened walls of a burnt-out shop being the immediate impression. But I'd been tipped the wink by Otto, so I drove on, over a leafy little hill, to Second Beach.

Which was as perfect as he'd described. A little sandy horseshoe of a cove, fringed with palm trees. On the far side, there were three whites with long hair sitting in the sunshine smoking a huge joint. There really were. Central Casting couldn't have done better.

At the top of the beach was a run-down looking bar. It was thatched, with a tatty terrace outside, and inside a restaurant whose pink tablecloths and white wicker chairs had clearly seen better days. Stage left a door led into a shop and off-licence. At a table by the restaurant entrance a black guy in a red beret was musing his way through a large bottle of Castle. Over a heavily distorting speaker came the sound of jazz.

I went inside and sat down. The back of my wicker chair gave way, and I just saved myself from falling backwards onto the floor. A large woman in pink overalls with one tooth appeared, handed me a grubby typed menu. It offered five different crayfish dishes, mussels, calamari, line-fish, kingklip and three different types of steak.

'What's the line-fish?' I asked.

'No line-fish,' she replied curtly. 'No crayfish, mussels, line-fish, steak or calamari. We got kingklip or T-bone.'

'What's the kingklip like?'

'It's a fish.'

'OK – I'll have a kingklip and a beer.'

I was mellowing into it. With a couple of beers and a kingklip inside me, the place had taken on a Graham Greene feel. Just over the other side of the terrace a blue public phone box – slightly askew – stood next to a blue plastic dustbin. Beyond, through the twisting green trees, the sea and surf was wonderfully – no, not blue, more turquoise and white in the bright afternoon sun.

Hm. This was definitely a place to hang out. I checked into a *rondawel* in the municipal campsite on the far side of the beach.

The sun set behind the woods. I sat against a rock as the sky went deep ochre, then threw up that familiar crimson blush; as the treeline darkened to a shimmering green-black silhouette.

By eight o'clock the bar was crowded with black revellers. At a table by the shop entrance sat a lone white who looked like Richard Branson after a bad acid trip. He was nodding and grinning toothily at his companions, three or four young black girls. The door to the restaurant was locked. But through the window I could see a white family – Mum, Dad, and three teenage kids – enjoying a meal.

'Can I get some supper?' I asked the woman in the shop. As she unlocked the door to let me in, a girl in a smart red and black jersey and a black baseball cap came through with me, sat at the adjoining table. She was no more than nineteen, with large liquid eyes and an exquisite figure. I looked over at her; she looked away. Looking away, I sensed her looking at me. I looked back, she looked away. The cycle was broken by the one-toothed waitress, who arrived with menus. 'Hello,' she said to me warmly; breaking into a huge smile I wasn't expecting.

I ordered steak and chips. The girl in the jersey just wanted chips.

'Not in here,' said the waitress. 'If you want chips you must eat them in the shop.'

The girl protested angrily in Xhosa. Then: 'I came in with him,' she shouted in English. 'He is my friend. I came in with him.'

The waitress went off: to return a minute later with the woman from the shop. Unceremoniously, they took one arm each and dragged the girl to the door. But as they unlocked it, five or six others tumbled in. A ferocious argument ensued, with the girl in the jersey leading the shouting, pointing again and again at me. Finally the big waitress lost patience: grabbing her arm, she yanked it into a vicious half-nelson and threw her out, pushing the others after her.

The door was locked and Security was summoned. Security was a doddery old guy in an orange boiler suit and a yellow woolly hat who carried a big stick. He stood just this side of the door, trying to look ferocious. He was clearly terrified.

Outside on the terrace, the girl in the jersey was now creating a massive scene, screaming and shouting and pointing through the window at me. 'Why *can't* I go in there? Is it because I'm not white? Is it because I'm black and he's white?' she yelled.

At the white family's table, Dad refilled his glass with sparkling wine and calmly explained the situation: 'She's just had too much to drink, and so you mustn't *warry* . . .' His kids didn't seem to give a damn, making faces at each other and giggling.

There was a hammering at the door. A friend of Security's. He unlocked it, and they wandered off to the kitchen, forgetting – oh dear – to relock it. Somebody outside realised it was open, and in they all tumbled again, the girl in the jersey and twenty-five others. Security came running out from the kitchen, rushed at them waving his big stick. Nobody took any notice.

Two large black guys had joined me at my table, sitting down on either side of me as I ate. 'They're students from UNITRA – University of Transkei,' they said. 'They've all had too much to drink. *You* mustn't worry about them.'

Michael was a soldier at the Port St Johns military base on First Beach. His brother Eliot wanted to be a lawyer, but at the moment was out of work. He was very friendly, with a broad smile and wide popping out eyes in an oval face. Michael was quieter. He had a triangular-shaped jaw, and thoughtful brown eyes.

'We will *kill* you,' screamed the girl in the jersey, as the waitress muscled her back through the door. 'We will *kill* you.'

'Perhaps I should go outside,' I said to my new friends. 'Maybe that would defuse things a little.'

'Don't *you* worry about it,' Eliot repeated.

I went through to the kitchen to pay, and found the waitress standing clutching the bar of the cooking range, shaking with sobs. 'Are you OK?' I asked. She didn't nod, just stared at me through her tears. 'Can I pay you?'

'I bring the bill,' she managed finally.

'It wasn't your fault,' I said. 'You were only doing your job.'

She looked blankly at me, carried on sobbing.

When she brought the bill, she was still weeping. Eliot jumped up, put his arm around her, escorted her off to the kitchen, comforting her in rapid Xhosa. Michael shook his head and smiled, gazed back towards the floor.

Outside, at a wobbly circular table, we were joined by Richard-Branson-on-acid, whose name was Dave. Then by a pretty coffee-coloured girl with a gap tooth, called Julie.

Michael was teaching me how to speak Xhosa. '"Molo"', he said, 'is "hello".' 'Mo-lo,' I repeated. '"Nkosi", he said, is "thank you".' This had an impossible Xhosa click. 'K-k-tch-k-tluk-tchick,' I went, trying to get it right. 'In Botswana,' I said, 'there aren't any clicks. You just say, "Dumêla rra – A o tsogile rra? – Ke tsogile sentle."' I ran off the greeting ceremony in a burst and Michael laughed. 'If you like a girl in Botswana,' I went on, 'you say, "A o batla ho jola?"' Michael laughed some more. 'In Xhosa,' he said, 'we say, "Ndiyaku thanda. Awundi thandi *na*?" – "I love you. Do you want to be in love with me?" And then: "Umuhle" [this last pronounced "Oom schleh"] – "You are beautiful".' 'Oom schleh,' I repeated. 'Ndyaka thande awundu thandi *na*?' 'No,' said Michael, laughing. 'Ndi-ya-ku thand*a*. Awun-*di* thandi *na*.'

A slim girl in a white jersey came over. She was very dark, with high cheekbones in a beautiful oblong face. She reminded me of one of the girls I'd taught all those years ago. I remembered how all the black faces had started off seeming the same, and then slowly you'd learn to differentiate, slowly you'd move away from Western types of beauty, to appreciate something much more African; until finally all we teacher aids had agreed that we found the white expat women, lounging around frazzling by their swimming pools, horrible to look at.

I bought some more beers. The edges were clouding. We were sitting in this romantic spot, in a crowd of Africans, chattering and laughing, Dave, Eliot, Michael, Julie and I. Out beyond the palm trees . . . the beach, the all-but-full moon, the surf . . .

'I've got an African wife now and she makes me very happy,' said Dave, 'but she's been away for three months, and tonight,' his lips twisted into lecherous grimace, 'tonight I just feel . . . *whoo-argh* . . . ready to go.'

The girls from the student party kept approaching our table, making some comment or other in Xhosa, then backing off. 'That woman in there,' said the girl in the jersey, appearing to the left of my range of vision suddenly, 'I want to *kill* her. We all want to *kill* her.'

I liked Julie. She had a nice laugh, and there was an appealingly straightforward quality about her. As we talked together, Eliot kept poking his head in, laughing to himself, shaking his head, singing: 'If I could have you-ou, bay-bee . . .'

Julie wanted to go to a disco that was going on round the back. It was five rand to get in. I paid for Michael and Eliot – no, I wasn't paying for Dave. Julie had managed to get in free.

It was like a time warp. Thirty or forty tousled hippy mops. Mostly white, some coloured, a sprinkling of blacks. The DJ was a magnificent specimen. He had hair down to his chest (just visible behind his beaded waiscoat), a painted face, a long beard.

Julie and I took to the floor. She looked bored. I tried to get her smiling, in that way that you do in discos, leaning forward as you're dancing and saying something in your partner's ear. It didn't work. She bopped on, looking a little swamped in my suede jacket.

I went to get another beer, left her to dance with Eliot and Michael. Outside, the smell of marijuana hung heavy on the air.

Later, after a long slow dance, I said, 'D'you want to go to the beach?' 'OK,' she replied, nodding. We ran out, down past the bar and through the trees, across the brightly moonlit beach to some dunes, where we held hands and watched the sea, eventually falling into a kiss.

'D'you want to come back to my little hut with me?' I asked. 'Can we go back to the disco, just for an hour or two?' she said, holding herself to me. 'Then I'll come back with you.'

Back at the disco, she vanished. There was some sort of fight going on at the gate to the road. I asked Dave what was happening. 'Julie's got a husband out there, making some trouble,' he said. 'You want to be careful, you get involved with these coloured chicks, you could end up with a dagger in your back. You leave here, you wouldn't even make it across the beach. I'm just warning you.'

It was time to go. Comatose with Castle as I was – no, I wasn't going to risk getting murdered over Julie.

But my jacket had gone. From the wicker chair where I'd left it. Oh shit. My precious suede jacket, half my wardrobe. Julie reappeared. 'Let's just see where those guys went,' she said, taking charge.

Eliot was wearing it. 'Can you get it off him?' I said. I stood in the shadows as he and Julie quarrelled, shouting at each other in Xhosa. Eventually: 'Hi, Eliot,' I said. 'Could I have my jacket back, I'm just cold, you know . . .' He calmed down suddenly and gave it to me. 'Thanks,' I said. But he wasn't too friendly any more.

'What was the fight about?' I asked her.

'Oh, just some guys.'

'Have you got a husband here, Julie?'

'No. I promise you – no, I haven't got a husband here.'

'D'you promise me? I'm trusting you, Julie.'

'You can trust me,' she said. 'You *can* trust me.'

'Dave said you had a husband.'

'He's only saying that because he wants me – don't worry about it.'

So we were dancing alone. Michael and Eliot sat on opposite sides of the disco, bent over on hard chairs, their heads in their hands, sleeping. Then the place had filled up again, and I was slumped in my wicker chair thinking: whatever else is true, that old cliché is true, boy can the Africans dance. Even *walking* across the floor they have ten times more style than the most frenetically grooving whitey.

Julie was bopping with three big black guys with shorts and sunglasses, laughing her head off, far more animated than she'd ever been with me. Lust and disappointment took turns in my drunken brain.

The last dance came on. And off. Silence. 'More music!' chanted the crowd. One of the guys in shorts was boogying around on his own: 'If music be the food of love, play on!' he shouted.

Half way across the beach, I stopped, looked at Julie and said: 'If you don't want to come back with me, you don't have to. Really.'

'You do what you want,' she replied simply.

In the night she told me she'd had four other white lovers. 'I'm not lying to you, Mark. Four.' She was twenty. She'd 'fallen pregnant' when she was seventeen, had a child who lived with her mother on First Beach. She had a boyfriend who lived in Umtata, came down to see her every other weekend.

I woke in the early morning in the dark. Oh Christ, what had happened? I'd slept with an African woman, unprotected. Oh god, only now did it hit me what I'd done. Been unfaithful to Sarah, and who knew what Julie's past was? Or what the boyfriend in Umtata got up to in his weekends away?

But that was it. There was no rewind mechanism. I lay awake as the daylight came up on the curtains.

In the campsite washroom all the showers were broken. I stood under a stream of tepid water, shaking my head from side to side and groaning – I didn't even have a towel . . . dried myself off with a damp T-shirt . . .

When I returned, Julie had made both beds, tidied the room, and was lying on one, fully dressed, with an unhappy look on her face. I sat down next to her. 'Are you OK?' I said, stroking her forehead gently. She nodded.

'What are you thinking?' I asked.

'Nothing.'

'Are you sorry you stayed the night with me?'

She shook her head. 'No.'

'I've got to go on today,' I lied. 'I've got appointments in Durban, which I've got to get to – for tomorrow.'

'It's OK,' she said, looking down at the floor.

'You go down to the beach,' I said, 'and I'll just take the hut key back to the office, and I'll see you on the beach.'

I was sorely tempted just to get in my big white Dolphin and go. Leave the whole stupid mess behind. But I couldn't leave her just sitting on the beach.

She was waiting for me on a rock. 'Let's go and sit in the sun by the sand dunes,' I said. I bought us some little cartons of orange juice from the shop, and we sat there, side by side, making desultory conversation. Every now and then a black guy would wander onto the beach, see us, come up and ask for money.

They have no jobs,' Julie said. 'They see you're white and want money.' In Xhosa, with them, she was fast and animated; with me, slow and straight-faced.

'Does it get very humid in the summer?' I asked.

'What's that?'

'Humid. You know – damp – in the air?'

'Dam . . .?'

'In the air. Does the air – get – hot and wet . . .?'

And so on. Language was just one of the things between us.

A white family trooped onto the beach, looking like something from a sepia snapshot of the 1930s. Father was wearing lace-up brown shoes and pale blue socks up to his knees. His three little girls had long dresses. One had a floppy straw hat. Mother and Nanny – in uniform – followed behind. Father looked over at me and Julie on our sand dune, and gave us a look that was more resigned than outright disapproving. He led his family on, well beyond us. From where I sat with Julie, their whiteness, their polite clear South African accents stood out in a new way.

I tried to get things moving by telling her about England. How cold and wet it was. The Welfare State. How you could get your rent paid and the equivalent of two hundred rand a week if you were out of work. Julie was incredulous. 'I should go to England,' she said. Then 'Do a lot of white men marry [she pronounced it "merry"] coloured girls in London?'

'Some,' I said. 'But it's different. There aren't so many coloured girls around.'

We sat in silence, watching a group of ten or fifteen kids playing football by the surf. 'Some of those boys break into cars,' she said. 'When people go on the beach or something.'

'To steal radios?'

'Yeah. Radios or whatever. Or they steal things from the beach. There are some bigger boys who use knives – but they are in prison now. They let them out in the summer. It's always the same. The police find them and put them in prison – but in the summer, they let them out.'

The idea of changing my mind, staying on for a while at Julie's place, came into my head. No.

'I better go now,' she said suddenly.

'Yes, I've got to go too,' I said. 'Get on to Durban. OK then,' I added, as she walked away. 'I know where I can find you if I come back this way.'

'In the café. I'm always in the café.'

'See you then.'

'See you.'

12

MASS ACTION

I crossed the Umzimvubu and drove up into the hills. A surprisingly lush landscape. Green wooded valleys, a functional stream. Bushes hung with yellow flowers thick on both sides of the potholed dirt road.

But I couldn't relate to it at all. I felt hungover and sick. The sun, shining hot through the windscreen, made me feel as if I was about to throw up any second.

There was nothing, *nothing* I could do. It had happened. Of course you haven't got AIDS, said an upbeat voice in my head. But what if you have, said an altogether more realistic one. *What if you have*? And what would I say to Sarah? I couldn't even be *tested* for three months.

I drove on, through a dried-out version of the Western Highlands, to Flagstaff. Originally I'd planned to turn right, swoop down the tar road to the Wild Coast Sun, the casino resort just this side of the Transkei border. But I was hardly in the mood for making satirical jibes about white South Africans who came over the border to gamble and have mixed-race sex. So I headed straight on. If I kept my foot down I could reach the mountains by nightfall. And not just any old mountains, but the Drakensberg, South Africa's most famous range, a walker and hiker's paradise, snow-capped in winter, awash with wild flowers in the summer. Something else I'd missed out on last time, something else a hundred white South Africans had urged me to see.

This way out of the Transkei, there was no border post. But a few miles over the 'border' a white with a lone ranger face under a baseball cap and a gun swinging from his denims waved me down. 'Just a routine police check,' he said, taking a good look at my suntan. 'You want to search in the car?' I said obligingly. 'No, drive on.' Two cars full of blacks were being thoroughly taken apart on the lay-by.

It was getting dark. And cold. I sped on, on a road with burnt black firebreak verges, through a low hilly landscape that looked as if it had been collaged out of cornflakes.

At Ye Olde Himeville Inn there was nobody at home. I rang the bell fruitlessly at reception for three minutes. Eventually I found a backroom where four black maids in pink caps were watching TV, and succeeded in persuading them to let me check in. My room was icy cold and stank of cleaning fluid. I felt dreadful; sick, tired and dreadful.

I had a bath, got into thermal underwear, two jerseys and a dressing gown, and went shivering to bed. Room service had never heard of Bovril. 'Have you got Marmite?' I asked. 'No, sah,' said the blank-faced maid. 'Isn't there a white manager in this place, somebody I could *talk* to?' I didn't say it; but the thought was in my head before I could stop it. Truly, I was back in South Africa.

In the end I had dry toast and *rooibos* tea. I sat up in bed, as weak as the tea, reading the *Mountain Echo.* FIRE DANGER ran the headline. 'This year there are all the signs of a difficult fire season, and the Fire Chief John Nicholson appeals to everybody to be more careful . . .' Another head-line said: WATCH OUT FOR HEAT STRESS IN RABBITS. Shivering, with the pong of cleaning fluid in my nostrils, it didn't even raise a smile.

So. It was 15 June. The day before the anniversary of the 1976 Soweto riots and the start of the nationwide ANC Mass

Action. I had moved along faster than I'd hoped, and was now only just over 130 kilometres from Pietermaritzburg, where Inkatha had demanded that the army be called in to control the potential violence.

So how could I be writing about South Africa, be an hour's drive from a potentially historic occasion, and miss it? Just because I was scared. Of what? Being hit by a stray bullet, pulled from my car by an angry mob? It was hardly likely.

I decided to drive up into the mountains and think about it. Just north of Himeville was the Sani Pass, the only southern route up into Lesotho, the little landlocked mountain kingdom whose borders are all higher than 1,000 metres above sea level, known by some as 'the Switzerland of Africa'. Despite being surrounded by and economically dependent on South Africa, Lesotho is not a homeland, but a genuinely separate country, with a king, a representative at the UN, and a High Commission in Collingham Rd, London SW5 – and I'd always wanted to see it.

The only thing stopping me now was the fact that the Dolphin didn't have four wheel drive; and without that they won't let you in through the border post. Nonetheless, I thought I'd test my white beast's mettle by seeing how far up the Sani Pass I could get on the South African side.

Not very far, as it turned out. After a promising start, the dirt road suddenly became alarmingly steep. On the tight curves above the drought-dry valley the Dolphin was doing its best, but the road had narrowed and I had a sudden vision of being stuck on a slope with no way of turning back and only the handbrake between me and a fiery explosion at the bottom. I took advantage of what may well have been the last medium wide stretch of road to do a nervous seventeen-point turn.

I put the car in gear, double-checked the handbrake and got out. It was wonderfully still; only the birdsong and the distant splash of the stream far below in the valley.

Ahead, the rust-brown grass, dotted here and there with

little green trees, climbed up and up to the towering rock face of the escarpment, still in dark blue shadow, though it was almost noon.

I sat in the sun and caught up on my notes. Every twenty minutes or so there would be a distant roar up in the mountains, the grinding of gears on the bends, and a truck or lorry would rattle past, a black face going back into South Africa. Then I heard a vehicle bumping up the other way, and suddenly I was no longer alone. A white of around my age, with straw blond hair and a bushy moustache to match, had parked, got out, and now stood silently a couple of yards above me. I squinted up at him.

'Beautiful spot,' I said.

'It is,' he replied, shaking his head slowly and pursing his lips. He looked at the plates on my car. 'You from Cape Town?'

'No – I'm English.'

'*English*. You on holiday?'

'Sort of thing. Are you going on up?'

'How far d'you reckon I could get?'

'If you want to go into Lesotho you need four wheel drive – they won't let you through the border otherwise.'

'Is that so? I may drive on a bit.'

He'd come up, he said, to get away from everything, do a bit of thinking. He was staying with his *boet* in Himeville for a few days.

'Your – boot?'

'Sorry,' he smiled. 'You're English. My brother.' He looked around slowly. Then: 'I'm actually up here avoiding the call-up.'

'The call-up?'

'Yeah. For tomorrow – June the 16th. You know about that? Mass Action.'

'Are you in the army?'

'I was. Everyone has to be. And once you've been in it they can just call you up at any time. They say they've called up 500,000 for tomorrow. I'm supposed to be at some bloody place in Pietermaritzburg. Got the notice on Friday. But if they ask, I'll just say I was away and the call-up was in the post-box.'

'What will it be like? If I drive down there. I'm quite interested to see it.'

'Oh, don't worry, it'll all be under control. Just don't drive anywhere near the townships, you'll be OK.'

He was Scottish, he told me. His parents had come out when he was seven and had never gone back. Now he worked at Pietermaritzburg University in the Maintenance Department.

'Which is, what – a white university?'

'No, not now. It's 60% black now.' He paused. 'And that's what makes me really angry. By the year 2000, it's going to be something like 80% black. I'm sorry,' he said, 'I'm not a liberal. I hate the blacks. The sooner they start putting bullets in them the better.'

I took a deep breath and looked out over the lovely valley.

'I think I've got more racist since working at the university,' he went on. 'You know, the white liberals that work there,' he shook his head, 'full of shit. Still, everybody knows my views now, we don't have any more arguments, we don't even start.'

'Right,' I said.

'But the blacks,' he went on. 'They don't even get proper degrees. They just push them through and hand out the diplomas at the end. OK, you get one or two intelligent blacks, but most of them are thick as pigshit. Thick – as – pigshit. I'm telling you, they're just animals, blacks. They're a different race. You're English. You don't know how it is unless you've lived here. You go to a university party, the white people will be there, they might just have a bit of whatever, but the blacks – they don't know how to behave. They're gulping down the wine like – like – ' he gestured furiously, 'then they're just going at the food, tearing the tinfoil off . . .' He shook his head.

'Students . . .' I said.

'Students, parents, whatever. I'm telling you, they're a different race.' He gestured at the empty mountains. 'Before we even got here,' he said, 'what did they do? Nothing.'

I couldn't quite work out why he'd picked on the mountains. For the whites hadn't done that much with them either. Indeed, the only person who had done anything with them, other than hike and build luxury hotels on them, was King Moshoeshoe I, the founder of Lesotho, who'd used the natural barrier they provided to protect his people from the murderous regiments of the Zulu King Shaka, not to mention the marauding Boers. I contemplated giving him a brief history lesson, but he was already on to . . .

'Take Zimbabwe. Ten years ago that was a beautiful country . . .'

He ranted on. Apart from the blacks, the English were the worst. They'd come out here, and *god* – [he pronounced this in the Afrikaans manner – *hut*] they were a terrible bunch of racists. And as soon as the shit started to hit the fan, they'd got out, just like everywhere else they'd colonised. The English and the Irish – they were the sort of people who would call a kaffir a kaffir to his face, just to annoy him. 'I mean,' he said, 'I'll call a kaffir a kaffir behind his back, but not to his face. I may be a racist, but I do know how to treat a black. They respect me, I respect them.'

'Right,' I said.

'The Zulus are OK. I don't mind the Zulus – but Inkatha – they're the slimiest bunch of blacks you've ever seen.'

'Inkatha *is* Zulu, surely?'

'What am I saying? Sorry – the ANC – the Xhosas, they're a slimy bunch. Look,' he went on, 'there may have been some things wrong with apartheid, but things were far better for everyone twenty years ago. The blacks were happier.

Now they're not happy. They don't smile in the way they used to.'

'I've seen quite a lot of smiling black faces,' I said. 'In fact, almost everywhere I've gone, that's been something I've noticed – the smiling black faces.'

'Zulus,' he said, pensively. 'Yah, the Zulus still smile. But not the others.' I didn't tell him I'd only met three Zulus so far, none of whom, come to think of it, had been great smilers.

'Why don't you just leave?' I asked.

'If things get really bad, I will.'

'You've still got a British passport?'

'Yes. But it's not that easy. I could go back to Scotland, but I don't think I could face it. The cold. This is a beautiful country.'

Speeding south-east in the late afternoon, the Drakensberg did indeed look spectacular in my rear-view mirror: the jagged outline of the highest mountains the palest blue; the lower ranges a series of cobalt cutouts; the flat sunlit streak of the burnt orange plain in front of them. A few cows made tiny silhouettes against the glow.

At the crossroads in Underberg, a big black guy had attracted a crowd with a puppet. It was a white girl with a mane of blonde hair, dancing to his tune.

I drove on in the dusk. Without a clue as to where I might stay. A sign said Ixopo, and I suddenly remembered that famous first line of *Cry, The Beloved Country*, 'There is a lovely road from Ixopo down to the sea . . .' Well, I thought, even if it turns out to be entirely full of Alan Paton bars and *Beloved Country* teashops, I'll put up in Ixopo. Then tomorrow I can take the lovely road down to the sea. That way I can get to Durban without going anywhere near Pietermaritzburg.

In the Plough Hotel there was no mention of Alan Paton, a beautiful coloured girl at reception, no loo paper in the

bathroom and an Afrikaans Bible by the bed. At midnight,
through my open window, the chatter drifting up from the
African bar sounded unusually wild and excited. Did they
know something about tomorrow that we whiteys didn't?
Were we all going to be murdered in our beds?

But in the morning sunshine everything in Ixopo was
peaceful. The *Natal Witness* had a huge headline, taking up
half the front page, which read simply:

JUNE 16TH

> The ANC today launches its national campaign of
> mass action to accelerate movement towards an
> interim government. The organisation's strategy to
> exert pressure on negotiations was triggered by
> hitches at CODESA II last month between it and the
> government.
>   The action is scheduled to start in main centres
> with rallies commemorating Soweto Day building up
> to mass stay-aways, disruption of business and a
> general strike to force the abdication of the
> government within months . . .

The lovely road from Ixopo to the sea wasn't quite as I'd
remembered it from the book. It now ran through one of the
forty-four pieces of the Kwazulu homeland. Although the
'border' was not marked by even a signpost, it was easy
enough to spot it. South Africa was huge green fields of
sugar cane, little signposts at the gates to farm driveways
saying J. VAN DER BYL or C. PRINGLE. Kwazulu was groups of
huts on the tops of over-grazed hills, smoking fires, the
roadside suddenly full of blacks with piles of luggage waiting for African taxis.

I arrived on the Natal south coast, drove up a coast road
dotted with dreary-looking little resorts. Here, the Mass
Action seemed to have taken the form of mass fishing. The
shore was full of blacks and Indians, standing out on the

rocks casting lines into the surf. More arrived every moment, unloading rods and wives in saris and endless children from their battered cars.

Before I knew it, I was on the motorway racing into Durban. JUNE 16TH. And Pietermaritzburg still only just over an hour away. Come on, I said to myself, gearing myself up for the *volte-face* that is the privilege of the traveller alone, you are turning your back on History.

So I completed the last section of my giant circle of funk and cut up through the rippling green hills of sugar cane to Pietermaritzburg, drove down the long hill into the town centre with my heart in my mouth.

But the streets were completely quiet. Smartly dressed white office workers walked briskly through a grassy square littered with autumn leaves. What blacks I did see were strolling, laughing, going about their business. There were a few soldiers, in pairs, but they seemed unaggressive, even casual.

So I walked around the empty central streets of Pietermaritzburg. I admired the fine forty-seven metre high clock tower of the city hall (completed 1900); I nodded thoughtfully at the red brick of the Supreme Court (completed 1871); I paid one rand and toured round the Natal Museum, which was full of stuffed wild animals and a well-laid-out history of South African costume. In Shuter and Shuter (the famous bookstore) I finally found a slim book on South African trees. And looking up *Cry, The Beloved Country* was appalled to see that my day had been even more absurd and fruitless than I'd thought. 'There is a lovely road that runs from Ixopo up into the hills . . .' ran the first line.

13

A MIXED MASALA

It was nice being with a family for a while. Just being able to mooch around the kitchen, microwave myself a bit of cheese on toast or make a cup of tea, slump in a chair with a book, watch TV. OK, so it wasn't very Jack Kerouac, but what the hell – I'd had enough of cold hotel rooms and splendid meals alone.

Gerald and Mari were contacts. Mari was the Irish aunt of a cousin-in-law, a warm, sensitive, gently humorous woman who helped out part time at the local primary school. Gerald was the South African she'd met while working as a nurse in what was then Rhodesia. He had an Afrikaans-sounding surname that turned out to be of German origin; though to look at he reminded me more of a turn of the century Russian. He had a pointed goatee beard and little round glasses, and would have looked perfectly at home striding onto a Chekhovian verandah: Yevgheniy Serghyeevich, the doctor; or Semion Semionovich, the schoolmaster.

He was a research fellow at the University of Natal and a great talker, taking a keen interest in politics and current affairs. He was full of suggestions of people I should go and visit in Durban. X at the University of Natal would give me the economic background, Y was an expert on the black-on-black violence, and I couldn't possibly leave without seeing Z at the University of Durban Westville.

Gerald and Mari had three children. Katie was thirteen and on the turn into adolescence, quiet and bright with an ironic smile, short brown hair and glasses. Peter was eleven and had the flu. Annie, seven, had blue eyes and tumbling ginger hair, and knew exactly how adorable she was. Katie spent most of her time in her room, working and listening to records; Peter and Annie lay on the floor of the sitting room alternately fighting and staring at the telly.

'How can you watch that rubbish?' Gerald would yell, as they flicked across to yet another American sit-com. Little, I thought, did Equity realise the effect of their long cultural boycott of South Africa. Deprived of all English TV, little Annie had adopted all the mannerisms of the sugar-pie American kids from the telly. 'Oh no, Daddee,' she would intone, fluttering her eyelashes. She could have jumped through the screen in her blue dressing gown and into *Roseanne* or *Loving*, no questions asked.

Their house – naturally – was heavily fortified. Here again were the ubiquitous burglar bars, double locks, alarms. I was staying in the old maid's quarters at the back, and to get to my room I had to let myself out through a heavy steel gate, walk ten yards through the garden, and let myself in – *clang!* – through another steel gate.

They lived in Kloof, a prosperous white suburb up on the hills to the east of the city. From there, Durban sprawled thirty kilometres down either side of two big urban freeways to the high rise blocks of the city centre, the port and the sea. From north to south it stretched equally as far, from the townships of Inanda and Kwa-Mashu in the north to Umlazi and the Indian location of Chatsworth in the south.

I had no idea where to start. Gerald sat me down and drew me a rough sketch map. You could picture Durban as built around a 'T' – or rather, a series of Ts – of high ground. Just inland from, and parallel to, the coast was the Berea Ridge. Running down towards it from the hills of Kloof, was the high ground of Pinetown, Westville, Queensburgh: on these

I would find the plusher suburbs, the universities and so on; down here in the valleys in between, and on the fringes of the main city, the African townships had sprung up. The first thing I should do was visit the townships.

I explained that I'd already seen Khayelitsha and Crossroads and Soweto-by-the-Sea and, really, townships was one thing I thought I could miss in this particular city.

No, Gerald said. Here it was very different. Because the Durban townships abutted onto the Kwazulu homeland, the blacks had a complex form of title that amounted to ownership of their plots. 'So with security of tenure you see a completely different story. They've started with the same basic housing units, but some of them have been improved out of all recognition. That's all you need, you see – security of tenure.'

The other crucial thing about Durban was the Inkatha–ANC rivalry. Township areas were strictly aligned to one side or the other. And the battle was not – as was popularly believed in the white community – a tribal Zulu-Xhosa clash, but more of a fight between the older traditional Zulus, loyal to their chiefs, Buthelezi and the Zulu King, and the younger urbanised Zulus, who had turned their backs on all those old-fashioned systems of tribal patronage, and supported the ANC.

So it was that I found myself doing a rather different sort of township tour, with Jackson, a burly middle-aged black working for an NGO which he was adamant that I didn't identify. 'In this city, you've got to be careful,' he said, as he drove me out along the freeway towards the airport. 'Ve-ry careful. I myself am not lined up politically.'

'Really not?'

'Really not.' Jackson looked at me, raised an eyebrow, and smiled. 'Or Mark, shall I say this – if I have any kind of sympathies, I keep them in my heart.' One hand on the wheel, he patted his chest. 'You see, politics is a power game. You just get a lot of people posturing. A fellow like me has a problem with that. And so, when you ask me who I support, I reply, "Let's wait and see." I don't know, man,' he went on, 'I'm despondent. I wouldn't be standing on platforms and saying this, no, not with the violence that's taking place. You've got children to bring up, you've got a family to look after . . .' He shook his head, and nodded thoughtfully. 'That's why people have said "Politics is a dirty game."'

'A very dirty game if people are killing each other,' I said.

'Exactly, Mark, ex-*act*ly. Now this referendum they've just had, back in March, this white referendum: in my opinion, the blacks should take note of that. These whites, they went through this referendum without any sign of violence. It went without a hitch. Now, why can't the blacks follow that route? That's why a person like me has a problem. You see, I sometimes feel that the concept of democracy in Africa has a problem. The leaders want to amass as much power as possible, you see. You see.'

We had driven off the tarmac onto dirt. Small homesteads, scattered on low green hills. There were trees, even grass. It wasn't perfect, but compared to the muddy squalor of Soweto-by-the-Sea it was a huge improvement.

'This place is very volatile,' said Jackson. 'This is all ANC. There were some Inkatha people here, but they were driven away.' He turned and looked at me. 'Perhaps you do have people here who are supporting Inkatha. But they are not showing it.' He chuckled, and sighed. 'No, man, they are not showing that.'

We were getting out of the urban area now, up a dirt track into hilly countryside. Sunlight on little green fields of sugar cane. The houses were not huge, say two-, three-roomed breezeblock cottages, but they were no longer shacks. There were hedges, palm trees.

'This is Kwazulu now,' said Jackson. 'Inkatha territory.' He pointed out a large blue bungalow with a little metal windmill to one side. 'That is the Chief's house. He has got electricity there, perhaps a borehole.'

We drove up a hill and stopped at the centre that his NGO had built. It was a warehouse-type structure with two or three outhouses. A large sign on the front said:

P--------- WOMEN'S CLUB
BUILDING MATERIALS
SALES OFFICE

THE FACILITIES OF THESE PREMISES HAVE
BEEN MADE POSSIBLE THROUGH THE DIRECT
SUPPORT OF THE FOLLOWING:
● THE BRITISH CONSULATE
● 600 GROUP
● MASONITE (AFRICA) LTD
● ASSOCIATION OF ROUND TABLE

'Now this place', said Jackson, 'used to look after sixty to seventy pre-school kids every day. Unfortunately this is no longer the case, as the transport to and from this centre is no longer operational.' He raised his left eyebrow. 'By which I mean, Mark, that the *bakkie* that was used to collect the children was taken away forcefully at gunpoint.'

There were new, stripped-pine wooden chairs and tables, a kiosk with newspapers laid out. 'We try to keep as wide a range as possible,' he said, 'even though we could antagonise the local leadership. You see,' he pointed, '*New Nation, City Press, Up* BEAT, UMAFRIKA. We are in Kwazulu here, but these are all ANC-inclined papers. So we are not serving one political party. You see.'

We walked through the warehouse and met Thomas the caretaker. 'Unfortunately we have no electrification here,' said Jackson. 'How are you placed on funding, Mark?'

'Well,' I dithered. 'I really – I'm not involved in funding in any way. I'm just doing a book, you know . . .'

'But we can perhaps utilise your wide circle of friends. Man, we *need* electrification here!'

Round the back, two women and two men were making concrete blocks to be sold locally for building purposes. In one of the four outhouses, donated, Jackson was quick to tell me, entirely by the British Consulate, three large women were making candles. We were introduced. African handshakes and laughter all round.

'These people, you see,' said Jackson, as the women continued with their work, 'are the only breadwinners in the house. Mrs M— here doesn't have a husband, so she depends on these candles for her survival. But there is a problem with marketing these candles. These women need to be promoted so that they can stand on their own.' Jackson turned to me. 'Is there any way you can facilitate this problem?'

'Really, I'm only observing . . .'

'Mark! I'm giving you some homework.'

'Why d'you call it a women's club?' I asked.

'We could only find women. We tried to get men, but they are hard to come by. This is a fact that needs to be documented, Mark.'

'So where are they?'

'They are in town, or they're . . . just around. But men everywhere, you see, are slow to take initiative. They weigh up a number of things before committing themselves. Some would say, "I don't have the candlemaking skills. I am not trained as a candlemaker". Others would not want to get involved at an early stage. For instance, until the British Consulate donated this shed, these women were actually operating in very dilapidated premises. In Mrs M—'s place, in fact.'

'What about the men making the concrete blocks?'

'Aha! Now the women are employing those men. Mrs M— is *employing* those men now. You see.'

On our way back, we passed a group of eight or ten restive-looking young guys, milling around at a junction. 'Look at those youths,' said Jackson. 'You have got to be ve-ry careful. As things are now, we are very jittery as we move around these areas. We are very scared of the youth. Many of these young boys have guns. You see. This is an area controlled by a warlord. Sometimes we have trouble if I bring a white visitor through here, but today I decided to take a chance. Last time I brought a minibus of white visitors through here, one of this warlord's henchmen stopped us, and they gave us a *lot* of trouble.' He chuckled. 'This is a land of contrasts, eh, Mark?

'We are living with whites,' he went on, as we drove back down the motorway towards town, 'and whites don't know our culture, which is pathetic. The vast majority of the whites haven't even *seen* the shacks where we came from. They're only interested in the labour and the amassing of profits. We take exception to that because it shows they don't care. By and large. We feel we have been let down by whites, some of whom we thought were on our side. And we fail to reconcile what they have done, with them being Christians. How can they be Christians, and have done these things to us?

'At the moment it's black-on-black violence, which is bad enough. I shudder to think what would happen if it ever became black-on-white.'

News of a major Inkatha–ANC massacre was coming in:

> 37 are dead in an armed invasion by 'hostel residents' of the Vaal township of Boipatong on Wednesday night [read the *Natal Mercury*]. By midday yesterday the *Weekly Mail* reported the death toll was 43 – including a nine-month pregnant woman and a nine-month old baby, both of whom had been speared to death . . .

'My prose piece is from *Great Expectations*, by Charles Dickens,' said the black student, standing in the centre of the empty stage in bare feet. '"Joe – what for? What for? There are some visits perhaps. But in regard of visiting Miss Havisham old chap, she might credit it, similarly she might not . . ."'

Then it was an Indian girl's turn. 'Please excuse me,' she said to the assembled teachers and students. 'I have flu.'

'Not to worry,' shouted the white Professor from half way up the stalls. 'That only affects the "mn" and "ng" sounds. OK, go on.'

'My poem,' said the Indian girl, 'is Shakespeare's sonnet, number 116, "Let Me Not To The Marriage of True Minds".'

When the oral exam was over the student group came to the front of the stage for their crits. Two Indian girls, a white guy with his hair in a ponytail, and the black guy, Penwell.

'Penwell,' said an Indian teacher, 'I didn't feel you related to the piece. That was written in dialect by Charles Dickens, and you didn't relate to the dialect at all.'

'Now why is it,' boomed the Professor, 'that nobody can say "women". "Wo*man*" you say, every single last one of you. Romora,' he went on, to the Indian, 'how do you say the word "h-o-u-s-e-s"?'

'Housses,' said Romora.

'Houz*zez*,' said the professor. 'Houzzes – not housses. Now the first step towards improving your work, all of you, is to be aware of where you are at the moment. There's a lot of problems with pronunciation, a lot of dipthong problems, a lot of dropped "h"s.'

'Penwell,' said the Indian teacher, 'why did you choose that piece? Did you have some feeling for that piece?'

At least Penwell was honest. 'I didn't get a chance to have much time,' he said. 'So I just picked up the nearest book in the library.'

The Professor was angry and disappointed. 'If you don't shape up,' he told the assembled students, 'there's going to be a massive failure rate this year. I mean you must, you *must* pick a piece that you actually like, and respond to. Of

course we can talk about enunciation, and projection, and
all these other things, but it must start with your response to
the work itself. The whole rich world of literature is there
for you to mine. And instead you pick the first book you can
lay your hands on.

'This isn't high school. You've got to make the grade. If
you want the help we're here to help – but we're not
teachers. So if you don't understand anything we've said
today – ask about it. If you disagree, come and find us and
challenge what we say. But there are so many of you that
you'll only get the help if you ask for it, because that's how
it works.'

We retired together to the Professor's office, which was
lined wall-to-wall with texts of plays, stacked high with
piles of scripts. A paperback called *The Master Farces* lay
central amid the clutter of papers on his desk.

'You can see some of the problems,' he said, with a shrug
and a smile. He was a big man, with small oblong glasses
perched on a long nose. On the top of his head, greying hair
was swept across an encroaching pate; below, his bushy
black beard was shot through with white. He spoke passionately, gesturing continually with the broad palms of his big
hands. 'We have a range of students from those who've just
come from black schools to those who've performed and
written plays. Add to that the problem of entrenched standards. With seventeen different educational establishments,
you get seventeen different matric levels . . .

'And the students,' he went on, 'are coping with a *tremendous* amount of culture shock. You get a black African sitting
next to an Indian for the first time in his life, being taught by
a white teacher. A typical scenario is someone who's worked
damn hard at a high school, often under atrocious conditions, maybe without books, with terrible overcrowding,
and they've survived that and actually got a good matric
result, and then they've come here and they go to a lecture

and they can't even *understand* what's going on in the lecture. That's when they become angry.

'This is compounded by an education system that never puts any initiative onto their students. "Underline that in the history book and next week we'll have a test." That sort of thing. There's never any questioning of the interpretation. It's "Who did Pip meet in the graveyard?" not "Why did Dickens start his novel at that point?"

'So they don't understand what is required of them, and they feel very aggrieved when they get low marks, because they have made a very stout effort, and they feel that they should be accorded some kind of mark commensurate with that effort. And then you have the painful job of explaining to them that irrespective of the amount of effort that's gone into it, they have to reach another standard that they may not even have *glimpsed*.'

I had gone to the University of Durban Westville – high up on the North Berea Ridge – looking for Indians. Until the formal scrapping of apartheid, this had been the Indian university, and despite being now 40% African and 10% white, it still had a 50% majority of Indian students. But the Indian teachers that Gerald had recommended were all busy, so I'd ended up sitting in on a drama exam, seeing yet again the dire legacy of Bantu education, and meeting a half-Jewish professor.

'The biggest danger, of course,' he went on, as our conversation took its natural course towards The Situation, 'is the kind of inflated claims that have been made in the past for what a black victory will produce. The kind of false promises that have been given. There was a case in Durban here: a black African woman worked in a house and the madam worked in town. One day the madam had to come back mid-morning for some reason, and found her maid up on the windows, with a tape measure. She thought this was highly unusual, so she asked, "What are you doing?" The maid said, "Measuring for my curtains." "What d'you mean?" said the madam. "Oh well," said the maid, "you know, in only another two years of payments I'll be moving into this house." It turned out that some local scam artist had been around and got a significant number of people, saying, "You know, the revolution's just around the corner, in two years' time all these white houses are going to be for black Africans, and you can buy them now: twenty-five rand a month from every one of you, over the next four years, and you can have this house. And she'd been paying, from a very meagre wage. He'd got different amounts, according to how much he could scam, out of a load of domestic servants, all convinced that they're now going to inherit this, come the revolution.' He laughed.

'The same house? Or different houses?'

'The same house. Because of course all the whites are going to be driven into the sea. And all the luxuries that the whites enjoyed will be ours. Very simple. For a basically uneducated people they don't see there's any flaw to that argument.'

'And they're quite happy to see their masters and mistresses driven into the sea?'

'Oh *ye-es*. There's no problem there. The problem is — when is the revolution, and when do I move in? How, of course, you pay for the electricity, or you pay for the curtains to put on the windows in the first place — that's not of concern. Because if that changes, everything else will change. And I will go and do madam's job. I will be sub-editor of the *Daily News*. I will be this and I will be that.'

'So when a black majority Government does get in — if it does — there's going to be a lot of disappointed people?'

'Vast numbers. And of course that will tend to split and divide people into camps again. Extreme left and extreme right. I've seen it happen on the city council here. The incredible turnabouts from left to right. There was a mayor here, Henry Klotz, who was originally a councillor. He was mandated by his constituency to stand against opening the beaches to all races. There was a public meeting in the city hall. This councillor got up and he said, "In no ways will I have my granddaughters and grandsons mixing with kaffirs and coolies on Durban Beach." Huge, overwhelming acclamation from all in the hall. Three, four years later, he was elected Mayor. Everybody thought: Oh *god*, now what's going to happen to Durban? But now he's actually got to deal with the problem – the pressures. And he was the person, who by the end of his mayorship, turned round and said, at a public meeting, that his greatest achievement – the thing he could be most proud of – was that during his mayorship, all the beaches of Durban were open to all races.'

We laughed. Before I knew it, we were onto Durban's other big problem, black-on-black violence.

'I mean the kind of human stories that come out,' said the Professor, shaking his head. 'In the first year that I was here, there was a lot of antagonism, and certain chain stores were targeted for boycott action. They were accused of underpaying workers, exploiting them and what have you. Now whereas in England there'd be some roughing up on the picket lines and that kind of thing, here the situation takes a very ugly turn. One of my students came back with a story about a member of his community, an aunt in fact. Her husband had been killed in political action in the area, she had five children – not all her own, some she'd inherited from members of her family who had since been killed in the violence – so she'd become the only breadwinner and organiser to look after these children. Anyway, she went to the picket line and said to them: "Look, I have to buy bread for these children. They're hungry: I have to have bread. I am too *old* to walk eighteen miles to the other shop, eighteen miles is too far for me." And they said: "Don't go into that store." And she said: "I've got to, I've got to. My children are more important than politics and you must understand that." So she went in and she bought bread. And at the opening to the supermarket, the big glass doors, they waited for her to

come out, and when she came out, they put a bottle of petrol
to her mouth, punched her in the stomach till she swallowed
this petrol, and then they set her alight and she went off like
an incendiary bomb. She just exploded in front of the store.
And those are the sort of actions where you think: Wow!
You know, gee, there's democracy for you. You know, those
are rough stories. Very rough.'

'What does all this leave you thinking?' I asked.

The Professor, head on hand, sighed deeply. 'Well it leaves
me with the thought that there is a growing number of black
Africans, ordinary folk, who are sick and tired of all that,
but they don't really know what to do about it. They are
caught in the middle. Like my friend Richard, who's one of
the black actors I work with. Richard's a training officer with
– I think – Creamline Dairies. He lives in Chesterville
township. Now he's a person who will be approached in the
middle of the night, and they will say: "Here's a *panga*, go
up there and demonstrate against the security forces. Join
the group." The point is there's no such thing as having a
neutral stance. You either join us, or if you don't we'll
assume that you're party to the others. So liberal humanism
gets a rough ride.'

He sat back in his swivel chair, smiled, shrugged, and
sipped his tea.

The Professor was a touch out of date with his friend's
movements. Richard, it turned out, had moved from the
township, and now lived in a big house in Westville – one
of the old white areas – up on the hill.

I called round to see him on the Sunday morning after
President F. W. De Klerk had been forced to flee ignomini-
ously after an ill-judged sympathy-visit to Boipatong. Richard was sitting on a big black leatherette sofa reading the
papers and listening to reggae, which thumped loudly out
from two enormous speakers on a ceiling-high rack behind.
He was big, burly, plump and warmly welcoming. He had a

half-beard and a deep, shoulder-shaking laugh. We did the African handshake and he took me through to the kitchen to meet his wife Hazel. A plump little girl of ten or so ran in and stood shyly by the fridge. 'And this is our ray of sunshine, Thandiwe,' said Richard, putting his arm round her. 'As you can see, she has inherited my build.'

Having fixed me a brandy and coke, we talked for a while about his acting. Now he wanted to get involved in directing. 'I have the picture of a very energetic play involving young people from the townships. I would really like to organise people into doing something like that.'

The school boycotts of the 1970s and 1980s, he told me, had created a generation 'who've been overtaken by time without having attained any significant educational achievements'. They weren't qualified to work. 'Maybe we need to look very closely at strategies to enable these people to have a meaningful adult role. Theatre could play an important part in that – even if it is only to send the message to everyone in the country that we need to address these issues.' He broke into a loud laugh. 'Well, that's the big noble picture. The reality of the thing is that there is a lot of talent among young people that needs to be brought out. Maybe the strength of something like theatre is that if you can have a success with a production like *Sarafina*, it makes people think – we knew those people, we were *toyi-toyi*-ing with those people, and what those people have done is to be constructive with their lives, and we might be able to do that too. At the moment we don't have anything except protest-type theatre. But if I want to watch protest theatre, I can watch the television, night after night. Or read the paper.' He flicked his hand down towards the sheaf of Boipatong headlines to his left. 'FW FLEES,' he read. 'This is "a raging mob".' He picked up the second: 'This is "an angry mob" – but FW flees in any case.' He laughed.

'So,' I said, a little later, 'it must be nice to be away from all that violence, up here on the hill.'

Richard shrugged. 'You know,' he said, 'there are times when I drive back into the township because I miss a certain life. Then there are times when I want to get out of the township because I want to sit down and write something on my computer.'

He looked out of the window, sighed, and gestured expansively. 'The life here . . . I've lived here since the 1st of December . . . I've got a black family on this side, and a white family on this side, and I *still* don't know who these people are. In the townships you know everybody. You can be walking on the streets and see people having a good time and you can just walk in.'

'D'you think you might be tempted to go back?'

'Obviously, being in a place like this has its advantages. Also, I don't know whether one could say that that type of township life is necessarily indicative of the way black people live in general. What it is indicative of is how people have had to cope with a lack of space. Look, in the space taken up by a yard like this there would probably be forty or fifty families. Because of that, people are always bumping into one another. As a result you develop a coping mechanism. "Brothers! Brothers! This is great stuff!" That sort of thing. But then, I know quite a number of black people that have moved up here into Westville – and if I was to thumbsuck a figure, I would say that right now about 70% of them are visiting people in the townships.'

I asked him if people down there had a different attitude to him now. Now that he was up on the hill with his big house and his fancy car.

'Well,' he replied, 'there is an awareness that this person has moved out of the township. This could mean, in their eyes, that this guy has a lot of money. But let me correct this – I don't have any money. They may want to believe that because I drive a company car, I hold a management position, my wife is a social worker, we have only one child – people may want to believe that we have a lot of money . . .'

He tailed off. He had been talking away from me, gazing out of the window. Now he turned with a shrug, and met my eye. 'As to how people *really* respond to that I may never know. As to what they're prepared to show us, it's that they're quite happy for us. They think, maybe: "Come on, guys, we can also do this." But then I've always been involved in the township. Even now I have a lot of young people coming up from Chesterville and getting involved in youth development programmes.

'I'm trying to be modest about this, Mark,' he smiled broadly, 'but – put it this way, if you went into Chesterville and said you were looking for Richard D—, it is possible that some people might not know who you're talking about. But if you go into Chesterville and you say, "I'm looking for Brother," *nobody* would not know who Brother is. I would like to believe that there are a lot of people there who think that I'm the nice guy. I *know* I'm the nice guy, because I've stayed there and done a number of things with them.'

'Such as?'

He told me about his last 'little project'. There'd been a problem of access in the township: a bridge needed to be built over a stream. 'There is a plantation of trees in the white area just outside Chesterville. We went in there one night, and . . . shall we say, when we came out, a number of trees that shouldn't have been felled were felled, so we built a bridge.' He laughed.

A white minibus had parked at the bottom of his drive. A group of smartly dressed young people made their way up the slope to his front door. Brother welcomed them in.

I had a lunch date with a barrister friend of a nurse I'd met in Cape Town. She'd described him as 'a lifty lawyer'. North Beach, on Durban's famous Golden Mile, was where we'd arranged to meet.

It was a beautiful sunny day, with the lightest breeze off the sea. The long, long curve of beach, divided here and there by concrete breakwaters, was full of people in bikinis, shorts, T-shirts – whites mostly, but with groups of blacks and Indians here and there. After the windswept wintry shores of the Cape and the Transkei it was a delight to be where the action was, lounging out in a crowd in this sub-tropical heat.

Tony was waiting for me on the steps up to the outdoor Deck Restaurant, wearing, as agreed, a black baseball cap. He was quite slight, with a thoughtful smile beneath a little well-trimmed beard; mid-thirties or so. His friend Dave, who'd bagged us a table with a view of the beach, was altogether more of a hunk. Tall, broad-shouldered, more obviously gay in appearance and mannerisms: for yes, they were clearly a couple.

We ordered three salads and three cokes, the restaurant not serving beer on a Sunday. 'This is something else you need to know about South Africa,' said Tony. 'All our ridiculous laws.'

Surrounded by whites in beach gear we discussed the Boipatong massacre. I'd missed some incredible footage on the news the previous night, Dave said. As De Klerk had fled, the soldiers had opened fire into the crowd, just like that. 'It was extraordinary,' said Tony. 'You'd certainly never have seen that kind of thing on South African TV – even a year ago.'

After lunch, Dave leaned over the balcony and pointed out the area of the beach where the weightlifters congregated. 90% white, their oiled and bulging muscles gleamed in the early afternoon sun. 'It's a poseurs' paradise,' he said.

'This was the last beach to be desegregated,' said Tony. 'Only what, Dave, two, three years ago?'

Since then, there had been a contention about New Year's Day. 'It gets completely packed with blacks now,' Dave said. 'It's like a tradition with them, to go to the beach on New Year's Day. It's caused a lot of problems, because all the Transvalers used to come down here for their Christmas holidays. I think quite a lot of them have switched to Cape Town because of the blacks packing the beaches.'

'Surely Cape Town's the same?'

'There aren't the same numbers of blacks down there,' said Dave, and suddenly our conversation had taken a serious turn. 'You just don't know about the future in this country. What's going to happen next, whether the next township uprising could lead to, you know, could lead to . . .'

'All the whites being driven into the sea . . .' I said.

'All the whites being driven into the sea,' he echoed, nervously. 'Yes.'

We went for a stroll along the front, an area just behind the main beach, of paved walkways, swimming and paddling pools, green lawns, bougainvillaea, palm trees. Here and there amusement kiosks; overhead a slow-moving cable-car ride; in odd corners 'Zulus' in traditional dress selling wicker baskets, carved African statues, beads . . . There were even blacks offering rickshaw rides. 'Not that the rickshaw has anything to do with Durban,' said Tony, 'they've just started doing this recently.'

In one of the smaller swimming pools a teenaged black girl played topless, wearing just a pair of semi-transparent white knickers. 'Now that's a problem since the beaches have been desegregated,' said Tony. 'In their culture baring your breasts means nothing, but a lot of the whites and Indians get offended.'

We walked out onto one of the four or five little concrete breakwaters, from where you could get a magnificent close-up view of the (all white) surfers. The swell was heavy, with waves ten to fifteen foot high. At the end of the breakwater you were right out there with them, sharing their excitement as they caught and rode a wave, chuckling at their disappointment as they missed one, plunged face-first into the spume.

As a package tourist, walking down the Golden Mile, it would be easy to think all was well in the New South Africa,

I thought. It certainly looked an idyllic picture, the sunlight on the sea, the blacks and whites and Indians strolling peacefully around, smiling, laughing, in each other's arms . . .

'Not bad for the shortest day of the year, eh?' said Tony, echoing my thoughts.

Camilla was a friend of Alex and Geraldine's. She was warm and pretty with long ash blonde hair. Only a couple of years older than me, but already she'd been married and divorced and had a big white house in the middle of town and two blond-haired little boys of ten and twelve. A radical free-lance journalist from a wealthy background she seemed to know someone from just about every department of Durban life: jazz musicians, trade unionists, teachers, socialites. You never quite knew who you'd find having tea or beer in the kitchen that led out through French windows to the bougain-villaea and the blue circle of swimming pool. Over supper the previous week she had showed me the book she had written attacking Buthelezi. 'It was something that needed to be done,' she said. 'It's more of an intervention than anything else – someone had to expose what he's up to.'

Now I found myself joining the end of a Sunday lunch. The late thirty-something guests were strewn around her wicker chairs, on their second coffee, talking about Boipa-tong. They were all white, all solidly pro-ANC. Of course the 'hostel residents' were Inkatha members. That went without saying. A thin dark-haired woman called Sugar was telling me how horrified she'd been by the TV coverage. 'The thing that shocked me was that those army guys just looked so young, and so untrained. I'm sure they just started shooting because they were afraid. And there was this female journalist there who'd just broken down, she was just sob-bing – I mean we never *saw* Sharpeville, that was the point.'

*

In the evening, back in Kloof, little Annie wanted to watch the video of *Charlie and the Chocolate Factory*. 'Oh plee-eeze, Daddy,' she said, in her best American soap imitation yet, 'don't let's watch the boring *news*.'

But having missed the dramatic pictures of the night before, Gerald was as keen as I was to catch up on the latest developments. 'We're watching it for fifteen minutes, Annie,' he said sternly. 'It's important for all our futures – yours too.'

So Charlie was left on hold at the gate of Willy Wonka's wonderful chocolate factory, while Gerald and I and the children watched (in Afrikaans) as Nelson Mandela told the assembled masses (in English) that in the light of Boipatong he would have to consider breaking off negotiations with the Government. We saw selected footage of De Klerk being chased out of Pholapark – but no crowds being shot at – and I gazed at the bright reflection of the happy family scene in the dark windows and wondered how things would develop, out beyond the steel bars, out, out beyond the bottom of the garden, where the palm trees shifted mysteriously in the breeze . . .

And when reality was over and Willy Wonka finally did take Charlie up into the sky and gave him the chocolate factory, the little town that they looked down on, with its red-tiled English roofs and its church spire and its neat green fields all around, looked so unbelievably safe and cosy . . .

Sugar had invited me to look round the school she taught at, an ex-white high school in the northern suburbs of Durban, that had now started to take blacks – which definition included Indians and Taiwanese. It was one of the richer absurdities of apartheid that the Japanese (who supplied South Africa with pig-iron) were classified 'white'; while Malays and Chinese, who'd historically been slaves and cheap labour in South Africa, were classified 'black'.

And so I found myself on a Tuesday morning break-time

being led through (predominantly white) hordes of shrieking adolescents in blue uniforms and into a crowded staff-room where I was placed at the centre of a semi-circle of white male teachers who were joking about the idea of Natal being Little England. 'That's how we like to see this school,' one of them said. 'Based on an English grammar school.'

There were differences, though, a man in a tweed jacket pointed out: they still had corporal punishment in South Africa.

'Long may it last!' cried an older man in a cream sweater and crimson tie, who was a born-again Christian. The best justification for corporal punishment appeared in 'Proverbs'.

They needed discipline in the school, he went on, because discipline in the South African home had deteriorated as a result of an overdose of American TV. The tweed jacket agreed: 'American sitcoms don't reflect the fine parental values of the ordinary American home,' he said. Through American soapies, true American values were misinterpreted.

The talk turned inevitably to politics and the issue of the moment – Boipatong.

'In the last few days', said the Christian, 'we are going headlong backwards from whence we came . . .'

'The trouble is,' said the tweed jacket, 'we don't know whether it's merely pointscoring, or . . .'

'The biggest problem with the ANC', interrupted another, 'is they've not given us anything concrete to work on. They can't do anything without consulting the grass roots, and if you're forever consulting the grass roots you never get anything done.'

'All we want', said a tall muscular young guy in a striped shirt, getting up to go to his class, 'is just for them to allow us to live, take some holidays, buy the cars we can afford . . .'

Our discussion ended up in a little spat: Sugar versus the born-again Christian. 'But there *are* no ANC Inkatha members,' Sugar was saying. 'Listen carefully,' said the Christian, 'I didn't *say* that . . .'

Outside in the corridor I met three representatives of the Ladies Voluntary Group, who were bent over a table cutting out new curtains for the biology laboratory. Recently, Sugar explained, with more State funds being diverted to black education, parents at white Government schools had had to start paying fees. Not enormous fees, but fees nonetheless. So voluntary help from the Ladies' group was extremely welcome. They raised their own funds, with fêtes and fun runs and so on. In fact, said the largest of the three ladies, who was wearing gold Dame Edna glasses and cream slacks, and described herself as 'the sewing convener cum general dogsbody', there was a fun run this Sunday, if I'd like to come.

I asked about black mothers. 'Yes, we do try and involve black and Indian mums,' she said, 'but . . .' She looked at Sugar.

'They tend not to have the free time,' said Sugar.

'Everyone does what they can,' said the sewing convenor. 'The Taiwanese gave eight computers. That's their contribution.'

Sugar was very eager that I should talk to Peter, the black man who ran the photocopying room. So we chatted briefly about the problems he faced. When he was in his own township he had to be ANC; when he went to visit his parents 'in the rural area' he had to be Inkatha.

'And how d'you find that?' asked Sugar.

'You have to do it.'

'And privately,' I asked, 'what do the people in the townships think?'

'They don't like it.'

'He reads Hansard,' Sugar said, as we walked off down the corridor. 'There you've got these white teachers, with no understanding . . . and here in the photocopying room you've got Peter, following all the Parliamentary debates . . .'

Sugar had sent her class to the library, to do some research into Lenin's economic policy. But not much appeared to be getting done. Round a table a group of six or seven white boys had their history books open in front of them, but there was a furtive giggling, and a note being passed. At the end of the table a large Taiwanese student was asleep, his cuboid head resting heavily on the pages of a novel in Chinese script.

Sugar woke him up. 'What are you meant to be doing at the moment? Afrikaans?' He grunted blearily. 'PE?' 'Yah, PE,' he nodded.

The only student who seemed to be doing any work at all was an Indian boy, who was sitting alone at the next table, studying Lenin's economic policy with all the intensity of the one who has been left out of the group.

The librarian – a neat brunette with bright pink glasses – was getting worked up. 'They're just doing *nothing* in here, a lot of them,' she said. 'I don't want to be an absolute bitch, but I'm going to be. It really gets on my nerves. They've got to realise that education is a privilege now.' She stormed off to sort out the Taiwanese, whose head had slumped back onto his book.

Camilla had another friend – Gugu – who taught in an ex-black school. I say 'ex', as technically the place *could* now have taken whites. Though, of course, whites were hardly falling over themselves to drive out along the potholed dirt tracks to get (or rather not get) educated in the township.

As I arrived the school seemed to be in uproar, black kids of all ages running around, tussling with each other, jumping up on desks, laughing, shouting, screaming. There was of course no plush reception area, no school crest in an echoing assembly hall, no green lawns, no comfy staff room and tea urn. Just a row of basic classrooms with broken, boarded-up windows, a central oblong of mud, and down the slope to the right a huge heap of uncollected rubbish: cans, bottles and plastic bags that looked as if they'd been piling up for *years*.

Being a senior teacher, Gugu had her own little office. She was younger than I'd expected, dressed in a stylish brown two-piece suit, as if she was just off for lunch in town rather than grappling with the problems of Bantu education in a township. She apologised – there was only the one chair. Would I mind perching on the desk?

'Is it break?' I asked, as the screaming outside reached a new crescendo. Gugu shook her head. 'No, they're supposed to be in lessons, but it's too cold for them, with the windows broken, so school's over for the day. I'm supposed to be teaching a class now, but . . .' she gestured hopelessly, 'the Principal's not here. And when he's not here . . . chaos reigns.'

'Does he use corporal punishment to keep control?'

'Yes. But it's not like before, when there was a strong arm. Even the Principal has to be careful, they can get physical.'

She had many complaints. As I could see, every window in the school was broken; they'd been like that for years, since the State of Emergency. The books she needed for Standard Six – well, she'd just got the kids' books this month; before that she hadn't even had the books she was supposed to be *teaching* with. The science students had no labs – so all the experiments they were supposed to do had to be done without equipment . . . 'Nothing is easy,' she said. 'When you go to a white school it's all provided. Labs, swimming pools, libraries, sports fields . . . but for us everything is *ad hoc*. She gestured to a stack of books on her desk. 'I had intentions of finishing a story today, but I can't do it now.'

They had one toilet for the entire school. A thousand pupils. 'The primary school don't even have toilets at all. They literally have to go to the bush.'

Two other teachers came in: in contrast to trim Gugu, large

ladies in flowing skirts. They squashed onto the desk to one side of me and there were African handshakes and African laughter.

Sobering up, we got into a discussion about class sizes. Gugu had fifty-two, sixty-five, sixty-seven and seventy-three. 'Oh you are teaching *good* classes,' said the larger of the two ladies, laughing.

'In the white schools,' Gugu said, 'they have forty per class, and they're arguing now that that's too much.'

There was a knock at the door. Gugu had to leave. 'You see,' she said, 'I have to go next door to the shop to answer the Principal's phone.'

'To the shop?'

'There's no phone in the school.'

Left alone, perched incongruously on the edge of the desk with the two large teachers, I asked about the children. What sort of age were they? They laughed. Any age. Some were eleven; some sixteen; some twenty-five. *Twenty-five*? Oh yes, some were even thirty. They'd missed their schooling because of the boycotts, or they just went to school because there was nothing else to do. Perhaps because their parents made them go.

There was no zoning. Some would come from one township, some from another. 'They just have to bring a report card. We can't send them away. There's no control. It's a haywire system.'

'It's just a mixed masala.'

'This is the legacy of apartheid. They wanted the system to be like this. Now it's difficult to reverse it. It would cost billions and billions of rands.'

I had a look around the place on my own. Below the oblong of mud was a long shed divided into two largish rooms. One was the library. No desks, just a few shelves of tatty secondhand books. There were two teachers waiting to help, but no kids. They were all next door, in a room which was absolutely packed; kids of all ages, practising dance steps; waltzing round arm in arm, girls and girls, boys and boys, girls and boys . . . no music, just the sound of feet on lino, the chatter and laughter of the onlookers.

'What's going on?' I asked a lanky teenage boy.

'They're preparing for a dance lesson.'

'Where's the music?'

He smiled. 'You're the one with the money, you can get us the music.'

Because I'm white, they look at me with suspicion. But when I smile . . . instantly they smile back, broad white grins in beautiful black faces. The girls are wearing the same flimsy nylon overalls they used to wear at Maru-a-Pula, and for the first time since I've landed in Africa I get a whisper of that magic. And even though the windows are broken, the sunshine is pouring in . . .

I came to my senses. I was just a foolish, sentimental whitey, I realised, as I walked back towards Gugu's office. From the shed came the sound of tinny Strauss. The dance lesson had begun.

'This is my other side,' said Tony, as we shook hands. He was out of his beach shorts and baseball cap and into blue pinstripes and a crimson tie. His chambers were not the wood-panelled staircases and rooms of Gray's Inn or Middle Temple, but a hi-tech office block with a brushed-aluminium lift, a lobby done out with tiles of cream, grey and salmon pink.

Tony's office was a strange mixture of ancient and modern: an antique desk, covered with ribboned briefs; bookcases full of thick green volumes of South African law . . . looking over to swish floor-to-ceiling windows and shiny black Venetian blinds.

There was a light double-knock on the door and Duncan joined us. Also in pinstripes – square shouldered, crisp haircut, mid-forties – he was the very model of colonial politeness. We were going to lunch at the exclusive men-

only Durban Club ('the last outpost of colonialism': from
Plett I could hear Alex's deep chuckle) and Duncan was our
host.

Three suits, we cut through the lunch-time crowd of white
and Indian office workers and turned into Durban Club
Place, dwarfed by the towering glass surfaces of the Nedbank
skyscraper above. There had been three Durban Clubs,
Duncan was telling us. The first had been on this corner
here, and had originally been set up as a coits club, but it
was felt that coits wasn't a suitable game for gentlemen, so
they'd switched to billiards. Tony and I chuckled and
nodded appropriately.

'It's quite a haven in here,' Duncan said, as we passed
through a stone archway into a lovely oblong courtyard,
shady with palm and fig trees, the sunshine dappling the
pale brown columns and balustrades.

On the steps we were welcomed by the broad smile of a
black man called Sunny. Not a fellow member: a club servant
in an impeccable maroon uniform, with SUNNY embroidered
in yellow on his chest.

Inside, the place was exactly as you might have expected:
dark wood panels, deep red carpets, black and white framed
portraits of the Royal Family climbing up the main stairway.

We had a peep into the library, which had . . . yes, two old
buffers snoozing in leather armchairs and four-day old
copies of English newspapers. Sunny told us that the post
was not what it had been; in the old days they'd have been
here in two days. The *Spectator* was prominent among the
magazines, as was the last ever edition of *Punch*, in which,
by a stroke of luck, I had an article.

My credentials as a bona-fide journalist now thoroughly
established, we proceeded to the bar to find a raucous crowd
of chaps with blue jackets and white hair swilling back pints
and whisky and sodas and g and ts. 'Interestingly enough,'
said Duncan, 'when we mooted the idea of changing the

membership to admit women, we got the greatest number of protests from the wives of members.'

We laughed. Were women allowed in at all, Tony asked, as we proceeded upstairs past Kings George V and VI, the young Queen Elizabeth II, the young Prince Philip, Prince Charles and Princess Diana.

'Oh yes,' said Duncan. There was a special dining room and reception area for women on the top floor. And black members? I asked. Yes, said Duncan, they had a number of Indian members and one or two African members. 'Obviously they've got to respect the way we are, and satisfy the right criteria and so on. In fact, we've got an African up for election at the moment – he's the President of the South African Federation of Black Taxis.'

Well, well! It seemed a long way from the fights-to-the-death over who controlled the N2 out of Cape Town . . . to us, lowering our bottoms on three sides of this crisp white tablecloth. Out through tall windows the palm trees of the Victoria Embankment shifted lazily in the breeze; beyond, the white masts of yachts in the marina; beyond that the serious chimneys of ocean-going ships in Durban docks.

More English than the English is the cliché. But looking round the dining room I didn't see evidence of any magnificently extravagant colonials; white handlebar moustaches *à la* Osbert Lancaster or whatever. Just South African versions of the same types you find in the armchairs of St James's. The difference was in the strictly efficient Indian waiters, who left the fumbling Spanish teenagers such London clubs now employ streets behind.

We helped ourselves to curry from a buffet, and Duncan asked me what I thought of South Africa so far. 'Very complex,' I said; and found myself adding that I'd met some very impressive people, who by and large were those involved with the future; and some less impressive people, who were those wrapped up in the past.

'But we don't want to throw out all of the past, surely,'

said Duncan. 'There have been some very good things in this country, as well as some very bad ones.'

Our talk turned to England. Tony hadn't approved *at all* of Mrs Thatcher. Just her voice was enough to put you off. I said I thought she was a victim of hubris. 'Now there's another woman out of a Greek tragedy,' said Tony. 'Winnie Mandela.'

'Was that Stompie stuff generally regarded as true?' I asked.

'It's on appeal at the moment,' said Duncan.

'Yes,' said Tony, 'I think it *was* regarded as true.' He'd had a friend who'd had direct experience of dealing with her. 'She just got to the point where she thought she could tell anyone what to do.'

They were both impressed by Nelson Mandela. 'You've got to admire the man for his integrity,' said Duncan, 'even if you don't agree with his ideas.' Cyril Ramaphosa had in fact addressed the Durban Club only a few weeks back. 'And he was very well received. He made a few cracks about nationalisation, but they were only cracks . . . but that's a good thing, surely, that people here in the Durban Club are tolerant enough to listen to the views of someone like that?'

On our way out Duncan said, 'I like this place. It's been here such a long time, it makes you feel secure, about the past, and the future.'

14

A NATIONAL DAMN SCANDAL

Boipatong had become an international issue. What had started as just another township massacre was now on the front page of newspapers across the world. My *Guardian Weekly* normally provided light homesickness-relieving stuff: Mr Major and the ERM, John Smith becoming leader of the Labour Party, quiet reassuring trivialities like that. Now it was full of South Africa.

On the phone both my mother and Sarah were concerned that I was 'all right'. I looked across to the family scene on the other side of the room: Mari bringing in the macaroni cheese, Peter and Annie in dressing gowns tussling on the floor over a video – I couldn't have seemed further from Boipatong. 'I'm fine,' I said, 'Boipatong's a long way away . . .' 'Everyone's worried about you,' Sarah said.

But if I was a long way away from the violence, I wasn't far from its roots. For it was in the Durban-Pietermaritzburg area that the ANC–Inkatha struggle had started; here that in the 1980s 'the unofficial war' had raged most strongly.

A man I had to see on this issue if I could, Gerald said, was Pierre Cronjé, the local MP, whose (all-white, of course) constituency ranged from Kloof right up through 'Maritzburg to Greytown on the far side. He was interesting because he was an Afrikaner who had been a staunch member of the Democratic Party but had recently defected to the ANC.

Furthermore, he'd become very involved in the local black community, in particular in monitoring the black-on-black violence on the ground.

He lived in a substantial two-storey house up in the hills above 'Maritzburg. There were wide green lawns, neat hedges, gravel paths, a pretty stone statue or two. As I crunched up to the big front door, two black garden boys in woolly hats passed me pushing a wheelbarrow full of leaves.

Cronjé (pronounced Cron-year) himself was swarthily dark, thick-set, wearing a patterned blue jersey and casual trousers. He gave me a powerful handshake, and ushered me through to a drawing room with tall windows, flowers in a vase, long sofas, a low coffee table. A maid in uniform brought us a tray of tea.

Pure South Africa! I'd come to learn about black-on-black violence and found myself hearing the story of an Afrikaner's political enlightenment.

Ever since he'd been a child, Cronjé told me, he'd had this feeling for the underdog. But I must understand, 'the black at that time was, to us, just a feature of the landscape, like an aloe or a tree . . .' Then he'd been at university during the Age of Rock and Roll, which had led to 'a dualistic thing': Friday nights at the Volkspieler, the traditional Afrikaner folk-dancing club, Saturdays rock and rolling. He'd qualified as a civil engineer, and that profession had brought him away from the Conservative Transvaal to 'this hurly-burly of people' in Natal. Through his work he'd got involved in building Government housing schemes for blacks in the townships. For the first time in his life, he'd realised that the resources of his country were 'being spent on fancy freeways to holiday resorts for whites, while the blacks over the hill were left in poverty'.

He'd started to take up these issues. In the early 1970s, with the build-up of resistance in black politics, his immediate group of professionals in South Africa were talking of emigrating. It was a hot topic. And he'd made a conscious decision that if he stayed he would have to work for change. So he'd got involved in the Progressive Party. No, he hadn't considered joining the black struggle or going into exile; at every stage he'd wanted to work through white politics.

In 1981 he'd come to Greytown, as the Democratic MP to 20,000 whites. In his constituency were one million blacks who had no vote. He'd found himself getting drawn into black issues on the ground: forced removals, the State of Emergency, then the Inkatha–ANC war.

He was uncompromising about the violence and its causes. 'People say it's complex and so forth. You want to make a simple issue complex, or you want to make a complex issue simple?' He leant forward and looked me candidly in the eye, before continuing in his thick Afrikaner accent. 'In Natal, we now have a move away from a traditional tribal system, which was very authoritarian, with still all the powers over every aspect of a person's daily life – access to land, access to other resources, and so on. Now, obviously this can work, and, like elsewhere in the world, it does work until a certain level of sophistication is required, when you're no longer just a hunter-gatherer, but begin to need to talk about the roads, about water, about this, about that.

'In the tribal system, the methods that are employed are almost verbal. You walk up to the Chief, and you say, "This is my friend, he needs a bit of land, I'm prepared to sacrifice part of mine." He goes out, he indicates it – and many of these things are not even recorded. So the lack of back-up administrative systems, in these tribal areas, and the lack of commitment of these tribal leaders to deal with much more urban-related issues, and not purely culturally related issues, means that they become obsolete, they can't cope with today's problems.

'So you now start getting embryonic structures developing, where people form a development committee, or an education committee, or a crèche committee, or whatever. Now, when many of these structures started affiliating to the ANC, they were immediately targeted by both Inkatha and the State. In many cases it was the white security establishment that went to the tribal chiefs and said: "Hey, crush these structures because they're there to undermine your authority."

'So the level of violence was determined by the resistance of the traditional leaders to the emerging democratic structures, as well as interference by the State in this political – battle is not the right word – in this *progression* towards democracy.

'Now with people in Natal living very closely – you know, Kwazulu is forty-four bits of land scattered within Natal – you'd have a person living in a tribal area, being locked into the modern industrial economy, and modern decision-making processes and so on, and then in his private life everything being determined by the Chief. It's a major conflict that was inevitably going to lead to a political battle. Now the fact that this battle became violent, to the degree that in Natal six thousand or whatever people have so far been killed, is a national damn scandal. Because we've got a very sophisticated police force that could, in fact, deal with those who've transgressed, who've stepped over from political struggle to violent struggle.

'When the violence started it was very much of a sporadic, incidental nature. You know, people got themselves into a shouting match, some protest around a school or whatever, somebody gets killed. The numbers of people killed you could count by the month. Until it became apparent that the ANC were very rapidly beginning to mop up first the urban areas, and then going into the fringes, which were the tribal areas. So in 1986 Inkatha entered on major recruitment drives to try and regain territory. And these became more and more vicious. More and more coercive.

'You know, from where I sit here, I can be at any one of the major trouble spots within twenty minutes. I had contacts in every one of the townships and the rural areas, and people would simply phone me and say, "Look, I'm standing here and I'm seeing a hundred armed men descending on this place." And I would immediately get in my car, get out there and see what was cooking. I'd just simply go down, and stand there, and see the thing unfold. I've seen many battles of this nature, in this war. I've seen the Inkatha recruitment drives, where it starts with a couple of people going into the next house, demanding that the boys come out, and just simply go down the line until there were perhaps a hundred people demanding that you sign up your Inkatha card. And if you don't that's just it: your house is gone – and always somehow with the tacit approval, right through to the active collusion, of the police force.'

Cronjé then gave me three or four accounts of fights that he'd witnessed, sounding, I began to think, like some general from the Crimean War, sitting up on top of the Natal hills watching the battles in the valleys below.

And in every case, he was adamant, the police did not play a neutral role. Everyone, as he put it, knows the script of Dallas. The *impis** gathered. Then the police met with them. Then for three hours or so the *impis* ran riot. Then the people watching would say, 'Now they're handing the guns back and picking up the cartridges to destroy the evidence.'

'On every occasion the police would have a story that they had false information of a conflict elsewhere. It's the same story as Boipatong. They've got their set pieces. I've heard them all.'

I liked Pierre Cronjé, and there seemed to be no good reason to disbelieve this Afrikaner who looked you straight in the eye and spoke with such quiet passion about the sufferings of people who could offer him no votes; who were not, historically, on his side.

> * not to be confused with an *impimpi* (an informer), an *impi* is the Zulu word for a small group of fighting warriors. The *impi* was invented by the legendary Zulu King Shaka, who modernised Zulu fighting methods, and was largely responsible for giving the Zulus their reputation for ferocity.

And there was one little description he came up with, in
the course of our long discussion, that struck me as particularly apt. 'You know,' he said, 'for someone like myself, it's
amazing to sit with even the most destitute of people, and
yet see in them this anxiousness about a New South Africa;
you know, a creative energy that's waiting to be released, a
will to succeed, to make it. And then you come back into
white society and they're all sitting there sulking and unsure
of themselves . . .'

I thought it would be only fair to get the other side of the
story, so I called on Gavin Woods, Director of the Inkatha
Institute, and spokesman for Inkatha. Another white man, in
a world of black-on-black.

The Inkatha Institute didn't exactly advertise its presence.
Finally, on the shabby second floor of the central Durban
address I'd been given, I discovered a tiny signboard and a
buzzer.

Woods was a slightly built man with a bad leg. Getting up
from his cluttered desk he moved across the room with a
crablike limp, shook my hand, slumped down gratefully in
the armchair opposite. Camilla had described him as 'terribly neurotic', but he seemed more sad than neurotic. With
his large eyes (magnified by the thick lenses of his spectacles), floppy blond hair and drooping moustache, he
looked, I thought, like the White Knight in *Alice Through
The Looking Glass*.

I was blunt: I told him I'd met Cronjé, heard bad reports of
Inkatha, eyewitness accounts of recruitment drives involving
armed *impis* and the active collaboration of the police.

'Everything is part of the truth,' he replied, in his soft,
rather weary voice. 'But things are very complex. And a lot
of subjects, especially the subject of violence, is something
that one can't talk about in simplistic terms. There's many
ways of looking at this violence. Some people see it as
modernism versus traditionalism, some people see it as a

rural–urban conflict, some people see it as youth versus the Establishment, some people look at it simply in terms of ANC and Inkatha, which implies ideological differences which are there to dispute. But there's also the haves and the have-nots . . .'

He continued in this vein for a while. Poverty, criminality, political labelling, all these things were part of the 'multi-causal arrangement of violence'.

'But what about the involvement of the police?' I asked, trying to bring us back to basics. 'It seems reasonably clear from Cronjé's account that in some instances the police have been directly involved with Inkatha . . .'

Woods nodded thoughtfully. 'In that violence is multi-causal,' he replied, 'people tend to have their pet causes and they exaggerate them, always having some substance. Indeed, Inkatha believes they've been the victim of police actions; have pointed to incidents where they believe the police have helped the ANC. One general statement is that Inkatha has lost the propaganda war on violence. The ANC are very resourceful, and have the sympathies and attention of people who always articulate their side . . .'

It wasn't the most convincing refutation I'd ever heard. Still, Woods was clearly sincere in his loyalty; eager to give me, in some detail, 'the Inkatha perspective on this violence'.

The fall-out had originated, he said, in 1979, after a meeting with the ANC in London, when Inkatha had refused to go along with the ANC's anti-apartheid strategy of 'the armed struggle'. After that, the ANC had declared Inkatha the enemy. Through the newspapers and magazines they controlled and through the Mozambique-based Radio Freedom, the ANC had vilified and denigrated Inkatha in many ways; ways, Woods said, 'which were very contrary to a particular African or black humanism which exists here. They *personalised* people. Buthelezi was called a dog who needs to have his throat cut. And a snake who needs to be smashed in the head.' For a moment there was real anger and upset in that soft tone. Woods looked straight at me through his thick lenses; his eyes were troubled. 'Inkatha has *never* responded to those character assassinations,' he said. 'Has never personalised the conflict to that extent.

'The ANC,' he went on, 'cottoned on to the black fomenting urban youth, and they just nurtured it in hate. The vehicle they chose in the early 1980s was to suggest Inkatha was a collaborator of the apartheid regime, part of the whole apartheid system in a very pro-active way. Inkatha argued that it wasn't, and in fact was able to produce documents to show that they became part of the system only with the blessing of the ANC leadership.

'So the collaborationist thing was untrue. But it's very understandable. You see, the ANC leadership, being in exile, found themselves at a distinct disadvantage. They could feed propaganda through, they could get a certain amount of people, but they couldn't lead in the direct sense. And there was Inkatha growing in leaps and bounds. They had to marginalise, discredit Inkatha. So this collaborationist thing became the way to do it. And once again what they used to say is all on record: the callings by Chris Hani to assassinate Inkatha Central Committee members, published in London in *The Times*; many other callings for murder of Inkatha leaders. ANC infiltrators were arrested on more than one occasion and under interrogation said they were sent to murder Buthelezi. We're inclined to believe that's the truth.'

It would be easy to tell you that there was something creepy about Gavin Woods; that his refutation of every anti-Inkatha criticism I'd heard was clearly motivated by a large salary, or the warped professionalism of the corrupt PR man. But that wasn't the case. As we talked through the details of Boipatong, and I sat listening to his patient repetition of 'And that's on record', and 'We're inclined to believe', and 'Everything's part of the truth', I found myself wondering what it was that had made this slight, crippled white man so intensely loyal to the Zulu cause.

I asked him about his upbringing, and with the pressure off, he relaxed noticeably. 'I'll tell you what influenced my life,' he said. 'Being part of a very big family which was a very poor white family. We started going to school without shoes, which was practically unheard of for whites in South Africa. We lived in a very humble home. My father was the market master, in a small town in the Natal midlands. That was the way he got food on the table, got us our schooling. And most of us went on to university, but we had to put ourselves through. We had a particular determination. But it was a humbling experience. We were somewhat left out of the white community in many respects.

'Mother and Father were both fluent in Zulu. And my mother had a great number of Zulu friends, usually the maids from around the district, who used to come to our house every morning with letters from their husbands, from the mines. And she used to read them their letters, because they couldn't read Zulu. Then they'd dictate, and she'd write them their letters.

'One of the very pleasant memories of my childhood is of our old kitchen, with all the black maids sitting round – because of their sort of communal, sharing way of doing things there was nothing personal about a letter from your husband. And everybody used to wail and cry and laugh together at everybody else's letter. And my mother used to make them each a huge cup of tea and a slice of bread and jam – it was lovely.

'And then my father had a major impact on my life. He was a founder member of the Progressive Party and a very astute man – a guy who could have gone a long way in his life if he'd had the breaks, but his father died as a kid and he left school a bit early, and even though he did further his education, he never quite found his feet. But he was able to teach us children why apartheid was wrong. I got caned at school for being too political when I was eleven years old . . . Funny things that come back to me. My brother and I used to go round on our bicycles at night and paint swastikas on all the Nationalist Party posters at every general election. And no other kids would understand why we had to do that.

'Then, many years later, I started part-time university after I'd been working for a few years. And I met students who'd come from Afrikaner families, and they'd had a great life but suddenly they developed a conscience and became more politicised than I was. And it used to irritate me a little. Even today a lot of people have taken good positions because they're anti-apartheid, but they've done it on a very comfortable route. With an easy education, the best private schools, they've never gone without a meal. And I get angry when people say, you know, "These blacks must get rid of their tribal structures. It's not democratic, and you can't afford to have that in your New South Africa." I think there are a lot of things they don't understand. The patronage of black politics might sound distasteful. But it has its place, and it's not something we can, by some clause in a new constitution, just get rid of.

'As to the violence – when it started, I was as appalled as anybody. But I felt a need to say: "There must be something that's making it happen." And at the end, I felt that it was just another story of human tragedy. Of everybody believing that what they were doing was justified, and even now in the violence, both sides always feel they've defended themselves. And it's not really about good people and bad people. There are people that exploit emotions. I think there are some bad politicians, from all sides, and there are other catalysts, including the police. But at the end of the day the people that manage to get involved in fighting – they are good people. A lot of the people in the party are just very lovely people. Buthelezi himself, if you get to know him, is just the most incredible man.'

It was time for some light relief, so I went downtown to a cabaret bar called Frankie's to catch the world premiere of a show which was on its way to the Grahamstown Festival (South Africa's equivalent of Edinburgh).

Frankie's had bright green walls and a wacky multi-coloured mural. A big plastic parrot hung from the ceiling. The barman had long blond hair in a ponytail. As did the manager. As did half the customers. The place was in fact full of the kind of right-on trendies you might have found in an Islington fringe venue in 1986; and every last one of them was white.

From outside the front door came a great shouting and shrieking. The ponytailed manager closed the door hurriedly. A street-fight was in progress and it was only ten minutes to curtain up.

A couple entered. 'Did you know there was someone bleeding to death outsard?' they said. 'Yiss,' said the manager, rather nervously. There was a rapid conferring with the barman, some worried looks at watches, then a decision to phone an ambulance. Nobody went outside to see the damage. No hysterical young woman got up from the red and green checked table-cloths and rushed to comfort the victim. There was no drama at all.

Every couple of minutes another groovily dressed couple would knock on the (now locked) glass front door and be let in. 'Did you know there's some guy lying in a pool of blood rart outsard,' they'd say. 'It's OK,' said the manager, 'we've called an ambulance.'

Upstairs, in the corridor by the Gents, the actresses were putting the final touches to their make-up. 'Of course I'm nervous,' said a young man in a tweed jacket and tie, pacing up and down.

The ambulance had arrived. But the stabbed man had either made off somewhere or been removed. The ambulance drove off down the narrow street, the Indian driver and his assistant peering carefully to left and right. Relief was visible on the plump manager's face; the problem had shifted elsewhere, with just five minutes to lights up.

The show was a spoof on South African TV advertising, and despite a complete absence of jokes, the two actresses – one in a pink nightie, one with a shaved head – soon had their audience in stitches. We waited for a good ten seconds for them to calm down from the first sketch before the third woman appeared.

'Psst!' she said. 'Hi! I'm a regular scientist and I'm here to tell you about *this*!' She held up an oversized mock-up of a soap powder box. 'The ultimate word in micro soap powder technology. We call it new Mega Mighty Micro Double Plus. Just think, housewife, at last a soap powder so concentrated that you only need a fingernail to clean your whole family's wash. Yes, new Mega Mighty Micro Double Plus actually devours all colours except for the whitest white. And here's proof. In the studio here tonight we've got our very own dullwit housewife and stupid mother.'

'I really am a regular housewife,' said the girl in the pink nightdress. 'I was always into micro-powders and I thought: Oh look, another one on the market! Big deal! But then I tried it. And just look how white my brand new Woolworths' long-patterned dress turned out. I was delighted with the result. And now my family is whiter than the whitest white and I feel fulfilled at last.'

'Psst! Tell us. Would you swap your new Mega Mighty Micro Double Plus for two thousand packets of ordinary soap powders?'

'No ways! I'm sticking with new Mega Mighty Micro Double Plus.'

'And tell us: how else did new Mega Mighty Micro Double Plus change your whole life?'

'Yah – OK,' said the housewife, pausing for maximum effect. 'Before I fell into the washing machine with new Mega Mighty Micro Double Plus – I actually – used to be – a *black prostitute*!'

Shrieks of laughter; a rustle of right-on uncertainty; general amusement prevailing. 'And there you have it,' said our housewife. 'The world's first non-racial soap powder, for the New South Africa. Putting whiteness where you've never seen it before.'

If I was interested in this whole ANC–Inkatha struggle, and the many ironies that surrounded it, there was one other famous local figure, Camilla told me, that I couldn't leave Durban without talking to: Roley Arenstein, a white Marxist lawyer who'd been a leading anti-apartheid activist in his day, had gone to jail for his beliefs, and had now, in his old age – paradoxically as she saw it – ended up as a key supporter of Inkatha. Indeed, I was to be told later, as Buthelezi's legal right hand man.

Thinking now of the vitriol I was to hear directed against Arenstein later in my journey, it's hard to recall how decent a man he struck me as being, that sunny June afternoon in Camilla's kitchen, as we sat drinking tea by the French windows.

He was in his seventies: white hair, a narrow, heavily lined face, a big nose, a small pointed white beard and moustache. But what you noticed were his large brown eyes, that fixed on you, clear, without even a flicker of the guilt or self-doubt of lesser mortals. That, and an endearing chuckle, which punctuated his speech throughout.

As a young man, he told me, he'd picked up a short book on Marxism by a writer called John Strachey. 'And when I read that, I knew that I'd found something that would keep me going for the rest of my life. Marxism seems to be able to explain everything. Not that you don't make mistakes. It's like a doctor. You learn how to treat disease, but that doesn't mean that you're going to treat disease properly every time. But that basic training of yours keeps you going for the rest of your life as a doctor. And this is what Marxism has meant to me.

'I never hesitated to say I was a Marxist. I stood trial a couple of times, and the first thing the prosecutor said to me was: "Are you a Communist?" "Yuh, I'm a Communist."' He chuckled. 'There was no substance in the actual evidence against me. But they convicted me on *my* evidence. They said: "Mr Arenstein says he's a Communist, he believes in Marxism, and whatever he does, he's hoping that in the end it will work out." On that point they found me guilty of furthering the aims of Communism. And for that I got four years.'

As for the current violence: well, the ANC–Inkatha crisis all had to do with the central question facing South Africa. Namely: *What is democracy?*

'This is the key question, Mark. It all goes round this one point: must there be power-sharing, or must it be universal franchise, full stop? What *is* democracy? Does it mean simply one man one vote, or does it also mean the rights of nations to self-determination? In a multi-national state you must always take into account the different national groups. If you don't there's going to be trouble.'

The prescription was Lenin's. It was Lenin who had said that nations had to fight for the right to self-determination; who had agreed with Stalin on his definition of a nation. 'Take this down, Mark,' said the old political prisoner, 'this is very important: A nation is a historically constituted, stable community, of common language, common territory, common economy, common psychological make-up, as evidenced by a community of culture.'

On this definition you could, he said, divide up South Africa as follows: 1) The Nguni language group: including Zulus, Xhosas, and Swazis; 2) the Sothos, North, South and West; 3) the Vendas; 4) the Shangaans; 5) the English; 6) the Afrikaners; 7) the Indians; 8) the Coloureds.

'One man, one vote yes,' said Arenstein, 'but there must be a second house, where the rights of nations are carried out.'

'But they're all living all over the place,' I objected, 'so it would be impossible.'

'That doesn't matter. Each nation doesn't have to have its separate state. It's useful if it does, but it's not a necessity. Take the Jews of Russia. They never had a homeland. Yet, every Jew in Russia carried an identity card, where his nationality was put in.'

Inkatha believed in power-sharing; the ANC in one man one vote. The other reason Arenstein supported Inkatha was because they had always said they stood for peaceful change. 'I'll give you one example. When Nelson Mandela came out, one day I phoned him, because he was calling for peace. His second speech, if you remember, was "Take your arms and throw them into the sea." And he was a great friend of Buthelezi's. The two of them were personal friends, before this whole business started. So I phoned up Mandela and I said, "It's about time you and Buthelezi got together, and together go to the people, and call for peace." He said, "That's fine, good idea, get hold of Buthelezi and let's talk about it." So I phoned up Buthelezi and he said, "Oh, fine." So they phoned each other. Mandela said to Buthelezi, "All right, find a good place to meet, and we'll call a big mass meeting, in the areas where there's violence. We'll call for the end of the violence." Buthelezi thought about it, and he came forward with a place called Taylor's Halt. And he phoned Mandela back, and said, "We can meet at Taylor's Halt." Hell!' Roley shook his head, and gave me a broad smile, 'as soon as the ANC chaps heard about Taylor's Halt, they went mad. They said: "That is a powerful constituency of Buthelezi, they'll kill us there, oh, what they won't do to us!" So Mandela then said, "No, we can't agree to Taylor's Halt." So Buthelezi said, "OK, I'm prepared to go anywhere, you name another place, it's only a suggestion." Mandela went back to his representatives and they said, "Nothing doing, nothing doing. Have nothing to do with Buthelezi." And subsequently Mandela said that if he'd gone on with the peace effort he would have been throttled. By his own followers.*

---

* A somewhat different perspective on these events is to be found in Matthew Kentridge's excellent account of the Pietermaritzburg violence, *An Unofficial War*, published by David Philip, Cape Town and Johannesburg, pp. 242–3. Kentridge's account suggests that

'And you see,' he went on, 'violence has it's own momentum. You can't just say, "Today we'll have violence, and tomorrow tell people to stop," because by tomorrow my brother might have been killed in the violence, and I, as a Zulu, will not rest until my brother has been revenged. I can't let his soul go on, not take any steps to revenge it. And a lot of the killings are revenge killings . . .'

WIMBLEDON SEX WAR [read the main headline of the *Natal Mercury*]

London. Dutch seed Richard Krajicek dropped himself in the middle of a sex war at Wimbledon yesterday by suggesting that most women players are 'fat pigs'. Krajicek admitted saying in a Dutch radio interview: '80% of the top 100 women are fat pigs who don't deserve equal pay.'

Gerald was disgusted. 'We're in the middle of a national crisis,' he said, 'and this is what they put on the front page. I don't know why we buy it.'

It was Saturday morning and Gerald was going to drive me up into Kwazulu to deliver some left-over fence poles and netting to Christina, their maid. 'I thought it might be interesting for you to see where she lives,' he said. 'We've been meaning to take that stuff up there for ages; it's a good excuse now you're here.'

Christina arrived promptly at 9.30 a.m., having travelled the twenty kilometres into Kloof by bus. 'Did you have to get up early to get down here, Christina?' Gerald asked, as we drove off, the trailer rattling precariously behind us. 'Yes, master – no master,' Christina replied, 'no, not too early, master.'

Mandela never gave his agreement for the Taylor's Halt meeting in the first place. He also contrasts Mandela's consistently conciliatory tone with Buthelezi's public attack of the ANC at the opening of the Kwazulu Assembly in March 1990, where he blamed the ANC for starting the war and keeping it going over the years.

The master was wearing shorts and a T-shirt, and having kicked off his sandals, drove his big estate car with bare feet. We turned off the main highway at a sign saying VALLEY OF THE THOUSAND HILLS. We were clearly on a tourist route: we passed viewpoints and tea rooms and curio shops, then a big Gothic-castle-like hotel, the Rob Roy. Here we turned right, off the white ridge and down into the black valley; for as well as being (from a distance) a tourist attraction, the Valley of the Thousand Hills was also one of the forty-four pockets of Kwazulu.

We bumped along a dreadful dirt road, suddenly in a world of mudhuts and goats and African women with plastic buckets on their heads.

'Amazing, isn't it?' said Gerald. 'You turn off and instantly you're in the Third World. Where do we go now Christina?'

'Straight, master. No – left – no, straight, master.'

Eventually we arrived at Christina's little house, which stood on its own on the side of one of the thousand hills. The ground sloped sharply away from her little plot to a tiny valley; then up to another little hill, and on into the lovely blue distance.

'It's funny, isn't it,' said Gerald, 'to think that if things were different, this would be an absolutely prime place to live. Look at that view.'

Shorty, Christina's little ten year old boy, rushed up to help us unload the poles and netting.

By African standards, Christina wasn't badly off. She had quite a large plot of land – half an acre or so – for which, she had, she said 'a receipt'. On our drive up Gerald had elaborated on what I'd already learnt of tribal land management. If a house was occupied, and 'being made the best use of', the family was allowed to stay; but if they upped and offed to be nearer to town, then they had no right to the land they'd left behind.

The house was made of mud and cement, with a corrugated iron roof. A tiny front room led off left to an even tinier bedroom, and through to a galley-sized kitchen. Round the back was a second little room, and behind that 'the fire room', a *rondawel* with a traditional grass roof. 'I cut the grass, master,' Christina said. 'Me – I cut the grass.' She laughed.

'You see the method of construction here,' said Gerald, patting the wall. 'You see how they've plastered on the mud with their hands, and then put cement on top which makes it more durable. What's this room, Christina?' he asked, poking his head into the darkness of the second room.

'This master – for the boys in school – not finished.'

'And where does Shorty sleep – in the *rondawel*?'

'No master – he fright – he pull mattress to the dining room.'

The kitchen was spotless. The paraffin lamps shone. A *Biscuits Au Beurre* tin was stacked neatly on a fabloned shelf by a row of tupperware.

'Ah look,' said Gerald, poking into the bedroom – 'that's one of the bits of carpet from our last house in Westville. And this old cabinet,' he patted a dark wood monster in the corner, 'that was one of the things we brought up here for her. This couch – I'll tell you about this couch in a moment.'

Christina went outside. 'This couch,' Gerald said in a low voice, 'this couch she got from some Indian furniture store in Pinetown – she uses our address to get it on hire purchase – for some incredible price – 600 rand or something. And when you think what she earns – she only works for us two days a week – that's a hell of a lot of money. I tell you, it makes me very humble when I think of what she's got here. It's only small – but the *pride* she has in it. You know, when you read in the papers of another hundred shacks being burnt down in the conflict . . . but if you think what Christina would feel if this place was harmed, after all the saving and scraping she's done to make it nice . . .' Gerald shook his head slowly from side to side.

Nailed to the wall in the little room with the couch was a

calendar saying TARGET FURNISHERS. It featured a little black family playing on a sunny beach. Black Mum and Dad, and two smiling happy black kids, a boy and a girl.

Outside, Gerald and Christina were looking at the view. On the next little hill was a substantial *kraal*: three or four huts within a fenced ring.

'Is that a very important man?' asked Gerald.

'Master?'

'Is that a very rich – important man – living there?'

'No, master – just one man and three wifes.'

We left. 'Is she married?' I asked Gerald, as we bumped back down the dirt. 'No,' he replied, 'she never got married. She's had five children I think, by different men, one of whom she's still very keen on – but she's never got married.'

We drove on, Gerald waving and shouting the Zulu greeting 'Sawubona!' at the passers-by, some of whom stared in amazement; some of whom, kids mostly, waved and shouted back.

'And so,' he said, as we bumped back onto the tar road at the top of the ridge, 'we go back through the looking glass.'

15

MOTHER-IN-LAW EXTERMINATOR

And then I got what everybody else in Durban had – the flu. I had such a great list of things to do, people to see: a black leader from the left-wing of the ANC; the last white trade union leader in South Africa; an 'amazing Swedish guy' called Matthew, who was known as 'the White Zulu', and could take me to meet an Inkatha warlord; the first black man to marry a white after the abolition of the Immorality and Mixed Marriages Acts; a famous sculptor friend of Otto's; a representative of what Camilla called the ONF's – the Old Natal Families – who had a huge sugar-cane estate . . .

Instead, I sat shivering under a blanket in Gerald and Mari's glass-fronted verandah, with a cup of hot lemon and honey, drained of all energy, watching Jessie the golden labrador chasing monkeys across the lawn.

It was mid-winter, and Wimbledon was on the telly, with a commentary in Afrikaans. Katie was in love with Agassi, who was *diffinitely* going to win. I struggled from my armchair for a Sunday lunch-time *braai*. 'How come black people can eat so much hot food, Daddy,' asked Peter. 'What d'you mean . . .?' 'You know, like chillies and things.' 'Well, I expect if you eat that sort of food on a regular basis, you'd get used to it, Peter,' said Gerald.

My greatest disappointment was that I'd failed even to

dip my toe into the Indian community. There they were, crowding the streets of Durban, and I'd barely spoken to even one.

So, dosed up with Day Nurse, I drove down to the city centre, to the Indian Market, and joined a collection of tourists in shorts poking round stalls that sold leather goods and brass elephants and rolls of silk and boxes full of live chickens and samosas. In the food shops two-foot-high pyramids of coloured rice and spices rose out of circular plastic dishwashing bowls: PINK LENTILS, BASMATI RICE, OIL DHALL rubbed shoulders with HONEYMOONERS' SPECIAL and MOTHER-IN-LAW EXTERMINATOR.

Outside, on Grey Street, I walked into a shop showing a video of a Muslim mullah preaching. Twenty or thirty people, Indians and blacks, sat watching. I was handed a leaflet which read: MORE THAN HALF OF ENGLAND'S ANGLICAN BISHOPS ABSOLVE THEMSELVES FROM BLASPHEMY AND REGARD . . . JESUS – AS ONLY A MESSENGER. Alongside a photograph of The Rev Professor DAVID JENKINS was a long rubric which concluded: 'The rejection of Jesus's divinity by more than half of England's Anglican bishops is indeed a flicker of light at the end of the long, dark tunnel of Christianity in which the Christians have been sadly groping for over 2,000 years.'

There was a general clapping and grunting. The video – produced, I noticed, in Ruislip – had come to an end. Everybody stayed seated while another identikit mullah was put on.

I asked directions to the Grey Street mosque, 'the largest in the Southern Hemisphere', and was led by a young black out of the shop, through a shopping mall, sharp left down a narrow corridor, and up four floors in a lift to be given tea in a silk-panelled drawing room with one Said Mohammed, a serious young Indian in a white kneelength smock. He had a white embroidered tarboosh on his head and a little black beard. Why did I want to see the mosque? Did I want to know about the Muslim religion? If I was seriously interested, I could join another group at ten the following morning.

The other group turned out to be a school hockey team from Cape Town. So twenty white sixteen year old South African girls, two teachers, Said Mohammed and I removed our shoes and passed through a room with a marble mosaic floor around a square shallow pool with goldfish swimming in it and low stools all around. I'd never visited a mosque before, and as we padded up the stairs I was expecting something magnificent: golden statues of Indian gods and goddesses, fabulously ornate ceilings, pairs of shaven-headed devotees, perhaps, walking solemnly as they waved incense by elaborate altars.

Instead we were shown into a huge empty room with nothing in it but an endless shabby green and red carpet. From the far end came the loud whine of a vacuum cleaner.

The disappointment was audible. 'Ezz thess – ett?' asked the South African teacher.

'This is the largest mosque in the Southern Hemisphere,' said Said Mohammed. 'Please sit down.

'You are all Christians?' he continued, as I sneezed, and the hockey team, now arranged in a semi-circle on the floor, nodded uncertainly.

With the hoover whining loudly in the background it was hard to hear Said, but it was clear he was doing his best to popularise his religion in the manner of trendy preachers the world over. 'I'm sure you all watch Western movies and find them most entertaining,' he shouted, in a voice too close to Peter Sellers to be taken entirely seriously. 'John Wayne, *High Chaperall*, *High Noon* and so on. When they are challenged they put their hands up. So, when we Muslims are in prayer, we put our hands . . .'

He was drowned by the approaching hoover.

'Now Princess Diana', I caught, a little later, 'is every-body's favourite. But if she gets a suntan, we wouldn't call her coloured. The devil we are dealing with in the Muslim religion is not the devil with long horns and a tail, but the devil within ourselves, racialism and . . .'

Hoover.

'The mosque is a keep-fit institution also, it keeps you fit mentally. The average person eats five times daily to maintain physical self, so we say . . .'

Hoover.

Suddenly, miraculously, after forty minutes or so, the machine was silenced, and lacking competition, Said Mohammed came to a rapid conclusion. 'Any questions?' he asked, smiling round. Before anyone could stop her, an earnest-looking girl in a pink sweatshirt had her hand up and was asking: 'How come you refer so much to the Bible, and yet you reject large parts of the Bible?'

'That is a beautiful question – have you got the time?' Said Mohammed smiled. Ten minutes later he was still talking and another girl had her hand up. 'Nah, Miriam,' came an urgent whispering from the teacher behind me. And then: 'Miriam – put your hand *down.*'

But over the far side of the semi-circle another hand was up.

'What are the beads for?' asked a girl with a blonde crew cut.

'I'm virry sorry, but I'm afraid we've got an appointment downtown at half past eleven,' interrupted the teacher. 'So we really have to go now. But we have enjoyed your talk virry much.'

'May I just answer this question?' Said Mohammed smiled seraphically. 'I see it is only quarter past eleven. Yes, when I am praying, all of a sudden my thoughts might start drifting to food – burgers, Wimpy, McDonald's, my thoughts can go wild . . .'

'We've really got to go now,' said the teacher.

'I'm keeping my eye on the clock . . .'

'It's quite a walk downtown.'

'Two more minutes, please,' said Said, holding up a finger.

'One question I'm surprised nobody has asked is: why women are not allowed in the mosque . . . Islam acknowledges the attraction between the sexes and if I came in here and there was a woman prostrating herself before me, and I am standing behind, it may be hard for me to think: a thousand praises be to God for creating such a perfect symmetry. I may not be able to concentrate on my prayers . . .'

I suddenly had an urgent appointment myself. As I left he was saying: 'We are not so different, at home we watch all the soaps, *Loving, The Bold and the Beautiful . . .*'

I found the splendour I'd been seeking, out in the Indian township of Chatsworth. The temple had four tall white towers with golden cupolas, a sweeping flight of steps up to the main entrance, and in the octagonal interior as many lavish surfaces as any hockey team could have hoped for. The ornate gold ceiling featured eight scenes from the life of Krishna; the rich marble of the floor was streaked with pale pinks and oranges; the central altar had coloured, fully dressed statues of Krishna and his followers, garlanded with fresh flowers: white-swathed devotees with shaved heads rang bells, waved incense, sprinkled me with water and flower petals.

But if I thought I'd found tradition and age-old Indian culture I was disappointed. The splendid building had only recently been completed; it was not a Hindu, but a Hare Krishna temple; a movement which had only arrived in South Africa in 1974 – and had been brought over by an Englishman.

Silently contemplating the altar I found I'd been joined by a party of forty Indian five year olds, all in neat black and white uniforms.

'So Krishna came to the earth 5,000 years ago,' said their teacher. 'How many years ago?'

'5,000 years ago,' they chanted.

'When he was a little boy he was very naughty. He began to eat sand, from the ground. And his mother told him off. But he said, "No mother, I'm not eating sand." And who knows what Krishna's mother saw when she opened his mouth? Yes, she saw the stars and the sun . . . and so she knew that Krishna was not an ordinary person, but that he was God.'

The teacher pointed over towards the statue of His Divine Grace Bhaktivedenta Swami Prabhupada, just at the end of the bench I was sitting on. 'And the person you see sitting over there is our holy leader, who took the message of Krishna from India all over the world.'

Forty five year old faces gazed at me with an awe I hadn't felt since I was a professional Father Christmas in Covent Garden.

Leaving the temple I took a drive round Chatsworth. The houses in this huge Indian township were of a completely different order to those in the black townships. Though packed closely together, there seemed to be none smaller than a fair-sized bungalow, and many were built several stories upwards, with elaborate verandahs, porches, balconies. The only thing lacking was the surrounding space of the white areas, the gardens and trees; and of course all except the main roads were dirt.

I stumbled upon the Chatsworth fair, which was on its opening day and packed with Indian senior citizens, sitting in rows watching a stage where a white-haired old Indian in a cream jacket was having the time of his life chanting into a microphone, while six sixty-pluses in saris did elaborate dances on the grass below.

In a square around them stalls and tents offered Life Insurance, Saucepans, Meals on Wheels, St John's Ambulance, Delicious Hot Chips, Durban Bible College, Al Galaxy Disco . . .

*

All indeed seemed fine on the surface of the Indian community. But Kriben Pillay, a young Indian playwright, told
me otherwise. Recently, there had been a great number of
murders in Indian Durban. 'Children murdering their
parents. Father shooting his wife and daughter. There's been
a horrific killing almost every week. Sociologists and crimi-
nologists are all putting their heads together and saying,
"Why is this happening?"'

Kriben had his own answer, which had to do with his
conviction that people (especially the Indian community in
South Africa) were too wrapped up with their own social
conditioning. 'I think we hold onto these notions of who we
think we are, of race and tradition and so forth, in an absurd
way. People hold onto these things, and they never question
why. You know, they say, "It's my religion," and so forth;
but if you speak to the average Indian – and you know I can
be knocked on the head for saying this – they don't know
what their religion is about. You know, they know the
rituals; and they can say, "Oh, you didn't do this when your
son got married, that's going to bring bad luck to the family."
But there's a lot of superstition . . .

'And for us Indians in South Africa to have this huge fear
that we're going to lose our values is ridiculous. There's
already a great deal of Westernisation, perhaps more than
we care to admit, and to have your daughter practising
Indian dance, or the fact that you do all your rituals on the
set days, doesn't necessarily make you an Indian Indian.
There's already been a transformation: you're now a South
African Indian. And you have to be open to the fact that
there will be other influences. There'll be greater inter-
marriage, as people relax. There'll be blacks marrying Indians, whites, all that will happen.

'But still, a Tamil may not easily marry a Gujurati. So
there is a problem. Where in India, it might not be such a
problem because Gujurat is 3,000 miles away from Madras,
here we're all together. So we're holding onto false notions

of things. And there's all kinds of psycho-social problems arising.'

'But how will this lead to someone actually murdering someone else?'

'Well, there's been a lot of suicides as well. And a lot of it's got to do with the fact that a Hindi boy, from the Hindi linguistic group, was in love with a Tamil girl, and the parents wouldn't allow it. So he went and shot himself, shot his lover, that type of thing.

'What I'm saying is that we are encouraged, especially in the Indian community . . .' Kriben broke off, then after four or five seconds of thought, began again. 'Most of our neighbours when I was younger had a name for an African, a black person. They would teach their children to say, I think the word is *billalloo*. I don't know what it means but, you know, "the *billalloo*'s coming for you." They train their dogs to bark at Africans. It's a strange thing, you'll find dogs not barking at anyone else, but at an African person, in an Indian area. Now that's got to come from somewhere. And if at the same time you say, "I've got this 5,000 year old civilisation, which I'm holding onto . . ." I'm just against any kind of blind adherence to something which, I think, limits us. If people want to have their particular faith, that's fine, I've no problems with that. I'm talking about using that to say: "This is your identity. And if you do this you're going to lose that."

'Now even one's faith, one's religious outlook, is just symbolic of another dimension of human experience which we haven't even begun to tap. For me, there is definitely a spiritual dimension, but it doesn't come out in the conditioning we have been exposed to, by way of so-called religious traditions and what have you. That's simple rote response, rote learning. But more than that it creates *fear*. Because if I've been brought up with the sense that I'm a Hindu, and my Hindu tradition makes me very different as a human being to that of the Muslim, or the Christian, then I'm going to try and preserve it. I'm going to get involved in acts that make me keep the divide even wider, never ever saying, "Can I see it in another way?" Now your average working-class Indian simply inherits this. He doesn't have the time, or the energy, to think about it, and is caught up in the momentum. This is where I feel we, as intellectuals, have a part to play. And for me this comes out in whatever I write. I'm constantly – I won't say attacking it, but unfolding it. I'll just quote the lyrics from one of the songs in this musical I wrote recently, which kind of sums up the way I feel about things.'

Kriben leant forward, and in a voice which had the complete sincerity of the artist with his own work, read:

> When you get to know
> each other
> Daring to say
> sister and brother,
> Knowing that you're
> not the same,
> In the way you look,
> In the sound of your name,
> But just the same,
> In all our pain,
> In all our love
> In all our death,
> And see the symbols of our Gods,
> As the symbols of our Breath,
> Which is the same for you,
> Which is the same for me,
> Then we touch our common roots,
> With eyes that finally see.

Above the main Grandstand stretched four, five tiers of expectant faces. Restaurants, bars, and above them the glassed-in boxes of the chosen few. On the sunny side of the track, the picnics had already begun. Extravagant cars with extravagant bootloads: cold chicken, salmon, champagne, lobster . . .

Women, women everywhere: tight yellow skirt, black and white striped top with yellow sleeves; crimson leather jacket over black velvet leggings; something from the 1920s, pencil thin in silvery glitter, two white ostrich feathers trailing from the hands; a breasty blonde in a leather miniskirt, shiny leather thigh boots, black lace *décolleté*. 'Christ!' gasps a passing suit to his friend.

An older woman, almost completely obscured by a gigantic white bow. Hats with little veils, hats loaded with flowers; a huge black and white saucer of a hat with matching stick of black and white beneath.

The guys mostly, of course, in boring old suit and tie. But also: white tux over black trousers, long blond hair, spreading shades (accompanying chick in gold chain mail with black knee-length coat over); brown corduroy jacket over crumpled sea-green trousers; impeccable white linen suit with long black ponytail; huge balding fatty in hand-embroidered shirt; a pair of chaps in grey tails and toppers; formal black tie . . . oops! she's over, his luscious companion in pink, tumbling ass over tit (and what tit!) down the steps under the track, not sure whether to laugh or cry, rubbing her bruised leg and laddered tights.

And who is *this*? JR in a cream stetson and broad pin-stripes, arm in arm with a fifty-something female in a baseball cap, jeans and a T-shirt that says KICK BUTT. Someone *very* wide coming now: black and silver spotted shirt, bottle-green satin jacket, and goodness, two magnificent *black* women, one in a tall red pillar box hat, the other in a black and pink lacy confection.

Johannesburg has arrived in Durban. For the day. The lovely late-September sun gleams and glints off a thousand pairs of binoculars. For this is the Durban July – the premier social event of the Durban 'Season', South Africa's Ascot Ladies Day (there are horse races going on in the background) and I have hung around for three days specially to see it, to be here alone with a gold badge that says ALEX CHIVERS, that

Camilla has told me will get me up through complex layers
of security and into Mr Chivers' private box on the top tier –
Mr Chivers being something Very Big in Durban Racing.

For the moment though I am mixing with the proles,
hardly bothering to gawp as a chopper descends amongst us
from the blue heavens, lands on track, disgorges three men
and a thin woman in yellow, looking mildly sheepish as
they run through the windy slipstream up to the bandstand.
'Ladies and Gentlemen,' says the tannoy, 'arriving on track,
Perry Stevens, the star of *Loving*, and his wife.'

Up by the giant scoreboard the search is on for the Best-
Dressed Lady. 'The prize, Ladies and Gentlemen,' says the
pigskin wallet tanned compere, 'is seven nights for four at
any one of the luxurious RCI Resorts.' 'How are *ewe*?' says a
voice behind me. 'First of all,' says the compere, 'we have
no 1, Gael Carruthers.' Gael steps up. She is the very baguette
in black and white I've noticed earlier, with the 'uge hat. Her
magnificent ruby lips crinkle into a wide smile and the
crowd ripples with applause.

The final line-up of twelve has two Indians and ten whites,
five of whom are dressed entirely in black and white. 'It's all
black and white this year, isn't it?' says an observant voice
behind me. 'We need some more kaffirs,' says another.

'Judges, are you ready,' says the compere. 'The judges
have been loaded into the starting stalls . . . the judges are
now conferring . . . you all look lovely, they've been up all
night, sewing away, Meg Jameson is looking deep in thought
here, and the decision is – our best-dressed lady is . . .
Number One, Gael Carruthers. Give us a twirl, doll, what's a
fashion show without a twirl?'

I ease off through the crowds to the Grandstand, ready
now for whatever Mr Chivers and friends have to throw at
me. I get as far as the second layer of security. 'That badge of
yours is five years out of date,' says the steward with the
dark glasses and the mobile phone. '*Are* you in Alex Chivers'
box? Alex has been moaning about these old badges . . .'

I make a hurried retreat back down the stairs and into the Yataghan Curry Tavern, which is full of Indians, with a sprinkling of whites. I stand in line and buy a curry. There is nowhere to sit. An Indian guy in a suit stands up for me. 'If you're chowing, you must sit,' he says. The white lady at the nearby table continues to guard her three empty seats.

To my left, an Indian mother sits on the floor with her two doll-like children. I smile indulgently at them, then warmly at the Indian next to me. He scowls.

'It's terrible for horse-racing,' he says.

'What is?'

'Letting children in.'

'Oh well . . . it's only for a day.'

'No it's not – it's all the time now.'

I head back out for the Celebrity Parade. 'Our first VIP passenger is Diana Tilden-Davis – Miss South Africa.' She grins, royally. 'In the Cher Corvette behind, Mr Perry Stevens, the star of *Loving* . . . and in our third car, a Plymouth Ragtop, our celebrity is Doreen Morris, South Africa's Best Dressed Woman.' Doreen is black, and yes, she is very well dressed.

'I'm so numb,' says a drunken guy at the rail next to me, 'I'm beyond numb. I'm what you call *local anaesthetic*!' He and his friend fall about.

And then the Big Race, the Durban July. Craning, you can see nothing, and then, suddenly, they've thundered past. 'Yo baby, yo baby, yo!' shouts a white winner in the crowd behind.

General Alan Fraser, the Chairman of Rothmans of Pall Mall in London, is presenting the Rothmans Sash to the winner, Spanish Galliard, owned by Mr and Mrs H. F. Oppenheimer. For it is of course the Rothmans Durban July.

16

GATSHA

In the Sunday morning sunshine I hopped up the resorts of the Natal north coast. Luxurious high-rise hotel-lined Umhlanga Rocks could have been in Europe, only there weren't enough blacks on the beach. A sprawling family lay about in their skimpy bathing trunks, while their maid, fully dressed in pink overalls and bonnet, sat upright a yard or two to their right.

The long stretch of dunes called La Mercy was clearly an Indian beach. Not a white to be seen. Outside the hotel a small crowd – women elegant in saris – stood by a parked bus, eating curry from paper plates with their fingers.

In Ballito, I stopped for lunch on a sunny terrace in a shopping mall. 'I wouldn't say the special is *that* special; why do they put it on special if it is?' said Davis the waiter, laughing loudly. Black humour, white privilege: I was back in the thick of it again.

On, on, over the undulating green fields of sugar cane I drove, coming to Mtunzini at sunset. 'You can have a walk on that beach that'll blow your mind,' Camilla had said; so I hid my shoes in the dunes and wandered barefoot along the edge of the surf for a mile or two. Being alone in a beautiful place again, watching the moon rising through the dying crimson glow, I missed Sarah dreadfully. A couple ran past me, laughing and tussling in the gloaming, just to hammer home the 6,000 miles between us.

But then the morning sun was shining on the green cane, and ahead was the blue outline of mountains, gently striped by horizontal bands of mist . . . or was it woodsmoke? Palm trees dotted the landscape. I was driving into Zululand.

Not that the whole of this area was technically Kwazulu. The Nationalist Government hadn't been that generous, keeping themselves a healthy corridor – 100 kilometres or so wide – bang through the middle of these ancestral lands. For the whites, too, have sacred memories here. Just outside Mtonjaneni is the grave of Piet Retief, leader of the Afrikaners on their Great Trek north from Grahamstown. And Piet Retief, as any Afrikaner child will tell you, was horribly betrayed by the Zulu King Dingane, who made a pact of peace with him and then brutally murdered his entire party: men, women and children. This incident, and the ensuing revenge of the Voortrekkers at the Battle of Blood River is the stuff of Afrikaner legend. Before the battle began they vowed that if God gave them victory, they would forever celebrate that day as a Sabbath. As it turned out, three thousand Zulus were killed for only three Boers, and 16 December, the Day of the Vow, has remained a day of national thanksgiving for Afrikaners ever since.

I was in fact driving into an area soaked in the spilt blood of warring tribes and nations. The Afrikaners and the Zulus; the British and the Zulus; and then, before the whites had even got here, the Zulus and all the other black tribes that the warrior King Shaka had driven from *their* ancestral lands.

Once again, the homeland boundary, though unmarked, was easy to see: empty stretches of white farm on one side, *kraal*-dotted hillsides on the other. For an hour or so the landscape was exquisite; then I was out of the hills and deep wooded valleys, and down, speeding over a plain of drought-brown bush, towards Ulundi, the capital of Kwazulu, and

the headquarters of Inkatha and its leader, Prince Dr Mangosuthu G. Buthelezi.

The 'G' stands for Gatsha, and this is the name by which –
up and down South Africa – Buthelezi is known. But woe-
betide you if you should ever use it to his face. It is a private
name, for use only by his closest associates. Later, in Jo'burg,
I heard an apocryphal story of a white man who'd been
thrown out of Zululand for using it, colloquially, among his
friends.

Mr Thami Duma was short, thin, and restless. Every now
and then, when I touched on some obviously pro-Inkatha
argument, he would break into a broad smile, which
revealed, up left, a single gold tooth. If I made some contrary
point, his fingers tapped impatiently on his large desk, and
the tooth vanished.

Mr Vincent Ngema was large and gentle, with a bushy
pepper-and-salt beard set off well by his ebony skin. He had
a soft voice, a warm easy smile.

On the wall behind Mr Duma was a framed portrait of
Buthelezi; to its left a colour photograph of the Chief Minis-
ter shaking hands with Mrs Thatcher outside Downing
Street.

We ran through the Inkatha story: how Buthelezi had been
the only one to tell the child comrades of 1976 to go back to
school, because education was essential to liberation. Once
again I heard about the 1979 bust-up with the ANC, how
Buthelezi had been called a snake, a dog; how Inkatha
members had only got into the violence to protect
themselves.

'You would appreciate,' said Mr Duma, as Mr Ngema
nodded silently beside me, 'the fact that self-preservation is
an instinct that precedes all other . . . so our members are in
the violence today because they have been forced into that
situation.' The ANC–Inkatha fight, added Mr Ngema, was a
tragedy holding up the liberation struggle. 'We have invited

the ANC to meet with us so many times,' said Mr Duma. 'If we could present a united front Mr De Klerk could do nothing.'

At the end of the interview, I asked Mr Duma if there was any chance for me to see the Chief Minister. It was unlikely, I knew, but . . . it would be a great honour. Well, he *was* in town, said Mr Duma. I would have to write a letter, outlining my purposes and credentials. He would see what he could do. Today was impossible, but tomorrow, maybe, or Wednesday . . .

I drove out of the dust and poverty of Ulundi and into the hallowed precincts of the Smallest Holiday Inn in the World. Low white buildings set round an octagonal swimming pool. Green grass, a bubbling fountain.

After lunch I lay alone by the pool in the warm winter sunshine. A little dog scampered up with a yellow tennis ball, dropped it by my hand, pulled up its right foreleg, gave me a meaningful look from large brown eyes. I chucked it, bounce, bounce, through the loungers, and doggy brought it back. We played like that for some time, and then I fell asleep.

I was woken by the large black forefinger of Mr Vincent Ngema, pressing on my shoulder. He looked me up and down with some amusement. 'Mr McCrum,' he said, 'the Chief Minister will see you now.'

'Now!' I said, springing up.

'Now,' said Mr Ngema. 'I will wait for you in the lobby.'

Twenty minutes later I was being shown through an X-ray arch manned by young Kwazulu soldiers at the entrance to the Legislative Assembly. A very substantial man in pin-stripes was waiting to meet me: Dr Buthelezi's Private Secretary. He looked me up and down rather coolly. 'We tried to contact you at the Holiday Inn this afternoon,' he said. 'But you were not available. Dr Buthelezi had two other journalists to see and we were going to suggest that you join them. But that meeting was at four o'clock. Now he is very busy for the rest of the day. He has a meeting now from five to six. And another from six to six-thirty. Then he has a dinner.' He shook his head slowly.

'I've driven up from Durban specially,' I pleaded. 'Is there any chance?'

'He might possibly be able to come out of one of these meetings to talk to you. But I doubt it now. You can wait here.'

I sat in the entrance hall, cursing the Holiday Inn dog. Five minutes later the Private Secretary returned. 'If you would come with me, please. Dr Buthelezi will try and come out of his meeting to see you.'

He led me down a long corridor and up in a lift to a small wood-panelled anteroom, which contained just a chair and a desk, on which was a copy of the Zulu language newspaper. 'Just wait here.'

Five minutes later he returned. 'Dr Buthelezi would like to know – what are the questions you will be asking him?' I hummed and ha-ed, fearful that this was some test I would fail, now, at the very last moment.

'You might,' said the Private Secretary, 'for example, want to ask him about CODESA.'

'Yes, CODESA . . .'

'And Boipatong . . .'

'Boipatong . . . his reactions to Boipatong, yes.'

The Private Secretary returned two minutes later. 'Dr Buthelezi will see you. You may come in here.' I was led from the dark cubbyhole into a spacious lounge. A low glass table was surrounded by large comfortable armchairs. The magazines and newspapers of the world awaited my perusal. The panelled walls were full of portraits and photographs of Buthelezi, in various settings. Two framed cartoons by Leyden – featuring Buthelezi – lay propped against the wall to one side. After ten minutes I was called in. There was a long dark polished wood table. And at the far end . . . Buthelezi. The half beard, the spectacles, the slightly hooded eyes – features I knew well from photographs – before me. He rose to shake my hand, meeting my eyes only briefly. Sitting back in his padded black chair, lit by yellow light from a lamp to his right, he looked weary.

So I switched on my tape-recorder and asked him about Boipatong, and he answered as you might have expected. He had already expressed it in his Press Statement. It was a terrible thing to find that kind of hideous violence between our own people . . .

He started to get worked up when we moved onto the attitude of the press, the international press in particular. Boipatong had got all the headlines, had been 'highlighted'. But what about the massacre of Inkatha members at Crossroads in the East Rand, in April, where *more* people had in fact been killed; that had hardly received a mention. Even a journalist in the *Sunday Star*, a man, he, Buthelezi, had sued in court, who had every reason to be bitter, had pointed out these double standards in the way Inkatha was treated, compared to the ANC.

'But you did have, didn't you,' I said, after a little more of this, 'a personal relationship with Dr Mandela that was very good. D'you feel sad about what's happened between the ANC and Inkatha, d'you feel that he's been taken over by his own members, or what's happened?'

Buthelezi shook his head wearily. 'I suppose it's him who can explain it really, because I've no quarrel with him. It's him who could not see me in 1990 after he'd phoned to say we were going to meet. It was not until almost a year afterwards that we met, on Good Friday, and talked for six hours about various things as old friends. And after that there was the ultimatum that they issued to the Government, which had attacks on the Government woven around attacks on the IFP. Which again created another cleavage. And then he contacted me because I reacted to that. I said to him that I'd been surprised that he had attacked us. No, he says, he was attacking the Government, not us . . .'

He worked through a list of apparent misunderstandings and failed meetings. 'But in your six hour conversation with him,' I asked finally, 'didn't you raise the fact that you've been trying to get him to meet to denounce the violence, and he's agreed to do it, and at the last moment pulled out . . .'

Yes,' Buthelezi replied. 'He did explain. He said that some of the ANC people almost throttled him . . .'

'Surely he can see that there's a tragedy looming. You and Dr Mandela are in a position to avert some tragedy that might otherwise happen, I think.'

'Yes, yes.'

'And as such you have enormous power between you. And this is a sort of historical situation that may not last very long.'

'Yes.'

'What is going on in his mind, d'you think?'

'I honestly don't know. I would think the ANC has an adversarial approach to the conflict. I would say that they regard the conflict as a black and white conflict between the white minority that has oppressed us, and the black majority. And they put themselves in the position of being leader of this black opposition. And of course I think that also some of them have not abandoned being revolutionaries. And looking at anyone else who doesn't follow their ways as a counter-revolutionary.'

'Wouldn't you think, though,' I said, 'that one of their aims at the moment must be to try and marginalise Inkatha?'

For the first time I saw a flash of anger. 'But how can I be marginalised?' said Buthelezi, leaning towards me, his voice rising. 'I represent a very big constituency. What can they do without the largest nation in this country? The Zulu people are the largest single nation in South Africa.'

'Yes.'

'And I don't see how you can *marginalise* the largest nation, with the kind of history that the Zulu people have had. There's no peace in this country, and there'll never be peace – unless there's a rapprochement. Anyone can see there won't be any rapprochement. You can't hold elections with the levels of violence being what they are – '

'There seems to be a cycle of revenge – '

'That's what I'm saying, Mr McCrum. I don't see them being in a position of advantage. Because as long as there is conflict and violence, I can't see that they're going to have an upper hand . . .'

Had he condemned himself out of his own mouth? Or was he merely stating the intractability of the situation? In the heat of the interview I hadn't fully taken in the possible import of his reaction. Instead I'd moved things on to ask about the role of the police in the violence. Sitting in the anteroom I'd read a press release which made reverse accusations from Pierre Cronjé's.

'In your statement you say that there have been many incidents where the ANC have been involved in killings of Inkatha members and then not been rounded up by the police.'

'Correct.'

'The same thing is said by them about . . .'

'The other side, yes.'

'What is the truth here? Are the police trying to fuel what fight there is?'

'I wouldn't say that the police force as such has a plan to do that, but it is true that – even on Thursday when I saw the Minister of Law, Mr Kriel, I mentioned to him that in Port Shepstone for instance, where some people were killed over the weekend, the police were not playing the game . . . and in Richmond, I had information that some of the police there were siding with the ANC . . .'

'And so', I said, after we'd covered a few more examples, 'the ANC allegations which you hear all the time, that the police and Inkatha are involved together, you would describe as nonsense?'

'It is nonsense, of course,' he said; and without prompting

brought up the notorious Trust Feed case in which it had been firmly alleged by local people that Inkatha and the police had been involved together. 'Even in that case where they quote those persons who were involved there, they were not really involved in the leadership of the IFP. There was a local dispute there with a certain man who happened to be an Inkatha member. And in fact they ended up killing Inkatha members.'

Clearly, one could argue this point indefinitely. 'So as far as you're concerned,' I said, winding things up finally, 'it's just carrying on with the peaceful struggle, and a hope that things will sort themselves out?'

'I cannot say that things will sort themselves out,' said Buthelezi. 'We have to try and cultivate a culture of tolerance and democracy. Even if it's difficult.'

'In the immediate future that doesn't seem like it's going to happen . . .'

'Well, it may not look like it's going to happen,' he said. 'But ultimately we would stop doing everything we are doing if we didn't have a hope that at the end the penny will drop and these things will stop. It's not the first area of violence in the world, and sometimes it does get to an end. There was a lot of violence in Zimbabwe, for instance, terrible violence, horrible violence. But it stopped. So even in this case we must hope; and work, for a situation where there is a rapprochement, and where the violence will end, because it is not in the interests of any one of us . . .'

With the tape-recorder off he relaxed, and began to look me in the eye. He seemed smaller when he stood up; and as he showed me back through to the anteroom, and we shook hands, and I promised to give him a fair treatment, he didn't exactly strike me as the devil incarnate, standing there genially in his three-piece pinstripe suit.

'Have they given you a copy of my book?' he asked.

'No, no.'

'Please give Mr McCrum a copy of *My Vision*.' The portly Private Secretary hurried off. Buthelezi and I shook hands again, and loaded down with printed material, I walked out past the machine guns into the cool starry night.

17

ANCESTOR WORSHIP

I didn't think I could leave Ulundi without at least having a look at the famous battlefield where, at the end of the Anglo-Zulu war of 1879, Lord Chesterfield had finally defeated King Cetshwayo and the Zulus, a defeat which had effectively put paid to Zulu power in Southern Africa.

So I drove five kilometres out of town, through the dry bush and over a little river where Zulu women were washing their clothes, and found not just the battlefield, but a full-scale reconstruction of King Cetshwayo's *kraal*, a museum of Zulu history, and Barry Marshall, the white director of the Zulu Monuments Council.

Barry had a bushy black and white beard, longish grey hair, glasses, a tweed jacket, and all the enthusiasm of the true historian. Yes, of course I could see the Ulundi battlefield. But how long was I staying? What about Isandhlwana, where the Zulus had first routed the English, and Rorke's Drift, where the Zulus had laid siege to a Swedish mission hospital. Then there was Piet Retief's grave and the tomb of the Prince Imperial, the last of the Napoleons. Not to mention all the black-on-black battle sites. Kwa Qukli, for example, just down the road here, where the crucial battle between the Zulus and the Ndanwas had taken place. 'Now if *that* battle had gone the other way,' said Barry, sipping his tea from the lid of a thermos, 'it would have been the

Ndanwas who would have been the dominant tribe – we wouldn't have heard of the Zulus.' He laughed. 'You should also see the Amakosini, the sacred Valley of the Kings. From the Zulu point of view, that valley is the holy of holies. And with a religion based on ancestor-worship, that's quite something. The Government left that valley out of Kwazulu when they were carving the country up – which makes you wonder how serious they were about creating a real nation.'

We walked through the dry noonday heat to the battlefield.

'They talk about black-on-black violence today,' said Barry, 'but the way the British treated the Zulus at Ulundi . . .' he tailed off. 'One of the Lancers wrote home to his brother to say that the rout of the Zulus had been better than "a good day's pig-sticking at Aldershot".'

Like all battlefields, it was, of course, just an empty field where a battle had once taken place. More interesting was the reconstruction of King Cetshwayo's *kraal*, a large oval of igloo-shaped grass huts. 'This is Cetshwayo's hut here,' said Barry, as we ducked out of the sunlight, through the three foot high arch of an entrance and into the cool dark interior. 'This is actually rebuilt on the original site.' He knelt down and pointed at a rough circle in the hard mud floor. 'This is the original fireplace – so you can imagine, on this very spot Cetshwayo would have sat and wondered what he was going to do about these guys in their red coats who were massing on the other side of the river.' He looked up at me with a gleam in his eye.

He pointed upwards. 'You see, there's no hole for the smoke. All this is natural stuff. Smoke just goes straight through it, and it would kill all the insects too, so it's a natural method of pest control. The insulation in these huts is incredible. When it's cold outside it's warm in here, and when it's warm outside it's cool in here. They knew how to use their natural materials. And now we in the West are just *starting* to get round to these kinds of ideas.'

Outside, we climbed up to the look-out point, a ram-shackle structure on poles with a long rickety stepladder.

'You see,' said Barry, looking out across the plain to the distant mountains. 'Take away that heavy settlement there is now and you get the feeling that it wouldn't have been so bad to be King of the Zulus.'

Walking back, we got onto the subject of Cetshwayo's grandson – Buthelezi. 'People either love him or hate him,' said Barry. 'I'm one of the ones who love him. He saw you last night – that's typical. He'll always make time to see people. Which means that he's forever keeping people wait-ing because he's attending to some old lady with some problem or other. He takes his duties as a Chief very seriously. He's trying to be both things, you see. Chief and Chief Minister.'

Was I sticking around till Saturday, he asked. There was an unveiling of Royal Tombstones, up at the Zulu King's Palace at Nongoma. 'There'll be thousands of them up there. Zulu pilgrims. Buthelezi and the King make speeches, and then they slaughter a few cows and have a feast afterwards.'

'So how do I get to that?'

'Oh you just pitch up – it's not a problem.'

So I checked out of the Holiday Inn and into a grass hut, one of several designed for guests of the Museum and the Kwazulu Government. I sat at a wobbly wooden table in the dappled bamboo shade and caught up on my notes. It was perfectly peaceful, just birdsong and the occasional distant yap of a dog; beyond the huts, the sun sank slowly over the empty plain.

Around five, a fat South African in shorts turned up with four blacks in blue boiler suits. 'Rart!' he bellowed at them imperiously. 'Ah'm going into town to get some provisions. Ah'll be back in one hour. One hour OK? You git some wood and git a fire going. And remember, we 'ave to leave 'ere at seven o'clock tomorrow morning.' Oh, go *away*, I thought, looking at his shorts stretched tight over his fat white bottom: just leave me alone to relax here.

But by 6.30 I was sitting cross-legged around a campfire with him, his silent forty-five year old Swiss girlfriend, and her equally silent seventeen year old son, drinking schnapps. Despite his accent, he was Swiss too. He had been in South Africa for twenty-five years, and was a monument and gravestone maker. Indeed, he was *en route* to the Zulu King's palace at Nongoma, to erect the monuments for the unveiling on Saturday.

'Most of my business is with Africans,' he said. 'In gravestones. There's not much business in the white community – they all get cremated. But the Africans, with this ancestor worship, if they don't do the right thing, they've got some ancestor sitting on their shoulder forever, so they really spend money on these things – have a proper gravestone, give themselves a proper send off.'

'You must have a lot of work at the moment . . .'

He laughed loudly. 'Yes, as long as they keep chopping each other up it's good for me. No, I've plenty of work. But you know, I've been out here twenty-five years and I've never felt so insecure as I do now.' He looked sideways at his girlfriend, whose knee he was gently fondling. 'Well, it's OK with me, if it all goes down the drain I've got my Swiss passport, I can just be on the next flight out. I'd lose a lot of money on my business, but', he shrugged, 'I've done it before,' he concluded cryptically. He got to his feet. 'I better go and see how my guys are doing.' He padded up to the grass hut where the four blacks were staying, rapped loudly on the little wooden door. 'OK! You all OK in there? You all in bed?' Loud laughter came from inside. He came back, sat down, poured himself another schnapps.

'You know, I envy those guys sometimes. I don't know what they talk about. They can talk and talk all day. It's incredible – just talk crap all day. Have you ever tried the beer they drink? It's thick, like cocoa in colour, but it's quite'

– he made a fist – 'strong.' He laughed. 'I give them one packet each, don't want them having too much, you know, they could turn . . .' He made a violent chopping gesture with his hand.

'Have you ever had any trouble like that?'

'No. We had some guys hold up the factory once . . .'

'But not with your own workers?'

'No. But you know, I've been here twenty-five years, and every year I understand what's going on less. You know, sometimes with my boys there, I think I understand them, but I don't. Something is making them do what they do that I cannot understand – something in the way they're brought up, in their ancestry . . .'

Driving through the rust-brown hills towards Isandhlwana the next morning, I asked my Zulu companion about ancestor worship. Sibusiso was the Museum's Education Officer, and in his zip-up blue cardigan, grey slacks, and thick-lensed glasses, hardly the Zulu from my childhood picture book.

'Actually,' he said, 'it's not that people worship their ancestors; more that they take the ancestors as people who form a link between them and God. They believe that those people are closer to God because they are dead.'

'If that's the case,' I said, 'surely they should find it easy enough to relate to Christianity?'

'Some people find it easy. But some do not find it easy, owing to the way the Christian gospel was brought to the people. Some people still feel that Christianity had no truth, because the missionaries came talking about religion, but what they actually wanted was to get a piece of land. Another thing is that Jesus is portrayed as a white man, and Satan as a black man with a long tail. So they say, "Why should I be a Christian if I am Satan? Christianity is for the whites." And other people say, "If I may one day meet God through Jesus then Jesus is one of the ancestors, only he is a white ancestor, so why can't I meet God through *my* ancestors?" Another problem is people saying: "How can I follow Christianity, which is followed by the Afrikaners, these people who have done all these terrible things to our people?"'

We'd turned off the main tarmac, and were bumping down a dirt track into the valley that contained both Dingane's *kraal* and Piet Retief's grave. It was right here, on this very hillside, that the never-to-be-forgotten act of treachery had taken place.

But it wasn't an act of treachery, Sibusiso explained, as we walked across the hillside through the reconstructed beehive huts of the *kraal*. 'We have our own oral history, and this says that Piet Retief was killed because the Afrikaners were patrolling around Dingane's *kraal* at night. The way Zulus think, anybody patrolling around the *kraal* at night was practising witchcraft – and in those days the punishment for witchcraft was death.'

Some misunderstanding! That had led to 150 years of mistrust and the mind-set that created apartheid. We drove back down to the Afrikaner side of the valley. The big granite headstone, surrounded by eight granite obelisks, was only in Afrikaans:

GRAF VAN P. RETIEF EN 70 BURGERS
RUST IN VREDE

Up some steps, shaded by trees, another monument listed the seventy murdered burghers: J. BOTHA, C. BREIJTENBACH, A. DE KLERK . . .

'If you are looking for trouble,' Sibusiso said, 'you can come here on 16 December. I don't think they'd be very happy to see any black people here.

'People have the wrong idea about the Zulus,' he continued, as we drove on towards Isandhlwana. 'They think that if you'll be meeting a Zulu he'll be carrying a stick and an assegai to stab you. But our people are so friendly. And visitors, strangers, in our history, they used to be given the red carpet treatment.'

Just over a hundred years ago, I thought, as we walked together across the dried-up scrub of the Isandhlwana battle-field, Sibusiso and I would have been at each other's throats. He with cowtails on his arms to bring the strength of his ancestors with him, in his left hand his white cowhide shield, in his right his deadly assegai; I suffocating inside my redcoat in the heat of a late January afternoon. Now we stood side by side, I in suede jacket and blue jeans, he in cardigan and slacks, before a pink granite obelisk which read:

JAMES ADRIAN BLAKIE
ELDEST SON OF THE LATE
ANTHONY ADRIAN BLAKIE
FORMERLY OF ABERDEEN
KILLED HERE IN BATTLE
22ND JANUARY 1879
AGED 19 YEARS

HIS DUTY NOBLY DONE
FOR KING AND EMPIRE
PRO PATRIA

As we left Sibusiso pointed out one of the huts in the adjacent village. 'There's an old man who stays there, and whenever you meet him he says: "You know what Macmillan says. Macmillan says there will be a wind of change."' He laughed. 'He never forgets to say that.'

On the drive back he said: 'We blacks have had to suffer so many things, like being denied access to places and so on. Why is there this hatred of us? If it comes out of some wars fought by our forefathers, then why do we have to bear that hatred now? All over the world people have fought, and these things have been forgotten and left behind.'

In the Babanango Hotel (otherwise known as Stan's Halt) there was a large handwritten sign above the bar:

THIS BAR IS FOR HAPPINESS
CABBAGES AND OTHER
POLITICAL ARGUMENTS
IS NOT HAPPINESS
THEREFORE CEASE!

Other notices read:

I'M A DIRTY OLD MAN BUT FOR YOU I'LL WASH IT

GIVE ME HEAD TILL I'M DEAD

HOW CAN I SAY I LOVE YOU WHEN YOU'RE SITTING ON MY FACE?

Up by the optics were two nudie calendars. The walls were papered from floor to ceiling with business cards; a couple of green POLIZEI armbands nestled among them.

Stan himself had a huge white handlebar moustache and bushy white sideboards sprouting from a chubby pink face. Above, his shiny pate was ringed with a frond of white hair. In his billowing yellow HARD ROCK CAFÉ sweatshirt and his tight blue shorts he looked like Father Christmas on a summer holiday.

A mid-afternoon party was in progress. 'You can't go *yet*,' Stan was saying to his two customers. 'It's only three o'clock.' He slammed a couple more beers on the bar top. 'And what can I do for you two gentlemen?' he asked, smiling without a flicker of racial discrimination at Sibusiso and myself.

'Are we too late for lunch?'

'Oh dear,' said Stan, looking at his watch. 'I'm afraid the

cook has just gone home. But we have a girl there who can manage a pie, I think, with some curry gravy. How does that sound?' He picked up a little silver handbell, which he rang imperiously.

Giggling suddenly like a naughty schoolboy, Sibusiso was showing me Stan's bartop array of collection boxes and vulgar toys. You put a coin on one and a skeleton opened its mouth, stuck out a great ivory tongue and scooped it in. Another wooden man (black) lived in a box. Lift him up from the box and . . . you guessed it . . . out popped his enormous tool.

Up at the bar, Stan and his friends were remembering, amidst raucous laughter, the day a girlfriend of theirs had sat up on the bar and exposed her tits. 'Were they good ones, that's the question?' 'Whoo-argh! groaned Stan, in a fair imitation of Scott from Wavecrest, 'they were perfect – like the ones you see at the end of the bar there.' His shoulders shook like Edward Heath's as he shot a longing glance at the nudie calendar and took a deep swig of his drink.

A black maid in uniform brought our pies and there was calm for a moment. 'Don't I remember you?' asked one of the drinkers, leaning towards Sibusiso. 'You were at that thing at the Ulundi Museum last year – and you gave a talk.'

'You have a good memory,' said Sibusiso, in his soft voice. We introduced ourselves. The tall thin one standing was called Roger; the shorter, plumper, seated one was Paul. Both of them had English accents; Roger's was unobtrusively public school.

Sibusiso grinned broadly while the conversation stayed merrily on sex. Politics was clearly a bit trickier; but Paul was very open, clearly determined not to behave any differently just because Sibusiso wasn't white.

'When you get up to the Transvaal,' he told me, 'you'll find those Afrikaners, whatever they say, they do look after their blacks.' Roger nodded agreement. 'Just so long as a black doesn't think he's their equal. But they're the kind to say, "You know, man, a kaffir is always a kaffir."'

With a kaffir right beside me, I felt more than a little uneasy. But Sibusiso seemed to be taking it well. 'If you want to stay,' he said quietly, 'don't worry, we can stay.'

Advice flowed as to where I should go in the Transvaal. The Royal Hotel in the old mining village of Pilgrim's Rest was a must. 'Very authentic,' said Roger. 'I tell you what else you should do, and that's go and try to find old George Marshall. He's probably the last of the original gold miners, must be eighty, ninety now; he's been living in a shack in that valley for years and years, still pans the gold by hand. A good way in is to arrive with a pint of milk, a loaf of bread and the day's newspaper.'

Before we left, I asked Stan about the notice above his head. 'Why 'CABBAGES . . .'? 'I don't allow political arguments in this bar,' he replied. 'There were two guys came in here once, and they started talking about cabbages. Before we knew it they were screaming at each other about politics.'

The young Indian guy who was staying at the huts was not a heavy drinker. 'How'z it?' he'd asked, as I sat alone by the camp fire. I offered him a beer. He preferred to share the ginger-beer shandy that I'd made up for myself.

'Try anything once,' he said, smiling broadly as the froth settled on his bushy black moustache. No, being a Hindu didn't stop him having a beer, every now and then. 'Things are changing, anyway, now – breaking down. There are guys who like to have a beer or two at the end of the day's work.'

I told him the reason I liked shandy was that it reminded me of summer days in England . . . being a teenager . . .

He laughed. 'You started early.'

'No, fourteen or fifteen is a normal age to start drinking in England. We used to drink cider at home when I was eleven or twelve. And then at eighteen my father would give me a drink before supper in the evening.'

'That must be a nice thing about your life. Being able to have a drink with your father. I would *never* have a drink in front of my father.'

'Even now?'

'Even now. Maybe once a year, on our special feast day, my father will come over and give me a beer, but only then.'

He was a shopfitter, working on a hospital near Newcastle, and he stayed here in the huts because it was the cheapest accommodation around. 'It's OK when other people are staying, but some weeks I'm here and there's nobody else around at night, and that's a bit lonely.'

Still, only one more night and he'd be back with his wife in Durban.

'Are you married?' he asked.

'No,' I said. 'Maybe – when I get back.'

'You have a special girlfriend?'

'Yes . . . I wish it was only one more night till I saw her again.' We laughed.

'Oh well,' he said, 'you're having an adventure.'

'Sure.'

His wife stayed with her mother when he was away. She, too, got lonely. At the weekend they went to his place in Chatsworth, which he owned, yes, but there were fairly strict regulations about what he could or couldn't build. 'And yet the blacks', he said, 'build their shacks just about anywhere and nobody stops them. Now they're building them in the middle of town, right on the street in Greyville.'

'You've had problems with the blacks?'

'Me – no – I've never had any trouble, and I'm staying in their townships quite often when I'm doing a job. Only once I had a problem. I was driving into a township, and this bakery van ahead of me turned right round in the road, so I thought if the bakery guy wasn't going to go in, it probably wasn't safe for me. What had happened was some black guy

had raped a girl, and when the police had come to arrest
him, all his mates had surrounded the van and were stopping
them from taking him away. That I couldn't understand. He
did wrong, yet those guys wouldn't let the police take him
away.'

Whites though, *had* given him a problem. Before the pass
laws were scrapped. 'I tell you, in a town like Newcastle or
Dundee, someone like me, all we could do in those places
was drive in, stop at the garage, get some petrol and drive
on. We couldn't go into the shops, the toilets, nothing.'

He'd been doing a job in a small town in northern Natal.
Had arrived in the town. Had got out at the station and seen
a toilet. 'It said WHITES ONLY. I went in there and when I
came out there were three guys standing there with guns
pointing at my head. I couldn't believe it! So I acted dumb,
as if I hadn't seen the notice. And they kept pointing at the
notice and saying: "Can't you read?" All over a toilet!' He
shook his head and laughed.

'His Majesty the King INgonyama [*sic*] Zwelethini Goodwill
kaBhekuzulu and Prince Mangosuthu G. Buthelezi cordially
invite . . . to attend Unveiling of Zulu Royal Tombstones in
honour of Kings Solomon Nkayishana ka Dinizulu, and
Cyprian Bhekuzulu Nyangayezizwe at the KwaDlamahlahla
Royal Residence,' read my invitation.

As I turned off the tar and hit the dirt road marked ROYAL
UNVEILING I wondered what fabulous African experience I
was letting myself in for: slaughtered cows, vats of tribal
beer, wild, wild dancing. Lunch would be late – of course –
but would go on all day . . . all night, probably.

Ahead of me were the dust trails, glowing in the morning
sun, of a long line of cars, every one of which was smarter
than mine. We crossed waterless rivers, ground up steep
hillsides, avoided enormous potholes, climbing up and up
into the sunburnt mountains. Here and there groups of

children, in tatty Western dress, stood by the roadside and waved, white smiles flashing.

Finally we seemed to have arrived. On a windy hilltop were two huge marquees, rows and rows of chairs, a big speaking platform, a line of flags, and a vast seated crowd, wrapped from head to toe in white linen, wearing tall circular flat-topped hats, a deep red-orange in colour, decorated with triangular motifs.

But the convoy passed on and came to a halt finally half a mile further in a grove of cypress trees. By a wire-mesh fence a small crowd had gathered. Costume was varied: half were turned out as if for an English wedding, the men in suits and ties, the women in dresses and hats; the other half were in tribal gear – naked under animal-skin skirts and leopard-skin shoulder-coverings and headbands, cowtails tied to their arms, clutching knobkerries or ceremonial axes. Hovering around the fringes were a sprinkling of sharp-looking dudes in shiny double-breasted suits and dark glasses. I didn't need to look to know that their waistbands were bulging.

And there, through a double-gate, standing by the cypress trees and the group of five or six veiled monuments, was Buthelezi – also in traditional chief's outfit, his only concession to modernity being a black poloneck under his leopardskin. Next to him a plumper, younger man, who from the superior size of his brass ceremonial axe, I took to be the King. He was wearing a skirt of what looked like rabbits' tails.

Beside them was a group of twenty or thirty chiefs and four priests in long red, white, and gold vestments.

The ceremony began. There were prayers that mentioned 'Jesu Christu'; then rousing Zulu chants which had the chiefs raising their axes and knobkerries high in the air. As each tombstone was unveiled, Buthelezi, the King and the chiefs stood solemn and silent, the only sound being the whirr and click of cameras from three white photographers, who wandered where they pleased. Two were in suit and tie. The third, tall and young, with floppy blond hair, John Lennon specs, and an embroidered African shirt, had – to my eyes – a distinctly Swedish look. Perhaps, I thought, this is Matthew, the fabled White Zulu! Equipped with my white skin and camera I slid through the gate, walked unhassled past the spooks in dark glasses, till I was a mere couple of yards from Buthelezi and the King. Click! I took a photo of my own. It could as easily have been a gunshot.

Back in the car park the crowd piled into their vehicles. Toyota Corolla seemed to be the favoured make for the guys in the suits, Mercedes and BMWs for the semi-naked chiefs. Buthelezi moved hither and thither in his leopardskin, grasping hands, greeting, smiling benignly – charm itself.

I got the Dolphin into line and we rumbled back on dirt to the white-sheeted crowd. Well-dressed VIPs of all colours were filing into the two marquees. The King and his more famous uncle took up seats on the central platform. I sat on my haunches far away at the back of the women's section of the crowd (the sexes were strictly divided).

'His Majesty the King, members of the royal household present, members of the Kwazulu Cabinet present, members of the consular corps, members of the Kwazulu Monuments Council, distinguished guests, ladies and gentlemen,' each speaker began in turn, before switching into Zulu. Lunch was clearly going to be a while.

Behind me, lounging out in the shade of a lone tree, I spotted the tall white photographer I'd noticed earlier, chatting with a guy with bleached blond hair. I went over. To my astonishment (and yet not to my astonishment, because these things just seemed to be happening to me now) he was indeed Matthew S—, Camilla's White Zulu. From her description I'd imagined someone much more exhaustingly far-out: spiky hair, leather trousers, a fat joint perhaps, dangling from sulky lips. But despite a certain languid cool, Matthew was easy enough to communicate with.

'Who are all these people?' I asked.

'This lot are the Shemba Church. Buthelezi likes to keep them on his side. Keep the Inkatha membership up. At least they can wear their uniforms here. In Durban they'd get stoned to death.'

'How long do we sit here?'

'Oh another couple of hours at least. Buthelezi'll be an hour minimum. Then we've got the King's speech . . .'

Matthew was writing a book too. About Zululand. He'd dug up all kinds of weird shit, he told me. 'When King Cetshwayo got crowned, the British were organising the ceremony. They couldn't find a proper crown, so they borrowed a papier-mâché one from the Pietermaritzburg Amateur Dramatic Society.' He chuckled dryly. 'This King Cyprian that we're honouring today, when he died he lay in state for a week with pictures of the British Royal Family all around him.' There had been another Zulu king whom they had crowned with a tin can. 'But he looked so ridiculous they ended up anointing him with castor oil.'

A familiar figure was striding towards us across the dry grass, spectacles glinting. 'So you made it, Mark,' said Barry. 'I've got some translations of the speeches if you're interested.'

'Did you write this one, Barry?' asked Matthew.

'No, Buthelezi wrote it himself. Every last word. I've written a bit of the King's speech though.'

An hour later we got to it. 'My uncle, the Chief Minister,' said the King (in Zulu, of course), 'and you ladies and gentlemen, must forgive me if I take a moment to digress here. One of the things that her Britannic Majesty Victoria did was to present a three-handled mug, lined with silver, to King Cetshwayo, to convey her personal esteem to him. That mug now has a history which must run its course . . .'

'Barry wants it for his museum,' said Matthew. 'He's trying to stir this up into a political issue.'

'Eshowe Town Council', the King continued, 'should now

recognise that this is a black thing we are dealing with, and no-one other than myself, as reigning King of my father's people, could be more knowledgeable about where that cup ought to be.'

Matthew laughed. 'He hasn't got a hope in hell. The Council aren't going to give it to him. What he's forgetting is the English won the war, not the Zulus . . .'

'I chose to make this digression today,' said the King, pausing for a moment to survey the sea of white-swathed pilgrims before him, 'because I was moved to do so. I did so looking down both sides of the mountain, and somehow this thing has come over the mountain, and is with us today, and is somewhat lost . . .'

After the King, another man got up to speak, or rather chant, high-pitched and very fast. 'This is the *nkosi*,' said Matthew. 'The Praise Singer. He goes into everything the King has ever done. He met with Mandela then, he was appointed by Botha then. If he does the full thing it takes over half an hour. De Klerk wasn't too happy when he met the King having to wait for half an hour while the Praise Singer did his bit.'

The King was on his feet again, this time speaking in English. Distinguished guests were invited to his residence. 'To the rest of you I say: "You know where the cows are."'

'So how d'you get into lunch?' I asked Matthew.

'Oh you just pitch up at the palace. I've been gate-crashing the King's functions for years. It's one of the advantages of being white. But it isn't lunch yet. We've still got the unveiling to go to.'

'I thought we'd had the unveiling.'

'No, that was just something they thought up yesterday. For some other minor royals. They were Letrasetting the inscriptions on last night.'

It was already after three and the wind had turned distinctly chilly. I stood shivering at the back of the crowd as Buthelezi, the King, the chiefs and the clerics prayed and chanted their way round another batch of monuments. After the last unveiling, they raised their swallowtail axes and danced down through the crowd to the dirt road that led to the palace, singing as they went. The VIP Mercedes jostled up behind them. A car alarm went off. I felt faintly incongruous, driving through the shouting tribesmen in a car that read DOLPHIN CAR HIRE – FOR THE BEST FLIP'N SERVICE.

The palace wasn't vast, just an elegant colonial house, with a long pillared verandah, and green lawns that led over to a cluster of outbuildings. My invitation got me easily through the machine-gunned security men at the gates. Inside, I found Matthew, standing in the middle of the lawn photgraphing a white *rondawel.* 'This is the house of the ancestral spirits,' he said. 'They have to have one, but as you see, they've made it in concrete.' He broke off, to point at a girl running past in a skimpy pink dress. 'That's the Zulu King's fifth wife, they're getting married next month, pretty little thing, isn't she? Here's an interesting titbit, she's a Xhosa – related to the Mandelas.'

Up on the verandah, the caterers were white, from Durban. The food was cold meat, quiche, the kind of trendy salads you'd get at a buffet in England. A waiter appeared with a tray of drinks, but they were all cans of Fanta. 'D'you have any beer?' I asked. 'No beer sir, just Fanta or Appletise.' 'Wine?' 'No wine, sir.' 'You won't get any alcohol here,' said Matthew. 'The Chief Minister is teetotal. He drinks Diet Coke and hates smokers.' He laughed. 'Here's a titbit for you – both those Kings whose monuments we've just unveiled died of cirrhosis of the liver.'

It was getting colder and colder. Sitting beside me at a long table on the verandah, Matthew was visibly shivering in his Zulu shirt. The large black man on my right was short of English and I had no Zulu other than 'Sawubona!' 'I've got some beers in the car,' I said to Matthew. 'Shall we go and get warm?'

We sat together in the front of the Dolphin, heater on full

blast, drinking Castle. 'I'll tell you the truth about Boipatong,' Matthew said, after a while. 'This has never come out
in any of the papers. All those hostel-dwellers are Zulus.
There are 1,500,000 Zulus living in hostels in Johannesburg,
working in the mines. They don't want to live there, they'd
never take their wives and families up there, to those rotten
places. They want to live here,' he gestured through the
window at the lovely mountains, bathed with pink in the
sunset, 'in Paradise. That's what they call this place. *Ezulwini*. In Zulu that means heaven.'

'They're sitting in those hostels for one reason only:
they've got good jobs and they're earning good money. Now
the squatters come along. They're the lowest of the low,
they're lower than a snake's arse, and a snake's arse is about
as low as you can get. Now those squatters go to the hostel
dwellers and tell them to boycott their jobs. The squatters
are unemployed, it doesn't matter to them if they sit on their
arses for another day. But the Zulus will lose their jobs if
they stay away. And they don't like being told what do to by
snakeshit, do they? So what they do is they go and beat the
shit out of those guys.

'I'll tell you something. I'll give this country another
eighteen months. Another eighteen months with the ANC
getting carried away and the Zulus will run amok. Mark my
words, they'll talk about a third force, but the Zulus will just
get the shits and go and fuck them up.'

Matthew had told me where to find a shebeen. 'You can
easily tell it – from all the cars parked outside.'

It was just the garage of a small beige-bricked Ulundi
bungalow, with the sliding metal door raised up and the
guys sitting around on tatty armchairs lined up along each
side. Posters advertising CASTLE were tacked to the walls. A
low table in the centre was covered with empty beer bottles
and cans of coke. There was a half-full bottle of white rum.

'Sawubona!' I said, a little nervously, as everyone had

turned to look at me. There was a fractional pause. Then 'Sawubona!' came a great cry back. 'Ninjani!' said a young guy in a pink tracksuit, smiling broadly and holding out his hand. 'Hello, sir,' said a little man in a beige waistcoat, down on the sofa to the right.

'Can I buy a drink?' I asked. 'Sit there!' said the pink tracksuit, pointing to a hard chair. 'We are just having a party here.'

The guy in the waistcoat was extremely drunk. 'Hello, sir,' he mumbled again, nodding and raising his glass. The pink tracksuit and his friend opposite me were just quite drunk. 'Where are you coming from?' they asked. 'England,' I replied. 'A long way away.' 'England – whe-*hey*,' they said, nodding thoughtfully.

I looked up the garage. Some of the guys at the far end were looking at me a little warily. But one man, lean, with a big circular Afro, grinned and raised his thumb. Now a drink had appeared for me. It was Dry Cane and Coke. No, I didn't have to pay, said the pink tracksuit. This was on him.

'What about the Cameroons?' said the waistcoat, springing into life suddenly.

'Yes,' I said, trying to remember, 'they're coming to play South Africa . . .?'

'Today,' said the tracksuit.

'It was 2–2,' said the waistcoat, waving his glass. 'It was 1–nil,' he raised a finger and paused for a few seconds, 'then 2–2.'

'Aha,' I said.

'Where are you coming from?' he added.

'England,' I repeated.

He nodded thoughtfully and sat up a little. 'Which is your car?'

'That one,' I replied, pointing nervously at my huge gleaming white machine. 'The Toyota?' 'Mm.' 'Aha.'

'We are Zulus,' the other two interrupted. 'We are Zulu *men*! Are you speaking Zulu?'

'Not much,' I replied. 'I can say "Sawubona!"'

'Sawubona!' they repeated, laughing. The tracksuit leaned over and grabbed my hand; shook it, African-style, with a third twist for good measure. His friend did the same.

'Then,' said his friend, 'we say "Ninjani". "Sawubona", then – "Ninjani". "Sawubona" – "Hello". "Ninjani – "How are you?"'

'Ninjani,' I repeated dutifully.

'Nin-jani.'

'Nin-jani.'

'Then you say: "Siphilile". I am – myself – very well.'

'Sip – hi – li – le,' I repeated carefully.

'Very good!' said the tracksuit.

The waistcoat had surfaced again. 'You must – speak – Zulu – because – you are – in – Zululand,' he said.

'Right.'

'You *must*.'

A few armchairs down they were ordering more drinks. They banged on the wooden door to the house, a woman in a headscarf poked her head through, took the order, brought it, and vanished, locking the door behind her.

The guy in the waistcoat was onto something. 'Why are you here?' he asked, fixing me with eyes whose whites were stained almost green. 'You must be here for something.'

'I'm just touring around, you know, having a holiday.'

'No,' he said, shaking his head. 'You have some . . . philosophy . . . something.'

I looked at him with a new respect. 'Clever, very clever,' I said.

He smiled and nodded. 'Don't worry, it is OK here. We may . . .' his voice sank into a mumble, then rose, '. . . but we will not *kill* you.'

'Right,' I said.

The tracksuit was now as far gone as the waistcoat. Shoving his chair across the concrete floor next to mine, he'd grabbed my arm and was telling me there was no way we could be friends if I didn't speak Zulu. 'You must speak Zulu,' he said. 'You *must*.' And then, aggrieved: 'Why do you not speak Zulu?'

'I haven't been here very long,' I said.

'Yes.' He waved a finger at me. 'But you must speak Zulu. I must teach you Zulu – so you and I can understand. OK?' He smiled.

'OK.'

'I like you,' he said, poking me in the upper thigh hard with his forefinger. 'I like *you* very much. So you will teach me English – and I will teach you Zulu. So,' he poked me again. 'We – *na*.'

'We – *na*,' I repeated.

'"Wena" – is – "you". I like you.' He fell on top of me. 'This is why I give you this drink because – I like you. I love you. I *love* you. You must speak Zulu, because I *love* you.'

It was time to go. I got to my feet and went.

Sunday morning. In the kitchen, Ernestina, the young maid who ran the huts, was doing the washing-up, and I was waiting for the kettle to boil.

'I went up to see the Zulu King yesterday, Ernestina,' I said. 'To see him unveiling some monuments.'

'Eeeya!' cried Ernestina, 'the Zulu King.' She shook her head slowly from side to side. 'He is a very nice man that one.' Then, with a gurgling chuckle. 'But they are saying he is a short-tempered so-and-so.'

'He has four houses, doesn't he, and four wives.'

'Yes.'

'Would you like that – to be married to someone who had several wives?'

'Me. No-o! I don't like that! I'm getting very jealous. Aiiyee!'

So I told her that in England you could go to jail for having two wives. She stopped in her washing-up, and turned, wet black hands on the hips of her pink overalls. 'Does the wife send them to jail – or the authorities?'

'The authorities.'

She raised a silent eyebrow. 'D'you think', I asked, 'that the Zulu wives who are married to these men – d'you think they like it?'

'Aijee! No.'

'They get jealous?'

'Of course.'

'Why do they do it?'

'They are just forced.'

18

'DO IT!'

I was in a sublimely good mood, driving up Route 66 through northern Zululand. The sun shone. After the light rain of the night, the landscape had taken on the palest blush of green. Fluffy white clouds purred across the sky.

Two young women in brightly coloured Zulu costume stood by the roadside with their thumbs out. They were Nomsa and Cynthia, a teacher of twenty-five and her nineteen year old student sister. And here, so you can get a feel of what it's like driving through Zululand on a Sunday lunch-time with two young Zulu women on board, is (part of) what we said:

> (CYNTHIA *remains silent.*)
> NOMSA: You are going alone?
> MARK: Well, I'm writing a book actually. I'm writing a book about South Africa.
> NOMSA: About South Africa. It's nice!
>   (MARK *laughs.*)
> MARK: So I don't know – I'm just going all over, seeing what it's like.
> NOMSA: Yes.
> MARK: But this is lovely here – beautiful spot.
> NOMSA: You are staying in England?
> MARK: I live in England, yuh.
> NOMSA: You live in England – oh, that's nice!

MARK: Very different from here.

NOMSA: No, we are staying right here. I'm a teacher in Nongoma. I'm also doing a diploma in teaching. It's a college here.

MARK: Oh right.

NOMSA: Yes . . .

MARK: Which college is that?

NOMSA: I'm going to show you, right in town. Yes, right in town. That's nice. When are you going back?

MARK: Well, I'm going on to Swaziland. And then I'm going through the Transvaal to Johannesberg.

NOMSA: Yes . . .

MARK: And then I'm going on to Botswana.

NOMSA: Oh Botswana. Oh, that's good.

MARK: And then I'm going . . .

NOMSA: You take a month?

MARK: Sorry?

NOMSA: You take a month driving?

MARK: Yuh. Oh no, I've had two months already. I've been travelling for two months.

NOMSA: Oh. That's nice . . .

By the time we got to Nongoma we were the best of friends. 'We like your company very much,' said Nomsa, as I dropped them in the centre of town. 'If I was not working tomorrow I would come with you to Swaziland. Yes. But I am working tomorrow. May God guide you wherever,' she added, as we parted.

Turning out of Nongoma I picked up two somewhat older ladies and drove them to the gateway of a school, in a village way out in the bush. There was quite a crowd here, and before I knew it half of them were trying to get into the car. When we eventually got moving, I had one man in the front, and a man, two women, a baby and a very drunk teenager in the back. 'Please sir,' the teenager wailed as we bumped along the truly terrible dirt road, 'please sir, my leg.' The guy in the front told him to shut up and we rattled on, the car now smelling very pungently of sweat and alcohol and woodsmoke and tobacco. 'Piss, piss, sir, piss,' shouted the teenager. I slowed. Was he going to wet himself if I didn't stop? Whatever. Our man in the front had no mercy. 'No, no,' he said firmly. 'Just keep 60k. sir, just keep 60k.'

Half way to Pongola I let them out. The guy in the front produced a ten rand note. 'Two rand change,' he announced. 'It's OK,' I said, 'it's on me.' There was a general murmuring of 'Thank you, sir, thank you . . .'

They were all getting out except the drunk teenager, who sprang into the front, strapped himself eagerly in. The whites of his eyes had the same greeny bloodshot quality as my waistcoated friend from the shebeen.

'I'm only going to Pongola,' I fibbed. 'I'm stopping in Pongola, OK?'

'I have nothing,' he replied. 'I have nothing . . . I want a *job* . . . you can give me a job . . . I come from Free State . . . please, sir, you must give me a job . . . where are you going? . . . I want to come with you, sir . . .'

I had no job to offer, I told him.

'. . . for the childrens, sir . . . I have two childrens . . .'

'You have a wife?'

He nodded. 'Yes, sir . . . I have.' He focused on me, and then, like the man in the shebeen, his drunken mutterings suddenly took a philosophic and strangely accurate turn.

'You are old,' he announced. 'You must marry.'

At the wheel I smiled to myself.

'Do it!' he shouted at me. 'You must do it! You have no childrens . . . and you are old. Do it – just do it!' He shook his head, slowly. 'You have a car. Who will take your car? Your brother? No . . . your childrens. Do it!

'You are a man,' he went on. 'Jesus . . . is a man . . . How can I do anything for you . . . for this . . . I want to thank you . . .'

But then: 'Please sir . . . have you got two rands? . . . I have nothing.'

'It's OK,' I said. 'When I drop you at Pongola I'll give you some money.'

'Oh thank you, sir. I want to thank you, sir . . . I can wash
your car . . .'

'Really, no, the car's fine. The money's on me.'

'Thank you sir . . . you are a *man* . . .'

We were crossing the little Bivane river, and all of a
sudden – bang! – we were back in White South Africa. The
burnt brown scrub was replaced with neat green fields of
sugar cane, the scattered huts and wandering goats with tidy
white bungalows. It was all too easy to see how, if you'd
never read the history of dispossession, you could end up
thinking that the white man had a way of making the land
productive that the black could never have.

I gave my passenger a handful of change, dropped him
at the Pongola turn-off, and turning right for Swaziland,
sped past the small crowd of waiting blacks. That was it!
No more hitch-hikers today. On my last visit to Swaziland,
I'd never got further south than Manzini, and now I wanted
to be selfish and enjoy the view on my own, with no
destination commitments, advice about my private life,
whatever. But slowing to take the sharp left turn for the
Lavumisa Border Post, I saw a young woman sitting forlornly
on her own with a little suitcase. I stopped. Her name was
Nellie, she was a Swazi, and she was not immediately very
forthcoming.

'Are you working?' I asked.

'Yes, I am working.'

Silence.

'What kind of work do you do?'

'I work at the Swaziland Water Authority as a lab
assistant.'

But once through the border (was I getting some strange
looks from the young white South African soldiers on the
gate, or was it just my imagination?) she loosened up.

'Are you married?' she asked.

'No.'

'Eeya! You are old though.'

'Am I? How old d'you think I am?'

'Twenty-seven . . . twenty-eight . . .'

'That's not so old to be married in England.'

'Here they get married at nineteen, twenty.'

'But you have men marrying many wives, don't you, here in Swaziland?'

'Some of them do.'

'What d'you think – about that?'

'I don't like it.'

'Why do people allow it then?'

'Oh they just say, "I am a Swazi man. I must be able to marry many wives." But it's mostly up here in the rural areas. I don't want that. I want one man.'

'Does your father have more than one wife?'

'Yes, he has three wives.'

'Is he rich then?'

'No, he is not rich. He is not rich at all. What he has he shares with all three of them.'

Her father was almost seventy. His three wives were fifty-six, fifty-five and forty-three. Nellie was a daughter of the second wife. How did he divide his time? Not, as I'd imagined, a week here and a week there, but 'on Monday he stays with one wife, then on Tuesday another, then on Wednesday another . . .'

'So where does he spend Christmas?'

Nellie laughed. 'With all of them,' she said.

We were driving across an immense flat plain. What Hemingway would have described as 'miles and miles of bloody Africa'. Way over to our right were the steep wooded Ubombo mountains – the border with Mozambique. Here and there a couple of teenage boys swerved cycles down the middle of the empty road. A very drunk driver steered a van erratically back and forth over the central white line, narrowly missing several oncoming cars and trucks. Just before Big Bend we came to a roadblock manned by black Swazi soldiers.

'Eeya!' cried Nellie, after we'd been waved through. 'I
don't like those men. If you try and run away they shoot to
kill.'

We drove on, up into the hills. Nellie was going to
Mbabane. I had several contacts in Manzini; an artist friend
of Otto's; a man who Gerald had told me 'would give me the
lowdown on the economics of Swaziland'; one of Alex's pals
who was the only white Cabinet Minister in Swaziland. But,
once again, I'd reached saturation point. I just didn't have
the energy to find out how Swaziland worked.

So I sped happily through crowded Manzini, and took
Nellie to the front door of her hostel in Mbabane. As we
passed through Lobamba she pointed out the Royal Palace,
high up on the hill. 'That's where the King stays. He already
has six wives, and he's only twenty-four.

'Goodbye Mark,' she said, as we parted. 'Next time you
come I will see you and your wife.'

The luxurious Ezulwini Sun was full of white South Africans, over in Swaziland for the gambling. Once again you
heard those shrill authoritative voices ringing across the
restaurant: 'And I want it naice and crisp, and I want naice
frish brid . . .' The waiters didn't tell them to go and boil
their heads, this was Swaziland – no, they bowed and smiled
and got on with the job.

In my bedroom I switched on the telly and was confronted
with the face of . . . goodness . . . John Gielgud. Of course! I
was out of South Africa, no longer in Equity-ban territory. It
was a lush drama, set in France. Gielgud and an actress
with hair as long and dark as my own girlfriend's chatted
their way through dripping green landscapes, stopped for a
picnic with . . . ah! red wine and cheese, rowed down a
slow-moving river, strolled through a deserted old country
house. 'Albert's family lived here for generations,' said the
actress, stagily, as they tripped together across an echoing
hall . . .

I was knocked sideways by a wave of homesickness. From the callbox in the foyer I phoned Sarah, but the lines to Swaziland, she told me, when I called back eventually from the bedroom, were constantly engaged. We had a thirty rand, minute-long, deeply frustrating conversation.

At breakfast I found that the newspapers had changed. In addition to the *Times of Swaziland*, there was – no, not the *Cape Times* or the *Natal Mercury*, but the Johannesburg *Star*. South Africa's leaders, I learnt, were taking the continuing CODESA crisis to the United Nations, 'while at home business and trade union chiefs pushed ahead with an emergency joint plan to avert a period of unprecedented strike action and protest.'

'The gloves were taken off,' read the urgent editorial, 'when CODESA broke down: now the bare knuckle fighting is under way. However hard one may choose to search between the lines for positive gestures in the recent letters exchanged by President De Klerk and Mr Mandela, the fact remains that they are overwhelmingly uncompromising, angry documents. They have had their effect in plunging our nation into a deep trough of despair and fear.'

Letters? What letters? Buried in Zululand I'd heard nothing of it.

Just down the road, in the Mbabane hospital, Tessa and John were playing with the last of the abandoned children. Sifiso was autistic and came from Manzini: his family were too poor to support him, nobody knew where to send him. Little Togozini in the yellow pullover – nobody knew where he even *came* from. 'We think he's from Mozambique,' said Tessa, 'because he doesn't speak Seswati – but then he doesn't really seem to speak anything. He'll sit and just talk to himself sometimes.'

'It's really sad,' added John, 'because he's also confused because all his friends were sent away. So last week I found really depressing, because he seemed so disorientated.'

'So all the other kids have gone back to their families?'

'Where they can find families,' said Tessa. 'Otherwise some vague relative or anywhere where they can just send them, because the hospital want to get rid of all the abandoned children.'

'Here it's considered bad luck,' John chipped in, 'if a handicapped child is born into the family.'

'None of these families', Tessa said, 'want a handicapped child. These children who've been abandoned here, I have a slight problem with sending them to relatives, because if the relatives have always been around they obviously don't want that child, so how is their life going to be improved living with people who don't want them?'

Tessa talked very fast, a serious grown-up look in her clear, dark, teenage eyes. John was tall, lanky, with blond hair that flopped down over his forehead. In another situation, I thought, he might have been a young soldier, boasting about how many kaffirs he'd shot. Instead he said: 'I think the most important thing is just to give the children physical contact, because they never get it from anybody. They're really hungry for it – you arrive and they embrace you right away, particularly this Togozini. I'd never even seen him before, and when I came here he gave me a kiss right away.'

Tessa and John didn't work at the hospital. They were down in these peeling blue corridors on their weekly Community Service from Waterford, Southern Africa's first multi-racial school, set high up on a hill above Mbabane.

They were fully switched-on to the ironies of a programme that their headmaster would later describe as 'excellent for a school of privilege and elitism like ourselves, in a Third World situation'.

But then, as Tessa took me round the wards, pointing out the smashed windows, taking me to meet a child who'd broken his hip lying in a bed next to a man who was dying of cancer, it was clear that this wasn't a once a week chore for her. She was spending a lot of time down here, and not just because she felt she ought to.

Waterford had been established in 1962 after the introduction of Verwoerd's Group Areas Act, by a white Johannesburg headmaster who'd found he wasn't legally allowed blacks in his school any more. In protest, he'd decamped to Swaziland, bought a farm from an Irishman (hence Waterford) and, like Deane Yates a decade later, set up a multiracial school from scratch, teaching initially from a group of old *rondawels*.

The place had flourished. The Mandela children had been educated there, the Sisulu children, the children of wealthy white Jo'burg liberals ... now it was part of the United World College Movement, with language labs and music rooms and computers and a handwritten sign on the door of the sixth form common room that read: 'Stealing is a criminal offence. Don't even *think* of trying.'

Waterford had been the inspiration for Maru-a-Pula, and walking round campus I got a strong whiff of that enchanted atmosphere. Black and white teenagers wandered round arm in arm in the sunshine. Three girls – a black, a white, and a Chinese – sat laughing together, textbooks on knees, legs dangling down over a wall. It was like one of those bogus photos you get on the front of a school prospectus – only it was for real.

It was of course an illusion. The school, like all schools, was bound to be riddled with problems. Tessa and John and the other thoughtful young people who'd been selected to show me round were of course the goody-goodies. There had to be bullying, drug problems, unwanted pregnancies ...

But no, the biggest thing I could dig up was some quarrel about bread being handed out after prep. Oh yes, and the lack of facilities for teenagers in Mbabane. 'Everything is so small and restricted,' groaned one languid girl from Mozambique. 'And teenage life is so – so small. We have these 120 people we're living with, every day, and that's all. That's all the teenagers you'll ever see, it's all the socialising you'll ever make . . .'

'Racism really isn't a problem?' I asked.

'No,' someone replied. 'People might joke about it. They might say "You nigger!" or something like that. But it doesn't mean anything.'

Talking to Dick, the young-looking white-haired English headmaster (he was a Geordie, from Durham) I surprised myself by discovering how hungry I was for reassurance. 'All along this trip,' I told him, 'I've heard this repeated white prejudice – that there is a problem with black people, that they never take the initiative, you know, they can't do these things . . .'

'Can't take on that responsibility . . .' he chuckled.

'Which has got to be nonsense – hasn't it?'

'It is nonsense,' said Dick, 'absolute nonsense.'

I was laughing; with relief as much as anything else. 'You hear it so many times that after a while you start to believe it.'

'Well, it's absolute nonsense. I mean, I've been here twenty-one years, and some of the students who've taken the most initiative, and have taken on most responsibility, and gone back into their societies and played a very import-ant role . . .'

He didn't add 'are black'; he didn't need to.

'So what you see in South Africa', I went on, determined to get something to hold onto, 'is just to do with what one would imagine if one looked at it on paper: lack of resources, impoverishment of . . .'

'Absolutely,' Dick interrupted. 'Nothing else. If you were saying it was anything else you'd basically be saying that you were racist, you know.'

I nodded, quietly.

'And that's wrong,' Dick said simply. 'It's deprivation. Educational deprivation that has been at the very root of the problem in South Africa. And will be, I reckon, for a long, long time.'

Makubetse was an Old Waterfordian, a student who had come from the townships of the East Rand and was now at the University of Natal. I found him in the sixth form hostel, sitting in the sunshine in the supervisor's flat. He had a smooth oval face, which was accentuated by the red and white spotted scarf he wore tight over his hair.

'When I came here,' he said, 'it was a totally different situation from the township. There it was all black, you know. And in South Africa you've got like an image of a white person, of an Indian, and you know, they tell you a white person's like that, it's sort of a stereotype thing. And I still had that in mind, and I had difficulty in relating to whites, and other groups, particularly in class . . .'

'What was your image of whites?'

'Whites, well they were always far from me. I thought: OK they just exist out there, and they might be intelligent because they've got opportunities, but on the whole I didn't really think of them, as, you know – I just thought of them as privileged. So I just had a little problem with my relationship with them. I mean, over the two years that I stayed here I had somehow to start thinking, you know, like: these are people, and not all whites are South African, and not all whites are like this, and not all Indians are like that. I got over that – then it was OK.

'Then the two years went over. And I experienced so many things: the international experience that I gained here – I related to so many people, so many different people from all over the world. And I was looking for a challenging life after Waterford. Well, I knew life would be different, and would be a bit tougher when I got back to South Africa – I always knew that racism was there – but when I got to university it was shocking, after my experience here. Those people don't come together. I mean they're just there together for education, that's it. There's no interaction whatsoever. Some people say: "Well, you're facing reality." But is that really it, that people should live apart?'

The rewards of privilege! No fewer than seven white men were eating dinner alone in the restaurant of the Ezulwini Sun.

There was the balding one with the thick moustache and the bright pink face, smoking and chomping down steak simultaneously; there was the long-haired ponytail in the sharp blue suit and tie, reading a book; there was the receding gingernut in the pinstriped shirt, drinking soup and staring into space; there was the sad-looking fellow in the white shirt, with the damp moustache, waiting for service and picking his nose; there was the good-lookin' dark-haired one in the sports jersey, ruminatively scratching his chin; there was the grumpy grey-haired one telling off the waitress: and I . . . I was the seventh lonely whitey, jotting in my notebook and listening . . .

The soundtrack was provided by the table to my right: a grizzle-faced old Jewish guy talking to the young French chef, who'd just been round to ask us how we found everything. Grizzle-face had a companion, also Jewish, who sat on his left, nodding silently. 'We're all in the same boat,' he was saying. 'I've been married for thirty years . . . I always said this to my daughter's boyfriend before she got married. There are two ways to go wrong in life, liquor and women. With liquor you're all right, you sober up, but with women, the problems never stop, every day it's something . . . so when he comes to me now, I say, "I told you so . . . you never will understand them, you will never." Of course it's two different personalities, but that's *good*. What have you got to talk about if not? Bugger all.'

I smiled complacently into my wineglass, grateful that I didn't have to think like this . . . that I had a woman at home I understood fully . . . that I was going back to marry and not have that kind of life with.

19

OOM GEORGE AND UNCLE TOM

The dirt road down from northern Swaziland into South Africa is famously spectacular. To both left and right of the Saddleback Pass, the mountains drop away breathtakingly into the valley far below. Beyond, layer upon layer of rounded hills – patchworked, this morning, with the shadows of the little clouds above – ripple away into the blue distance of the eastern Transvaal.

I'd done it before, fifteen years ago, during the week I'd spent driving around this area with my school-friend Justin. Justin was a bit miffed because the VSO-type job he'd managed to pick up was teaching in a school for handi-capped white children in Pietermaritzburg. I, unfairly, had landed the much more authentically right-on work in black Botswana. He listened to my stories with undisguised envy.

All of a sudden I was back in South Africa. In the Barberton Post Office the blacks and whites now stood in the same queue – but they were still from different worlds. The whites in their khaki shorts, long blue socks, sensible shoes; the blacks run down and scruffy, not looking up to catch your eye.

I drove to a big town called Nelspruit, which straddled the main N4 west to Jo'burg and was like a South African version of Reading, full of smart young women with short hair. I stopped for lunch in a sandwich bar called Juicy Lucy's. An old white woman with a face from a Hogarth cartoon sat wearily over her coffee, her heavy eyelids shuddering with disapproval as a young black couple took the table one down from her.

We drove on, the Dolphin and I, up a long flat empty road, through forests of pine and gum. Just before Sabie we came round a corner, and suddenly it was all there: the beautiful eastern Transvaal, blue mountains rising above the green-black trees. The afternoon sun broke through the cloud to cast biblical rays upon the scene. Another watercolour I wasn't going to get round to painting.

Up here it was holiday time. The roads were busy with slow-moving caravans, and every now and then you'd see groups of hearty walkers, dressed as if for a pre-war hike: khaki shorts, khaki rucksacks, long socks.

Around five, I arrived in Pilgrim's Rest. Set in a street of old corrugated iron miners' houses, the Royal Hotel was (as Paul and Roger at Stan's Halt had advised me) entirely authentic. Green-painted wooden pillars held up the corrugated iron roof. The bathroom – marked MANS' BADKAMER – was a draughty walk across a paved courtyard. My room had two single beds with brass bedsteads, a little table with fresh flowers, a mahogany wardrobe and dressing table, by the bed an English–Afrikaans bible.

It wasn't a room you could exactly lounge around in, so after my bath I picked up my *Weekly Mail* and headed over to the bar to take the last remaining stool in a row of burly, middle-aged, moustachioed men contemplating existence over a pint of lager. Promising, very promising. My quest for the right-wing viewpoint looked as if it was going to be easier than I'd thought.

To my immediate right were a couple who didn't quite fit in. They were drinking shorts, and wearing the kind of clothes that tourists wear. The man was late thirties, I reckoned, ruggedly good-looking, with short dark hair. The woman was some years older, with a rumpled face and greying hair. Idly, I wondered what they were doing together, and came to the conclusion that he was gay and she was an older friend.

Now she had turned on her stool, and was smiling at me in a tipsy kind of way. I smiled back. 'Are you touring?' I asked, Mr Lonely making friends. They laughed. They were from Jo'burg, and they thought it was hilarious that I was reading the *Weekly Mail* in the Royal Hotel in Pilgrim's Rest. 'We've just driven all this way up into the mountains to get away from that kind of thing,' said Kathy, laughing. They wouldn't tell me exactly what they did, but it was 'on the lift'.

'You've got the right on your left and the left on your right,' said David, gesturing at the moustache sitting beyond me.

Before I knew it, we'd agreed to share a table for dinner. What a pleasure it was to be getting drunk with some people from the city! Irreverent lefties who were full of sharp urban ideas, jokes, opinions; who swore and wanted to drink, no, not just a glass or two of wine, but three or four bottles, and then progress to brandies afterwards.

They seemed to know everybody, everything. Oh the ANC – well they *worked* for the ANC. David called Cyril Rama-phosa 'Squirrel'.

They could fix me up to meet just about anybody in Jo'burg. Mandela? David looked at Kathy; and Kathy looked at David. Look, they couldn't *promise* anything but a very good friend of Kathy's was Mandela's Press Secretary, and surely if she met me . . . Kathy looked at David. 'Look,' he said, 'Mandela's First Prize for you, isn't he? So we can have a crack at getting you to him, and if we fail, we fail. Your problem being that every journalist in the world wants to meet Mandela.'

They also seemed to know half the people I'd already met. 'I went to this extraordinary place called Stan's Halt,' I said. Oh yes, Kathy knew Stan. She'd been there many times. And

Buthelezi. Well, Mike, the guy they shared a house with in Jo'burg, had been closer to Buthelezi than anyone. I'd stayed at the Ulundi Museum. It was Mike who'd laid out the battlefield and the reconstructed *kraal*. 'He can tell you a thing or two about Buthelezi,' said Kathy. 'Look,' said David, 'Mike used to be known as Buthelezi's White Man, he was that close to him.'

I was back in anti-Buthelezi territory: and how! Camilla had never been so openly critical as these two.

'So you think he really knows everything that's going on all the way down his organisation?'

'Of course he does,' said David. 'Don't be naive. Look, he has these meetings every Tuesday evening in Ulundi where he tells the Inkatha guys exactly what to do next. Seriously. Ulundi is an extremely sinister place.'

'How does that tie in with what I found there? With all the people around him being so full of praise for him?'

'Because they need him. He's an Uncle Tom figure.'

'But I'm talking about white people, the Head of the Monuments Council, for example.'

'He's given him a job. He's hardly likely to say nasty things about him, is he?'

Then I mentioned Roley Arenstein and the shit really hit the fan. Kathy's eyes were bright with hatred. 'He's the one that sends out the writs for Buthelezi. His son and daughter are Buthelezi's legal firm. He's the most accomplished operator you've ever met.'

'But he struck me as being totally decent. Really. A genuine idealist.'

'Then he took you in. Totally.'

'Why would he go to jail for his beliefs then?'

'OK, name one thing he's sincere about.'

'Federalism for a start.'

It was that kind of dialogue. Drunkenly we continued, until it looked as if Kathy might get up and leave. 'I'm not sure I can sit at the same table as someone who likes Roley Arenstein,' she said.

'Look,' said David coming back from the loo, 'can you two *stop* arguing about Roley Arenstein. You can talk about that in Jo'burg.'

So we got onto racism. 'There are two *lunatic* misconceptions about this that I cannot understand how anybody who knows the system can have,' said David, waving his brandy glass at me. 'One is that blacks are inferior to whites; and the other is that they're identical. Put it in the animal kingdom. If someone came along and said a leopard is infinitely superior to a tiger you'd laugh him out of court. If he said to you that a leopard and a tiger are identical, have identical behaviour patterns, they react identically to the same stimuli and so on, you'd also laugh him out of court . . .'

'So you *are* a racist . . .'

'No I'm *not* . . .'

'. . . in that you think these two races . . .'

'Look,' David interrupted loudly, then paused to swig his brandy. He sighed deeply: 'The problem is that racism's become one of those words like . . . rape – that's used incredibly loosely. And has acquired, in the modern Western world, connotations of almost paranoic proportions. You can't be racist describing someone as "a black person", that's ludicrous.'

He wanted to give me an example. Some American professor, he couldn't remember his name, had presented a paper on some research he'd done on monkeys. What this professor had found, was that in a given troop of monkeys, there was an adolescent group who'd leave the troop for a period of two years or so, and go in for extremely violent behaviour. The professor had identified the most violent, and since they were monkeys, had been able to kill them and analyse their brains. And what he'd discovered, was that the greater the shortage of a chemical called serotinin in the brain, the greater the degree of violence.

'And this guy', said David, 'presented this paper, in New York or somewhere, and trod on every anti-racist corn in the world. Because what he was saying is that there's a correlation between this kind of behaviour and the way young' – he drew the quotation marks in the air – '"blacks" behave in America. OK, so he phrased it stupidly – but that doesn't matter. What's important is that here's an example where a genuine scientific breakthrough appears to have been made, and it's not even able to be held up to scientific analysis in any way – because the guy's been branded a racist. Now that's just counter-productive – for blacks and for whites.'

We were arguing alone. Kathy had sunk into a stupor, her eyes half-closed, her brandy glass empty, a flickering grin on her face. Everybody else in the restaurant had left long ago. It was time for bed.

But still we continued, on into the night. Eventually, having invited me to stay at their house in Jo'burg for as long as I liked, Kathy and David left to go to their room. *Their* room. So they were a couple. Or were they? I looked forward to finding out in Johannesburg. Already, their company had given me a powerful whiff of the Big City ahead.

I felt a little stupid the next morning as I stopped in Graskop to buy George Marshall a loaf of bread, a newspaper and a pint of milk. For all I knew, he was dead.

I followed Paul and Roger's directions, out of Graskop, then off the main road and down a winding dirt track through the woods, the little mountain river below me to my right. After three kilometres I saw a shack, at the bottom of a little valley. There were a couple of rusting cars beside it, an old caravan, a big pile of logs. I parked my car and walked down, rather nervously, as there was a ferocious barking of dogs.

A man with unkempt straw-coloured hair, a crimson face, and a beer belly rolling over his khaki shorts, emerged from the shadows of the shack and yelled at the dogs in Afrikaans. They fell silent.

'Hello,' I said. 'I'm looking for George Marshall – does he still live here?'

''E duss,' replied the man, in the thickest Afrikaans accent I'd yet encountered. ''Ees in town at the moment. Gone to see the doctor. No, old George 'ees gone into town.' He nodded slowly.

Koos was his name; and I reckoned I couldn't have found a finer specimen of rustic Afrikaner. His thighs, emerging from those khaki shorts, were truly as thick as small tree-trunks. He'd been a butcher in Nelspruit; had sold up everything, he said, to come down here and 'look after old George'.

Old George had eighty-two claims. 'Hell [Koos pro-nounced it 'Hull'] but that's a lot of money to pay over so many years.' He looked slowly round, hands on hips. 'There's plenty gold here, plenty gold.' He shook his head and pursed his lips.

'This is a mine here,' he said, stamping his foot. 'We're standing on a mine right here.'

The shack had two corrugated iron rooms off a central covered space, where a wood fire burned in an old petrol drum; there were three or four wicker chairs, a small table, and any amount of other clutter on a bare earth floor. 'We built this for him,' Koos said. 'He used to live up there in that Kombi. Lived up there for forty years – all on his own. This is only temporary here. We're going to build a proper house, up on the hillside next year.'

He didn't seem to mind telling me everything; even though I'd pitched up, just like that, out of the blue. 'You want a beer,' he said; then, as we sat in the sunshine drinking, 'No, you can't leave this old man here. They robbed him three times you know. Three times. There's another old miner down the valley, Tommy – they burst into the kitchen, pinpointed the gun to 'ees 'ead and said "Gold, gold, gold!" But 'e didn't have any that time.

'I'm staying here with my wife,' he went on, sipping slowly

at the lip of his glass. 'She's got a pistol, a very good pistol; she's a good shot.' He looked slowly round. 'We've got to cut all thiss trees down, thiss black wattle trees. You can't see a black man behind those trees at night. Can't see 'em.

'Still, it's nice here, eh? He's got no problem with water. Hull no. There's a spring right there – the water comes right out of the mountain. What a pressure!' He took me into the kitchen, pointed at the stainless steel sink and taps. 'This building had no water inside. I connected it up, you see. Here's his gun. This is a very old Winchester. Point 22. He gave it to me now in his will.' Koos pulled a big knife out of a drawer, ran it down against his forefinger. 'Look at this. This is a Joseph Roger. This is more than 150 years old, this knife. Hull, it's as sharp as anything in the world. Murder weapon. It's actually a murder weapon.' He pointed over at a white enamel bread bin, which had BREAD written on its side. 'You see that bread bin,' he said, shaking his head in wonder. 'That is more than three hundred years old. Belonged to George's grandmother. Hull no . . . old George . . . 'ees got some stories to tell you I reckon. Of the old days. If 'ees in the mood . . .'

There was a car coming down the track, driven by a woman with steel-grey hair and glasses. Old George climbed slowly out, levered himself upright with his stick. He was dressed like Baden Powell: a wiry old boy in long khaki shorts, long khaki socks, sturdy brown leather shoes; the only faintly up-to-date thing on him being his maroon lumberjacket shirt.

'Here they are now,' said Koos. 'Now don't you say anything until I've given him a bit of beer.' He winked. 'This is Mark, Uncle George!' he shouted.

Uncle George blinked at me vaguely and said nothing. He was feeling a bit weak after his blood test, Koos' wife said. They sat him down in the shade. 'You want a beer, Oom George!' shouted Koos. Uncle George nodded, smiling vaguely. 'I'll give him one,' said Koos, winking again. 'You just sit there, Mark.'

Koos' wife Marye had that same soft female Afrikaner voice, those same gentle eyes. With her newly done short grey hair, her smart white blouse and black slacks, she was still dressed for Nelspruit, incongruously tidy by this shabby shack and its clutter-strewn surrounds. 'Put the nice side, won't you try,' she said, when Koos told her I was writing about South Africa.

'OK Mark, we'll try now,' said Koos. 'You go right up close, ask him the questions.'

'Mark's going to ask you a few questions now, Oom George,' he shouted. 'Put you on the television.'

But Uncle George wasn't playing. Answers to my shouted enquiries ('So what was it like in the old days?' and so on) were just not forthcoming. He mumbled a little and then went silent.

'He needs to trust you a bit,' said Marye. 'He's got lots to tell.'

'These old prospectors,' said Koos, standing by shaking his head, 'they were used to having people just turning up, trying to find their gold. They don't trust anybody. What we'll do, is drive him down to the waterfall in the *bakkie*. He'll tell you some stories then all right.'

So the three of us men crammed into the *bakkie* and bumped a hundred yards down the steep track to the river. Koos pointed out a hole in the hillside. 'That's one of the old mines. Hull, there's plenty gold in there. Plenty gold.'

The river was low, but still flowing: too wide for the old man to get across. 'Elliot!' bellowed Koos across the valley, '*Kom herso*! Kom here!' A black man in a green boiler suit and woolly hat appeared, carrying an axe. 'Bring a log here,' Koos commanded. 'No, not that one, that one.' Elliot obliged, tugging a big log down through the stream, laying it gently in front of Uncle George, standing there to steady it with his foot as the old man teetered across.

'See that up there,' said Koos, pointing half way up the steep crag which overhung the waterfall. 'Wild beess.' He shook his head again. 'Nobody can get the honey in there. You see?' I could: against the dark shadowed sandstone, the tiny bees stood out, clearly sunlit.

Old George had started talking! In the clipped phrases of a colonial English accent. 'You see that cave there,' he said, waving his stick at the dark shape behind the trees. 'That was called Billy Davis' cave. He used to live in there. He came here when there were no white people here. A native attacked him one night but he managed to chase him away. They killed his dog. The next day he built a wall there with two loopholes to shoot through. He was prospecting in this valley in 1884. He discovered a wall of gold on the other side of the river.'

1884! Two years before gold was discovered on the Witwatersrand and the crazy mine-settlement of Ferreira's Camp became the gold-rush town of Johannesburg, attracting adventurers from round the world, and becoming in less than forty years the biggest city in South Africa.

'Elliot!' bellowed Koos. 'Elliot. Kom here!' Rapid instructions followed in Afrikaans and Elliot got to work clearing the trees in front of the cave. Soon it was clear, blocked only by Billy Davis' wall of stones, with the two 'loopholes' in the centre.

'There it is,' said Koos proudly, as Elliot stood panting to one side.

Marye had joined us. She needed to go back into town. Before they went, she insisted on sitting us down in the shack for orange squash. Johann, another scraggy, unshaven white, was there too. And by the end of the shack, neatly turned out in white cap and apron, a black maid, doing the family ironing. We sat around drinking the squash, as she got on silently with her work.

'So how did you vote in the referendum?' I asked.

'"Yes",' said Koos. 'But we didn't want to.'

'You see,' said Marye, in that soft voice, 'we voted "yes" for the business. We had to, because things are so bad. But if not, we'd have voted "no". That's the way we were brought up.' She looked over at Koos and Johann, who were now rattling away in Afrikaans. 'But you can't change an old Boer like him,' she said, with a shrug. 'I don't know, perhaps you can start the change with the little ones.'

'I tell you what, Mark,' said Koos. 'You should drive further on down this road. Another five ks. There's another old prospector down there. Tommy Hancock – now he'll tell you some more about those early days.'

He lived in a clearing among tall trees, right by the fast-flowing mountain river. His house was not much more than a shack: two rooms, with clay walls and a flat green tin roof. Opposite was a white *rondawel* and two or three corrugated iron sheds.

A couple of dogs yapped up to me as I approached: a big brown boxer and a black and white collie. The old man was sitting at a wooden table outside his front door, eating a plate of eggs and bacon. He was wearing a flat cap, a black plastic leather-style jacket, baggy brown trousers and big leather walking boots. When he spoke, it was straight out of *Passport to Pimlico* – that chirpy old-fashioned London accent – not a trace of Seth Effrikan. He didn't seem at all surprised to see me.

'I'm just having a late breakfast,' he said. 'Well, it's Saturday. I don't work on Saturday.'

There was a good reason for this, as it turned out. As we sat drinking tea from tin mugs, making friends, discussing the problems of South Africa, the world, Tommy suddenly said, 'Today is the biggest culprit of the lot.'

'Sorry?'

'Today being the biggest culprit of the lot. To the world – as to the state it's in today – is the Sabbath. Saturday is the Sabbath.'

'Right.'

'We're supposed to keep that day. And very few do. We're supposed to work for six days, including the Sunday. Sunday's number one. Monday is number two. But no – we have to switch it round. Everything we're told to do, like bad children, we don't listen to. And that is why we are in such a *hell* of a mess.'

'Because we don't take Saturday off?'

'That's the first thing. The main thing. But you've got to abide by the rules of it too. It's no good taking it off and then going to a booze party and that sort of thing.'

'So what – you just do nothing, and not drink?'

'No, you drink. Wine – or you drink beer. An ordinary decent living life. But if you don't do that. Hell now! You go round murdering people today.'

He paused and sipped his tea, fixed me with his bright entreating brown eyes. 'We're living in a very, very dangerous world now. I was robbed down here. Four blacks. About eight o'clock at night. I didn't have my security door up, and I was in bed, taking my legs off – I've got wooden legs you see, result of an accident, years ago. Anyway, when I'm taking my legs off I've still got the use of my knees – not very successfully, but I can get around on them. Knock knock knock at the door. "Who's there?" "Aeneas." That's my boy. Good, faithful boy – I don't worry about him. So I come to the door – there was Aeneas standing there – and the next moment he just disappeared. They got him by the back of the neck, pulled him away, and then four of them come in.

'Big heavy revolver at the back of my neck, down on my knees. One hand down there trying to stop my face from getting to the ground. On my knees it's not so easy to stand up straight. And just next to me, oh, about a foot away, a lovely big army boot that he had on his feet. "Goma! Goma!" That's "Talk! Talk!" He wanted to know where I kept my gold. But first of all I just shut up. There were four against me. And without your legs on, you're not feeling very secure at all. So all I did, I just prayed out loud, and the person that helped me there is the person upstairs, you know. And these coons were startled in the first, they just looked at me – What in the hell! This chap's crackers, as well as what d'you call it. But in the end I just gave in and showed them where the gold was. Crawled round on my knees.

'They were two and a half hours in there. They stole about five thousand rands' worth of stuff. Cameras, crockery, cutlery, everything they could get their hands on.' He broke into a chuckle. 'I must tell you one thing, though. While they were here – I even burst out laughing myself. I have a spare pair of legs. I leave the trousers on, shoes on, and put it in the corner of the wardrobe. With an overcoat hanging down over the top of it, so all you can see is just from the knees down. And this boy opens the wardrobe, sees these legs there. "Eiya! What's there, who's there? Who's this?" And if I was a ventriloquist then he'd have been off like a streak of lightning. Honestly.'

We took our cups back into his little kitchen. He showed me his bedroom: a tiny oblong with a bath across the end, a bed against the side wall, and in the other corner a toilet. On the wall by the bed was a handle, which he pulled: from outside came a loud foghorn-like noise. 'That's to bring the boy,' said Tommy.

The 'boy' duly appeared, a young black in a red nylon jacket whose name was Mick. He was instructed to wash up and clean the little house while we went off to look at the diggings, which were thirty yards or so further down the track. We came to a big L-shaped pit, about eight to ten feet deep. To one side was the log that Tommy sat on while 'the boys' (he had three) dug to his instructions with pick and shovel. You had to get deep down, under the big boulders, to the black sands underneath, which contained the alluvial gold. To the left of his log, Tommy had a wood-framed contraption to filter out the gold-bearing sand from the gravel. It had a long sieve-like metal grille with corduroy underneath to catch the tiny particles of sand.

From there we went back to the clearing, to see the next stage: the amalgam barrel, driven by a home-made water wheel. Another honk on the foghorn and Mick appeared, to operate the sluice. Along a channel from further upstream the water came, through the sluice, splashing over the water wheel that turned the barrel.

Finally, we huddled into the dark shed where the gold mixture and the mercury were put together (mercury attracts gold) and the mercury was burnt off ... 'And so,' said Tommy, with a gleam in his eye, 'you've got your little button of gold. You take that to the police station, they give you a permit, then you take it to the bank, they weigh it, send it off, and sooner or later they credit your account with the value of the gold.'

Over a lunch of steak and eggs – and beer poured by the faithful Mick – Tommy invited me to stay. 'It's wonderful here in the evenings,' he said. 'I sit here with my beer and just watch it all, the night life, the moon coming up, different sounds. Nature's orchestra, I call it. There's frogs, every blessed thing, there's sound everywhere, the trees rustling and squeaking up there. And the big point in me enjoying it so much is the expense. You know how much rent I pay down here? Twenty cents a month. Well forty cents – I've got two of these claims. Your water's free.'

He shouted for Mick. 'I'm teaching him to be a valet,' he said, as he got Mick to pour the beer into our plastic cups at an angle so that it wouldn't froth. Over Tom's head, Mick smiled at me and raised his eyebrows. But when in his boss's line of vision he was clearly nervous.

'They've got to be obedient,' said Tommy. 'If they forget once, twice, three times – they go. You see, forgetting's an excuse for not doing something. And if they steal – that's it. I might drop a spoon – and if I look around and it's gone – that's it: I say "Pack up!" No, I'm strict enough, but I'm kind-hearted too. I know their ways, you see. You people from overseas, you don't understand. But I was brought up with them. And now they want to take over. Well, I don't know about that. Don't know that they'll be able to manage it. You look at Zimbabwe – that's in a terrible mess.'

After lunch, we looked at his poems. They had titles like 'Vanity' or 'The Devil's Workshop'. The one he was fondest of was called 'Freedom of Choice'. 'I sent that one over to London – *The Golden Book of Poetry* they were publishing over there. But they wanted eighteen pounds from me to publish it. So it didn't get published.' He chuckled. 'Still, it must have been good if they wanted to publish it in a book like that.'

ALLUVIAL GOLD by Thomas Hancock

Have you ever heard
The song of blacks
At work
Or the scraping of a shovel
Against a stone?
Have you ever heard
The murmur of water
Splashing about
Or the rumble of a barrow
With a load?

Have you ever seen
The glisten of a pick
Held high
Or the twist of a shovel
To gain a load?
Have you ever seen
The wobble in the wheel
Of a barrow too old
Or the mountain stream
Working with ease?

Have you ever felt
The sun, the wind

And the rain
Or the grip of a shovel
Ready to twist?
Have you ever felt
The load in a barrow
A fortune may hold
Or the weight of a nugget
Against your cheek?

I'd decided to move on; on into the sunshine that shone on the opposite hill. 'Oh well,' said Tommy. 'I'm sorry. But I'll see you another time, I hope.' We shook hands. 'I'll tell you one thing, though, before you go, Mark. If you're ever in trouble, you know what to do, don't you? Just send up a prayer to the person upstairs. He's up there, you know. No, he is. He's helped me many times. I've been through hell, man. With these legs and what have you. But he's always there, if we listen for him.

'If you've got a car, a Citroen or landrover or whatever, they give you a manual don't they? Little book, tells you how to work the thing. Well, we've got a manual as well. Little black book, that wasn't written by man. Oh no. Parts of it, maybe, but not all the wisdom in that book. I've studied it over many years. You have a look in that book, it'll tell you what to do next. You'll remember that, Mark, won't you?'

I drove north and west along what the guide books and tourist boards call the Panorama Route. At 'God's Window', where the escarpment breaks to give a spectacular view out over the Lowveld far far below, the Kombis were piling into the car park and everyone was queuing to take the same photo.

I sped on to the Blyde River Canyon: a hollow so gigantic it is hard to believe it has anything to do with the tiny Blyde River, which runs along the wooded bottom far beneath, a barely visible wiggling silver line. Projecting from the tree-

hung cliffs on the far side of this enormous chasm are three
– 'rocks' is not the right word, as they are far too huge; 'hills'
won't do either, as they've been cropped, as if with a giant
piecutter, so that their curved sides are sheer cliffs, while
their conical tops are covered with bush. They are known as
the Three *Rondawels*, which isn't a bad description, though
it somehow seems a bit crass to name them at all.

When Justin and I had driven up fifteen years before, it
had been out of season and early evening, and the whole
canyon had been an astonishing chiaroscuro of blue shadow
and slanting ochre light: so astonishing that I'd insisted on
sitting and painting a watercolour.

Now, in the early afternoon glare, it didn't have quite the
same impact. On a rock by the viewpoint someone had
scrawled GOD IS A SUPREME BEING. A couple halted right
behind me: 'Ah think this is that photo on the front of the
phone die-rict-ory,' said the woman, snapping it anyway.

20

A MISSION TO LEADERSHIP

In the heart of the Transvaal, I went to pay my respects to the God of the Afrikaners. The Lydenburg Dutch Reformed Church was like all those others I'd passed, a simple white building with a tall needlelike spire. Inside, it was just as unpretentious. No stained glass, no embroidered drapes or statues of Jesus, no altar even; just bare white walls, a half-circle of wooden pews, and a raised-up wooden desk at which stood a man in a grey business suit, the Dominee, leading the service in Afrikaans.

The congregation was entirely white; which was not unexpected, as the Dutch Reformed Church still worshipped in separate congregations and only in 1986 came to the reluctant conclusion that their theological justification for apartheid was not valid.

> Every nation and race will be able to perform the greatest service to God and the world if it keeps its own attributes, received from God's own hand, pure with honour and gratitude . . . God divided humanity into races, languages and nations. Differences are not only willed by God but are perpetuated by Him. Equality between Natives, Coloureds and Europeans includes a misappreciation of the fact that God, in His providence, made people into different races and nations . . . Far from the word of God encouraging

equality, it is an established scriptural principle that
in every community ordination, there is a fixed
relationship between authorities . . . Those who are
culturally and spiritually advanced have a mission to
leadership and protection of the less advanced . . .
The Natives must be led and formed towards
independence so that eventually they will be equal
to the Europeans, but each in his own territory and
each serving God in his own fatherland.

> (Report of a commission of the
> Nederduitse Gereformeerde Kerk,
> 1954)

Yes, here indeed were all the people I'd come to the
Transvaal to find. At the back, the old men with their white
hair and moustaches. In the centre, the red-faced middle-
agers, sitting forward with their arms crossed. At the front,
an angelic-looking blond boy, his hair neatly brushed, sitting
with his fingers in his mouth.

It was strange to worship in a foreign language – like
watching TV with the sound turned down. You see the
gestures and responses that much more clearly. The self-
satisfied smile as the Dominee adds a joke to his sermon, the
passionate look upwards as he makes a point that sets the
old men nodding.

When we prayed, we men stood, while the women
remained seated. Everyone had their eyes tightly closed,
except for me and a sulky looking teenager in a flowery shirt.

Before I knew it, there was the swelling singing of the last
hymn, and we were out into the sunshine, shaking hands,
hurrying for cars, stopping to chat to the Dominee.

I drove west on a straight empty road that took me up into
hills so dry the grass was rust-coloured. By the roadside,
long-tailed monkeys loped. I half-expected to see one turn
and stick out its thumb.

The road curved sharply down through a mountainous
pass; then I was back on another cultivated plain. Ahead
was a new range of dry-as-a-bone mountains, the closely
packed homesteads trickling down their lower slopes indicating the edge of the North Sotho homeland of Lebowa.

I turned right, onto a narrow girder bridge over the
Steelpoort River, and yes . . . I was back in Black Africa. The
big black letters of the Maloma Liquor Store; the huge OMO
hoarding; the red-brown dirt strewn with a thousand strips
of weather-aged plastic; the goats, nosing hopelessly after
the non-existent grass; the broad white smiles in black faces
of dressed-up women returning from church.

Francis and Margaret originated from Cape Town. Francis
had taught at Bishops (the Diocesan College) which was one
of South Africa's leading British-style public schools –
whites only, of course.

But for the last seven years they'd been out here, at Jane
Furse in the dusty heart of Lebowa, reviving and expanding
the old black mission school of St Mark's, and clearly having
a far more interesting time than they'd ever had in that
privileged corridor between Table Mountain and the sea.

Now they were no longer dealing with kids whose parents
were white businesspeople and lawyers and doctors. These
were the children of local chiefs, children from polygamous
marriages, children from the townships of Transvaal and
Jo'burg: and they were deep into the problems of the Looking
Glass World.

'More or less every week,' said Francis, as we left the
clatter of school Sunday lunch and walked back across
campus towards his bungalow, 'there'll be someone at school
who's involved at the funeral of a mother, a father, a brother,
a sister, or an uncle. And lots of them will be violent deaths,
like the one you've just heard [there'd been an announce-
ment] where the elder brother was shot dead in Alexandria.
We now go to a funeral I should say once a month – something

that we are obliged to attend. Whereas, before, in Cape Town, that was more like once a year.'

Francis was not a tall man, but he had a natural authority. He reminded me of other headmasters I've known: the same core of seriousness, of respect for values deeply believed in; but also the same desire to get it across that his vocation and his religion didn't make him a square, that he knew how to have a good time.

Margaret was recovering from the flu. She was sitting up in their double bed in a flowery nightdress, her mid-length grey-flecked brown hair slightly awry. With her crisp Cape Town accent, and her bright, humorous, practical manner she could have been (probably had been) one of those Black Sash women I'd met two months previously. Now she described the kind of 'schizophrenia' they'd developed, working in Lebowa and then returning to visit their white friends in Cape Town or Jo'burg. 'Usually we just ignore the things they say, but every now and then it blows up into a row.' She laughed. 'I remember some men at a dinner party in Jo'burg started saying to me, you know, "I was brought up with these people, I know their ways," and I'm afraid I just exploded.'

In the afternoon I went for a walk with Francis, Sebastian the new Afrikaans teacher – a grizzled, nervous, bespectacled man in his fifties – and twelve fourteen year old girls. We drove out past a sprawling village to a little *koppie* of giant boulders, set above a gentle slope of sparse bush. There were giant euphorbias, cacti, dried-up acacia trees.

It was the strongest reminder I'd yet had of Botswana. The girls were exactly like the little girls I'd taught in George's garden, ambling along arm in arm, the chatter and laughter flowing back and forth in that exquisitely laid-back African way.

'Joyce Molefo?' Francis called.

'Yes, sir.'

'If you were a goat, Joyce Molefo, what would you eat up here?'

Joyce Molefo looked down at the bare red earth, the few broken white grass roots that survived. 'I don't know, sir.'

'Well, what d'you think? Looking round?'

She shook her head slowly from side to side, then looked up at her headmaster with a smile. 'I would just go beck,' she said.

We climbed up on top of the boulders, looked out over the huge dry plain. With the girls at his feet Francis improvised a short history lesson, then we ambled back. '. . . and that's Joyce, and that's Tumi, and that's Mahlotsi, and that's Mr Breytenbach, our new Afrikaans teacher,' said Cynthia, concluding the list of the girls' names.

Mr *Breytenbach*!

As we drove back, Francis told me a tale of two villages. On the right hand side of the road I could see Marishane, which had been evangelised extensively by missionaries, who'd established some very good schools. 'And as a result you find now that if you go to Marishane, you know, this son is away at UNISA, and that daughter has got a scholarship to Wits, and it's a thriving little place . . .' While on the left side of the road was Mamone, where the royal Chief resided, and the missionaries had not been welcomed, and so, 'if you go to functions at the Chief's *kraal*, all of a sudden you look at these children who are singing or parading, and discover that they've got bandy legs or they're blind and so forth . . .'

At seven o'clock, there was a service in the chapel that was about as far removed as you could get from the Afrikaans worship of the morning. Yet up went the prayers of black teenagers to that same Jesus Christ, and in between He was praised with boisterously sung Sotho hymns. Outside, the warm dusk had the same smell as Maru-a-Pula, of dew-dampened dust and distant woodsmoke.

'Nelson Mobote,' called Francis, through the gloaming, to a boy and girl standing under a thorn tree.

'Yes, sir.'

'I thought you were supposed to be ill with a fever, Nelson Mobote.'

'Yes, sir, I was.'

'And yet the sight of this pretty girl whose face I can't see has miraculously cured you.'

'Yes, sir.'

Mr Breytenbach, the new Afrikaans teacher, was indeed related to the South African poet Breyten Breytenbach: he was his younger brother.

They were an interesting family, the Breytenbachs. The eldest brother, Colonel Jan, was a famous South African soldier; who'd set up and commanded the anti-terrorist 32 Battalion, led the notorious 1978 paratroop raid on Cassinga in Angola, and still enjoyed military hero status with the Establishment. The second son, by contrast, was Breyten, the dissident poet who'd been jailed for nine years for allegedly starting a white wing of the ANC (defined as terrorism) and now lived in exile in Paris. And here, suddenly, holed up in out-of-the-way Lebowa, was another brother, Sebastian, a teacher who'd been thrown out of the white educational system, he told me, for his involvement with the emerging multi-racial teachers' unions.

He was very nervous, sitting on his single bed smoking his pipe, and half way through some definition or description would suddenly gesture sharply at my tape-recorder. 'Cut!' he'd say; and then, before proceeding, 'I must get my thoughts in order.'

He told me a sad story. After Breyten's trial and conviction, his mother and father had made an appointment with John Vorster. Perhaps, as fellow Afrikaners, they had hoped they might have some influence over the notoriously hard-hearted Prime Minister.

'The appointment was for eleven o'clock,' said Sebastian. 'They arrived at his office at half past ten, and waited till about half past twelve, till the Private Secretary of John Vorster eventually came through and said, "Well, sorry, Mr and Mrs Breytenbach, but the Prime Minister has been in consultations and very busy, but he can see you now." And my parents being very perturbed and outspoken, wanted to know what was happening, and how come Breyten had been in solitary confinement, and how come he'd been sentenced to nine years. They asked him some pertinent questions, but John Vorster, no scruples at all, said: "All this leaves me stone cold, because, in certain families in South Africa, in the past, there's always been some rebels and some real people to be proud of. General de Wet was a hero; his brother was a *hensopper*, a joiner . . ."'

'A joiner?'

'A joiner is – during the Anglo-Boer war – those people that joined up with the Britishers. But General de Wet, of course, he was a famous leader of the Boers, and his brother, who nobody knows about at all, joined up with the Britishers. So he said, "In your family also, we have this tragic case that your eldest son, Colonel Jan Breytenbach, was a hero of Angola. He went into Angola, he instigated everything in Angola, he fought there, he got medals. But then you have another son, Breyten, who is a rebel, he is a joiner, he joined the Communist Party." And he went on and on and on about it. And he said, "As far as I'm concerned, he deserves his nine years. Not even nine years – death. He should have hanged. To set a good example. Because he's a Communist." So my Dad said, "Well that's never been proven by any court."

'So after these famous words of John Vorster, what happened seven days after that, my mother attended the funeral of her best friend at Hermanus, and this must have been the shock building up, because at the graveyard, she collapsed, and she died, on the spot.

'Three months after that, my father was getting very lonely and disillusioned and you name it, perturbed, upset, and he had a bad stroke. He was hospitalised at Settlers' Hospital, for nine years, and then he died. His brain was still very sharp, but he couldn't communicate at all, he couldn't walk at all.'

Sebastian was clearly very bitter, trembling visibly as he talked. It was such an *Afrikaner* story, I thought, as I left him. It had all the elements. The disputatiousness, the hard-heartedness, the rebelliousness, the sense of being a race apart, the nepotism and favours that were almost unwittingly expected from such a sense, the betrayal. If ever a family were victims of their own race, these were they.

Over a whisky that evening, Francis and Margaret told me about their experiences during the State of Emergency, shortly after they'd arrived at St Mark's.

'In 1985,' said Francis, 'we started here. In 1986 we got ourselves going and we had tents up and all the rest of it because the school had expanded, and there were months – Easter time in 1986 – when there was a complete breakdown of law and order. And the young children went from school to school and they demanded the stopping of this particular school, or they commandeered the teachers' vehicles – they simply said: "Hand over the vehicle to us or else!" And people would then do it. Sometimes they said: "If you don't want us to drive, you can drive, but we will tell you where we want to go." And so you had this extraordinary business of headmasters and teachers driving their pupils on through the bush to the next school where they'd do the same again. And this snowballed through the country. So that you had hordes of 500 or 1,000 kids going up and down the roads, moving on to the next school and stopping it.

'And they passed us by, which was quite mystifying to us, and also quite alarming, because you wanted to know what on earth was going on. So we got in touch with the leaders, they came one night, and they said, "No, no, we want to make the point that the kind of school we believe you're starting at St Mark's is what we *want*. We're not against education, but we are against the kind of education that we've been offered." So then we lived.

'There are several stories about this that fascinate me. You remember today at Assembly there was a senior boy gave out a messsage about detention . . . Well that boy is called Jeremiah, and when he was a small boy, one morning, down the avenue here came a group of ten or twelve comrades man-hauling Jeremiah. They thrust him at me and said, "This boy has been playing truant." Now it fascinated me, because the whole world was playing truant at that stage. There wasn't one school that was functioning. But they said, "This boy is playing truant. He's one of your pupils and he should be going to school."'

'And then,' said Margaret, 'the comrades also used us as a meeting place. Because if they met anywhere near the road the soldiers would come and beat them up and chase them away and shoot them. So they used to say: Could they come and use the bottom of our grounds for a meeting place. And that's one of the reasons the police and army became suspicious of us.'

'The whole world was molten,' said Francis. 'When you drove off, you just didn't know what was going on. On one occasion, Margaret and I were driving off to a school near here and our car was stoned. And when we came back again with all these broken windows and so on, we met the leaders of the comrades and we said, "Look, what goes on? Here we are stoned etc etc . . ." And they said, "That's because the people don't know who you are yet. You need more exposure. Can you please come and attend the next funeral that takes place." And that was interesting because by that stage the army had just arrived, but it hadn't yet exercised its power. And we had to go off to this funeral that was in the hills over here. It was a time when the comrades thought they were still supreme.'

'And a child had been shot,' Margaret cut in.

'He'd been shot by the police,' said Francis. 'So we went off and there was this coffin covered by an ANC flag, which was forbidden at that stage. And we had this funeral where all the army vehicles were parked round, but not interfering. And the people there were definitely aware that things weren't right, that things might not go their way now. And there was a kind of hysteria. But the army did not intervene. And then it was a day or two later that all of a sudden the army just rolled up their sleeves, piled in, and beat up anyone in sight. Anyone that was vaguely school-going age, they beat up. There were horrific stories about kids who would go off home during their lunch-break and be beaten up. Or when a child was sick at home, the army would see them and beat them up. And then, all of a sudden, there was just no-one. Everyone had disappeared.'

'And d'you remember,' said Margaret, 'I had a stream of people coming to give affidavits. I sat down in that library and we must have had thirty, forty people a day coming to give affidavits about brutality. Some of them had been taken off and given mock-burials and mock necklacings . . . it was very, very horrible.'

'And it was in the course of this,' said Francis, 'that one morning there was a knock at the door, and we found it was a dawn raid, we were completely surrounded by the army, just sitting there, in the bushes, pointing guns at us. They searched the house, they searched the school – and of course there was nothing. But it's extraordinary how traumatic it is to have that kind of dawn raid, to have the surprise where you open the door and you discover that you are surrounded by what is a completely alien force. And you suddenly discover that you're totally powerless. It was the only time that we had an inkling of how a lot of people lived. Because if we compare notes with other black friends now, you discover that actually a dawn raid was something they were pretty used to.'

'There was the army,' said Margaret, 'and also the Security Police, and they had cars that had largely Cape Town number plates. Which was interesting, wasn't it, Francis? They were a very frightening bunch.'

'And one wonders', said Francis, 'where those guys are now. Because they haven't annihilated themselves. They're out there somewhere, you know.'

21

MAHWELERENG AND P-P-RUS

In the main street of Potgietersrus I asked a haunted-looking black in a stained boiler suit where the African taxi rank was. He didn't seem to understand. 'The place where the taxis – the minibuses – are,' I repeated. He shook his head. 'Is only for the black nation, sir,' he replied.

'Where are you going on to?' Margaret had asked the day before. 'Potgietersrus,' I replied. 'I'm going to interview the local leader of the Conservative Party.' 'Ah Mahwelereng. We've got plenty of friends in Mahwelereng. It's funny, having worked with these kids for a while, you start to think of these places by their township names. All those whites thinking these are their towns, and the country the blacks know is something entirely different – like a shadow.'

Geoffrey, one of the kids at the school, had family in Mahwelereng; it was arranged that I should stay with them. Someone would meet me at the main black taxi rank in P-p-rus (how much softer that sounded) at 10 a.m.

Eventually I found it. There were no less than three people waiting to greet me: Geoffrey's father Lesetja; his burly friend Albert Chokwe; and an older man with white hair and some missing teeth who was Geoffrey's grandfather, Lesetja's father-in-law. He was going to come with me now; we would meet up with the others later.

Once in my car Grandpa held up a bit of card. MOTHAPO it

read. 'My name is Mothapo,' he said. 'My name is Mark,' I
replied. We then spent the next twenty-four hours in a state
of misunderstanding. I thought he was called Mothapo, when
he was Mr Mothapo; he, in turn, thought I was Mr Marks.

First things first. As an honoured guest and (second
misunderstanding) 'Geoffrey's teacher', Mothapo wanted to
take me to meet the local Chief. We drove out, past the
P-p-rus Industrial Area, through the edge of Mahwelereng
(row upon row of 'matchboxes') to an area of tribal land
beyond.

The Chief's place was on the far side of the tribal land,
right up against a low *koppie*. We walked up to two bulky
stone gateposts. Up a short drive was a substantial bungalow,
painted in cream and maroon. A tall, distinguished-looking
bald fellow in a grey shirt, khaki shorts, long pale yellow
socks and black *takkies* approached us. We shook hands.
'Morning sir how are you I'm fine,' he said in a burst. 'Yes
. . .' I managed belatedly.

But he wasn't the Chief. Outside a double garage in the
sunshine sat a withered little man in a pinstripe suit that
was a fraction too large for him. He wore a black and white
tie and a straw hat with a red band. Beyond and below him,
on a wicker mat on the concrete, was a large woman in an
orange flowery dress and green woolly hat. A teenager in
shorts and T-shirt was summoned and three chairs, one with
a broken back, were brought from inside. Mothapo blew the
dust off them and we sat down.

'We wait until someone greets the Chief for us,' said
Mothapo. The tall bald man obliged, in a rapid blur of Sotho.
Then we were standing again to shake the Chief's hand. We
sat again, and the conversation continued for a while in
Sotho, the large lady silent and smiling as the men talked.
Beyond, a maid knelt on all fours, polishing and polishing
at the shiny maroon surface of the *stoep*.

'Erm, Mr Marks,' said Mothapo, eventually, 'it is our

custom here that when you greet the Chief, you bring him some sort of present . . .'

'Such as?'

'Something such as ten rand would be very good.' He reached into his pocket. 'I can give him ten rand for you.'

'No, no, I've got ten rand . . .'

The Chief seemed delighted with his present. He crackled the green note into his top pocket. 'Could I perhaps see inside the house?' I asked.

Of course, of course! Now that the Chief had been greeted, anything was possible. The lady in the orange dress rose, and I was escorted past the maid into the front parlour, which contained a three-piece suite covered in plastic, and a palewood sideboard on which were arranged a large number of porcelain dogs, several vases full of silk carnations, a cruet set, and some battered gold and crimson Christmas cards. On the wall was a group photo of the Kaiser Chiefs and a framed colour poster of New York by night.

We proceeded to Mothapo's house in Mahwelereng. It was a far cry from the Cape Flats and Soweto-by-the-Sea, so pleasant you could almost have mistaken it – bar the dirt roads – for a white area. Mothapo had a good-sized bungalow full of comfortable furniture; from his garage he was running a small shop, a 'tuck shop' as he put it.

He introduced me to his wife, a large courteous lady in pink. 'I hope you will enjoy your stay with us,' she said, bowing slightly as she gestured me through to the lounge and offered me tea.

We sat on brown lycra settees, in front of a low darkwood coffee table, covered with a white lace tablecloth. The burden of entertaining his white guest was clearly starting to tell on the old man. 'Yes . . . yes . . . yes . . .' he repeated, running his fingers loosely over his forehead. 'I have six children by my former wife . . .'

'Six children?'

'Five girls and one boy.'

We stop-started like that for a while, then he seemed to pick up confidence and began to tell me about his life. He'd been a policeman. For a while he'd been very happy because he'd been working for 'a Dutchman who was very very good. He was just ... the surname was Dutch, but his way of living, with people ... he was a man. I'm telling you.'

'He had respect for you?'

'Yuh. He comes to your house, he stands there, they give you tea, you drink together. You go to his house, he'd call you into the house, you sit, he'd call for tea, you drink together. *In* his house.' Mothapo gestured firmly, to make the point. 'And when he wants to go to the bioscope in the evening, he will ask me, "Man, where are you going today, this evening?" I said, "No, well, I'm doing nothing." "Can you come and remain with my house in town? I'm going to the bioscope with my wife." So I would go and remain with his house. I wouldn't remain outside, I'd remain in the sitting room. He'd give me the magazines to read. He'd say, "There's the TV, there's the magazines, what kind of liquor do you want? There are the glasses, there's the fridge – take what you want." And the wife was also just like that. Very very good. I could drink what I want from these people. Yah – no, he was a man. The day he went away I said, "Now I'm in trouble." I couldn't even finish six months. After he went.'

'Did you have to work with somebody else?'

'Yes, now that was bad. Because every little thing I do they say, "That man has spoiled you. He has made you white, he has made you *white*." No, I had to leave. Buy my own discharge.

'Some white people,' he continued, 'Dutch, are very good. But some are just wild. They just treat black people like animals. We are not allowed to go into church. Even if you have got a friend, a European friend, or a European family – if there is a death, you don't enter into church there. As a black man. No. Dogs and kaffirs not allowed.' He laughed and shook his head. 'God is also angry now. No more rains.

Those big long-time rains. No more. Two clouds only in six months.'

'You think that's why?'

'I say He's angry – the owner of the place is now angry.'

Lesetja reappeared. We drove off to his house where the women of the family had prepared lunch. Lesetja said grace, and before we ate, one of his daughters brought round a plastic washing-up bowl of warm water for us all to wash our hands at the table.

Being a teacher, Lesetja had a subsidised bungalow, surrounded by a patch of garden, complete with all mod cons: TV, inside bathroom, loo. The only problem was a lack of water. 'Ah,' he said, shaking his head, 'they say it is the drought, and what-what. But I don't know. In town they get water all right. Here we only get it in the middle of the night.' So the smart avocado bathroom suite was full of plastic buckets and containers; and when you went to the loo you had to refill the cistern by hand.

The burly Albert Chokwe reappeared. We stood in the driveway and admired his brand new Toyota truck, which he'd won in Pretoria at the National Arm-Wrestling Championships. Chokwe was, in fact, South Africa's current champion arm-wrestler. I was suitably polite.

After lunch, Lesetja was very keen that I should see *his* home village, so he, Chokwe, and I drove out of town in the Dolphin to further-flung tribal lands. *En route* we passed a new platinum mine. There was, apparently, a problem because platinum had been discovered on tribal land, and now the entire village had to be moved. Lesetja didn't object. The Chief had negotiated with the mine company and the tribe would be compensated. Chokwe, however, disapproved: the villagers would have to move against their will, and more than likely would never see anything of the money.

After I'd seen the school where he taught and been on a brief tour of the other schools and clinics in the village, Lesetja, too, wanted to take me to visit his Chief. But this proved to be a rather more complex business than in the morning. The Chief's *kraal* was protected by two tall wire-mesh fences, topped with barbed wire, and two guards with machine guns. 'These are the war police from Lebowa,' said Lesetja. 'They are guarding the assets of this building – the tribal authority.'

The Chief, it turned out, was away. Lesetja was disappointed. 'We will go instead to visit one of the most high regents,' he said. We drove round the corner, but the regent was not at home. Next stop was the Chief's chauffeur. This was more fruitful. With the chauffeur inside the Dolphin, when we returned to the soldiers at the gate we were admitted. We drove up through a second fortified gate and into the Chief's *kraal*, a large bungalow with a cluster of varying one-storey buildings and *rondawels* in the surrounding dirt yard.

Well! We were in luck. Another of the regents was at home, though how 'high' he was no-one told me. He was a slight man with a huge potbelly, dressed in a baggy brown V-necked pullover. Underneath, he wore a khaki shirt and a green tie; on his jersey a silver sheriff's star. He propped himself on a wooden knobkerry.

Chairs were brought and we were granted an audience. The regent sat to one side of us, staring grandly into the middle distance as Lesetja translated my questions about the platinum mine. I'd clearly picked the wrong subject. 'There is still a controversy,' said Lesetja, 'as the present Chief has not in fact been officially installed. The Lebowa Government has stopped them because they want to go through his references and what-what. The present Chief is also the local Lebowa MP, you see.'

I didn't see. At all. The whole system seemed to be ridiculously complex. The Lebowa Government. The Acting Chief. And who the hell was the regent for, if the Acting Chief was fifty-two? The last thing on anybody's minds seemed to be the displaced villagers.

I got to my feet to leave. But I'd forgotton something. It wasn't just the Chief who had to be greeted. I scooped up ten rand in loose change from the baseball cap in the boot of the car. The regent inclined his head and favoured me with a smile.

'The regent thanks you,' said Lesetja. 'And if you come back next time you will be highly welcome. Even a beast can be slaughtered.'

The regent gave me a final benediction. 'In our language,' said Lesetja, 'he is saying, "Grow and become huge as an elephant, but don't frighten people."'

Rattling back into town in the sunset, things became clearer. 'We could not talk about the controversy there,' said Lesetja, 'but this Acting Chief is not popular with the villagers. The Lebowa Government is trying to force this Chief onto the people.'

'The controversy started with the death of the old Chief,' said Chokwe.

'Yah,' said Lesetja. 'Now there are four people vying for it. Each one has got his group. The regents don't agree on one Chief.'

'The Chief's office is important,' Chokwe interrupted, 'because the Chief gets paid by the Lebowa Government.'

'Yah. Then he's getting monies from cases he's settling, fines, visitors . . .'

'It's a lot of income . . .'

'And he has a big house, electricity . . .'

'There's going to be a civil fight,' said Chokwe. 'Yes, there's going to be, over this thing . . .'

'This thing,' said Lesetja, 'we call it Verwoerdism. This was started by Verwoerd. And they did not understand this, the white people, when he – this man Verwoerd – installed this system of homelands, that he was separating these people . . .'

Ministers of the Pretoria-funded Lebowa Government got

a new Mercedes Benz every two years, said Chokwe. 'He's living in a Government house, free of charge . . .'

'He's just supplied with everything,' said Lesetja. 'Even the furniture . . .'

'And they give him Mercedes Benz subsidy . . .'

'Subsidy. If he stays there ten years he can get five Benz.'

'Five Mercedes Benz!' Chokwe was shouting from the back. 'Five!'

The sun had set and the sky behind us glowed crimson, the hills to our right in crystal-clear silhouette. As we bumped along the road we passed groups of young women with whitened faces, carrying bundles of long sticks. Lesetja explained that they had just come from Initiation School. 'They have the sticks to fight the men off,' he laughed. 'If they could start now they would *sjambok* you.'

'What happens at Initiation School?'

'Oh, they dance, and do all these things, and get circumcised.'

'The girls get circumcised? Nowadays?'

'Yes,' said Chokwe, as if this was an odd question. Lesetja laughed. 'Then we say they are ready to be family women. Boys and girls, when they have been circumcised, then they are ready for a family.'

The Initiation School was nearby. We turned right, drove down a narrow track towards the flickering orange light of an enormous fire. Over the wattle fence, under the trees, you could see the silhouettes of the young girls dancing.

Lesetja went over to the old ladies in charge. We weren't – as men – allowed to go in, but for ten rand they could arrange for the girls to dance for us. Ten rand! Ten rand! Fifty girls, in linen skirt-wraps dirtied by dust, with faces and bodies whitened with clay, lined up three deep to dance a dance of welcome in the pool of light thrown by the Dolphin's headlamps. At each end stood the old women clutching their bundles of sticks.

'Akela – eeh – eeh!' the girls chanted, slapping their knees

as they danced and the drums beat time behind, 'Akela –
eeh – akela – eeh, akela – eeh – eeh . . .'

'They are greeting you,' said Lesetja.

We were only eight kilometres from the centre of Potgietersrus, but I felt like Dr Livingstone, deep in the heart of the
Interior.

Back in Mahwelereng we went to visit Geoffrey. 'He is a
good man,' said Lesetja, 'a very good man.'

Geoffrey was tall and distinguished-looking. He wore
light-sensitive tinted glasses and spoke with an altogether
more sophisticated English accent. He'd been at Fort Hare
with Buthelezi and Mandela, had taught in Zambia for
eighteen years, now worked for the Government of a nearby
homeland. Not Lebowa, but KwaNdebele, the tiny area south
of Potgietersrus reserved for the Ndebele people.

We sat in his front parlour and drank beer, while in the
room behind, his daughter supervised his grandchildren's
supper.

'And from here,' he said, 'you're going straight to Jo'burg?'

I decided to be honest. 'Well, in fact,' I replied, 'I've come
really to interview the leader of the local Conservatives, Mr
Van Tonder.'

Through his half-dark glasses, Geoffrey fixed me with a
long, penetrating look. The others turned in their seats. 'I –
I'm trying to get all points of view,' I wittered. After five long
seconds Geoffrey nodded slowly and chuckled. 'Mr Van
Tonder, eh! Whoh! How come you're seeing *him*?'

'I was given an introduction to him in Cape Town. So I
made an appointment to see him up here.'

Geoffrey shook his head and laughed. 'I wish I could just
make an appointment to see that bugger.'

A little later there was a double knock at the door and two
young white men walked in. They were clean-cut young
Americans in grey suits, one dark, one blond.

'Good evening, how are you all?' they asked, giving careful

African handshakes all round; until they came to me, sitting behind the door. I rather threw them; the dark one gave me the African handshake, the blond opted for something rapid and European. Geoffrey invited them to take a seat.

'We are missionaries,' said the blond. 'And we've come here tonight to share the word of our Lord Jesus Christ with you.'

'I see,' said Geoffrey, observing them closely through his dark glasses. 'And what church do you represent?'

'We are from the Norman Bible Church,' said the blond nervously. 'We have a service here in Mahwelereng every Sunday at nine, and if any of you would care to join us you'd be very welcome.'

'Nine o'clock,' said Geoffrey. 'Hm. That is unfortunate. Very unfortunate, as it clashes with our own Anglican services.'

'So,' asked the blond, as if talking to a collection of highly intelligent monkeys, 'what do you all do – what are your jobs?'

'Well,' said Geoffrey, with just a flicker of a smile, 'Mr Chokwe here is a mechanic, Mr Mofomme is a teacher, Mr Mothapo is a retired policeman, and Mr McCrum is a journalist. Indeed we were saying earlier how unusual it was for us to have a white person amongst us, and now I am beginning to feel that this is my lucky day.'

The missionaries nodded seriously.

'And do *you* have a job?' they asked.

'Yes, I have a job,' Geoffrey replied. 'I work 130 kilometres from here. I was in education for a long while. Now I have retired, you might say, into an administrative position. You might say I am', he pursed his lips wryly, 'a migrant labourer.'

'A migrant labourer,' said the missionaries, nodding.

With sincerity in his voice, Geoffrey now congratulated the missionaries on their efforts. 'It is important', he said, 'that the word of Jesus Christ is spread amongst us – so you are doing good work.'

'But we can't expect to see you in church?'

'Well as I say,' said Geoffrey, 'it does clash with our own Anglican service. But you never know, one week perhaps you might see us.'

The missionaries got to their feet. 'May I ask you a question,' said Geoffrey, as they turned to leave. 'D'you make a habit of knocking on people's doors round here at night?'

'Oh yes,' said the missionaries.

'Hm,' said Geoffrey. 'Well, I wish you luck.'

We returned, Chokwe, Lesetja and I, to his house for supper. Again there was the hand-washing ceremony, grace, and we men ate alone: thin chicken legs, with a spicy sauce, thick white bread and thin potato cakes. I had brought in some beers from the car, so after Chokwe had left us, Lesetja and I sat drinking and talking. 'You see this,' he said, pointing to the label on the bottle. 'L-A-G-E-R. This stands for: Let Africans Get Equal Rights.' We laughed.

Pieter Van Tonder, prominent local businessman, Chairman of the Managing Council (the Mayor of Potgietersrus, in our terms) and leader of the local Conservative Party, was not only convinced he was right; he was determined to convince *me* that he was right. During the two days I spent around him, I kept getting the feeling that he really thought that if he kept on enough at me I would suddenly see the light, say, 'OK, blacks and whites *are* completely different,' and go back to England and write a manifesto for the South African Conservatives.

Why? was the repeated burden of his argument. *Why do we think like this?* 'We've been here roughly 300 years, as a white people. And that includes people from Britain, France, Holland, some Scandinavian countries. And through some,' he paused, seeking the right phrase, 'through some . . .

chemical composition, everybody to a certain extent becomes racist. And my question always is – *why*?'

Through his thick glasses, his enlarged bright eyes fixed me with the force of his reasonableness. 'I must admit, ' he went on, 'now, that if I came from Britain, or from Germany, and looked at the South African situation from the outside, I would have exactly the same sentiments as you. You can't but otherwise. These are human beings and they have been gangwayed into a situation that is abominable in many ways. That is so. But living with the situation, working with the people every day, it puts a completely different perspective on it. Why do people that grew up in a non-racist situation, come to Africa, spend a certain amount of time here, and start to think like I do. I've got friends from overseas, I've got a hotel manager in town, and after ten years here he thinks and does as I do. Why? Did all the white people that came from all around the globe to settle here – did they all come here with inherent prejudices? Why did they react that way?'

I put it to Pieter that the blacks his hotel managers would be reacting to would be, by and large, the blacks the system had created: poorly educated, not trained to take initiative, and so on.

'Have you moved into the rest of Africa yet?' he asked.

'I've been to Zimbabwe when it was Rhodesia,' I said. 'I've also lived for nine months in Botswana.'

'OK, Botswana and Zimbabwe. Let's say they're very close to South Africa, and economically are dependent, to a large extent, on South Africa. So let's say white influences from within the country spread there. But look at the rest of Africa. Where they've had all the opportunity to forge their own educational systems. To bring people up to whatever level they wanted to. And except, to a certain extent, for the Ivory Coast, where they've retained a very strong French presence, in fact the French are effectively running the country, we have,' – he paused – 'a peculiar African situation. I wish I could be more specific.'

'I've heard this many times . . .'

'I think', Pieter interrupted, 'it was Albert Schweitzer made the comment, that if anybody comes to Africa, thinking that he will uplift the African to his level of thinking, education, whatever – he's going to be sadly disillusioned. Africa will eventually force him down to their level. It's a harsh statement. But look at Africa, objectively – I'm right.'

We argued on, round and round the same old mulberry bush. I wasn't going to be shaken in my convictions, nor he in his.

'The difference as I see it,' he said, 'is that the whites always had the inherent will and ability to pull themselves up by their boot-strings, whereas the blacks always looked to the whites to pull them up. Maybe it's an unfair comment, because I'm generalising now, but after the Boer War there were people in this country, whites, my own forefathers, who were unbelievably poor, who lived in shacks – I've still got the photographs. The system gave them the opportunity, that's what you're going to tell me. But they still had the will, to uplift themselves, to get education for their children . . .'

And so did the blacks. Unfortunately a combination of callousness on the part of the independence-granting British, (who in 1910, for the first and last time in history, handed sovereign independence to a racial minority), and the subsequent denial to non-whites by the Afrikaner state of such simple rights as the ownership of land and the vote, meant that all the boot-string-pulling in the world couldn't have helped the average dispossessed black of the early part of this century. But there was no point in arguing about history. Quite apart from anything else, Pieter would have been taught a very different history from the one I'd read in the British Museum.

Instead I told him about my visit to Mahwelereng; about Lesetja and his family. 'What about *him*?' I asked. 'He desperately wants to get his kids into decent schools, he's got one into St Mark's, he's thrilled, he's hardly lacking the will to uplift his family . . .'

'You're not making exceptions here?' Pieter held me with those bright eyes, and a fixed, almost semi-circular grin. 'Mark,' he said. 'I think basically all human beings, irrespective of skin colour, want the same things. Russian or American or . . . What we're looking at here is a system that was created; and the question I keep asking is: Why? Why did the whites want to entrench certain rights? Why didn't they want to share with blacks on an equal basis? Why did skin colour become such a focal point? And I say: I find it difficult to believe that all Europeans that settled here were inherently racist. Some were. But the blacks had a share in turning us into the unacceptable people we have become.

'I'll tell you what,' Pieter went on. 'I look at myself, and I frighten myself sometimes. And I wonder why? Why am I nice to Mr McCrum, whom I've never met in my life, I've invited him to my house tonight . . . yet the black that's worked for me for twenty years, I won't have him in my house.'

'Why won't you have him in your house?'

'I think it's because we are completely different people. It's deep down, inherent, inbred. Call it what you want. And I look on myself as a reasonable person. And you will say to me, "You are not. Because if I was a black journalist, with the same education, the same standard of living, arriving on your doorstep, you would most probably have turned me away." And you're right. I would have spoken to you and everything. But I'd never have invited you to my house.'

'Even if I had exactly the same . . .'

'Even if you sent me Martin Luther King. I will speak to him, I'll be civil to him, and decent to him, but I won't invite him to my house.'

'Are you frightened of him? Is that the problem?'

'No, I'm not frightened. I'm not frightened of him.'

'So what is it? What *is* it?'

'That's the definition. That's what I'm looking for.' He paused for a while, then said slowly: 'Every time I have expected anything from a black, in the end I was disappointed.'

'And these are your farm workers, or . . .?'

'People that work for me in the factory here. Somewhere or other, I think that when you go back over the ages that the whites have been in this country . . . maybe that's a starting point. Maybe our expectations of them were totally – too high, I don't know. And eventually, we just gave up.'

'And got tough . . .'

'And got tough. We said, "Look – if you steal our cattle again, or you do that, or you do that, we're going to do this." And we started to harden attitudes. And that's been handed down from father to son. That you can't trust them because they're bound to nail your hide to the wall if you do.'

That evening I went to Pieter's house in a leafy street off the main N2, and met his son, Manie. He'd just been out on his father's farm shooting kudu, and now he was in the kitchen cutting the meat to make *biltong*, that peculiarly South African delicacy: strips of sun-dried and salted lean meat, originally the protein staple of the trekking Boers, now degenerated to the status of a universal snack, handed out like crisps with the beers before the *braaivleis*.

'Kudu *biltong*,' he said, smiling as he rubbed his bloody hands. 'It's the best.' He reminded me a little of Geraldine's children. He had the same long hair, was dressed similarly in T-shirt and jeans. When he heard we were talking politics he grabbed a beer and veered off again.

'One thing we must agree on', said Pieter, giving me the semi-circular grin again, 'is not to talk any politics tonight.'

Pieter's pretty blonde wife Kate hardly looked old enough to be Manie's mother. She didn't want to talk politics either. 'We just have an agreement', she said, as Pieter went off again to get some more beers, 'not to discuss it, because he's Afrikaans, and I'm English, and we don't agree.'

Kate had had guests for four days running and wanted a break, so we went out to the steak ranch in town, which was of the Mike's Kitchen variety: red and white striped outfits, trendy looking white waiters with hair flopping down over their eyes.

The steaks were enormous. We drank beer and tried to avoid politics. Unsuccessfully. 'Dad, you can't say that,' Manie burst out eventually. 'Look, I know some very intelligent Zulu guys at varsity. Really.' He shook his head. 'You just can't say those sorts of things, Dad.'

As they argued, Kate smiled at me. 'You see,' she said, gesturing sideways with her eyes, 'it'll all come right with the young ones – they don't think the same way.'

In the lounge back at Pieter's place we shared a nightcap. The bright confidence of the afternoon had given way to an altogether more despondent mood. 'To Afrikaners,' Pieter said, 'land is the crux of everything. Every one of us wants to own a farm. It's inbred into us. If you want to see a bloodbath in this country, they must try and take away our land. Let them take away everything, all the ensconced white privileges – take them all away, I won't fight. The day they touch my land – I won't allow them to do it.'

'So what would your reaction be – if the ANC legislated to take away your farm?'

'Violent.'

'Literally.'

'Literally.' Pieter shook his head slowly over his tumbler of whisky. 'Unacceptable as it is to me . . . totally . . . I hope never in my life do I have to take up arms against a fellow human being. I'm a religious man . . . I'm not a fanatic . . . God forbid that ever. But at the moment in this country, the way things are going, with all the talks, with everything . . . I think that bloodshed is inevitable.'

*

Mrs Magde Neethling had the softest of voices, and those same gentle Afrikaner eyes. She sat on the sofa in her elegant drawing room in a green and black suit that wouldn't have looked out of place in Knightsbridge. She and her husband had a farm, twenty kilometres or so out of P-p-rus, to the south. It was a lovely spot: the biggest, oldest house I'd yet been in in South Africa, surrounded by lush foliage at the end of a long dirt drive.

'Yah,' she said (and I wish you could hear that quiet, unassuming voice), 'I voted "no" in the referendum. You see, I believe that the Afrikaner has a right to a piece of land in this country that he can call his own. Just the way the Zulus, Vendas, Xhosas and everybody else has his own ground from which he works. I don't want to dominate the black people. But I don't think it's right if they dominate me. I would like to have a country of my own. And I don't think that's asking too much. That's why I'm a member of the Conservative Party. I think they will try to get something like that for us.'

'D'you think that if the ANC came into power in the next year or so that they would take away some of your farm, or all of your farm . . .?'

'I don't know whether they will take away,' said Magda. 'But that's not the point, I don't mean my farm. I want a country of my own. I don't want the whole of South Africa, I mean that's not possible. A minority group like the white people can't own the whole country. But I would like to see that we get a part of it. A small part – that we could call our own.'

'A homeland?'

'A homeland. Because all the black people of this country have their own pieces. Their homelands. Their countries. And it's only the white people that haven't got it. I think that's the right of every person on earth to have somewhere that he can call his own.'

'And you don't want black people there?'

'No, they can be there, that's no problem, but the white people must be in the majority there. If it can be. That will be a place where we can have our own culture, our own schools . . . everything the way the Afrikaner people would like – just the way you do in Britain.'

'Sure, sure. But you're not happy with the idea of multi-culturalism, multi-racialism. You don't want to say: here is this nation, separate from any other – the Afrikaners. And we will now become one of the nations within – like the Welsh, or the Scottish are within Britain.'

'Yah. But the difference is – they have their own piece of land. That's all we want. We don't mind a federal type of Government, but we want a piece of land that's ours. Otherwise I don't think we'll have peace. I can't see it.'

'Whatever we do,' I said to Manie as we left Potgietersrus behind in the rear-view mirror, 'we should try and keep off politics tonight.'

'Diffinitely,' said Manie. 'Let's just see if we can have a nice relaxing evening. Otherwise, if we get onto politics, we'll just have an argument, and then the whole thing ends up with bad feeling.'

It was around four in the afternoon, and we were driving out past . . . goodness . . . Mahwelereng, Dire Straits blaring from the stereo, to go for a *braai* on Pieter's farm.

From the way Pieter had talked about defending his land I'd got the idea that this farm of his had been in the family for generations. But it turned out that he'd bought it only four months previously. As Kate and Manie and a black lady who'd emerged from a nearby hut loaded up the *bakkie*, Pieter enthusiastically showed me the improvements he'd already made. 'It was in a terrible state . . . all these buildings here derelict. You see, I've already painted it up, repaired it . . .'

Over the other side of the hill we stopped at a site where five blacks and a white foreman were building a new cattle enclosure. Pieter was keen to show me how solid it was, how well-aligned the poles were, how well his 'boys' had put it all together. I was introduced to Hans, the white foreman. 'Dit is 'n Engelse joernalis . . .' said Pieter. 'You see,' said Hans, shaking my hand and gesturing at his workers, 'I 'ave only given them nine strokes of the *sjambok* this morning, not the usual ten.' He laughed.

'Johannes!' Pieter barked at one of the kneeling workers. Rapid instructions in Sotho followed. Johannes left his work and started loading up the *bakkie* with firewood.

'That guy', said Manie, 'is the husband of the woman who helped us earlier. They came onto the farm and wanted to work for nothing. They were prepared to work for just food and accommodation, which shows how desperate they were. But Dad insisted on paying them the proper wage.'

We drove on, Pieter and Kate in the front, Manie, Johannes and I standing in the back with the food and the firewood. Johannes looked permanently terrified of his master, jumping to his every command. And the commands *were* commands, far from our quaint English 'Would you mind . . .?', 'Could you possibly . . .?'

We arrived at a beautiful little clearing in a wood. There was the ashy smudge of an old fire. Johannes jumped out first, started humping the firewood from the *bakkie*.

'Can I help with the wood?' I asked Kate.

'If you want – well – no,' she said, smiling uncertainly. I helped with the food instead, loading it onto the camp table Pieter had set up.

'This is one thing they are good at,' he said, standing over the fire as Johannes knelt and expertly built it. He grinned. 'Of course, they've had generations of practice.'

The fire was soon ablaze. Kate had set out the spread on the table and was busy chopping the salad. The sun was setting behind the mountain, half-obscured by the leafless trees. It was pleasantly warm.

'Spring is in the air,' Kate said brightly. 'Definitely. We haven't had an evening this warm for ages.'

'Have you given Johannes a beer, Manie?' asked Pieter.

'Yes. Can I take him back now?'

'No, he can stay and cook the *mielie* porridge. They work till sunset.'

Mielie porridge – or *pap* – is an African speciality, and, as they say, an acquired taste, being a tepid thick white lump of porridge, cooked on the open fire in a cast-iron pot. Africans live on it, Afrikaners regard it as essential for a true *braai*; they could no more have barbecued steak without *mielie pap* than we could have roast beef without Yorkshire pudding.

His tasks completed, Johannes was driven home. We sat, in the gathering twilight, listening to the sounds of Africa all around us. Anne must have said something to Pieter: political discussion was so clearly off the agenda there was something of an awkward gap.

'D'you hear that bird there?' said Pieter. 'Partridges.'

We ate enormous kebabs on sticks. Mellowed by food and wine Pieter told the first Van der Merwe joke I'd heard since I'd been back, Van der Merwe being the stupid Afrikaner farmer who is the butt of the typical white South African joke. 'OK,' said Pieter, 'so Van der Merwe goes to London. And he's riding along with the Queen in the royal carriage, when the horse makes this terrible loud . . .'

So we talked about the Royal Family, what the Queen was really like; about this new book that had come out about Diana, whether she and Charles would get divorced; about the new Brahmin cattle Pieter was bringing onto the farm; about the leopard that Manie had seen, which weren't dangerous, unless you separated a mother from her cubs . . . and not a word was said about the Conservative Party, or the Afrikaner homeland, or the rights of Africans . . .

The following morning I met a man who was politically to the right of Pieter. I'd done a stupid thing. In town the previous day I'd managed to lock my keys into the boot of my car. I'd called the local garage and two moustachioed whites had appeared. After they'd taken the car apart and retrieved the key, I drove them back to their machine-shop. Seeing a group of five white mechanics standing round an engine, I heard Otto's voice in my ear and asked whether any of them knew anybody in the AWB.

They stopped what they were doing, looked seriously from one to another. One, a kindly looking older man, walked off. But a tall young guy with longish blond hair had no problem: the *oke* I needed to talk to was called Andreis Dunlop. He was the leader of the AWB in the northern Transvaal.

Having read the international press coverage of the AWB, I'd expected, at the very least, a hatchet-faced generalissimo in full uniform. But Andreis was a plump, mellow-looking individual, with a creamy-skinned face, a receding hairline and a drooping black moustache. He met my eye candidly, spoke softly, broke frequently into a warm inclusive smile. Though he was mostly Afrikaner, he told me, Dunlop was a fine old English name, and he was hoping one day to get over to the UK, and try and find records of his ancestors, who lived, he thought, in Suffolk.

It turned out that he'd recently resigned from his senior position in the AWB. There'd been a dispute over some money and he'd fallen out with Terreblanche. He shook his head, sadly. 'And I would 'ave died for that man,' he said. 'Really. I would 'ave died for 'im.'

The AWB's position was simple, he explained. They didn't just want an Afrikaner homeland: they wanted the Transvaal, the Orange Free State, and Natal north of Blood River. The old pre-Boer War Boer Republics, in fact, plus that juicy bit of Natal that included Ulundi and traditional Zululand. 'That was the land that belonged to the Boers,' said Andreis. 'I don't want a centimetre of land of other countries: I only want what is mine.'

'OK,' I said. 'Say you got all that land, where would all the black people go?'

'Oh, that's quite difficult,' Andreis admitted. 'I don't say they must go away. I don't think AWB policy says they must move out. It's just that they won't have any voting rights there. Because if you understand the problem – you got Transkei, you got the Ciskei, you got Bophuthatswana. All those places. Most of those people got voting rights in their own countries. But if he stays in Soweto, works near Jo'burg, he wants voting rights there as well. So you show me any nation in the world that's got two countries.'

Andreis was full of such well-reasoned felicities. He'd agreed to talk to me because I'd said what I'd said to everybody on my trip: that I was keeping an open mind, that I would try and present everybody's point of view from an unbiased perspective.

But something was happening to me in Potgietersrus. Way back at the start, a Cape Town liberal had told me that South Africa forces you to take a stance, that however dispassionate you try to be, you can't remain outside politics. And listening to Andreis, I was realising that my gorge was rising and I did have a stance: I was, whether I liked it or not, a white English liberal. I wanted to stop listening and start talking, point out to Andreis just how sketchy and preposterous were the AWB's demands; just how absurdly misguided he was when he said things like (this was in justifying why blacks weren't allowed in white churches): 'But if I go to Mahwelereng they will put a tyre round my neck . . .'

'You think?' I said.

He chuckled. 'I know. I *know*. I don't say the people in the church will do it, but long before I reach the church, comrades and stuff like that will do it.'

'Has that ever happened in Mahwelereng, to your knowledge?' I asked.

'No,' he replied, floored for all of two seconds. 'And that's another proof', he went on, 'of how the Conservative mind is having a very good effect towards the black people: I mean why in Potgietersrus don't we have any boycotts, strikes, necklaces and stuff like that . . .?'

Well, I did promise him a hearing, so here goes: Andreis's definition of the difference between blacks and whites (and please bear in mind that English is his second language):

> I think it's the First World and the Third World.
> That's the difference. It's not that we got to step on
> them and stuff like that. We got to help them. But we
> don't never get it right in one generation. Never.
> They think otherwise. They think about their
> stomach today. We think about our stomach
> tomorrow.
>   I personally think that if you go back in history.
> You take a black. He walked barefoot. He never ever
> think to himself to make himself shoes. Just take him
> a piece of wood and something to walk on, you know
> what I mean? He walked over diamonds in the west
> Cape. He never picked one up and said: 'I wonder
> what this is worth?' He came to the great sea. He
> never ever thought: 'What is on the other side of this
> big water?' I mean you take South Africa.
> Everybody's blaming Verwoerd for apartheid. I
> personally think apartheid was meant good. There
> was honesty in apartheid. But the blacks never took
> their opportunity from apartheid. To develop
> themselves, you know, and own communities, stuff
> like that. They'll all just look up to the whites, you
> know. And that's another fault of the white man.
> You know, he uses the cheap labour for many years,
> and today we've got to pay for it. And that was our
> fault. We used the blacks to do our work, we should
> have done it ourselves.

As we walked out to his car he said: 'And I'll tell you something else. All this stuff about Eugene Terreblanche and Jani Allan. It's true.'

The South African journalist Jani Allan had sued Channel 4 for libel over a TV programme that implied she'd had a relationship with Eugene Terreblanche, and the case was making headlines in all the South African papers.

'It's true?'

'I was there,' said Andreis, 'the first night. I've got video material of the two of them together.'

'I could get you a lot of money for that,' I said. 'If it really does show them together.'

'It does. But I wouldn't sell it. Not at any price. Even after what he's done to me. For the sake of the AWB.'

'He's a pussycat,' said Kate, when I went back into the house. 'Strange to think he's a member of the AWB. Still he's not my kind of man, I'm afraid. Gives me the shivers. Wrong class, too.'

Pieter and Manie drew up, back from a morning in Pietersburg. Pieter was very pleased: he'd bought himself another farm. As we finished lunch he said, 'I must give you some wine to take with you to Jo'burg.' He returned with six bottles – two red, two white, two sparkling – which he insisted I accept. He and his wife had been, as befitted the cliché about Afrikaners, extravagantly hospitable.

22

THE CITY OF GOLD

'Mark!' shouted David. 'You made it! All the way from Potgieters-the-Rus. Welcome!'

It was five o'clock on a Friday afternoon and an end of week booze-up was in progress on Kathy's *stoep*. David, Kathy, a hippyish guy with long hair and a grey beard, two young blonde women, and about forty-five empty bottles of Amstel.

'We went to a meeting of the ANC Women's League this morning,' said Kathy, 'then we went out for a quicklid lunch.'

'A *quicklid* lunch, Kathy?' asked David. They collapsed into shrieks of laughter. I gulped at my Amstel; I had a lot of catching up to do.

The two blonde women left and three more visitors appeared, rattling the thick green bars that completely enclosed the *stoep*, making it more of a giant cage than a *stoep*. A teenage girl, a thin young guy in a black poloneck and John Lennon specs, and a spivvy looking character in a shiny grey suit: whiteys all. 'Look what we have here,' shouted David. 'Chantalle, Rick, and Gary the Gate.'

Chantalle was Kathy's younger daughter; Rick was an astrophysicist from 'Wits' (the University of the Witwatersrand, pronounced 'Vits'), and Gary sold security gates – was closing in on selling one to Kathy. 'I never used to drink until I did this job,' he confided, sipping at the neck of his Amstel. 'Now, everywhere I go I get offered beer, wine . . .'

'*Voetsek*!' Kathy was shouting through the bars at a dog that was bounding across her little front lawn. 'Go away! There's a horrible dog in the garden.'

'It's Gary the Gate's,' said David.

'Is that your dog, Gary the Gate?'

'Yes.'

'I can't buy a security gate off someone who has a *dog*,' said Kathy, giggling. She was wearing the same black top, black leggings and pink ankle socks that she'd been wearing the last time I'd seen her. 'I haven't changed since Pilgrim's Rest,' she said. 'Well, there was one day I sat in the nude and washed this outfit.'

'And here comes the Madam!' shouted David, as a crinkly-faced little old black lady, carrying two bags of shopping, walked up the steps, let herself into the cage. 'Yvonne, this is Mark. Mark, this is Yvonne, who runs the house.' Yvonne chuckled and shook her head; we did the African handshake.

More people pitched up. Kathy's older daughter Tania and a silent young man with cropped hair. Two girls who were friends of Chantalle's. An older guy in a tweed jacket who had to phone his wife. 27 Blackthorn Street was clearly where it all happened on a Friday night.

Gary the Gate left. 'I'll come back on Monday when they've sobered up,' he said.

The grinning hippy was Kathy's older brother, Joe. He'd been in exile for some years, was now running an aid organisation in Canada, was back in South Africa for two or three weeks working out where the money should go.

'This is a guy', Kathy was saying, waving in my direction, 'who likes Buthelezi. He thinks Roley Arenstein is a wonderful idealist.'

'Agh come on!' said Joe. 'Roley Arenstein is . . .' He broke into a string of unrepeatable names. 'No, really, I mean that,' he concluded. 'I lived in Pietermaritzburg for twenty-five years. That guy was so negative, his influence on what was going on was so negative . . .'

'Don't take it out on me,' I said, 'I'm just telling you what my impression was.'

'Nah, nah, I'm sorry,' said Joe. 'I'm just saying – if you're talking about Durban, Roley Arenstein is . . . is . . .' he shook his head, '. . . irrelevant. Really. I can't believe you bothered to interview him. In the history of this country the contribution of that guy is a footnote, it's less than a footnote . . .'

It got cold and dark on the *stoep*, so we went in and sat in the big double reception room, round a log fire. The place clearly doubled up as an office: there were desks and in-trays and a fax machine and a row of word processors against one wall. 'You see this,' said David, waving a magazine called *The Rock* at me. 'This is the magazine of the ANC Women's League – which makes us all laugh because "rock" is a word English South Africans use about Afrikaners – short for rockspiders – because of their long and hairy legs. Just like the Afrikaners call the English *soutpiel* – saltdick. People with one leg in South Africa and one leg in England, so their dicks are in the sea.'

Much later, much drunker, sitting at the round table under the striplight in the kitchen, Kathy was in rhapsody mode. 'The people are so much more vibrant here, that's why I love South Africa . . . I'm seventh generation and I love being looked after by my maid, I'm sorry but I love it . . . I don't care what I do when I'm drunk, really, I'll take my clothes off and dance in the nude, as far as I'm concerned that's other people's problem . . . God I hate grown-ups, I went to this dinner party the other day and the people were so *did*, you know, it was *dridful* . . .'

Lots of people dropped in for drinks the next morning. Kathy's other brother Toby pitched up: a big guy with a huge black and grey beard, flashing dark eyes, long hair swept off his head in a ponytail. He was a well-known Jo'burg jazz musician. There was a shortish black guy called Lolo, who was a famous drummer, and a couple of other white friends. Loud barks of laughter came through the kitchen door.

'This is the guy who likes Roley Arenstein,' said Joe as I came in. There was loud laughter.

On Saturday afternoon David and Kathy wanted to take me to the rugby. 'This you have to see,' David said. 'This is *the* South African institution . . . it's the national religion.' He gathered up a handful of the small tangerines they call *nartjies*. 'These are for throwing. Here, take a couple.'

As we got into the car it juddered horribly. 'This is one of the devices you have to have to get insurance in Johannesburg,' David said. 'Not only d'you have to have an immobiliser, but also this thing that fakes engine failure if you don't press the right buttons. So when someone comes up to you at the robots and points a gun at your head and forces you out, they think the car isn't working and abandon it.'

At Ellis Park stadium the fans were pouring out of their cars. We took seats behind the goalposts. It was an all-white crowd. The only blacks in the place were the ones walking up and down the aisles with the trays of ices, cokes and *biltong*. David and Kathy were having great fun pointing out, 'typical rugby *okes*'. 'There! There!' shouted Kathy, indicating a hugely fat guy in a maroon jersey and a bush-hat with a leopardskin headband, who was swigging from a two-litre bottle of coke, eating *biltong* and simultaneously watching the game through his binoculars. 'And that won't be just coke. That *oke* doesn't drink coke, for sure. Either he's got a hip flask, or he's got the rum already mixed in. Spook and diesel they call it.'

The Xerox Transvaal were on 20 and the Minolta Orange Free State on 16. The teams were down by the Transvaal touchline and as the excitement mounted, the little orange *nartjies* whizzed through the air to land on the pitch.

'I'm going to ask you to please stop throwing *nartjies*,' came the voice over the tannoy. 'Thank you.'

A guy who was wearing a brown checked jacket over a grey checked shirt was standing cutting chunks of *biltong* with a gleaming eight-inch hunting knife. Sticking his tongue out, putting a chunk on his tongue, chucking another chunk at his friends.

And yes, the Minolta OFS had converted the try and gone into the lead 27–25. The guy in the red shirt with the yellow 15 on it had stood up, was hugging an *oke* in a camouflaged army top. Another *oke*, eyes closed, was kissing his hand. His own hand, that is. With an expression of the deepest rapture. Above us, in the reserved seats, the whiteys were banging the steel advertising hoardings – SMIRNOFF, PHILIPS, RANDTORIA BREWERIES – like drums.

Then OFS do a drop kick and the *okes* go haywire. They are 30–25. It's all over for the Xerox Transvaal. 002 minutes to go on the big video screen. 001 minutes. They're looking like a losing side, then suddenly one of the quarter backs breaks free ('he's the nearest thing to an albino gorilla I've ever seen,' shouts Richard over the din, 'no brain, no fear,') races down to land a try. 30–30. The match is shivering on a knife-edge – but then the guy who has missed three drop-kicks already this afternoon screws up the last one and it's a draw. The *okes* stumble out into the street, dazed.

In the evening Blackthorn Street was buzzing again. Genial Joe nodded mellowly over a tumbler of brandy and ginger by the fire. David strode around noisily with a glass of wine. Jazzman Toby was back, with a thin, large-eyed, dark-haired wife called Lindsay. Chantalle grooved through with two girlfriends, saucily dressed for a night of *jolling*. Tania – the older daughter – swished through in leggings, off on the town with a black guy called Frank. Then Rick, the polo-necked astrophysicist, stumbled in, bringing two friends: Peter, who taught at a multi-racial school in north Jo'burg, and Judy, his girlfriend, who worked for a Jewish newspaper. We were all going to Rumours, the famous local jazz club, to see Lolo the drummer.

Rocky Street, Yeoville, was some venue. There were bars, there were jazz clubs, there were discos. There were girls in thigh-high suede boots and tiny miniskirts. There were hippies, lounging around on the saddles of motorbikes. There were even four skinheads, striding dangerously down the middle of the pavement yelling something depressing about kaffirs. Whites all; the only blacks were polite fellows selling hot-dogs from stalls.

Rumours was small and dark and packed. We occupied a long table up by the stage. Between sets, Toby went up to chew the fat with the guys: slapping Lolo on the back, throwing back his head, laughing.

Rick's friend Peter knew a guy who taught at Maru-a-Pula. And Judy had been at Rhodes and knew Otto 'really well'. Truly, White South Africa was a small world! 'He's another ageing lifty,' she said, 'like this lot.'

Rick seemed very hyped up about something. 'Steak, potatoes and peas,' he said, pointing at my plate. 'You go half way round the world and eat steak, potatoes and peas.' On my other side, Lindsay asked about my journey. 'Go to Soweto!' she said. 'Everywhere else in Jo'burg is just a suburb of Soweto now . . . And it's so dangerous there. The blacks, when they say goodbye to their children in the morning don't know whether they'll see them in the evening. AK-47's,' – the whites of her eyes were growing ever larger – 'we don't even know the *sound* of those guns – but the blacks live with that every day. They know the difference between the sounds of all the types of guns . . .'

Rick had sat in Toby's chair. When Toby returned from the stage, there was an angry tussle: big bearded jazzman versus angry astrophysicist in poloneck; eventually Rick withdrew, came and sat next to me.

'That guy really is a *total* asshole,' he shouted in my ear.

'. . . but it's a very vibrant country,' Lindsay was saying. 'It's on the edge, yes, it's on the edge.'

Kathy had run out of drinking options. 'I want something *different* to drink,' she cried. 'I'm tired of everything.'

'Southern Comfort?' I suggested.

'No.' She shook her head, deep in thought. Five minutes later she had settled on chilled white wine. She swigged away cheerfully, nodding and smiling as the music and chatter swirled around us.

'D'you want to stay?' asked Rick. 'There's a party in Brixton we could go to. Or we could go and score some beers at Bebita's – see whether Tania's there – not gone off with any nubile young men.'

Bebita's was heaving with the young in one another's arms. Chantalle was there; her two sexy girlfriends were there; Tania was there – without black Frank. There was a guy with round glasses, two teenage hippies with hair as long as Lennon *circa* 1969, and a silent girl with cropped black hair, a white face, a smudge of red lipstick and a black T-shirt. We sat around in the smoke drinking Castle from the can and Rick told Tania how pissed off he was with Toby, and she sat on his lap, and with Frank out of the way his thin smile had turned to open laughter.

Then one of the hippies had invited us all up to his flat for a joint, and we were off, out of the bar, past black guys asking for money and other black guys frying hot dogs and hamburgers and in a silent sidestreet we trooped up the stone stairs of a block of flats and sat in a room with a double futon on the floor and a little guttering gas fire and watched as one of the hippies pulled out a plastic bag full of grass and crumbled it and rolled a fat joint and we all passed it round and . . .

'Where are you staying?' asks Chantalle.

'At your mother's,' I reply. 'You are her daughter, aren't you . . . or perhaps I've wandered into *The Twilight Zone*.' This gets a howl of laughter from the hippies, and there is more giggling when I tell them about Yeovil being a country town in England and really not at all like this Yeoville, though why anybody is laughing god knows, as only I know how absurd the contrast is . . .

Then I'm walking back with Chantalle through the empty streets and she's telling me how wonderful her mother is, and how she was married for twenty-seven years, and last year the marriage broke up, and it's really upsetting, and now David's around, and he's also just split up with his wife, and Tania likes him but she doesn't, and as I wish her goodnight and slump into my narrow bed I remember that white Johannesburg has the highest divorce rate in the world.

At eleven o'clock the next morning Kathy was sitting in her nightdress in the kitchen, bleary over tea and toast. 'I can tell you exactly what a party in Brixton would have been like,' she said. 'Nothing happens till eleven. Then about two hundred people turn up half out of their heads on some drug or other. And all the *okes* want to do is get laid. And the place will be a third full of Rastamen who are trying to persuade the white girls that all they've ever wanted to do in life is have a good fuck with a Rastaman, and around two or three in the morning they'll all go home except for a few weirdos and people who are too pissed to move. I hate those parties. I hate them even more than I hate grown-up things.'

David was on the *stoep*, reading the Sunday papers in the sunshine. 'This will interest you,' he said. 'The Government are running rings around the ANC. They're actually secretly looking forward to the Mass Action. It isn't going to work – and you're going to be here at a time when there's a fundamental shift to the right.

'Of course, coming from England you'll be more interested in the lead story.' He waved at a headline which read CELL DEATHS – GRIM DOSSIER, 'but it's hardly news to us that the police are killing people in detention. Another forty-nine people murdered in detention – yawn – what's new?'

*

The party goes on. After lunch, in another jazz club, I emerge from an afternoon sleep to find a noisy supper in progress. Joe, Toby, David, Tania, Chantalle and three new people: a middle-aged couple, and a young guy who tells me that if you're a white South African and you go to London you're either a fascist or a freedom fighter. 'When we first arrived we were fascists, but then, when we got to know people, we became freedom fighters.' He laughs. 'We didn't disillusion them. I spent two years in England telling the cute London chicks I was a freedom fighter.'

After supper we're all going off to . . . goodness . . . *another* jazz club. A famous one called Kippies, down by the Market Theatre, to hear a singer called Dorothy Masuka.

It's a smallish place, with round tables and a mainly black crowd. We sit right at the front and David explains that Dorothy could have been as big as Miriam Makeba only she screwed up. She had the lead part in the musical that made Makeba famous, but messed it up; Makeba took over and became the international star.

Whatever the truth, Dorothy has a wonderful voice. She sings a township jazz version of 'Summertime' and I am swept away into a dreamworld where I chuck in everything and come to live in vibrant on-the-edge Jo'burg, with this voice, and this music, this music . . .

Dorothy bows to the applause. 'I'm looking for a nice handsome guy,' she croons, and makes the mistake of picking on a very drunk Indian who has been muttering 'We love you – oh we *love* you mother,' ever since she came on. He leaps up on stage, puts his arms right round her, and she has to wrestle to get him off. 'Won't somebody save me,' she gasps; but nobody moves.

After that, her delivery is a little less confident. She keeps her gaze well away from the Indian who stands up and dances wildly on his own, shouting, 'We love you – oh we *love* you mother! More, we want *more*! Africa . . . eesh Africa . . . eesh eesh Africa!'

Lolo is there, takes a turn on the drums. Another black guy, who is so wrecked that he can barely stand, does a spectacular solo on the guitar. 'Just look how out of it he is,' says David. 'Look how his bottom lip's drooping, and yet look at the intricate stuff he does with his fingers. I've seen him when he was twenty-five times more fucked-up than that.'

Tania fancies the bass guitarist, a tall saturnine black guy with a woolly hat. 'I just *know* he'd be good in bed,' she says.

A fantastically sensual black girl is dancing on her own, to one side of the stage. 'That's Suzanne,' says Kathy. 'There are two identical twins, Suzanne and Suzette, and they fuck anything in town.'

'Suzanne's got a white guy with her,' says David, 'what we'll have to do is fix Mark up with Suzette.'

'I'm fine,' I say, 'I – I'm fine.'

Kathy is having the time of her life, throwing all cares to the winds. She's wearing a short black and turquoise skirt and green leggings and now she's up by the stage dancing wildly with her daughter.

As we come out into the cool winter night, David shouts: 'Hey! Watch out! There's an unexploded Pom on the pavement.'

The Eugene Terreblanche case continued to dominate the news. Foolishly perhaps, I'd told David about Andreis's videotape. His ex-journalist instincts were up and running. 'But you could make a *fortune* out of that,' he said.

'I know, but, you know, he didn't want to be persuaded.'

'Come off it! You're not telling me you've got scruples about the AWB. Look, if Jani Allen loses that case Terreblanche is finished. Those northern Transvalers are all good Christians and adultery is not allowed. You could actually assist in that process.'

'Well, I want to get home in one piece, you know.'

'Look, nobody's going to shoot you – you're a journalist.

This guy's out of work you say, he's had a quarrel with
Terreblanche over 500R, you could offer him, what, 5,000
for the video, that's a grand in English money, and god
knows what you could sell the material for in London. You
should ring George Carman, the English newspapers . . .'

'I know, but . . .'

'Look,' said David. 'I'm going to take you to *see* Eugene
Terreblanche. He's speaking at the Portuguese Hall in Turf-
fontein on Wednesday night. Perhaps that might change
your mind.'

You and I know all about Eugene Terreblanche. You've
probably seen him on the news: a big, bearded figure yelling
into a microphone; or watched footage of his supporters
marching up the main street of Ventersdorp in those swas-
tika-like 'three 7's' armbands. But going to a rally was
something else.

The most chilling thing was the audience. I was prepared
for all the cliché stuff: the long table of uniformed comman-
dants up on the stage of the huge echoing hall; the big flags
draped behind; Terreblanche bellowing in Afrikaans, stabbing the air with his index finger; the thin-lipped spook in
beret and dark glasses just behind him to his left; even the
row of hooded figures in black (only their eyes were visible)
standing at attention with their rifles in front of the stage.
This was all as Hollywood would have designed it.

No, it was the people packing the hall that shocked me.
The modern looking young women with children on their
knees; the men in patterned jerseys and jeans; the toddler in
the transparent plastic-covered pushchair; the kindly-faced
old boy in spectacles. These were characters from a shopping
centre in Croydon, not faces from film footage of the 1930s;
people like you and me, not monochrome weirdos from an
evil twist of history. A few seats away from me was a young
lad who couldn't have been more than seventeen, fully
togged-up in his green uniform and maroon beret, his mother

– looking as wholesome as a woman from a washing powder advert – sitting proudly beside him.

The other surprise was the humour. 'What's that?' I asked David, as yet again the audience broke into laughter. 'He's having a go at the press,' David replied. 'Whatever you do don't take out your notepad and start writing.' Then: 'Now he's saying that the blacks from Mozambique come to this country under the feet of the elephants, past the claws of the tigers – he's talking about the Kruger National Park – so keen are they to get to apartheid South Africa.'

Terreblanche grew serious again. I heard the words 'Jani Allen' repeated amid the Afrikaans. 'He's saying all the witnesses in London are liars,' David translated. '"The focus has shifted from the sport in Barcelona to the sports of Jani Allen."'

At the end he switched languages. 'And this I must say in English,' he bellowed. After David's warning, I didn't take out my pad and write it down, but the gist of his words was that the ANC was the party of the Communists and the Devil who were trying to drive Jesus Christ out of South Africa. The audience erupted into a standing ovation and suddenly it was all over: the faithful were standing solemnly to sing a hymn and everybody else was leaving.

The next morning I phoned Andreis in Potgietersrus. He wanted to think about it. A day later he phoned back: he'd thought about it, and he'd do it: signed statement, everything. 'There's only one problem,' he said, 'I think my children have cost me a lot of money here. I've got the shots of them going into the cottage together, but the bit after that they've taped over – some Mickey Mouse video or something.'

So my career as international investigative reporter came to an abrupt end, twenty-four hours after it had started. I can't say I was too unhappy. Kathy had told me that her house was bugged, and all day I'd been on the alert for members of the Security Police, coming to take me away. As I'd driven off at lunch-time, a guy in uniform had swung out and followed me . . . but it was only next door's chauffeur. No, I just wasn't cut out for it.

I cruised around Johannesburg's famous northern suburbs . . . Westcliffe, Houghton, Melrose, Hyde Park, Sandhurst, Hurlingham, Sandown, Parkhurst, Morningside. It was like Hampstead multiplied fiftyfold. Splendid mansions in huge gardens. Glimpses of pools, tennis courts. Black gardeners watering banks of lush foliage. Bright yellow 24 HOUR ARMED RESPONSE signs. Maids on street corners in white headscarves. A clear blue sky, endless sunshine.

At the robots on the big intersecting main roads north, black men sat with brown cardboard placards saying NO FOOD NO JOB NO MONEY PLEASE HELP WITH JOB OR FOOD.

By a lucky coincidence, the Baron was in town, staying with friends in Melrose. It was dark when I arrived, so I could only make out the looming bulk of the house and see a maid in brown uniform and white apron and cap through a lighted window.

Inside, the long drawing room had a ceiling made of criss-crossed stripped treetrunks. A huge log fire blazed in the grate. I sank into the bright yellow cushions of an enormous sofa and gazed at a row of boxes full of lavender plants that ran along one side of a chunky glass coffee table. A quick scan of the walls revealed quality art, interesting prints and originals in heavy frames.

Simon was in his fifties, quite short, with greying hair and a stomach that spoke of more than the occasional business lunch. Ruth was diet-thin, dressed all in black, her dark hair swept back off her forehead and held in place by a gold clip shaped like a shell. She talked fast, with a way of fluttering her eyelashes so that she didn't fully meet your eye. Despite being out of his natural habitat, Alex was the same as ever; it was good to see him and I didn't remind him of the wicked things he and Geraldine had said about northern Jo'burg liberals.

Over drinks Ruth told a funny story about the famous ANC leader Oliver Tambo, who had recently become a neighbour. 'They're what we, in the northern suburbs, call our NBFs,' she said. 'Our New Black Friends.' As a foursome, they'd recently gone to the Market Theatre, to see the new Atholl Fugard – *Playland*. Ruth explained how awkward they'd found it sitting there with Oliver and Adelaide Tambo.

'When they're coming up with these lines like "these fucking *kaffirs*",' interrupted Simon, 'I mean, of course it's authentic, but . . .'

'So we're sitting there,' Ruth picked up, 'and I was getting very tense, with all that language, and at the end of it I said to Adelaide, "So what did you think of it?" And she said, "To tell you the truth, I hate bad language."'

We laughed.

'Of course Tambo's had a stroke now,' Simon said, 'so he's not what he was. But I find it very moving, you go round there on a Sunday afternoon and he's sitting there in a chair on the lawn, and all afternoon people keep turning up, to greet him, almost to pay homage to him . . .'

We talked of the phenomenon of these legendary black revolutionaries moving into mansions in the northern suburbs. 'I think it's right', said Ruth, 'that they should.'

At dinner we had vodka with our Russian starter, then two kinds of wine with our two kinds of seafood, served to us by a tall elderly black man in a white chef's hat. We were joined by Ruth and Simon's son, a curly-haired student who was at college in America and wanted to be an actor. He terrified his mother by taking black taxis into town. 'But our son says we have the cheapest and best system of taxis in the world,' she laughed, proudly.

Nonetheless, despite the taxis and the luxury, they were moving to London at the end of the year.

*

In a lovely mansion in Westcliffe, I had lunch with Edward
Jordan, the composer who was responsible for South Africa's
current pop No 1. He was twenty-four, a short-haired, affable
ex-public schoolboy (Bishops), ex-Wits University, and desperate to get to London, where he was prepared, he said, to
do anything – 'be a roadie, work in a pub' – to make it in the
international music business. 'I get a hard-on just walking
down the street in London,' he said. 'That's where it all
happens. Last time I was there I passed Paul Weller in the
street and I nearly fainted.'

He lived with his parents, and his studio was also his
bedroom. There were posters on the wall for current hits
alongside an old college playbill: 'The Wits Players present
RANDLORDS AND ROTGUT.' He sat up by his console laughing
loudly as he took me through the various musical styles he
could muster: reggae; rock; 'of course as a pianist there are
just piles and piles of ballads'; compositions for the multi-
racial band Mango Groove, who were pals of his from Wits;
black 'bubblegum music'. . . 'Write this down, Mark,' he
yelled at me, over the beat, 'all the protest music for Black
South Africa gets written in Westcliffe.

'When Nelson Mandela was released, I had this fantastic
idea. Why not – as he was released – get his speech on
digital audio tape, whack it on a house beat and push it in
the clubs. OK, now everyone else is going to have this idea,
but why don't we have it first. So we sat there with our tape,
and eventually on the Sunday night that he got released he
came on and said, "Ladies and gentlemen of the world, I
don't know what to think, and I'm not going to say anything
now, I'm just going to go back to the ANC office where
they'll tell me what to say – thank you."' Edward laughed. 'I
mean did you see the speech, that was basically the substance . . . I mean, what kind of leader is that?

'Anyway, we did it, and we called it *Choice*, and we didn't
sleep and we worked right through the night and we made
this really brilliant record in three days. And then SAMA –

that's the South African Musicians' Alliance – which is ANC affiliated – put a ban on it. Two white kids doing this – there was absolutely no ways.

'D'you want to know why? Because we didn't pay them. I don't know if it's more true in the Third World or not, but at the end of the day here, it all comes down to money. If you want your record to be put in Soweto, you have to fork the bucks out. Paul Simon wants to come and play, he can't just come and play, he has to pay the right people. To say that it's OK. And not just nothing – ridiculous amounts of money. Which goes straight into their pockets. It doesn't go to the education of young black children, which is what it's meant for. This is a corrupt Third World country and that's what happens. I just wish the Westerners would understand it and say, "Stuff you, we're playing anyway." But then they say, "We'll blow you up." When Paul Simon came out here, there was AZYGO, the Azanian Youth Organisation or something, who said, "We'll blow up the stadium if you don't pay." Eventually, afterwards, we found out that AZYGO was only about eighty people and a fax machine. But that's why Paul Simon concerts were only half full. And why he'll never come back here, nor will any big international act. Why? To run at a loss? To play in South Africa? It doesn't make sense. All that gear. 137 crew. People here don't appreciate the amount of effort that goes into putting on a big stadium show. And all these little groups saying, "We, the people, have not been informed about ..." Agh!' He shook his head with irritation.

Edward's girlfriend Sue-Anne Braun was the beautiful TV presenter I had gawped at in many a hotel bedroom. Now we sat side by side in a spacious drawing room in Parkhurst – at twenty-four, she too lived with her parents – sipping tea and leafing through her portfolio.

'It's my mother's, so it's very soppy and sentimental ... this is me at fourteen, looking dreadfully toothy ... this is

the first film I ever worked on, it was one of those dreadful
American films. They made a hell of a lot of them out here
in 1987, 1988. And this is just appearances, and commercials
and boring, boring . . . And this is *Nunsense*, which was the
biggest smash-hit this country has ever seen, it ran for two
years . . .'

She told me what it was like being a South African
celebrity at twenty-four. 'I went to Hyde Park one day to do
some shopping and this woman approached me and said,
"Aren't you Sue-Anne Braun from M-NET?", and I said,
"Yes, I am," and she said, "Oh! Can I have your autograph?"
So I said, "Certainly," and we start chatting, and she says,
"Oh my husband thinks you're lovely," and chat-chat like
that. And then she turns round and says, "What d'you think
of our new lounge curtains? We bought them last week."
And I said, "I – I . . ." And I suddenly thought, Oh my *god*,
how do I get out of this? And I looked at her, and I said, "I
haven't seen them, I can't *see* you." She just looked devas-
tated. And I walked away thinking – Oh boy, oh yeah.'

But now, despite her nationwide fame, she too was planning to go overseas, 'to start all over again' in England or
America. Partly, it was because she'd succeeded in South
Africa, and now she wanted wider exposure; partly because
there were very limited opportunities for actors in South
Africa; partly because she just wanted to live in a First
World country. 'I don't want to have to live in a country
where – you know, we have friends in Zimbabwe who phone
us and say, "Please can you send us this, because we can't
get it any more . . ."

'I have a tremendous heartache for South Africa, because I
do believe we're going to have to go through five to ten years
of major shit before anything is done, and I have a horrible
feeling it's going to end up terribly Third World and poverty-
stricken, and I feel so disloyal saying that – but that's really
what I feel.'

'So what is it particularly about First World countries that

you like?' I asked. Sue-Anne leant forward with enthusiasm:
'The commodities, the lifestyle, the capitalism, I suppose.
The fact that you work *bloody* hard, you get rewarded for it;
you can live in a good home and have a good lifestyle; there
are opportunities, you can study, you can take it further,
things are available to you which are not here . . .'

William Kentridge, the well-known South African artist,
told me about dual projects. We were having coffee in a
sunny room adjoining his studio – also in his parents' house
in the northern suburbs. Kentridge actually *lived* in an
altogether more downmarket suburb near Ellis Park, but as
his parents were resident in London for all but six or seven
weeks of the year, it clearly suited him to work where there
was peace and space and light and a view out over a large
and lovely garden.

We were talking about the three characters who featured
in the animated films that were a central part of his work –
and an extension, he explained, of the large charcoal draw-
ings stacked up everywhere in the studio. There was Soho
Eckstein, 'who owns half of Johannesburg'; Felix Teitelbaum, 'whose anxiety floods half the house'; and Mrs Eckstein, 'who is the lover of Felix Teitelbaum'. And a crowd –
'there's always a huge crowd.'

'This is a black crowd?'

Kentridge smiled. 'They're charcoal marks on a white
sheet of paper. I'm not specific as to who they are. These
films are not political tracts; rather, they're records of the
way in which politics, particularly here, impinges on ordinary daily lives with a more neurotic effect than, I would
say, it does in Britain at the moment. It might be that in
Britain people get angry, or they have particular views – but
it's not the sort of thing that creates a deep level of anxiety,
or neurosis, or ulcers.'

'And it does here?'

'I think so. I mean the uncertainty – the number of people

who have dual projects, one project being to leave the
country and the other to try and continue. Various projects
that have in a sense to be made ready for different possible
futures that may happen here. There's a general malaise –
certainly in white South Africa, white middle-class South
Africa – a malaise and an anxiety that's extraordinary. A
sense of things being too hard to solve ... I mean the
scenario of things completely falling apart, of violence just
escalating and escalating, unemployment and anarchy
becoming greater and greater, relatively safe areas becoming
smaller and smaller, and more and more contained ...'

'So have *you* got a second project, to move overseas or
...?'

He smiled. 'No, no, no, I think my work is much too rooted
here to be able to move like that.'

The Berman Gallery was on the tenth floor of a block of
offices on Smit Street, right in the skyscrapered mini-Man-
hattan of central Jo'burg. I pressed a buzzer in a brass grille
and eventually a black guy wearing a baseball cap appeared.
This, as it turned out, was not a trendy doorman, but the
artist himself – Fikile. He seemed weary, not particularly
keen to talk to me.

Upstairs, the show was being taken down. The gallery
ladies were smart and white. One had half-moon specs round
her neck on a gold chain. Another, black jeans and a tight
black cardigan. They were looking through another black
artist's work, giving him advice in their clear Seth Effrikan
voices.

'Lovely colours; I love mixed media,' said one. 'Wouldn't
you do some more mixed media for us?'

'I can do it,' said the artist, a big man with a beard.

Half-moon specs was looking at one of his landscapes. 'It
must be more open – the land. Doesn't have to be too
cluttered, you know. Maybe just the lodge, and the village,

and the waterhole, and the vehicle – it doesn't want to be too busy, you know.'

'I'm capable of doing that landscape.'

'I'm sure you are.'

'I'm capable.'

'I'm sure about that.'

Fikile's paintings were abstracts with figurative details. They were called 'Who Knows What Lurks In The Dark', 'Mourning of a Dying Nation', 'On These Barren Plains'.

In the back room a very drunk black guy was lying slumped on the smart cream couch. He smiled at me, then frowned. 'Thass smart,' he said. (That's smart? That's some art?) 'Thass *smart*,' he repeated. He pulled himself up and stumbled next door. I stood looking at a painting entitled 'For Brothers', which had words scrawled into thick smears of paint against a metallic background. YOUR DIGNITY WILL STALK THE DARK NIGHT UNTIL WE'RE LIBERATED. FOR STEVE BIKO, read one of the scrawls.

'I want to go with you,' I could hear the drunk guy saying, just beyond the doorway in the next room.

'You're messing my shit off,' Fikile replied. Then the gallery ladies had rallied round, and I watched as they eased him towards the main door. 'Would you like to skitch something for us,' they said brightly, as he tottered off, 'so we can look at it – OK. Take care, hey?'

The drunk guy turned, nodded, gave us a long and solemn stare. 'I – take – care,' he said slowly.

Fikile came through to me in the other room, shaking his head. 'That guy is a friend of mine. He was high when he woke me this morning, and when we came here they gave him a glass of wine and then he started drinking himself to bits.'

Fikile's eyes were pink-grey and rheumy with liquid. There was a buzz coming off him, a tangible feeling of anger. He was polite to me, but impatient also. Another journalist in a blue suit and ironed shirt. Fikile was the flavour of the month. Outside, the interviews were stacked up in the cuttings file.

He quizzed me about what I was doing, what activists I'd spoken to, which townships I'd visited. So much that had been written about him was wrong, he said. That he was a black power artist; that he was an angry young man. He told me of his meeting with one woman journalist. 'She came to me and I said "Fuck off." Why should you say some kind of yes to everything?'

Fikile had not had an exhibition in a gallery for thirteen years. 'It was a way of fighting. I was fighting my own little war, to show that an artist is a human being, and an artist is the very source of their income, and they must realise that. But now, I think – this is the right time to project.'

Two whites had joined us, moving thoughtfully from painting to painting. A Jewish guy in his fifties with a grizzled stubbly chin, and a pretty dark-haired young woman in a black cape. 'Excuse me,' Fikile said to me, rising, greeting the man warmly with an African handshake.

'He's a patron,' he said, when he returned. 'An advocate. He saw my work, eventually when he met me we got very close. He helped me through financially, through very difficult times. And, I would say, spiritually, to still have sanity.'

The advocate was musing on a picture. 'I've seen all this stuff before, Fikile,' he said.

Fikile stood, showed him 'For Brothers'. 'Too obvious,' said the patron sternly. 'You're copying yourself.'

'He's an artist and a human at heart,' said Fikile, as the patron headed off next door. 'He's not the kind who's just a philanthropist. If he sees that you're in dire straits, he'll give you five hundred rand. And if he sees that's not enough he'll offer you a thousand. He's not phoney. I'm the kind of person who senses phoniness right from the start.'

'D'you mind him being so critical of your work?'

'Everyone has got the right to an opinion. He knows my poetry and he knows my painting and now I'm putting them

together. I think that's what he means when he says I'm
copying myself.'

He told me about his time in detention. 'It was the usual
thing. Ninety days without trial. Solitary confinement. In a
room no bigger than this.'

'They beat you up?'

'They beat you up to pulp. Detention is not a matter of just
sitting in the cell. You are being tortured. And that's
enough!' he said, suddenly; and with a downward-sweeping
gesture of his hand, he got up and walked out of the room.

Of all the politicians that I'd heard about in my long
progression up the coast, Van Zyl Slabbert was the one who
had sounded most intriguing. Everyone had mentioned him.
'If you really want to get the low-down on what's happening,
try and get to Van Zyl,' they had said. 'In the morning he's
in De Klerk's office, in the afternoon, Mandela's — he's the
man.'

An Afrikaner who had turned against the Establishment,
he had become Leader of the Opposition in Parliament, and
had then resigned, declaring that Parliament was no longer
relevant to government in South Africa. He had then set up
IDASA, the Institute for a Democratic South Africa, a nationwide NGO dedicated to forging links between the separate
communities of South Africa. In 1987 he'd been responsible
for the extraordinary (by South African standards) initiative
of flying sixty leading Afrikaner reformists to Dakar in
Senegal for talks with leaders of the still-banned ANC. (Who
in England would fly sixty 'wet' Conservatives to Dublin to
have talks with the IRA?) The session had been described as
'a remarkable meeting of minds', and had laid the founda-
tions for CODESA – indeed, for the very 'transition' I'd been
witnessing.

Now we were having tea together in the Gazebo Restaurant
of the luxurious Sandton Sun. Golden gazebos rose above
plush yellow-gold upholstered armchairs. A white lady

pianist trinkled up and down the keyboard of a grand piano, producing Kleidermann-style versions of 'Memory' or 'Michelle'. To our right, brightly lit gold lifts sailed silently up and down enormous transparent tubes.

I was excited. Two evenings before I'd seen Dr Slabbert address a Black Sash meeting in Houghton, and had been impressed. A tall, burly, brown-haired rugger-player of a man, he'd combined an academic's intelligence and comprehensive grasp of the issues with an endearing humour and lack of pomposity. Now, through a contact of the ever-influential Baron's, I'd got him to myself for an hour or so.

We skimmed over his early life. It sounded familiar: the farm in the northern Transvaal, the black childhood friends, the enlightenment at university, the slow move away from the Establishment, to the point at which he was being bombarded with rotten eggs and tomatoes at public and university meetings. He chuckled. 'But now,' he said, 'universities that used to declare a ban on me . . . I can't stop the invitations. Stellenbosch, Potschefstroom, Bloemfontein . . . Before, when I went and argued against the tri-cameral constitution at Stellenbosch, they punched holes in the tyres of my car; they killed the meeting by bringing in megaphones and throwing chairs all over . . . Now, Breyten Breytenbach and I, about a year ago, went to Stellenbosch, and we were walking on the campus, and the students started clustering around, and before we knew it, in an amphitheatre, there were five or six hundred students just asking us questions, and wanting to *know* . . . you know.'

So what about Parliament, I asked, and his inspired move of leaving it, declaring it redundant? He was, as ever, down-to-earth: 'The disillusionment with Parliament', he said, 'was basically because Parliament itself had become totally marginalised – I mean it became a kind of grandstand ticket at the Wimbledon Final: you're sort of watching the game but you're not part of it. Because basically the Government at that time had begun to ignore Parliament, they were

governing through the Security Establishment. And I
increasingly felt I was performing a kind of decorative role
for their intentions. That, and the fact that there was no real
dialogue going on with the ANC, which was banned at that
time. So when I resigned, I quite deliberately used my status
as Leader of the Opposition to do things which under normal
circumstances would have brought a lot of hardship to an
individual. Like letting them take my passport away. I said,
"I'm going to talk to the ANC, so take my passport away."
And for Botha to say: "Former Leader of Opposition's passport is taken away" – that was a bit tough . . .'

The resignation had led to the Dakar meeting, and to the
present. 'Would you say', I asked, 'you were now in a fairly
unique position, in that you're up there with all the key
players and yet you're not affiliated to anything? It must be
a nice position to be in.'

'It is. It is – an extraordinary position to be in. It's not an
unenjoyable one. I enjoy talking to the Right wing. I think
that there are elements within the Communist Party that do
not like me at all, but apart from that . . .'

'You're in a position where, whatever happens over the
next few years, you're still there, in the middle . . .'

'Oh yuh . . .'

'As a facilitator, or whatever . . .'

'Sure, sure. Whatever capacity, I'll be there.' He chuckled
as he reached down to pick up his tea cup. 'I'll be around.'

'D'you fantasise about being back in politics? You were
joking the other night that you weren't the State President,
and during the questions afterwards somebody said that you
should be. D'you ever think it would be nice to be back in
Government?'

Van Zyl leant forward. 'I have no desire whatsoever to
play any kind of formal political role. I never enjoyed
Parliament; from that point of view. I never enjoyed being a
politician; I always found that extremely uncomfortable. But
having said that, I can tell you now that if I think it has to be

done, for whatever reason, I will do it. In other words, if I believe that it can play some kind of a role to ease the transition, to contribute to some kind of rationality in political debate, I will do it. I won't particularly enjoy it, but I will do it.'

On paper it might sound like a line; but confronted with his unflickering gaze over the tea table, I found it easy to believe him.

'I can see,' he went on, 'that we could reach the situation of a kind of deadlock, where the debate just bogs down because the parties are overburdened by the legacies of the past, and they can't move. Well then you have to see if you can do something about it . . .'

'I can't see', I said, 'how you're going to end up with a Government that doesn't have some sections of white in with the black . . .'

'No. There has to be an interim Government. And that interim Government will be a multi-racial Government, if you want to call it that, no question about it.'

'And that may stay in place a lot longer than people . . .?'

'I've never had any doubts about that. I mean people from both the Nats and the ANC side get irritated with me when I say, "This is going to take longer than you think." And I say to the ANC in particular, "The reason it's going to take longer than you think is because you want it to be shorter than it's going to be." And I also say to the Government, "Every time you make that point, you add another six months to our transition."

'You know these people pretty well. The Government are sincere in what they're doing? Or are they playing a sort of waiting game?'

'Some of them are playing games, but basically De Klerk has no choice – to follow through, even if he's not a 100% sincere about it. He's just got too much at stake . . . but following through doesn't mean he's going to roll over and hand over power. You know the ANC tend sometimes to treat the whole thing as a morality play: we now deserve to be in power. One thing I can tell you about Afrikaner politicians is that they have no great concern about the morality of politics. For them it's power. And they'll work with the power thing. If they're satisfied that the relinquishing of power would not lead to repression, or breakdown and so on, they'll go through with it . . . I'm sure they will; I've no doubt about it.'

Far over to our left the lady pianist had switched to 'Don't Cry For Me, Argentina'. I felt it was an appropriate moment to bring up the second big question I wanted the insider's view on. 'So how far is De Klerk involved in what the security services are up to?' I asked.

For a moment Van Zyl's voice dropped almost to a whisper: 'I don't *think* he's personally involved. I think he's confronted with a very difficult problem; he has inherited a security apparatus over which he did not have much control when it was created. In fact, he was deliberately excluded. He came in on the assumption that he could deal with this problem quite comfortably; he never really expected the depth of destabilisation and involvement that went on. And now that he's confronted with that, it's in a sense threatening his fallback position. Because the fallback position for any incumbent regime is armed force. So it's becoming increasingly difficult for him to avoid becoming involved. Like now, this guy that was killed the other day, yesterday, what does he do? All the circumstantial evidence is beginning to narrow down. And the sense in which he becomes involved is by default, rather than by cognition. But to say that he has a sort of command headquarters where he throws the switch on a Monday and says, "This week we kill forty people," that's not on. I've never believed that.'

'There obviously are people in there who are doing that. Who are they?'

'Let me give you a plausible response to that — because if I knew, of course I would tell the whole world exactly who they are. They've killed three of my friends, close friends. We have five defence forces, each one has a third force. In other words, each one has elements out of control, unaccountable, who can take almost unilateral and arbitrary action whenever they want to. Why would they do this? They do this because they fear transition; they fear for their jobs; they do this out of conviction; and they do this with criminal intent. Now that is not an uncommon phenomenon, in repressive societies . . .'

'If that's the case, if they're not involved, why don't the people at the top put all their energies into finding out who these people are, and getting rid of them?'

'Well, I think part of the reason for that is that some of the people at the top were involved, from the outset, in setting this thing up. So you have kind of a peer group discomfort there. You know that it was, say, General X who was part of that unit which must take responsibility for special recces in such and such a place. But now those special recces have become rogue elephants, General X is turning his head the other way and so you begin to say: "Oh my god, is X implicated?" And X gives you the hard look and says: "As a matter of fact, the Minister of Y and the Minister of Z, as well as the former Speaker of the House *and* the President, they were all in on it." So then De Klerk looks where the rot is extending to and he says: "If I have to start cutting out here, I'm starting to cut pretty close to the bone. I'm going to have to dump some of my colleagues." So he says, "Let's go for amnesty," which is I think what's going to happen . . . There is no real way other than, as old Vance said, wiping the slate clean, trying for a fresh start.'

Under the circumstances, the forgiveness of the black community, Van Zyl agreed, was 'extraordinary'. Would there ever be a formal apology?

'It's not just a question of an apology,' said Slabbert. 'It's a question of who apologises. A lot of whites have said they're sorry. Some Cabinet ministers have said they're sorry. But they want an official confession and apology from De Klerk. And I agree with them. I agree that he should say, "Listen, we have stuffed up this country good and proper. And we are sorry for it." But it's a very difficult thing for him to say.'

'And I don't think he will . . .' I said.

'He won't. And it's crazy, because it would have an enormous – what is the word I'm looking for? – soothing effect for him to say: "Yes, you know, we really made a fine mess of this whole show." They talk about how apartheid didn't work, and caused a lot of harm and so on. He does about everything except say he's sorry.'

Kathy's maid Yvonne had agreed to take me into Soweto. She had to go 'down there' to visit an uncle of hers who was seriously ill in hospital. Nonetheless, as we set off on Saturday lunch-time, she was in a bubblingly good mood. 'Last night,' she said, 'Kathy went out at ten o'clock and gave me a beer, and then she said, "Is that enough?" so I had two beers, and I was sitting there in my room, drunk, and when a song came on I liked, I just stood up on my own and jived. Oh Mark, that was nice.' She chuckled, the big map of Jo'burg spread out over her knee.

I was nervous, excited. All the tales about getting hijacked, shot, and so on spinning round in my head as we cut through the centre of town, down through the unfashionable southern suburbs, out on West Reef road, past the factories and warehouses and coloured townships, and finally down the Sowetan Highway into the same old story, mile upon mile of little 'core' township houses, dirt roads, African taxis, kids playing in the street . . .

'This is the box of matches where I stay,' Yvonne chuckled, as we bumped off the road and into a little backyard cluttered with a corrugated iron shack, a washing line, an outside loo.

Inside the 'matchbox' was a main room – perhaps nine foot by fifteen – and two tiny bedrooms, all done out in shiny pale green. In the main room was an assortment of non-matching kitchen items: an old Aga in one corner; an electric cooker bang next to it; a fifties-style stand-up kitchen cabinet; a modern Hoover deep freeze; an old-fashioned white fridge. By the window that looked out on the dirt street was a white-painted sideboard. In the centre of the room was a wooden table with a frayed fablon top. On the wall a calendar for TOBY'S FORD GARAGE – A JEWEL IN SOWETO which featured a large-breasted blonde falling out of a skimpy red dress in the surf.

In the backyard, grinning, was little Tshepiso, Yvonne's eight year old grandson; wandering around rather sulkily in a white dressing gown at two o'clock in the afternoon was Pheello, her twelve year old grand-daughter; at the kitchen table, John – otherwise known as Titi – her adopted son; emerging from the bedroom, Winnie, her daughter; and in Winnie's arms, the baby.

Titi had a huge smile in a square face. 'I'm pleased to meet you,' he said. Yvonne produced a big bottle of Castle from the fridge and opened it with a block of wood which had a triangular arrangement of screws at one end. 'You see in Soweto, Mark,' she said, laughing, 'our bottle opener.' Titi sat next to me and wrote in my note book:

> MY NAMES
> TITI JOHN REMERE PROFEREFERE – IT MEANS A VIOLENT
> PERSON

He laughed. 'It's a contrast because I'm not like that. I prefer to stay home and read books. I don't like to go out and fight.'

Underneath he wrote:

> 30 YEARS SINGLE
> I MEAN NOT MERRIED WITH ONE KID HOPE TO BE MERRY
> SOON.

Titi asked me if I was merry. 'No, not yet,' I replied. 'I hope to be soon though.' He laughed. Another little girl ran in from the sunny yard. She was called Marvellous. 'What's that mean?' I asked, thinking I'd misheard an African name. 'Lovely,' said Yvonne. 'You know – marvellous.'

With Marvellous was an exquisite girl of nineteen with braided hair and a white woollen top. She was Rahab. 'You are welcome,' she said softly, giving me the gentlest African handshake I'd yet had. 'That's my – what's the word? – nephew,' said Yvonne. 'Your niece.' 'Yes, my niece.'

Yvonne had been cooking her invalid uncle a meal. Of *boerewors*, *gemsquash* and mashed potato. She crammed it into a little tupperware box and we drove off to Baragwanath Hospital, a huge barrack-like building high on the ridge that marked the edge of Soweto. It was visiting time, and the place was packed with the friends and relatives of patients.

Yvonne's uncle was in the middle of a long, busy ward, refusing his food. A cheerful young nurse was trying to feed him milk from a syringe. He lay flat on his back, only his head visible above the sheets: a wizened, ancient face, his tattered grey beard stained yellow from old nicotine, splashed white with new milk. His eyes stared benignly upwards.

'He recognises me,' said Titi. Yvonne leaned over him. He mumbled to her for a while, a slight smile on his lips. Suddenly she burst into tears.

'We'll leave him now,' she said. As we walked off, she dabbed at her eyes with a big handkerchief and took my arm. 'He just told me where his money was,' she said, 'and said that I must make provision for him and give the rest to the little boy. Those were my mother's last words. The same thing. I will have to come back tomorrow – but', she shook her head slowly, 'I don't know whether I will find him here.'

In the huge warehouse of a shopping centre I got some strange looks: the only whitey in the place. I got out my wallet and we loaded up with steak and *boerewors*, and then drove to an unofficial Off Licence, operating out of the back of someone's house. The man was doing incredible business, his fists stuffed with notes, his garage crammed with people walking out with cut-price crates of beer.

On the way back, Titi pointed out a hillside full of long grey buildings – the notorious hostels. 'You see those houses over there,' he said, 'that is where the violent men live. The Government pays them to go out and kill people. You see, they are not working, many of them, so they are easily manipulated.'

We dropped Yvonne home and went out to a shebeen, which consisted of a few guys sitting outside a small bungalow in plastic chairs in the sunshine. They rose to their feet, greeted me with enthusiastic African handshakes.

Titi and I had a beer and talked about his marriage plans. He'd been with his girlfriend for ten years and they had a child. He wanted badly to get married, but he couldn't afford the traditional *lobola*, the bride price. 'How much will it cost?' I asked. 'It is expensive, 1,200 rands.' 'How do they work out how much to charge?' 'They look at you and if you look rich, they ask for a lot, perhaps 10,000 rands. If the wife is well educated.'

Back at the matchbox Titi got matier. 'I have always wished for a friend from overseas,' he said, putting his hand on my arm. 'I can't tell you how happy I am. It's like my first day at school.'

News of the feast had clearly got out. More friends turned up to cram the tiny house. Mandy was big; her husband Reginald was bigger, wearing a grey Aramis sweatshirt. Maliyeza was squat, lean, with a nasty scar on his chin; he was Winnie's boyfriend.

'What does Maliyeza mean?' I asked.

'It means "money's coming". When he was born he was very rich.' They laughed.

Sitting beside me, Titi touched me on the arm. 'Mark,' he said quietly, 'I'm afraid I'm going to get drunk.'

The others were asking me about overseas. How big was my place? Did I have a car? Reginald wanted to know about the English President: where did he live? I explained that we had a Queen. Mandy knew all about the Queen.

'D'you have a truelove?' Winnie asked.

'Yes,' I said. She smiled a broad smile, and nodded. Titi nudged me. 'But why buy a book when you can get it from the library for free?' He laughed. 'I mean, why *buy* that book, when it is *free* at the *library*.' He laughed some more.

Yvonne and Winnie had got everything ready. Steaks, *boerewors*, a pasta salad, a green salad, the bread rolls that Yvonne had refused to let me pay for at the supermarket. 'I'm getting these,' she'd said firmly.

Reginald's grasp of world politics was a little vague. 'Is Bush – where is he from?' I told him. He shook his head. 'The American army is very strong. They almost killed Saddam Hussein.' 'They did.' 'I wish they could come here and fight for us.'

Yvonne was still standing, still going out to the *braai* in the yard to fetch the meat, chopping it up small to put on plastic plates for the kids. They were eating in her tiny bedroom, five of them, sitting on the floor.

'You must come and sit down, Yvonne,' I said. 'You can't do all the work.'

'Aiyee!' she cried, shaking her head. 'I have to feed the children. Now you see why I want to go home. I'm all right in my room – I dance with my radio.'

After supper Titi wanted to take me back to the shebeen. 'There'll be a lot of chicks there by now,' he said. But Yvonne wasn't happy for me to go to 'that place'. 'I don't know who some of those men are,' she said. Eventually Titi gave in to his adopted mother. 'So we're not going?' 'She has refused,' he said.

'We will take you to a nice place, a cool place,' said Mandy, 'where there is no trouble.'

The cool shebeen was a large, beige-brick bungalow with

all mod-cons. There was a big kitchen, an indoor toilet and bathroom. In the lounge, a group of middle-aged men and women were sitting round a long, polished-wood table which was covered with a white lace tablecloth. A coal fire burned in the grate. The smart green-upholstered easy chairs had shiny transparent plastic covers. It was all extremely genteel.

After a couple of minutes in front of the fire, we were invited to join the group at the table. Polite African handshakes all round. One of the men was called Lerato.

'That means "love",' said Mandy.

'At the time that I was manufactured,' said Lerato, 'my parents were very much in love. That is why they gave me that name.'

'And this is our Shebeen Queen, Mercy,' said Mandy, introducing me to a large woman in an electric blue evening dress. 'This is her *place*.' If it was a man here, he would be the Shebeen King.

Mandy and Winnie and I were chatting about TV. 'Don't you know *The Bold and the Beautiful*?' said Mandy. 'No, we don't have that American rubbish in England,' I said. 'American rubbish!' she laughed. 'I love *The Bold and the Beautiful*. If I'm returning from work and I'm going to miss *The Bold and the Beautiful*, I say to the driver "Drive fast, please!"'

After a while, Mandy's husband, Reginald, decided to take us somewhere livelier. A guy called Donald was coming too; with Lolo, another friend. 'This is more of a tavern than a shebeen,' said Mandy. We bumped across Soweto to the DJ Inn. They were keen that I didn't park the Dolphin on the road, but round the back of a cousin's house, where it would be safe.

The dirt street was empty and silent; the night was cool; there was a whiff of woodsmoke in the air. There were no streetlights, only the giant township lights, beaming down from forty, fifty foot steel masts some way off.

At the door of the DJ Inn we were frisked. 'Because people will kill each other in these shebeens,' Mandy said cheerfully.

It was just like an English pub inside. Round pub tables, a dartboard, a tiled floor. The far bar was packed, the near bar empty. We sat round a table in the empty one. As we drank and talked the place filled up.

Donald leaned towards me. 'We are safe here,' he said, nodding. 'If they go out from here, they start to kill each other – but here, we are safe.'

A large group came in, pushed two tables together, loaded themselves up with beers, cokes, bottles of rum. The music got louder. People got up to dance. 'They call this jive CODESA 3,' Mandy said, pointing at three women dancing around by the slot machine.

'CODESA 3?'

'They just go round and round in circles.'

A huge broad-shouldered guy came and shook hands with Reginald. He stood back, 'I *like* this table,' he said. 'You know why? Because it's multi-national. We have one Xhosa, one Zulu, one Swazi, one coloured, and one *white* man.' He laughed loudly.

'Move your *shoulders*, man,' he shouted at me when I got up to dance. 'Yeah! Left one, right one, that's better. Eeya!'

It was late when we got back. Yvonne had gone to bed. 'Sorry Yvonne,' I said. 'We were supposed to be driving back, weren't we?' 'I don't mind,' she said, 'as long as you are happy.' She switched on the lights in her little bedroom. Three kids were moved sleepily from the single bed to share the narrow double with Yvonne. I fell asleep in the single, fully dressed under a blanket.

When I woke, sometime in the small hours, Yvonne and the children were snoring merrily. From way off in the distance came the sound of African drums.

Of course I was horrified by Boipatong. Weren't we all? Sitting at our breakfast tables reading accounts of a pregnant woman, a baby bayonetted to death. But now, suddenly, in the middle of Soweto, the reality hit home. It would have been Winnie's laughing baby, speared. Little Pheello, no longer sulking around in her white blanket dressing gown: a corpse for that worldwide TV audience to shake their heads at on the News.

Was this the dawn coming up at last? Or just the continuing glare from the towering overhead township lights, lights that said to the population of this place: *You are all hooligans*.

With Yvonne beside me, I drove back through deserted early Sunday morning Jo'burg. In Kathy's spacious kitchen, I had half a melon and a cup of fresh coffee, then lay soaking in the bath with the *Sunday Star*. It seemed utterly luxurious.

I was trying to get my interview with Mandela and listening to a lot of jazz. Kathy's friend had passed me on to the ANC Press Officer, a white Afrikaner called Carl Niehaus. Three times a day I phoned:

'Hello ANC.'

'Could I speak to Carl Niehaus, please?'

Jazz. Phone finally rings.

'Hello ANC.'

'Could I speak to Carl Niehaus, please?'

Different jazz. Phone finally rings.

'Hello ANC.'

'I'm trying to get through to Carl Niehaus.'

Different jazz.

So I faxed him; then phoned about the fax.

'Hello ANC . . .'

'It's the ANC culture,' said Kathy. 'That's what they're like.'

One fine morning I finally got through to him. 'Carl Niehaus?' I gasped. 'Did you get my fax?'

'I get a lot of faxes,' he said coldly. Mandela was busy;

Mandela was going abroad; no, Mandela would clearly not be available for the likes of me.

'So how would you dance your journey?' asked Beverley.

She was the first of my old Maru-a-Pula friends, the tomboyish coloured girl who'd climbed up onto the roof of the boys' boarding house and asked me to teach her how to paint. My crumpled photo showed her standing outside the dining room holding a bowl of porridge, her other arm round the neck of her best friend, Barbara. Now she was living in an ex-'poor white' suburb of Jo'burg, working at an NGO called the Institute of Race Relations, where she was producing a report on education.

She looked much the same: taller and older and wearier in the eyes, but the same short fuzz of hair, the same creamy-coffee coloured skin. We met at a bistro on trendy Rocky Street, and sitting with her and her friend Jasmine – also a coloured – I suddenly felt the whiteness of the place: for despite the long hair and the right-on gear and the heavy metal band in the courtyard at the back, the young people coming in and out were almost exclusively white.

'Dance my journey?' I asked.

'I mean, what kind of music would you set it to. African music? European music?' It was just that Jasmine was a dancer, and they'd been trying to think of how they would dance a journey they'd made, in the opposite direction to me, from Port Elizabeth (where Jasmine came from) to Cape Town.

It had been shortly after the 1990 scrapping of apartheid, and Jasmine and Beverley had set out with high hopes along the Garden Route, looking forward to seeing this famously beautiful part of the country that had effectively been denied to 'blacks' like them before. It wasn't simply that some of the prettiest beaches – Plettenberg Bay, for example – had been whites only; it was more that all the resorts and campsites had been whites only, and if you had nowhere to stay, then how could you see these places?

But now they found that despite the formal scrapping of apartheid, they *still* couldn't find anywhere to stay. At every campsite, they were told it was full up. 'It was the holiday season,' Beverley said, 'and at the first spot we stopped I think it was a genuine case of being full. But then as we carried on down the road . . . it just came across that the guards, the black people at the gates . . . it was as if they'd been told to tell people that there was no place if you were black.'

'Did any of them actually say that?'

'Yes, some of them said so. After the owner had come forward and said, "Look, there's no space for you," we heard from them that – actually we haven't been letting blacks into this place, and that's what you can expect.'

Like many 'blacks' talking about the sort of minor injustice that would have you or me screaming with anger, Beverley seemed remarkably sanguine and objective about her story. Perhaps that was the only way to deal with it. 'It's interesting . . .' she kept repeating, putting her emotions strictly in the passive: 'I thought it was quite interesting because, in a sense, when we left PE, there was so much excitement about the journey, and the possibility of stopping, seeing places, exploring the coastline, and knowing that things were open now, like you could go where you wouldn't think of going before . . .'

Even the mentality that had created these divisions, and continued to perpetuate them was 'interesting': 'Just the mentality that they have a right to take over the air.' She laughed. 'I mean that's what it boils down to. It boils down to the air and the sea and the sand and, you know, the kind of leaves in the trees. How can you want to keep those things to yourself? It's so silly. And they won't share it. Even now that the central State might be wanting to take those things away from them, or might be saying, in simple terms,

"Share!", they're finding all kinds of ways of not sharing. What's happening now the beaches are opening up is – I've heard a lot of this – wealthy whites talk about buying places, privatising it, in other words. Then you can put up little fences and prevent people coming in . . . It just shows that here you have people who have just been spoilt beyond repair, and it's such a pity that that's the case. And I think it's interesting, because everything about the beauty is *African*. That's why I wanted to know how you would dance it, because if I visualise a dance and what kind of music would go with it, for our journey, it would have been African music, and it would have been African sounds and an African rhythm.'

Dennis had been the troublemaker in the second year English group that I'd taught on American George's verandah. Now he was Creative Director of Herdbuoys, South Africa's first black advertising agency, which had swish offices in Sandton City, one of the smartest of the northern suburbs. He'd grown tall and distinguished looking, with a peaceful, fulfilled air about him. We had an appointment for five o'clock, but it was nine before I finally got to see him. 'There's been a real train-smash today,' said the pretty black receptionist.

He was sitting at the end of a long table in the boardroom, eating spare ribs from a foil container and drinking beer from the can. He was presenting in Cape Town at two o'clock tomorrow. The client hadn't liked the original concept. They were going to have work through the night on the rethink. From my own short spell in advertising, I recognised the scenario.

Waiting outside, in the beige lobby with the stylish backlit HERDBUOYS sign, I'd had a look at the ads in the frames.

SHEEN CURL RELAXER
Go for style, Go for Sheen

They signed it in ink to stop the blood
NATIONAL PEACE ACCORD
PEACE NOW. NOT ANOTHER DEATH LATER.

HERDBUOYS. ADVERTISING AND MARKETING PRACTITIONERS.
IT'S ABOUT TIME.

Why herd*buoys* I asked my former pupil. He chuckled.
'There is a bit of a double play in there. We're trying to take
the mickey out of the industry, out of this whole society
where guys of our ilk – of our hue – have always been called
"boy".' He leant back in his padded chair. 'Right across
society you'll find a sixty year old gardener being called
"boy" by a ten year old ... And your typical herdboy is
always herding cows from the back, you know. However,
the "buoy" that we're talking about is always at the front – it
gives direction to ships at sea coming into dock. So that's
the meaning: that we will lead, from the front, you know,
not the back.'

They'd been going for just over a year, and already, Dennis
told me, they were looking at projected billings to the end of
their second year of over twelve million rand. But then, the
markets in South Africa were predominantly black. Blacks
accounted for 80%, for example, of beer consumption. 'So
many people claim to know the black market,' Dennis said.
'But we don't say we know the black market, we say we
know who *we* are, and can write to people much like us,
and actually touch the – you know,' he patted his chest, 'the
strings inside here. We know the nuances, we've been there,
and no-one else has been there.'

It was, as they say in advertising, a good pitch – and I felt
sure that however the New South Africa developed, Dennis
couldn't fail to be one of the coming men. He clearly loved
his job. Working for yourself was 'an incredible satisfaction'.
And advertising was most exciting, it really was. 'As somebody once said – it's the greatest fun you can have with your

clothes on.' Just before he rushed back to 'hit the night' with the creative team I asked him how confident he felt about the future.

'Very,' he replied, lounging back in his padded chair. 'Ve-ry.'

It seemed strangely appropriate that the last thing I should do in South Africa was visit the Lost City. If you'd sat down for six months with a team of top design consultants you couldn't have come up with a more ironic monument to the absurdity of apartheid in practice.

The year that I'd been at Maru-a-Pula – 1977 – had also been the year when the Tswana homeland of Bophuthatswana had been made an 'independent national state'. Shortly after that, an enterprising Durban millionaire hotelier called Sol Kerzner had seized the opportunity that the proximity of the new 'nation' to Jo'burg offered, and built Sun City – a luxury casino resort, plonked down, green grass and swimming pools and golf courses and all, in a dried-up valley in the empty Pilansberg Hills. No longer did the citizens of Jo'burg have to drive the six hours to Gaborone to play blackjack and roulette and watch stripshows and maybe indulge in a little (in South Africa still illegal) mixed-race dalliance: in two hours they could be in Sun City.

It did so well that the first hotel spawned a second, the Cascades, complete with three new swimming pools and an artificial 'African jungle'. Now Kerzner was completing his dream with the fantasy of a lifetime: the Lost City.

Dick O'Brien was architect-in-chief. He was in his early sixties, with raffishly long grey hair, a little grey moustache, and large designer-dude square glasses. He was taking a couple of his juniors, Lindsay and Theo, out for a day trip to show them the site. As we sped westward in his blue BMW he explained the concept, or rather, the 'myth' of the Lost City. As dreamed up by Sol:

Three thousand years ago an African tribe had built this

palace and this city. It had been destroyed by a violent
earthquake, and had crumbled into the jungle. 'The idea is',
said Dick, 'that someone's just found this palace, and we've
restored it to its former glory.'

We sped on, down a remarkably good tar road. 'Would Sol
Kerzner have had anything to do with the making of this
highway?' I asked.

'No comment,' said Dick, with a dry chuckle. We reached
the Pilansberg Hills. An advertising placard loomed up
across the veldt, then a giant silver bow-tie. We'd arrived,
turning right through a toll-gate marked STAFF ONLY. Dick
presented his card. A uniformed black smiled silently and
waved us through. 'That's a shame,' said Dick. 'If I put it in
the machine it says, "Welcome Mr O'Brien."'

The old Sun City complex was much smaller than I'd
expected. Outside a sign read SUN CITY WELCOMES TUPPER-
WARE. 'What style of architecture would you call that?' I
asked, looking at the creamy yellow facade of the main hotel.

'Disgusting,' said Lindsay.

'South African boring,' said Theo.

But we had no time to dwell on this, or indeed the two-
dimensional pyramid of the Cascades with its attendant
jungle; for there, looming above both like some monstrous
hybrid between a French *château* and the Taj Mahal, was
the Palace of the Lost City, the magnificent climax of Kerzner's dream, beige fake-stone towers, topped with green
fake-copper cupolas, rising from the central 'stone' block of
the hotel. Even the architects were taken aback. 'It's just so
enormous,' said Lindsay.

Dick took us on a tour. The site was like something out of
Ben Hur. Hundreds and hundreds of blacks in blue boiler
suits beavering away in the sunshine. Up scaffolding, down
holes, kneeling, standing, walking, running, shunting back
and forth in mechanical diggers. Despite the heat, there was
furious activity. The whole thing had been built from
scratch, Dick explained, in seventeen months, and was due

to be finished in five weeks' time, ready for Sun City's first Miss World contest. Kerzner was a hard taskmaster, obsessed with every single detail. 'He blasts everybody if things aren't exactly right,' Dick said. He waved at a crane on our right, which was lowering a tree from the sky. 'Three weeks ago we built this parking garage. We're just busy putting swamp forest on the top of it.'

The main structure, he explained, was concrete over a steel frame, finished with age-painted plaster. All the ornamentation and carving on the exterior was fibreglass. 'Those fronds are fibreglass, over there you see kudus. They're also fibreglass.'

'This, Mark, is a cheetah fountain. Two cheetahs chasing four impalas in double life-size. At their feet bubbles and fog.'

'Bubbles and fog?'

'Yah,' he smiled and raised an eyebrow, 'there's going to be a mist spray.'

We'd arrived at the huge front entrance door. 'This will look like old bronze. Fibreglass on a steel frame. Visual impact will be intricate, almost Minoan.'

Inside, in the cool shade of the vast central hall, there was a surprise. 'This marble floor is marble,' said Dick.

'Real marble?'

'Real marble, from north Italy.' He pointed at a boiler-suited white hunched over a noisy polishing machine. 'That's a real Italian there. You see, he won't even let the black guy polish his floor.'

We looked upwards at a dome painted with colourful jungle frescoes. 'Designed by Americans on an African concept,' said Dick. He chuckled. 'I've never seen a fox up a tree before, but they've got one – third branch up – see it?'

We moved through to: the Tusk Bar, where fibreglass tusks filled with sand complemented a ceiling whose design was based on patterns scratched in dung in the floor of Ndebele huts; the Royal Chamber, which had walls of yellow-gold silk and . . . goodness . . . real timber cheek-by-jowl with fibreglass elephants' heads; then on, through a courtyard dominated by a full-sized sculpture of an elephant, and out through the massive East Gate, down a flight of stone steps – 'the Royal Stair' – to the lake.

'Everything is used,' said Dick. 'You see those dungeons – that's fresh air intake for the kitchens.'

'And then,' I said, 'when you get the water, the whole thing'll be reflected.'

'Yah. I'm dying for that day.'

Below the Palace, in a vast dustbowl, the Lost City proper was coming into being. It had sure been a strange tribe. We stepped through the artificial jungle, past the biggest man-made waterfall in the world, to an enormous wave pool, with three palm-tree covered islands, and a long crescent of sandy beach. A Scotsman called Doug showed me the giant shutes that would produce the two-metre-high surf, and then the ducts on the side of the islands that would suck the water back again. The sand was coming up from the Cape. 'All the islands will have slot machines, obviously,' said Dick.

We drove out to a nearby Game Reserve for lunch. 'Sol wanted it to be totally African,' he said. 'When we started, we were doing all sorts of Roman features, but Sol kept saying, "Make it more African." We said, "Well, you'd better thatch it then."' He laughed.

'But there's never been a building like this in Africa, has there?'

'No,' Dick replied. He looked into his wine glass, then thoughtfully back at me: 'You know Mark, I'm not a great one for gambling. There's something essentially false about gambling. And I don't know, but I . . . I wonder sometimes whether this whole thing isn't a reflection of that.'

Later we saw the haunted rows of grannies at the slot machines and lost a couple of hundred rand on the roulette tables. Walking down the ramp, out of the hotel, we heard the true sound of Africa, a hundred large black women singing and dancing in the road. It was the Tupperware Conference.

'What are they doing?' I asked Dick.

He laughed. 'Oh, probably just waiting for the bus home.'

'What are they singing?' I asked one of the chocolate brown and gold liveried porters. He grinned. 'They're singing that they're winning,' he said. 'That the black people are winning.'

23

A FOREIGN COUNTRY

Approaching Botswana I was filled with a mounting excitement. This was a road I remembered, out past Rustenberg and Zeerust and then sharp right up into the hills towards 'Gabs'. In 1977 it had been corrugated red-brown dirt, a wild track through the African wilderness, and a hell of a bumpy ride in the back of a *bakkie*. Now it was tar: a smooth 140 kilometres per hour at the wheel of my beautiful Dolphin.

I was leaving South Africa behind me now. The more-English-than-English voice of Radio South Africa's Paddy O'Byrne was fading and breaking up, there was a dead dog by the roadside, little settlements of African homesteads, and then, coming over the top of the hill . . . no question about it . . . that vast plain stretching away, the little isolated 'mountains' rising like rocky islands from the blue-green sea of bush. I stopped the car, sat on the bonnet in the sunshine, hardly able to believe I was here again. Just about to swoop down on this country that had been a dreamscape for so long.

It was only a fortunate quirk of history that had prevented Botswana from being incorporated into South Africa. Since the 1880s, the Afrikaners of the Transvaal had wanted to bring this substantial chunk of territory under their control. But the area had become the British Protectorate of Bechuanaland, partly because Cecil Rhodes wanted to keep a road

north open for the commercial interests of the Cape, partly
because he wanted to prevent the Afrikaners in the Transvaal
linking up with the Germans of South-West Africa. With
such motives are nations founded . . .

When the two republics and the two colonies were brought
into a Union in 1910, the South Africa Act provided for a
later incorporation of Bechuanaland (together with the other
two protectorates of Swaziland and Lesotho) and between
1913 and 1949 the issue of these three areas of British
hegemony was raised repeatedly by South African leaders.
Luckily for present-day Botswana, the British Government
had continued to reply that 'the time is not yet ripe',
inspiring the founder of apartheid, Dr Malan, to describe the
situation in 1949 as an 'intolerable encroachment on the
rights of South Africa'.

I sped down to the border post – the Tlokweng Gate.
Unfortunately the guys on passport control didn't know my
status as Botswanophile returning after fifteen years, so I had
to wait in a long line of NON-BOTSWANA NATIONALS and then
requeue at Customs to declare my four remaining bottles of
Potgietersrus Pieter's wine. Then, my knowledge of the local
greeting ceremony notwithstanding, the car had to be zeal-
ously over-searched by a young customs guard getting his
own back for years of being kicked around by whiteys.

Suddenly I was through, onto a broad tarmac road that
certainly hadn't been here before. On either side, beyond a
neat wire fence, the bush was clear. Surely there had been a
little village on the right; certainly goats and cows had
wandered all over the dirt road. Now there were giant
advertising hoardings: THE GABORONE SUN – THERE'S STILL ONLY
ONE HOTEL IN GABORONE . . . KENTUCKY FRIED CHICKEN . . . and
then I was seeing Gabs up ahead, and already it was more
changed even than I'd imagined. The Oasis Motel *certainly*
hadn't been there. Nor had these office blocks. Nor had these
rows of smart flats. What had happened to Naledi, the old
squatter camp? I just couldn't locate myself at all. There

were junctions and traffic lights everywhere, not just one four-way stop and one set of lights. In 1977 the roads had been empty: now the traffic was bumper to bumper in two lanes; a slow urban crawl.

After an hour of getting lost, I finally found the old centre, the old Mall. Right, so if The Mall was there, the Museum had to be there; yes, there it was, unchanged behind its surrounding trees, looking much the same. So if the Museum was here, surely the school was down here and left. Wasn't this the road we used to ride along on the Honda 50, barefoot and without a helmet, to collect the mail from town? That mosque was a new addition, and ... goodness ... a vast stadium where the scruffy football pitch used to be. But yes, there up the end on the right was the Holiday Inn, now in a swish new incarnation as the Gaborone Sun.

The old dirt road round the back was tar, complete with speedbumps; and, rounding the corner I came, past a golf course, to a security gate with uniformed guards. Where once there had been ... what? ... a gate; no, there hadn't even been a gate.

Maru-a-Pula! There it was. Changed and unchanged. To the right, those familiar octagonal classrooms, the dusty paths, the little thorn trees, the bougainvillaea; to the left, the swimming pool I'd helped to build. But what was this car park? And this monstrous double-storey building ahead? I bumped on down the – thankfully still dirt – track to where the headmaster's house had been.

And *that* was the same; that same grass circle out front where a cobra had reared up and hooded at us one time, the same little porch. I rang the doorbell. A young woman with short hair answered, holding a baby. She was Kate, the wife of the new headmaster. She offered me a beer, and I sat, staring in a rather shell-shocked way out onto the little garden. I really *was* back. There was the same circle of sun-whitened grass, the same lone thorn-tree in the middle, the same bush beyond. Although now, through the trees, I could make out rows of small houses where once it had just been empty Africa, stretching as far as the eye could see . . .

'That's a low-cost housing area,' said Kate. 'Site and serviced. They erect their own houses.'

Her husband Peter arrived: a man not much older than me, with neat haircut, tweed jacket and tie.

So I was eating lunch at Maru-a-Pula . . . and we were talking about the changes. The splendid new building by the car park was Mait-i-song, the Maru-a-Pula 'cultural centre'. There were many other new buildings too: a new art room, a new library, new science labs – mostly paid for by George's 'American Friends of Maru-a-Pula'. So those summers in Maine had not been wasted.

I'd come at a very good time, Peter said. George himself was flying out from the States for the annual meeting of the School Council and would be here on Tuesday. Sadly, he'd suffered a stroke, and was not all he had been; but the old spirit was there. And then, in ten days' time, there was the annual M-a-P Reunion. Would I still be around? That would be the time to see everyone.

Over coffee we were joined by a plump, rather camp teacher who'd come to try on a pair of the Headmaster's trousers, which he needed for the end of term concert at Mait-i-song. The first piece they were doing was the World Premiere of a work by a local composer, called 'Requiem for an Elephant'. 'He's dying from the drought, you see. There's this long section where we go "No – no – no – no – no – no-o-o war-ter"; then the bass section comes in with "The elephant stum-bles". Philip and I got into absolute *hysterics* yesterday imagining this elephant coming in and saying: "Actually it *wasn't* like that at all, it was more of a *trip* than a stumble."' He shrieked with laughter and went off to try the trousers, but unfortunately he was too fat. 'Woolworths is having a sale,' Kate suggested.

Peter took me off to show me round the school. New this, new that, fragments of memory in between. The girls' boarding house was still there, but no girls were braiding their hair on the balcony, no boys calling up in the warm evening air . . . The old workman's pre-fab that had housed my art room was still – incredibly – intact; but it was stacked full of old chairs. There was no Bennett, bent earnestly over his oils, no little Archie trying to keep up with pencil and paper, no Thabo hanging around on the steps suggesting they go and play football instead.

'I expect you'd like to see Tom Sullivan,' Peter said.

We'd never got on too well with Tom Sullivan, us teacher aids. I remembered him as a rather tetchy character in a shabby purple cardigan, seemingly forever out to spoil our youthful fun. He wasn't exactly the person I'd journeyed all this way to see.

But now, as I sat with him in his little cluttered office looking through my stack of photographs of the old days, it was hard to remember what the problem had been. The bald head, the thick-rimmed glasses were exactly the same; the hacking smoker's cough much worse: but adult to adult, he seemed immensely affable; indeed, as a white South African who'd made the choice to spend his life teaching in this idealistic school, rather admirable.

'Oh *yes*,' he said, chuckling over another of the photos, 'that's Thabo – yes, he's around; he's working for a design company in town. Now Nicodemus – he's a lawyer, he's done *very* well, drives a huge Mercedes and speaks with that same impressive voice. Now Michael, here, d'you remember him? He's now a lecturer at the university.'

'What about Primrose?'

Tom laughed. 'Primrose is virtually running the local hotel industry. And I was just talking on the phone to someone else who's very keen to see you. Sophie. She's done terribly well. Involved in all sorts of different areas. But she's leaving for Tanzania first thing tomorrow, so if you're going to catch her, you'd better phone from here.'

Sophie's number was engaged. Typical.

'You remember Kwame,' Tom was saying. 'Very much the quieter of the two brothers. When he was here he never used to say anything very much at all. But then he went to Oxford and is now a Professor in America.

'I was actually interviewed on his behalf in Oxford. And I remember they said to me: "All we want is for you to guarantee us that he'll get a 2(2)." And I said: "Well, I hope very much that he'll do better than that, a 2(1), or a 1." And then,' Tom laughed, 'of course he got there and opened out totally. Got his first and rowed for the college and was a leading light in the Debating Society etc etc . . .'

Sophie was still engaged. I went to find Walker, who was in Mait-i-song having tea with a cleric who was even camper than our trouserless friend from lunch.

Walker looked as if he'd been aged by a none-too-competent make-up department. What they'd decided to do was brush his blond brown hair slookly back from his forehead, fleck it with grey, and give him the lightest sprinkling of lines under his eyes. Otherwise he looked exactly the same; the same endearing slightly nervous laugh, the same mildly flustered air, as if he was glad to see you but had something more important on his mind.

It was so odd, suddenly being here like this. To me, Walker was a central figure in the memory, the guy with the ever-open flat and the ever-boiling kettle. To him, I was just another teacher aid, who'd been here for a couple of terms fifteen years ago. 'Give us a call on Sunday morning,' he said, as I stood there awkwardly with my tea. 'I'll be less frantic then. Sorry, I'm a bit wrapped up at the moment with this concert tonight and everything.'

Sophie was *still* engaged. This was it, the perfect ending: I come all the way to Botswana and miss Sophie.

Eventually I got through. Her voice, her laughter, was exactly as it had been fifteen years before, with that same slight catch that now I remembered well. She was going to the supermarket at five, but why didn't I go round there now?

She had a long, low bungalow in the nicest, oldest part of town; which is to say, the 1966 part of town. A blond guy with a neatly pointed beard let me in. 'I'm Jens,' he said, 'Sophie's husband. Sophie's on the phone. Come through.'

So I sat, in a shaft of late afternoon sunshine, in Sophie's elegant grown-up sitting room, talking to Jens, and in the other room Sophie made phone call after phone call, and the clock ticked closer and closer to five, when she was going shopping.

Eventually she came through. She was just the same. 'Sorry Mark,' she said, kissing me warmly. 'I just had to set up all these meetings for next week.'

Jens went off to the supermarket, and Sophie and I sat on the long white sofa and swapped life stories. After Maru-a-Pula, she'd been to university in Cape Town. Before she went, her parents had suggested that she spend some time in Rustenberg, staying with a white Anglican priest and his family, to prepare herself for the experience of being black in South Africa. 'And yes, they prepared me, they prepared me in a way. Because Cape Town was not nearly as bad as Rustenberg. It was useful.' She smiled. 'And then I had all sorts of funny experiences in town.'

'Like?'

'One of them I remember . . . I had a pain in my tooth, and I was trying to get hold of a dentist. And Sarah, the priest's wife, tried to phone to make an appointment for me. And they'd say, "Ogay"' – Sophie laughed as she mimicked the Afrikaans accent – 'and then Sarah would say, "Well, she's black." And they'd say, "Oh we're very zorry we dan't 'ave sipp-rett amenities." Eventually she found one; and the person said it was OK. Sarah explained that I was black and the woman said, "That's fine." So I went along to the dentist, together with some chap who was travelling around with something called Youth for Christ. He was staying with us at the priest's house, and he was very nervous because he'd been in detention, and he'd had his eardrums burst.'

'Black?'

'Yuh, he was black. Anyway, I went through the front door, because that's the most logical place to go, you know, you go to the reception, say you've arrived for your appointment, which is what I did. And I got this incredibly dirty look from the receptionist, a woman with a beehive hairstyle and – you know – cat-eyes glasses. And she looked me up and down and she said: "Dooth eggs-tragshun. Round the beck." I said, "I haven't come to have my tooth pulled out, I've come to have my tooth looked at, because it's sore." And she just repeated: "Dooth eggs-tragshun. Round the beck." So of course this chap who was with me was becoming rather nervous, the chap who'd experienced prison, and he said, "Well Sophie, I think we should really go round the back." So I went round the back and a lot of black people were standing there, waiting to be served between white appointments. And I was leaning against a car and somebody said, "Hey! Don't lean against *baas*'s car." So I was really getting very tense, and about twenty minutes after my appointment had been due I became rather irritated and I said to this chap that I was going to go round the front, to find out what had happened. And he said, "Well, I'm going home," and he left me. So I was there on my own. I went to this woman again and said, you know, I'm still waiting to see the dentist, and she ignored me. There was a younger woman there who said, "Well, could you please go round the back and I'll attend to you." I said, "But I've been waiting to see the dentist, and I told them I was black . . ." and blah blah blah, and she said, "Well, please go round the back." So I went round the back and . . . anyway, eventually I was attended to, because everyone was staring at me. And they found out I didn't have a hole in my tooth, it was wisdom teeth coming up, which was rather embarrassing, after all that.' She laughed. 'But that was one – you know – typical, trivial example.'

When she'd got to Cape Town, Sophie had studied law. 'And again I had to deal with incredibly racist attitudes which proceeded from total ignorance. Because I was one of only two black women in an entire residence of whites.'

'For example?'

'For example, if I didn't finish my food, they'd say, "Och, so what d'you usually eat, hey?"' Sophie exploded with laughter. 'I also experienced what it meant to be barred from places.'

'Apartheid was still in place?'

'Yes. I remember there was a cinema not very far from the res – this was my first year – and we were all going to go there, some students invited me to join them, and I said I couldn't go. They said, "Ach. Why not?" I said, "Because I'm black." Of course they'd never encountered this in their lives! All their friends, their entire environment had been white. White schools, white churches, white clubs, and white universities. So they found me very weird – I was a total enigma. Added to which I didn't speak like their domestic workers, and of course that was how Africans spoke, so what was wrong with me, you know.

'I was also a bit of an enigma in relation to black South Africans. They didn't understand me either. I had a white accent – that was how they saw it – and therefore I must possibly have some sort of whiteness about me, and there-fore, politically, was possibly suspect as well.'

During her first year there'd been a couple of boycotts, and she'd found it very difficult to know how to react, 'because while I was aware that things were not OK in South Africa, I was also very aware of the fact that I'd gone there to study. And that my parents were paying for my education, and I was determined to leave there with my degree. So it was like walking a tightrope – because one didn't want to appear to be totally insensitive to what was happening around you; on the other hand how d'you explain to your parents you've been kicked out of university because you participated in a march? Particularly when one looked at the experience of Botswana – it just didn't really make much sense.'

Later, there'd been an attempt to start a black students' organisation, which she'd refused to join. 'Those were very difficult times. I remember standing there and arguing with an acquaintance of mine who was trying to get me to join this organisation, and I was trying to explain to him that within my own terms it was racist. Imagine trying to start a black students' organisation in Botswana!'

We laughed. It was good to be out of that nightmare world across the border. As the light faded around us, we talked on, and Sophie took me through what she was doing now. She was a lawyer; she was involved with a group called Women and Law in Southern Africa; she was on the General Committee of the All-Africa Conference of Churches; on an ad-hoc advisory group on economic justice; she'd just done a case report for the Botswana Christian Council on Human Rights of selected communities of Basarwa; she was hoping to set up a Human Rights Centre; she did counselling for battered wives . . . the list went on. And I wished I could have just got in a car with her and driven up to Pieter Van Tonder's house and said, 'Now are you going to tell me this is the exception that proves the rule?'

And even when we got onto relationships and marriage we didn't mention our long distant romance or the teenage heartbreak that had followed, when I'd come back from my hitch-hiking trip to find she'd got involved with a fellow student, an Indian called Naynesh. She did mention him, apropos of something else. 'I don't know whether he was here at the same time as you,' she said. 'Yes, he was,' I replied, wondering whether she was dissimulating, being tactful, or had just forgotten.

By the time Jens returned with the shopping it was almost dark in the room. Sophie switched on the lights and insisted on finding me a wedding photo. She, black in white; he, white in black. 'Just to show that I did finally get married,' she laughed. Outside the sky was crimson, and yes . . . I took a deep breath . . . there was that familiar magical thorn-woodsmoke smell in the air.

Tom Sullivan had recommended Tebogo as someone who would know how to get in touch with my favourite ex-kids. Though he was featured in one of my photos, I didn't remember him at all.

It was the smile that had been missing: a warm, slightly shy smile that brought him straight back. How could I have forgotten Tebogo? On the fringe of the art room gang, I even had a drawing I'd done of him at home. In his flat ivory cap, he hardly looked fifteen years older, though he now had a thin beard and moustache.

We met at The Village, a new yuppie-style sports-cum-shopping centre which you had to pay to get into. Once inside, you had access to smart clothes shops, three or four inter-linked swimming pools, a gym . . . I shook my head in disbelief: in 1977 'The Village' had been just that: the original Gaborone village – a few *rondawels* and a run-down bottle stall.

Tebogo was now a town-planner, working for the Government. Over a coke in the Oasis Motel we talked about Maru-a-Pula.

'Some of us feel it isn't what it used to be,' Tebogo said. 'That some of them are a bit spoilt now. You know, they have computers, and science labs, and', he laughed, 'a library. You remember the old library?'

I did. American George had set it up in the second of those workmen's prefabs; a few dog-eared encyclopaedias and paperbacks. Not that Tebogo objected to the facilities *per se*. It was just he thought the school had lost some of the old ideals. 'Of service to the community, things like Gabane, that sort of thing. But I don't know, it's only an impression.'

'Things have changed anyway since Seretse died,' he said. 'There is much corruption in Government now, and it goes fairly deep. We had two big scandals earlier this year and last year. Maybe we've learnt our lesson.' But after Seretse had gone the Ministers had been paying themselves more; and now they all drove Mercedes Benz. Tebogo frowned. 'I don't think there's any need for them to drive Mercedes Benz.'

In the old days we teacher aids had scoffed at the expatriates: lying around roasting by their pools, never getting involved with the locals. Now I was staying with an expat couple, Paul and Susie, who lived fourteen kilometres out of town in a large one-storey house set back from the spanking new tarmac road north to Francistown.

Then, Broadhurst had been a run-down little farm, out in the bush. Now it was one of Gaborone's largest residential areas, and Paul and Susie's eldest son, Thomas, was at Broadhurst Primary school.

So it was that I found myself sitting at a table full of expats in a hall decorated with Union Jacks and huge cutouts of red London buses (not the ugly square ones of today, the charming rounded ones of yesteryear). The food was Lancashire Hot Pot, Bangers 'n Mash, Steak and Kidney Pie, Roast Beef and Yorkshire Pudding. As we'd come in, we'd been handed a songsheet with things like 'Daisy, Daisy' and 'Oh, you beautiful doll' on it. For this was a fund-raising evening for Thomas' school – a British Pub Night, in fact.

As we queued for food the expats talked about how badly the evening had been supported by local parents. They weren't grumbling, they were just surprised there weren't more of them here. 'But maybe a British Pub Night puts them off,' said Susie. 'It does sound rather exclusive, doesn't it?'

'Frank's experience', said a woman from Manchester, as we tucked into our grub, 'is that the Batswana are surly. It's so different from Zimbabwe, where people are instantly friendly. I don't know what it is about the Batswana.'

'Well things must have changed,' I said. 'That was the main reason I came back. Because I found the people so warm.'

But what about the Botswana Defence Force, they said. Some of the incidents had been quite horrific. There'd been a man who'd got lost one night in Gabs, found himself in State Drive, been warned off by the BDF guard outside State House, three hours later was still lost, found himself back in State Drive, and the BDF had shot him dead.

Another horror: Returning from a holiday in the Okavango, a man had been double-booked at a hotel in Francistown. There was nowhere else for him and his family to stay so he'd decided to drive the long road south to Gabs. Half-way home he'd got stopped at a roadblock. When the soldier wanted to search his car, utterly exhausted, the man had started to get angry. The soldier insisted on going through his suitcases, and finding a pair of the man's wife's knickers had chucked them onto the road. The man had lost his temper and the soldier had shot him dead.

I sighed. Deeply. I remembered the BDF when it had first started, as a reaction to the unprovoked forays of white Rhodesian soldiers, over the northern border around Francistown, spilling over from the Zimbabwean War of Independence. The story then had been that they'd just come in and murdered innocent people in the villages, though doubtless some of them too had their reasons and their commands. So Botswana, a country without an army, had started the BDF: 500 young men in khaki marching up and down on the old airfield, looking like something out of an Evelyn Waugh novel. Indeed, it was one of the things I'd talked about with Tebogo, earlier that day. The BDF couldn't ever hope to compete with the South African army, he'd said, so what was the point of further expansion?

There was a disco. 'Route 66', 'Lady in Red', 'Brown Sugar': the engineers and architects and accountants who were so crucial to the building of the new Botswana took to the floor, and grooved to those hits from the good old days. Susie leant towards me. 'It's time for us to leave,' she said.

'Now?'

'No, no – I mean Botswana – in December. It's such a small world, everybody knows everybody else, what's going on, who's having affairs with whom. I'm just aching for the anonymity of London. Just to be able to go out to the shop dressed in any old thing and know you're not going to run into anyone.' She sipped her red wine, looked out over the gyrating white middle-aged throng. 'We've got plenty of friends here,' she said. 'But I wouldn't say we'd met any soulmates. In four years. That's sad, isn't it? A lot of them are pretty empty. Rich and empty.'

I'd slightly lost my nerve. In South Africa it had become so easy, pursuing influential strangers. I'd been the Commissioned Overseas Journalist. Now I was just Mark the ex-teacher aid, who was writing a book about . . . what? why? . . . Maru-a-Pula. I found it twice as hard to pick up the phone. Why should these ex-kids want to see me? What would I think if *my* old English teacher had turned up in London out of the blue saying he was writing a book?

Archie restored my confidence – and my spirits. I'd wondered whether he was even going to remember who I was, but he exploded with enthusiasm down the phone. 'Mark!' he bellowed. 'Good to hear from you after all this time!' How long was I staying? We must meet for lunch tomorrow. But that wasn't enough. There were lots of people who'd want to see me; he would arrange it.

I felt quite bowled over.

We met for lunch at Park's Restaurant – in the African Mall; yet another new venue in yet another new part of town. Archie had been a short skinny kid of fifteen, with a big smile and a loud laugh. In the photo I had of him, he was wearing a skimpy patterned T-shirt and a little bush hat squashed down over his head.

Now he was my height, a rather dapper man of thirty or so, stylishly dressed in a thigh-length black and white jersey jacket, smelling discreetly of expensive perfume. He seemed to know half the people in the restaurant; before he sat down with me he made a shaking hands tour, then invited two young women at a nearby table to join us for a drink. 'D'you remember this girl, Mark? She was in Standard One, I think.' Brenda didn't remember me and I didn't remember Brenda, but what the hell – it was all very pleasant, being thrown back into the centre of Happy Happy Africa, not a surly face in sight.

'What are you doing on Saturday night?' Archie asked suddenly. 'I'm going to have a party – for Mark. Spread it around, will you, girls. Party. Saturday night. My place.'

Left alone we swapped CVs. After Maru-a-Pula, Archie had gone to the university of Botswana. 'I discovered girls, they discovered me,' he said, with a little gurgle of laughter. Then, having got his diploma, he'd become a teacher, working for three and a half years 'surprisingly enough, in my home village'. Then he'd been to Florida for two years to do a Master's – 'a splendid time'; now he was at the Ministry of Education, developing curriculum material for Government schools.

Over a plate of scorched lasagne we remembered the old days. Like Tebogo, Archie thought things had changed at M-a-P. Part of it was 'an inevitable consequence of development'. The students were wealthier; there were greater income disparities in Botswana than there had been; in Gabs in particular.

'But it wasn't as materialistic then as it is now. There's a desire amongst some of us to see some defining characteristics of Maru-a-Pula stay in place. That may sound conservative, but I don't think it is . . .'

The product of a very different society, I felt – in my jeans and T-shirt – almost less grown-up than my ex-pupil, who was now well on his way to becoming a substantial citizen of Gaborone.

Turning to the topic of my book, I felt strangely diffident. Colour – which I'd all but forgotten about – had reared its ugly head again. How could I tell Archie about the Van

Tonders? Or laugh about Acacia Lodge? I was suddenly conscious of just what a white time I'd had; how much I'd got sucked into seeing things from a white point of view.

'I have relatives in South Africa,' Archie told me, 'and I've visited them a lot. And I hate it. I *hate* interacting with the institutions of apartheid, but – by virtue of the fact that to get there I have to go through the border-post, and I drive a motor vehicle, and so on – I have to. And put up with police harassment and all those things.

'But the most painful thing is talking to them – a lot of my cousins. Many of them have been through Bantu education.' Archie shook his head. 'Very poorly educated. And they've trivialised everything. They're really a good example of the success of Bantu education, in that they've taken on those values. And thinking processes.

'If you converse with them, you can hardly hold a fifteen minute conversation with them. It becomes completely unintelligible in less than ten minutes. They drink – I don't – so they go off to drink, and what can I do ... pick up a newspaper ...'

Primrose had a deep red Mercedes Benz, which purred along the Lobatse Road, past the old industrial estate, to Chatters, where she was taking me for dinner.

In 1977 she'd been starting on her A-levels, a girl I'd remembered more for her gentle disposition and helpfulness than any great beauty. Now she was Marketing Manager of Botswana's main chain of hotels. Her long hair was swept back, braided and decorated with beads. There was something around the lips that was the old Primrose, but otherwise I was out on a date with a glamorous black woman – and she was paying!

As with Sophie, it was an extraordinary relief to be genuinely away from the whole black-white problem area. There was no need to be on guard, worry that one might suddenly say the wrong thing, hit some deep vein of hurt or anger. I even felt mildly embarrassed, raising the subject of racism, asking Primrose how things had been for her in Ireland, where she'd done her training.

Oh it had been fine, she said. She'd found the Irish culture very similar to the culture in Botswana. 'The people were very, very gentle, very slow, very friendly; there were queues, and you know, it was very much like here.'

If there had been a problem 'it was more the fact that as a black person, you know, the kids would point fingers and say: "Mummy, why is she different? Why is she black?" And you know, Mother slapping the wrist, "Don't *point*, don't talk so loudly." And the parents would be embarrassed. And the thought that went through my mind was: This is how prejudice starts, because now the child is not told why that person is not white – so they're going to think there's something wrong, because their mother was scolding them, instead of just being told, very openly, "Oh no, she's from a different climatic area . . . pigmentation . . . the whole bit . . . maybe the child wouldn't understand it at the time, but it's not then going to seem unnatural.'

Unlike Archie, she was entirely relaxed about her experiences in South Africa. 'Yes,' she said, 'I've experienced patronising attitudes – but they're just momentary, and then you're out again. You know, South Africa's not one of those places where you turn around and you say, "All Afrikaners are this way." Because you find that the Afrikaners in the rural areas are actually much more down-to-earth, because they mix that much more with', she paused momentarily, 'the blacks.'

'But in a very patronising kind of way . . . often . . .?'

'Yes. The problems come in the towns, with the poor whites. Who are these? These are the guys who are your security guards, your immigration officers, your border guys, because they're the ones that are feeling most threatened, most vulnerable.

'Then when you look at your rich Afrikaners, they are . . .

depending on who was introducing you, would depend on how they reacted. If you were being introduced by somebody who's important enough in their eyes, and they're white, then they're going to be very, very hospitable, to the point where they're falling all over you. I was laughing in Pretoria, because I became a celebrity for the day. An ex-minister – we're running this hotel on his behalf – '

'South African minister?'

'Yes, this is in Pretoria . . . he was Minister of Information or something . . . so we're having an official party, and we met his wife, and were taken to the home, went out for dinner – extremely nice, and the whole bit . . . The following day his partner came along, and his wife came along, and it was, "Oh you must meet my mother." So, now I had to meet all these old Afrikaner women, and then it was, "Oh you must meet my son," and I was sitting there going, "Oh my gosh, oh my gosh," you know . . . They were going all out to show that they were so . . . you know this was the New South Africa, we've accepted the situation, and the fact that you're black doesn't really matter.'

We laughed. Just a little twist of history and all Primrose's gentle objectivity could have been something entirely other.

It was the last school assembly of the year, in the huge auditorium of Mait-i-song. The school sat on raked seats, while round the balcony at the top sat the . . . forty? fifty? . . . staff. Looking round I could see what Tebogo and Archie had been getting at. These kids were in an entirely different league. Trendy jackets, lipstick, patterned tights, designer jumpers. In the row just below me was a pretty black girl in – of all things – an ANC beret.

They were in an end-of-term mood. Cheers and wolf-whistles greeted a fifteen year old Indian who'd run down onto the stage to thank a leaving teacher.

The headmaster got up to speak. 'We have with us today an ex-teacher-aid . . .'

Wolf-whistles, cheers, catcalls. The entire school had turned to look at me.

'. . . who was here fifteen years ago . . .'

A lessening in volume.

'. . . which means that he was teaching here before half of the people in this hall were born.'

Silence. It was true. I was middle-aged.

George had arrived, and was staying in one of M-a-P's (as I was learning to call it) 'guest flats', in what had once been the upper floor of the assistant headmaster's house. Even from the bottom of the stairs I could smell that familiar pipesmoke. It took me straight back to that brick verandah where night after night George and I had sat drinking gin and tonics and playing backgammon, while the crickets sang in the warm darkness and strange rustles and squawks came from the bush at the bottom of the garden; that same bush that had stretched out endlessly to the horizon . . . to the Kalahari beyond . . .

Now there was gin, but no tonic. 'I'm sorry,' said George, in that familiar American sing-song, 'there's no vermouth either. I'm having water with mine.' He clumped next door and broke up some ice from the fridge. I heard him swoosh some water from the tap into his glass.

George's stroke had left him with a left eye that was wide and staring. He had shrunk a little inside his clothes. His tie was clumsily tied. His smoker's cough was that much more elaborate. The smile had vanished from his lips.

It wasn't quite the fond reunion one could have hoped for. He was friendly, but there was more suspicion than affection in the look that accompanied the words. Well, I hadn't been the most loyal of pals. Though my memory of George had always been warm, I hadn't kept in touch and I'd never taken up his invitation to stay with him in Maine.

'So you're writing a book about Maru-a-Pula and what — schools in Southern Africa?' he said, from the centre of his cloud of pipesmoke.

'Well, not *just* schools . . .'

But like Gerald in Durban and everybody else, George had his own clear idea of what my book was about. 'I can tell you a little about the early days here at Maru-a-Pula,' he began; and we were off, on a History of the Teacher Aid; from the days when they were *really* needed, to wash up, and dish out the food, and answer the phone . . .

'In those days there were – what – 140 students only. I was able to say, "Come on over, listen to some records."' He caught my eye. 'I was *known* for that. The kids knew they could just come round to Uncle George, and play records or have a Fanta – but you *can't do that* with five hundred students . . .' George shook his head sadly, swigged his gin and water. 'I miss it though,' he added.

We talked for an hour, then I walked with him through the gloaming to the dining room. The suspicion had faded, and the old affection had returned. 'Keep in touch,' he said. We shook hands, warmly. But as I walked back towards the car, I wondered whether, things being what they are, I would really ever see him again.

Ludo. Sixteen, tall, lean and strikingly beautiful. I had picked her out of the crowd on my first day. Headstrong and difficult, the scourge of poor old DY. Her father was a South African, and had spent some time as a political prisoner; Ludo had been, consequently, very angry on that subject.

One particular memory: me, lying in bed at George's house with gastro-enteritis; Ludo coming to visit, standing at the doorway in the sunlight. 'I could kill a white man just like that,' she'd said. And her foot had darted out and crushed a chameleon. I'd been shocked, unable to understand the depth of her anger.

Now she was married. 'Oh Mark,' she cried, when I phoned. 'How are *you*? I'll get some of my naughty friends round to see you.' She laughed that loud familiar – shriek was more the word than laugh.

Like Sophie, she, too, now had a spacious bungalow in the old part of town. House and garden were idiosyncratic and stylish. A bowl of pink carnations on the hall table, framed African art on the walls. 'It's all done by local artists,' she said, showing me through to a room with white sofas, a low glass coffee-table, white walls, a log fire.

Her husband Solly was pale-skinned, with hair cut almost to the scalp and thin-rimmed glasses. He was quietly spoken, with an air of great gentleness. There was a girlfriend there too: Nicky, a Zambian architect who'd studied in the UK.

Ludo had quietened down. A little. But she still shouted rather than talked; she was still all arms and legs.

After M-a-P, she'd won a Rhodes scholarship to Oxford, but had flunked out and returned to Botswana. 'I just got so *lonely*,' she said, leaning right forward out of her chair. 'You can't imagine it. Now I think I could handle it – but then I didn't understand how England worked. I was the first African woman at Magdalen and *nobody* talked to me. I used to phone here, I used to phone Nicky in Zambia. But then I'd put the phone down and I'd be alone again. It was *dreadful*.'

Nicky had had part of her education at a girl's school in the Quantock Hills and agreed that the English were very unfriendly. She remembered a time when she'd got onto a train and said, 'Hello, how are you?' to a woman opposite her. 'And this woman looked so terrified I thought she was going to get up and run away. All because I'd said "hello".' She laughed.

'And then the Oxford dons,' said Ludo. 'I couldn't believe them. One of them used to give me a tutorial from his – what d'you call it? – his cupboard, his closet.' She shrieked at the memory. 'I remember when I first went in there with my essay, and I looked around and there was nobody there, so I went down to the porters and said, "Look, it's three o'clock and I'm supposed to be having a tutorial with Mr So-and-so and he's not there." And they said, "Oh don't worry, just go back in there and start reading your essay." So I did, and after a while I heard these sounds coming from the cupboard,

things like "hmm" and "yes", and then when I'd finished –
still in the cupboard – he gave me an assessment, and then I
went. And all the porters told me that was quite normal.

'And then in the summer, we went punting, you know, on
one of those Oxford punts, and there's an island there where
all the dons bathe naked. These same dons who are so mousy
and so on, dancing around naked on this island. And some
of the naughty ones would come towards you in the punt,
pretending they were about to pee. I couldn't believe it!'

After a while Nicodemus turned up. He'd also been in that
fourth form, the star actor of the school, with a magnificently
deep voice. Now he was a barrister in a charcoal grey suit;
and though he didn't lean over and call me "m'friend", he
had something of the Lincoln's Inn manner. He defended
the thirty pula entrance fee to the nightclub we were thinking of going to in Gabane. 'The guy has to pay his mortgage.
Lower the price and the thronging hordes will be there,' he
said wearily, wiping his brow.

Over a take-away pizza, we discussed South Africa. Ludo
explained how the townships were run by children with
AK-47s. 'Mark, these kids that man the barricades – they're
just children – ten, twelve, fourteen. And you know what
children are like: they've got no real moral sense so they can
just do anything. I've got a cousin of eighteen in Sebokeng –
and I'm telling you, he's too old.'

With this talk of South Africa, Nicodemus' urbanity had
faded, and anger creased his brow. What would disconcert a
London barrister so, I thought: bring them back from fat to
nerve?

'Rage, Mark, is what I feel,' Ludo was saying. 'It's what we
all feel.'

'So how does that tie in with what I kept hearing about
forgiveness?'

'Yes, we are prepared to forgive, but we want some
recognition of that. We want them to say, "We're sorry, we
did you wrong." We want an *apology*.'

Nicodemus went home and we moved from rage to Winnie Mandela. Whether Nelson had done the right thing in leaving her. Both Ludo and Nicky felt that he'd treated her wrong, 'even though she did have a lover.'

'The point is,' said Nicky, 'she was there for him, all those twenty-seven years.' Ludo talked passionately of Winnie's solitary confinement in Brandfort, in the Orange Free State, far away from her friends in Soweto. 'There wasn't even a *floor* in that house,' Ludo was shouting. 'There was just *sand* on that floor. And who would Nelson be without Winnie? It was Winnie that kept his memory alive while he was in jail. It was Winnie that created his reputation.' It was totally unfair they'd picked on the Stompie thing. They'd hounded her, when they should have made some attempt to heal her. Everybody who knew her when she was young said what a wonderful woman she'd been. She hadn't been cut out for such a life. She was just a beautiful young member of the Royal Family. In fact – Ludo was losing her thread – she'd got more beautiful as she'd got older – what was she *supposed* to do? Nelson Mandela had prostate problems. Everybody knew that. So why did he worry that Winnie had a lover?

On that issue, Solly agreed with me. It was because she had a lover that Nelson had had to leave her. 'By taking a lover,' said Solly, in that gentlest of voices, 'she was showing that he was no longer a man; and that was intolerable.'

My angle was a simple one of the anger and jealousy a lover would engender. 'OK,' I was arguing at Nicky. 'Imagine it was the other way round. That you'd been in jail and then you came out and your husband had another woman, and he wanted to move her into the house. How would you feel about that?'

Nicky had her head in her hands. 'I'm thinking about it,' she said.

By English standards, Ludo was saying, letting Winnie off, not sending her for trial would – of course – have been selective justice. But in the South African context, where justice was a joke . . .

It was time for me to go. 'I'm still *thinking* about it,' said Nicky, as I shook her hand.

It was Saturday night. Archie's party in my honour. Was this going to be the ending I was looking for? Flashing lights, wild dancing, all the old friends . . .

Archie had said 8.30, so I got to his little bungalow at 9.30, ready for action. To find: Archie and four guys sitting on a white plastic sofa watching the Olympics.

Archie was very welcoming. 'Mark!' he shouted. And then, showing me into his little kitchen: 'I've bought you a bottle of wine. And tonight, in your honour, I'm going to have a drink.' So we sat and watched the Olympics. After a while Brenda turned up, with her flatmate, a beautiful girl with eyes like a cartoon Bambi whose name was Lesego. 'Aren't you going to get your future wife a drink?' Brenda asked Archie sweetly.

It was 10.15 and Archie's sound system wasn't working. He was trying to persuade one of his other guests to go and get one from somewhere else. We sipped our drinks and watched the women's hurdles, the 400 metres, the men's hurdles. Brenda was laughing at the blacks in the English team.

'Oh, the British have got a *brother* now – and the Italians, they have a brother too, oh no, where did they find *him*?'

In the men's hurdles the British came third. The four victorious American blacks hugged each other, draped themselves in the American flag. The British – two black, two white – smiled and shrugged. 'The British needed two more brothers to win,' said Brenda, doubled up with laughter.

A trendily dressed whitey turned up, clutching a bottle. His face fell. 'Hey, I can see this is one of those Saturday night rave-ups,' he said. 'Dave!' shouted Archie enthusiastically.

Luckily, Dave had a little ghetto blaster in his car. The TV was switched off, a fire was lit, and soon three of the guys were dancing in a corner. Two more whites turned up, a short broad-hipped woman with her hair tied back, accompanied by a weasly looking guy in a denim jacket.

Dave was a photographer from Watford. He'd come out from England on a photo-shoot of the Okavango and stayed. Now he had a good business in town, lots of work, and he wasn't planning to go home. 'I hate England,' he told me. 'Englishmen, really, they're so self-seeking. I find them all immensely boring.'

The white chick had hit the floor, was doing a wild hip-wiggling dance. 'You see,' said Archie, 'she's very African-ised, isn't she?' I nodded. It wasn't at all bad; just a *little* too earnest to be entirely authentic.

Finally, at midnight, Thabo appeared. He seemed as enthusiastic to see me as I was to see him. Little Thabo: model, artist, eager beaver of the art room. He had been put into a photocopier and enlarged by 25%, and somebody had etched on a pointed beard – but the grin was the same, everything else was exactly the same.

We laughed over my old photos; then some more over memories of the art room. 'I still remember those warm colours and those cold colours,' Thabo said, shaking his head. 'Still!'

At the end of the party, Thabo and Archie and I had made enthusiastic plans to spend Sunday afternoon listening to jazz. On every roundabout in the sprawling new city were big handpainted sheets advertising JONAS GWANGWA 4 PM SUNDAY BODIBA CLUB, MOGHODITSANE.

In the old days you'd bumped over the railway on a level crossing, and then out down through the empty bush on dirt. Moghoditsane had been a little cluster of huts where the road forked. It had had a village idiot who shouted harmlessly in the middle of the green. To the right the road wound on into the wilderness towards Kanye; to the left was the low magical range of Gabane hills, the village at its feet. On all sides were cattletracks and *marula* trees, and on a warm February afternoon there was no sound but the distant clang of cowbells and the singing of African women mooching along at their own sweet speed, a kid or two strapped to their backs. To the English boy who'd seen the gentle landscapes of his own country sliced up and ruined by bypasses and motorways, it was a paradise.

Now a flyover swept you easily past the railway, and a big tar road got you to Moghoditsane in five minutes. The old village was there like a torn painting in the background, but up by the road were the tatty bottle stores, a garage or two, a pile of car tyres, a Cafe Takeaways.

At the Bodiba Club there was no jazz. Jonas Gwangwa had been postponed till seven. I persuaded Archie to kill the time by taking me for a drive round Gabane. 'You can see the old dirt road there,' he said, 'running alongside.' I tried to imagine myself thundering along on the Honda. Pointless. Before I knew it we were there.

Some things were the same. The rocky wooded hills behind; with the same GABANE picked out in large white stones. Off the tar, down riddled tracks to left and right, were still plenty of mud and thatch homesteads, their surrounding yards enclosed by low green hedges.

We found the little breezeblock 'destitutes' house, which Archie and the other fourth formers had built. The destitutes had all died. But the thin, broad-hipped lady who had looked after them was still there, and she seemed to remember me, stood holding my hand with tears visible in her eyes, shaking her head slowly back and forth. I'd taken a photograph of her, she told Archie in Setswana, sitting on the step. She ran inside and returned with a crumpled photo of herself between two whites neither of us knew.

We drove along the dirt road by the bottom of the hills. The river had been here, where the little black herdboys had brought their cattle to drink in the glinting water; now it was just a dry ditch. Then the shebeen – where was that? I couldn't locate it among the ugly new breezeblock and corrugated iron houses.

And then you'd come round the corner of the hill, and . . . there was the endless plain, that sense of being at the edge of the world, the road meandering away towards villages too distant for the inadequate Honda; villages I'd had it in mind, one day, to travel to; in a donkey-cart, or on a more powerful motorbike.

Now it would have been all too easy. You came round that same hill, and . . . *whoosh*, there was the great tar road, with a big green sign saying KANYE 60. Beyond, a row of tall pylons stomped off into the distance.

It was sunset, and all the red-brown rocks and the red-brown earth and the green-brown trees were suffused with that same exquisite red-orange light.

'It's sad,' I said, 'all this Westernisation.'

'Modernisation,' said Archie. 'It's inevitable. I heard they could run all these electricity lines underground. But it's more expensive, so they don't.'

We sped back to the Bodiba Club. Two little hills whose sharp silhouettes I'd once laboured to render now had winking white lights on top. They were right by the new Sir Seretse Khama International Airport.

Finally, it was the night of the M-a-P Reunion. Lying in the bath at sunset I was a little nervous. What twist of fate was going to hit me now? Was the climax of my journey to be – me, wandering around, unrecognised by everybody?

As it turned out, truth was stranger than any imagined fictions. For who should appear, weaving his way through the crowd of black-tied ex-kids . . . but Greg. He'd left America, was working in Swaziland, was engaged to Jodie, who was now a nurse in South Africa.

'I am so *glad* you're here, Mark,' he cried, putting his arms around me, shaking his head, standing back in exaggerated American disbelief. 'I can't *believe* you're here. I was just saying to Jodie as we drove up from Jo'burg – wouldn't it be great if Mark and Nina were here, and Sam and Matt and

Jitika,' he broke into that infectious giggle, 'and then we could all gang up and say how much we hated Matt.'

And there was Kgotla, the naughtiest boy in form four, who used to take out his penis and wave it around at the back of the class to make the girls giggle. Now he was resplendent in wing-collar and blue bow-tie, a dignified wife on his arm. He looked so respectable I hardly felt I could remind him of his adolescent antics. But when I greeted him, he didn't remember me at all. 'I'm sorry,' he said, shaking his head with that familiar triangular smile. 'I don't.'

You get back what you put in. Wandering around, Greg was greeted by far more of the men than I was. But then, I thought, Greg lived in the boys' boarding house and gave English lessons and got thoroughly involved; while I scarpered off and sat on George's terrace writing children's stories and teaching myself to type, and vanished to Gabane for whole days to eat *marulas* and dream and paint on my own.

But then an Indian woman whose face I only dimly recollected came running over. 'Mark! Mark! How are you?' 'It's, it's . . .' I dithered. 'Sally.' 'Sally – of course!' Slowly she was coming back. 'I remember you taught me how to sweep,' she said. 'I was sweeping in the kitchen and you said, "No, you mustn't pull the brush towards you, you must push it away." I've never forgotten that.'

And here was Rachel, who'd flown in from Israel. Then, a rather over-plump brunette with a scowl; now, a beaming blonde in a low-cut dress with a bearded English fiancé gripping her right hand. 'Mark, of all people,' she cried. 'Now what were you famous for, something . . .'

'The art room?'

'No, no – that motorbike. Always on that motorbike.' She laughed.

And now, there, across the crowd was DY and Dot, both preserved in aspic. DY had the same shiny pate, bushy eyebrows, firm welcoming handshake. Dot the same dark curls, that same concerned question-mark of wrinkles on her brow. DY too was having problems recognising people, as one after another his grinning black ex-students approached him through the darkness. 'And you are . . .?' 'Kgotla.' 'Kgotla! Of *course*!' said DY, magnificently.

'I'm so glad to see *you*,' said Dot, in that cut-glass English accent. 'We have a watercolour you did, of a storm coming up over the playing field, that we have in our drawing room. A friend of ours said she knew *exactly* the right frame for it, and it looks *lovely*.'

'I heard a rumour', said Greg, appearing from one side, 'that you and DY were living in Alexandra township.'

'Three streets away,' said Ma Y. 'DY is trying to solve the rift between Inkatha and the ANC. We have them sitting in our drawing room, and then he's quickly able to get out to the troubles.'

We went in to dinner. Long tables laid out on the stage of Mait-i-song. Above us, on the walls, bunches of blue, white and black balloons, streamers making the initials M-a-P. We were each given a commemorative T-shirt, with a neat triangular logo, and the slogan M-A-P REUNION 1992.

Greg and I and Jodie and Sophie (back from Tanzania) and Jens and Indian Sally and a couple of others made a table together. Archie was – of course – the Master of Ceremonies. Before we'd even begun, there was a speech, by 'one of the first students of M-a-P'. Then we'd barely finished our starters before Archie was on his feet again, to introduce a speech from 'the new headmaster, who will welcome us here both officially and officiously . . .'

Beside me Greg chortled. 'Archie's English is as good as ever.'

'I hope I am neither official nor officious,' Peter began.

After our main course DY took the floor; after pudding the Honourable Minister for Education; it was only left for former bad-boy Tennyson (oh the problems I'd had stopping him smoking *dagga* behind the art room) now a father of four and Chairman of the M-a-P Alumni Association, to make yet another speech over the coffee.

Greg was full of anecdotes. 'Don't you remember the Scrooch Patrol?' he said. 'Oh gad!' he shouted with laughter. 'Ma Y', he said to his little audience at our end of the table, 'had called us teacher aids in, told us that she was very *woe-rried*' (he'd slipped into her accent) 'that some of the *young-sters* were *scrooching* in the *bushes*. We knew about smooch-ing, and we knew about screwing, but we weren't *quite* sure what *scrooching* was. So we tied a couple of those big torches to the front of the moped and drove out into the bushes and we were ... The Scrooch Patrol! And all the kids who were there just shouted, "Eh Mark-we, eh Greg-we, go away!" Oh gad!'

At a table by the door I found three members of my little twelve year old English class, none of whom remembered me. I showed them the photo I had, six enthusiastic little girls with their hands up in the air. 'Is that *me*?' said Merapelo. 'Oh *no*, it isn't *me*.' She screamed with laughter and embraced her friend Mpho. Merapelo was married now, and a mother of three. Her parents, refugees from South Africa, had become naturalised Batswana. She herself had been sent to Moscow for three years by the ANC. 'Yes, I remember you now,' she said finally. 'I remember you now.'

There was dancing, to the Botswana Police Band, who played old favourites from the 1970s and 1980s. I found myself sitting alone at the half-empty table, tears in my eyes at the thought that that dream of mine really had come true. I'd come back. I was at Maru-a-Pula; and here, amazingly, they all were: DY and Greg and Sophie and Archie and Primrose and Merapelo and ... I had done it, I had lived the dream, and now I could go home to Sarah.

In the morning we had a final breakfast with Walker. With Greg and Jodie, and tea and toast, it was a fair approximation of the old days, but for the presence of a rather camp Rural

Dean – plump and white as a turkey, with breadcrumbs tumbling down the front of his cassock.

Walker was going to Sunday lunch with Lady Khama and didn't know how formal he should be. 'What am I going to wear?' he called from the stairs. 'Oh, just the simple twinset and pearls, I should think,' sang the Dean. 'Nothing too busy.'

For old time's sake, the three of us ex-teacher aids drove out to Gabane, and sat outside the destitutes' house in the dust with a beer. It was a magical afternoon; and this, I thought, as we sat there, is the perfect ending. Above us were the Gabane hills, where Greg's brother John's ashes were scattered. John had gone out with Jodie, all those years ago, and now she was with Greg, who'd been gay, and nursed his lover for five years as he'd died of AIDS (which Greg had escaped) and now they were out here together, trying to conceive a child.

Jodie had had it with England, she was never going back. It was 'static and depressing'. Paradoxically, the little town in the western Transvaal where she worked as a nurse – Brits – was the headquarters of the AWB. 'They don't have fences in Brits,' she said. 'I asked one of the guys why he didn't just take some vegetables from this field if he was hungry, and he said, "If I did that, I'd be shot."'

After we'd laughed our way through all the old stories, we each told each other a new one. Each of us had had something happen to us all those years ago that we'd never dared talk about. Now, years later, we confided in each other, and laughed, and promised to keep our shameful secrets. And Greg and Jodie drove off one way, and I drove off another, and mentally, in the woodsmoke-scented Botswana sunset, I wrote:

THE END.

A FALLING STAR

But it wasn't of course the end. There was something I'd been hiding from myself. Only now, as I turned to head for home, did it return to haunt me.

I left early the next morning to take the car back to Cape Town, driving at speed through the pretty low hills of southern Botswana, through the border gate at Ramatlabama, down past the joke-capital of Bophuthatswana – Mmabatho – and then on, across endless miles of empty bush and up into the Kuruman Hills.

Buying a South African newspaper I discovered that the Mass Action had come and gone; Nelson Mandela had addressed a large peaceful rally in Pretoria; the General Strike had only lasted two days.

Beyond Kuruman a vast yellow plain opened up: there was land enough here for ten million Africans. I raced on, the only car on the road. At Upington I crossed the Orange River and the terrain changed again, to a black knee-high tundra that my guides told me was Bushmanland. It grew dark. I stopped the car and switched off the lights. The stars were intensely bright. I took a last deep breath of Africa.

At Calvinia I checked into a hotel as depressing as any I'd been to yet. I sat alone in a garish crimson and white dining room, while the white moustachioed owner drank lager alone at the bar, and a little uniformed coloured maid stood two yards away, attentive to every flicker of my eyebrow.

I had come back this way, the longer emptier way, for the flowers: in August, at the start of spring, Namaqualand is famous for its flowers. Coachloads of elderly whites, I'd been told, came annually to see the extraordinary 'carpet' of blooms that the first rains release from the ground.

The next morning found the grannies, but not the flowers. It was a bad year, the Afrikaner chemist in Niewoudtville told me. The rains had been late and insufficient. He had some postcards of better years. Up and down the roads in cars and minibuses the old couples cruised, with only a splash or two of white or yellow here and there to satisfy them.

Just after Niewoudtville, I had a shock: I came round a corner . . . and there, a thousand feet below me, was another plain. I twisted nervously down the edge of the escarpment and drove out to the sea. Beyond the little port of Lambert's Bay the coast road became dirt, winding through a lovely Alpine landscape. Now there was vivid green grass, copses of trees in bud; here and there a track led to a little Afrikaner farmstead. And here, suddenly, were plenty of flowers: white, orange, purple, yellow: patches, hillsides, yes, even carpets. In the far distance were the snow-capped Swartruggens Mountains. It seemed a shame that I was flying home to be with Sarah at the wrong end of summer in England, when if we'd arranged it differently she could have been here with me now, we could have been picnicking in this lush valley at the start of spring.

I came out onto tar, and suddenly Cape Town was a mere 105 kilometres away – less than an hour. I put my foot down. At the 70 marker, Table Mountain came into view, that familiar flat-topped silhouette. Visible, then invisible; then, rounding a corner, there it was in magnificent close-up. This, if not from the sea, was the way to approach it. The sky was blue, the sea was bluer, the mountain was green and sunlit, the city a sprawl of white houses on the lower slopes. Even the smoking industrial chimneys in the foreground couldn't spoil it.

The parrot in the Tudor Hotel was either dead or asleep. With heavy heart I returned the Dolphin, became a pedestrian again. There was no flight from Cape Town till Saturday. I had three days to kill.

I sat in Greenmarket Square, wondered how it would seem if I was arriving now. Four tables away there was a girl with thick blonde hair tied back, looking eagerly down at a map, then looking up and round and smiling at the Rasta singing the Bob Marley songs. No, my impression would have been different: today there were no less than two black couples on the cappuccino terrace; and when the Rasta was finished he was joined by a white girl with red lipstick and ginger hair who kissed him and drove him off in a battered hatchback.

At Camps Bay, outside the café, a little white girl and a little black girl danced along the pavement hand in hand. In the spring sunshine the beach was fuller. A speedboat swerved and banked beyond the gleaming surf. Para-gliders jumped off the Lion's Head, swooped slowly down, landed with a thump on the sand.

In Lebowa, Francis and Margaret had given me their son Andrew's number. I phoned him. He was getting married on Saturday. Would I be around? Would I come to supper tonight and meet his fiancée? Would I come and see him get married?

So it was that I found myself on my last day in South Africa attending a white wedding at the very Anglican Cathedral where I'd spent my first morning. I looked around for Trevor the tramp, but he wasn't to be seen.

The priest was white and trendy. Having asked whether there was any just cause or impediment, he waited for a good ten seconds, before saying 'That's lucky'. 'On an occasion like this,' he went on, 'we have many different emotions. We feel joy, we feel admiration, we may even feel

"at last".' There was laughter: Andrew and Rebecca had
been together for five years.

Apartheid had done its job well. Despite Francis and
Margaret's work and life in Lebowa, despite their son's
liberalism and desire to be a writer, despite the fact that I got
a lift out to the reception from the local branch organiser of
the ANC, it was a completely white affair. Indeed, looking
round the garden at the guests, at the cherry blossom and
the daffodils and the newly mown green grass, but for the
Cape Dutch architecture and the magnificent backdrop of
Table Mountain behind, we could have been in England on
a lovely day in April.

Ros, one of the teachers from St Mark's, drove me out to the
airport. I kissed her fondly goodbye. 'Have you got someone
to meet you at the other end?' she asked. 'Yes,' I replied
smugly. On the phone from the Tudor I'd told Sarah I
couldn't wait to see her, and she'd replied in kind. I could
hardly believe that it would be her I would have in my arms,
not a phone receiver. With my last few rands I bought her a
soapstone hippopotamus and bottle of duty free champagne
for our long Sunday reunion.

I hardly slept as we crossed the world. Five hours, four
hours, three hours till I saw her again. After all these
strangers, someone at last who was not a stranger. Just one
hideous nagging thought, that had returned to bug me ever
since I'd left Botswana: what would I tell her about Julie and
Port St Johns? I would have to tell her; it had only been two
and a half months ago; it would be the middle of September
before I could have a test. But she would surely understand.
She *would* understand. Anyway, I wouldn't, couldn't, have
. . . no . . .

We bumped down at Heathrow. Grey clouds in a dirty
ochre sky: I was back in England, at the fag end of August.

And there she was, waiting for me loyally at the exit gate
at seven in the morning. Not dressed up as I'd imagined,

with lipstick and make-up in my favourite brown jacket; but looking scruffy, almost prettier in her torn jeans and loose white top and boots. Looking at her from the side, she had a lovely light in her eyes, and seeing her again, I thought: Yes, that was, as the Africans say, the correct decision, I will marry you. We hugged deeply, and kissed, just cheek to cheek. There was no need for any more; all I wanted was to get her home and into my arms. It was the middle of the August Bank Holiday. We had two whole days to be together, before we need surface and see *anyone* else.

It was strange, being back with her after all this time. Readjusting to the way she talked, her preoccupations. I felt different too, plump in my blue jacket. I started telling her some of my edited highlights, filling in the details we hadn't had time or money for on the phone: Buthelezi, Soweto, finding all my friends, Greg. She nodded along, and we rattled on up the familiar motorway – my Renault was on its last legs – and down into the Cromwell Road.

She was having a show in Los Angeles at the end of September, she told me. 'Aren't you happy for me?' she said. 'Yuh, yuh, of course I am,' I replied. (What about our holiday in France?) 'That's wonderful. Great!'

We got back to her flat, unloaded my four cases. What a lot of rubbish I'd picked up. Books, journals, African carvings.

Now I would have to tell her. I would open the champagne, we'd get into bed, and then I would tell her, and she would understand. After all, I'd forgiven her once for a one-night stand.

'D'you want some tea?' she said.

'I bought some champagne in Cape Town.'

'No, I . . . it's too early to drink.'

'Sarah! I've been away for four months. Let's have champagne and . . .'

She was walking towards the kettle. She turned abruptly in the narrow kitchen: 'Mark,' she said, 'I've met somebody else.'

GLOSSARY

Azania – the name given to South Africa by freedom fighters (from the Latin for Africa)

baas – boss (Afrikaans)

badkamer – bathroom (Afrikaans)

bakkie – open pick-up truck (Afrikaans)

billalloo – black person (Indian slang: unknown origin)

biltong – sun-dried lean meat, often game, eaten as a snack (Afrikaans)

Boer – literally farmer (Afrikaans); has come to mean Afrikaner

boerewors – long sausage, staple of the *braai* (Afrikaans)

boet – brother (Afrikaans)

braai, braaivleis – barbecue (Afrikaans)

Broederbond – Band of Brothers, Afrikaner secret society

chibuku – thick white African beer (Setswana)

dagga – marijuana

Dumêla – Setswana greeting

ezulwini – heaven (Zulu)

gemsquash – a round, orange, marrow-like vegetable

hardegat – hard-assed (Afrikaans)

hensopper – literally 'a hands-upper'; a traitor, one who surrendered to, or joined up with the British in the Boer War

hippo – nickname given to fortified police lorries (township slang)

impi – small regiment of Zulu fighting men (Zulu)

impimpi – an informer, a sellout, a lover of whites (Zulu) *jol* – a party; as a verb, *jolling* – to party, have a good/wild time (Afrikaans)

kaffir – literally 'unbeliever': now offensive slang for 'black' (Afrikaans)

kgadi – sweet African beer; also honey, anything sweet or lovely (Setswana)

kingklip – South African white fish

kitsconstabel – literally 'instant policeman': a black township policeman given fourteen days' training (Afrikaans)

knipmes – short stabbing knife (Afrikaans)

knobkerrie – a thick wooden stick with a round top, which can be used as a club (from Afrikaans *knopkierie*)

koppie – low hill (Afrikaans)

kraal – a homestead, group of huts comprising such a homestead (from Afrikaans)

lekker – lovely, delightful (approx) (Afrikaans)

lobola – bride price (Zulu)

marula – sweet lychee-like fruit (Setswana)

mielies – sweetcorn; hence *mielie pap*, the porridge made from *mielie* flour, the staple diet of rural black South Africans (Afrikaans)

nartjies – orange tangerine-like fruit (Afrikaans)

nkosi – royal praise singer (Zulu)

Ninjani – Zulu greeting

oke – bloke (SA English slang)

Oom – uncle (Afrikaans)

panga – a broad, heavy African knife

pondokkie – a meat stew, generally made with game (Afrikaans)

pula – unit of currency in Botswana, similar buying power as a pound; from Setswana word for rain.

robot – traffic light

rondawel – a round hut, usually with a grass roof (Afrikaans)

rooibos tea – a popular South African tea, made from 'red-bush' (rooibos) leaves (Afrikaans)

Sawubona – Zulu greeting

sis – expression of disgust, equivalent to 'ugh' (Afrikaans)

sjambok – a whip of dried hide (Afrikaans); as verb: to flog

soutpiel – saltdick: Afrikaner slang for a SA Englishman

stoep – covered verandah or porch (Afrikaans)

takkies – trainers, sports shoes (Afrikaans slang)

tokoloshe – evil spirit that some Africans believe haunts the
   floor of their huts

toyi-toyi – a war dance

veldt – open, unforested country (from Afrikaans *veld*)

APPENDIX

A Short History of Southern Africa

B.C. Yellow-skinned Khoikhoi (Hottentots) and San (Bushmen) people established as cattle herders and hunter-gatherers across Southern Africa.

300–1500 A.D. Tribes of Sotho, Tswana, and Nguni peoples drift down from Central Africa to northern areas of Southern Africa.

1652 Jan Van Riebeeck, founder of white South Africa, arrives at Table Bay to build a fort, hospital and vegetable garden to service ships of the Dutch East India Company. This settlement is to become Cape Town. (Van Riebeeck stays only nine years.)

1657 Dutch soldiers released from service granted status of 'free burghers': allowed to cultivate land and raise cattle on 28 acre farms along Liesbeeck River. Khoikhoi people – whose grazing lands these are – rise up to fight black South Africa's first war of resistance. Having crushed the Khoi, Van Riebeeck claims title to the land by right of conquest.

1660–1800 Dutch 'Boers' (farmers) venture further and further into the Cape interior, establishing farms as they go. Khoisan people who survive European diseases (notably smallpox) are dispossessed and taken into servitude. Their miscegenation with whites and black and Malay slaves produces the 'coloured' people of today.

In the Eastern Cape north-westerly moving Boers encounter resistance from Xhosa branch of Nguni tribe. After a series of

frontier wars, the Xhosas are driven back to the Great Fish
River.

1795   At the start of Napoleonic Wars, a British expeditionary
force seizes Cape of Good Hope. Returned to Dutch 1803.
Reoccupied 1806. At end of war Cape formally ceded to
Britain. British enforce policy of Anglicanisation on reluctant
Afrikaners. Dutch language abolished as medium in
administrative service and judicial system and phased out in
schools and churches.

1820   4,000 British Government sponsored settlers arrive at
Algoa Bay (Port Elizabeth) to establish farms in Eastern Cape;
the undisclosed British aim being to secure the white frontier
behind the line of the Great Fish River.

1834–54   The Great Trek. 6,000 Boers, accompanied by 4,000
'coloured' servants, sick of British rule and impositions, set
out northwards from Eastern Cape into the unknown. Known
as Voortrekkers. (Voor = Ahead)

1816   Shaka becomes leader of the small (2,000) Zulu clan,
which he builds into a formidable military power, conquering
and dominating surrounding Nguni tribes and eventually
commanding an army of 40,000 and ruling large sections of
Natal. This sets in train a vast chain reaction known as the
Difaqane (forced migration). Defeated tribes flee north, south
and west. Moshoeshoe I escapes to Drakensberg mountains to
establish Sotho kingdom. Sobhuza flees to mountains north of
Pongola River to establish Swaziland. Mzilikazi leads Ndebele
north to Transvaal.

1828   Shaka assassinated by half-brothers Dingane and
Mhlangana. Dingane subsequently murders Mhlangana and
takes control of new Zulu kingdom.

Feb 1838   A party of 69 Voortrekkers led by Piet Retief meet
Dingane to negotiate a land transfer. During the festivities to
celebrate this agreement, Dingane betrays Retief and murders
him and his party, before sending his soldiers to slaughter 281

Boer men, women and children, and two hundred 'coloured' servants at nearby Boer encampment.

Dec 16th 1838   Survivors of this massacre, reinforced by newcomers under the command of Andreis Pretorius take on a Zulu force of 12,000 by the Ncome river, killing 3,000 for three slightly wounded Boers. Before the battle Pretorius and the Boers have sworn a solemn oath that if God grants them victory, they will build a church and remember the day for posterity. Known as The Day of the Vow, the 16th Dec is still the most sacred date in the Afrikaner calender.

1850   Having driven Ndebele out of Northern Transvaal, Boers establish two independent republics: The South African Republic in the Transvaal, and the Orange Free State by the Orange River. The British continue to rule colonies of Natal and the Cape.

1856   Xhosa prophet girl Nongqawuse has a vision that if Xhosas destroy all their cattle and burn all their grain, famous Xhosa warriors of the past will rise up from their graves and a great wind will drive the whites into the sea. Cattle are duly slaughtered and grain burnt, but warriors and wind fail to materialise. Thousands die of starvation and Xhosa power is effectively broken.

1879   British-Zulu war. After being defeated at Isandhlwana in January, British rout Zulus at Ulundi in July. King Cetshwayo is deposed and deported, and Zulu power broken.

1868   Diamonds are discovered by children playing in Orange River. Mining for alluvial diamonds begins the following year. In April 1871, Sarah Ortlepp picks up a diamond while picnicking on a hill in the Orange Free State; by August there are 5,000 people digging on the hill. Mining town of Kimberley founded. Disputes between Boers, Griqua and Tswana chiefs over ownership of territory settled by British who take control.

1877   British annex Transvaal. Paul Kruger, leader of the Boers, travels to London to plead with Queen Victoria to revoke annexation. Her refusal leads to:

1880   First Anglo-Boer War. British defeated at Majuba Hill.
Independence granted to Transvaal with Kruger as State
President.

1886   Gold discovered on Witwatersrand. Entrepreneurs from
Kimberley and elsewhere set up settlement of Ferreira's Camp
(subsequently Johannesburg) thirty-five miles from Boer
capital of Pretoria.

1896   Jameson Raid. Cecil Rhodes, leading gold rush
entrepreneur and Prime Minister of Cape Colony, plots
uprising among British in Johannesburg, with aim of
overthrowing Kruger's government in Pretoria. Uprising a
fiasco, and Dr Jameson, leader of British support commando, is
arrested.

1899   Boer republics give British Government ultimatum: all
mutual differences to be put to arbitration; British soldiers on
Transvaal borders to be withdrawn. British failure to respond
leads to 2nd Boer War. 26,000 Afrikaner women and children
die in world's first 'concentration camps'.

1902   Peace of Vereeniging. Colonial status imposed on Boer
republics.

1902–10   British Governor Lord Milner attempts to
restructure newly colonised republics on British lines, and
Anglicise new generation of Afrikaners. Afrikaans prohibited
in schools. Defeated Afrikaners receive support worldwide.

1905   General Election in Britain brings Liberals to power.
Affected by international opinion and a visit from Boer leader
Jan Smuts Prime Minister Campbell-Bannerman gives Boer
republics back their independence (1906–7).

1910   The South Africa Act. Campbell-Bannerman establishes
a Union of the two Boer republics and two British colonies.
Rights of Africans, 'coloureds' and Indians ignored. Louis
Botha becomes Prime Minister of the Union.

1913   New sovereign Parliament passes Land Act. Blacks
prohibited from buying land outside designated 'reserve' areas
(10% of total country). It becomes a crime for blacks who are

not servants to live on white farms. At a stroke a million black 'squatters' are made homeless.

1912   Pixley Seme, Oxford and Middle Temple educated Zulu lawyer, founds African National Congress (ANC), initially as attempt to stop Land Act becoming law. The ensuing decade sees the start of half a century of non-violent black resistance.

1914   Barry Hertzog, Afrikaner Cabinet Minister, breaks away from the ruling South Africa party of Botha and Smuts to form Afrikaner National Party. His manifesto: to reverse 'Milnerism'; education in Afrikaans to be compulsory; bilingualism in public service.

1914   Short Afrikaner civil war erupts over issue of support for British or Germans in First World War. Botha and Smuts pro-English; Hertzog pro-German.

1918   Broederbond founded. This 'band of brothers' dedicated to restoring fortunes and national pride of Afrikaners becomes eventually an all-powerful secret society with enormous influence over key appointments in Church and State.

1920–38   Slow build up of radical Afrikaner strength and support for National Party. Legislation passed to protect 'poor white' workers from African competition. Informal colour bars established. 1936: Blacks lose voting rights in Cape.

1938   Centenary of Great Trek. 200 Afrikaners 'trek' from Cape Town to Pretoria, leading to further upsurge of Afrikaner nationalism.

1939–45   During Second World War Afrikaners again split over English/German support. Pro-Nazi Ossewa-Brandwag Movement forms to sabotage South African war effort.

1948   D. F. Malan, advocating policy of 'apartheid' (apartness) wins General Election for the National Party by just five seats, deposing Jan Smuts. This and succeeding Nationalist Governments, believing that separation of the races is the only solution to South Africa's cultural diversity, set about realising their ideology with a whole structure of radical legislation. In 1948 the Prohibition of Mixed Marriages Act

makes marriage between whites and non-whites illegal. In
1950 the Group Areas Act legislates for complete residential
separation of the races; and the Immorality Amendment Act
bans sex between the races. In 1952 the Abolition of Passes
and Co-ordination of Documents Act imposes hated 'pass-
book' system, whereby all non-whites are legally bound to
carry identification documents at all times. In 1953, the
Reservation of Separate Amenities Act legalises already
informally existing separation of buses, railway carriages,
toilets, beaches, park benches. In 1954, the Resettlement of
Natives Act gives the Government authority to remove entire
existing communities of non-whites from areas deemed to be
'white'.

1952   Nelson Mandela leads 8,000 in campaign of defiance
against apartheid: he is given suspended prison sentence and
'banned'.

1955   At an ANC-organised 'Congress of the People' the
Freedom Charter is drawn up: a vision of a democratic and
non-racial South Africa.

1956   Mandela and other Congress leaders tried for treason
and acquitted. Mandela goes underground to set up Umkhonto
we Sizwe (Spear of the Nation) the military wing of the ANC.

1958   Committed apartheid ideologue Hendrik Verwoerd
becomes Prime Minister.

1959   Robert Sobukwe breaks with ANC to form Pan
Africanist Congress (PAC).

1960   Sharpeville massacre. Peaceful ANC and PAC anti pass
law protest turns violent as police open fire on unarmed black
crowd, killing 69 and wounding 180. This outrage, followed
by the 'banning' of both ANC and PAC, becomes a turning
point in black attitudes to resistance; and in 1962 'the armed
struggle' is formally adopted.

1960   After white referendum Verwoerd establishes South
Africa as an independent Republic; Harold Macmillan, visiting
the new Republic, delivers famous 'wind of change' speech in
Cape Town; in 1961 Verwoerd withdraws from the

Commonwealth in protest at international criticism of apartheid.

1961   Helen Suzman founds anti-apartheid Progressive Federal Party; for thirteen years she is the lone voice of opposition in Parliament.

1963–4   The Rivonia Trials: Mandela and seven other black leaders sentenced to life imprisonment for sabotage and conspiracy.

1963–73   Economic boom. With ANC and PAC banned, black leaders jailed, and order restored, foreign investors pour capital into South Africa.

1966   Verwoerd assassinated by white 'lunatic' as he sits in Parliament. John Vorster becomes Prime Minister.

1969   South African Students Organisation (SASO) founded. In 1970, Steve Biko and other leaders break away from white students to develop ideology of Black Consciousness (BC) – a rejection of white values and inculcation of a positive black world view.

June 16th 1976   Inspired and organised by the BC movement, the schoolchildren of Soweto rise up in protest against the enforced teaching of Afrikaans in black schools; this issue is the focus of deeper grievances about Bantu education and apartheid generally. Army disperses students with gunfire, killing several. This provokes further sustained demonstrations and violent riots.

   Post Soweto, P.W. Botha, the Minister for Defence, devises 'total strategy' as a means of saving South Africa from what he describes as 'the total onslaught' of enemies of South Africa, internal and external: Communist Russia and her satellites being the prime threat. This 'total strategy', which involves the relaxation of petty apartheid in combination with an intensification of repression of militants, is strongly opposed by Right-wing factions in the National Party.

1977   Steve Biko, founder of the Black Consciousness (BC) movement, arrested on suspicion of distributing 'inflammatory pamphlets', dies in police custody. Shortly afterwards BC inspired Azanian Peoples' Organisation (AZAPO) founded.

1978 'Muldergate'. The Minister of Information, Connie
Mulder – one of P.W. Botha's key right-wing opponents – is
caught siphoning off secret funds to mount a massive pro-
South Africa propaganda offensive overseas. John Vorster is
forced to resign after it becomes clear he was aware of
irregularities. P. W. Botha succeeds as Prime Minister. 'Total
strategy' becomes central government thinking, and security
forces are schooled in the theory of 'total onslaught'.

1979   ANC meet in London with Chief Mangosuthu
Buthelezi's Inkatha movement. Buthelezi refuses to agree to
the armed struggle. A year later ANC start attacks on Inkatha
and Buthelezi, who is denounced as a collaborator.

1982   After row about increasing 'liberalism' in National
Party government, Andreis Treurnicht leaves Nationalists to
form Conservative Party.

1983   'The New Dispensation': having abolished some aspects
of petty apartheid, P.W. Botha holds a whites-only referendum
on replacing whites-only Parliament with a tricameral
Parliament with separate Indian and coloured chambers, but
still excluding blacks. The new Parliament is approved by
whites, but voting poll among Indians and coloureds is less
than 20%. Those who participate are generally denounced as
'sell outs'.

1983   Mass opposition to these half-hearted reform initiatives
leads to the formation of two 'umbrella' anti-apartheid
movements: the United Democratic Front (UDF) and the
National Forum (NFC). From its inception the UDF is multi-
racial and non-violent, committed to campaigning within the
letter of the law.

1984   Five days after tricameral Parliament established the
'Revolt of the Eighties' begins – once again in Sharpeville
township. Black unrest continues for three years, resulting in
3,000 deaths and over 30,000 detentions.

July 1985   In the face of continuing black unrest a State of
Emergency is imposed. P.W. Botha tells nation that
extraordinary powers are needed to deal with 'external
Communist agitators who are inciting the people of South

Africa to unrest'. South African police replace tear gas, rubber bullets, and birdshot with selective 'shoot to kill' policy.

August 1985   After aggressively anti-reform speech by P. W. Botha American banks call in short term loans, sending rand currency plunging 35% in 13 days.

June 1986   Second State of Emergency imposed. Journalists not allowed to mention police by name or film suppression of violence in townships.

1987   In townships around Pietermaritzburg and Durban, the level of ANC–Inkatha violence becomes such that some commentators talk about 'an unofficial war'.

1989   De Klerk replaces P. W. Botha as President of South Africa. In October, he releases Walter Sisulu and seven other high profile political prisoners.

Feb 2nd 1990   De Klerk announces formal end of apartheid. Shortly afterwards Nelson Mandela is released, and the ANC is unbanned.

March 1992   After Conservative Party victory at Potchefstroom by-election, De Klerk holds white referendum on his reforms, which he wins with 68% majority. CODESA, the Council for a Democratic South Africa, comprised of representatives from almost all the political parties and homeland Governments, meets to try and work out formula for new South African constitution, details of transitional Government, date for eventual democratic elections.

June 1992   Boipatong. A massacre of squatters by alleged Inkatha supporting 'hostel dwellers' brings the issue of black-on-black violence to international attention.

August 1992   ANC Mass Action and General Strike, threatened to 'bring the Government to its knees within days' lasts two days, and is almost entirely peaceful.

April 1993   Chris Hani, leader of Communist Party, murdered outside his new home in a white suburb of Johannesburg. A week of violence follows, and a right-wing Conservative is arrested in connection with the murder.

July 1993   Date set for Democratic Elections.

Further Reading

I would recommend anybody whose appetite has been whetted for a greater understanding of South Africa's extraordinary and complex history to begin with Allister Sparks' excellent *The Mind of South Africa*. David Harrison's *The White Tribe of Africa* is a very readable history of the Afrikaner people. A superb outsider's view of the complexities of modern South Africa is to be found in Joseph Lelyveld's *Move Your Shadow*; and Rian Malan's *My Traitor's Heart* is a compelling series of case histories of violence told from the anguished point of view of a radical Afrikaner.